WHAT'S THE USE OF LECTURES?

WHAT'S THE USE
OF LECTURES?

Donald A. Bligh

JOSSEY-BASS
A Wiley Company
www.josseybass.com

Published by

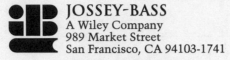

JOSSEY-BASS
A Wiley Company
989 Market Street
San Francisco, CA 94103-1741

www.josseybass.com

Jossey-Bass books and products are available through most bookstores. To contact Jossey-Bass directly, call (888) 378-2537, fax to (800) 605-2665, or visit our website at www.josseybass.com.

Substantial discounts on bulk quantities of Jossey-Bass books are available to corporations, professional associations, and other organizations. For details and discount information, contact the special sales department at Jossey-Bass.

We at Jossey-Bass strive to use the most environmentally sensitive paper stocks available to us. Our publications are printed on acid-free recycled stock whenever possible, and our paper always meets or exceeds minimum GPO and EPA requirements.

Library of Congress Cataloging-in-Publication Data

Bligh, Donald A.
   What's the use of lectures? / Donald A. Bligh.—1st ed.
       p. cm.—(The Jossey-Bass higher and adult education series)
Includes bibliographical references and index.
   ISBN 0-7879-5162-5 (pbk.: alk paper)
   1. Lectures and lecturing.   I. Title.   II. Series.
   LC6515.B55   2000
   378.1'79'6—dc21   99-006979

FIRST EDITION
PB Printing 10 9 8 7 6 5

THE JOSSEY-BASS
HIGHER AND ADULT EDUCATION SERIES

CONTENTS

ix

PART FOUR: ALTERNATIVES WHEN LECTURING IS INADEQUATE

PART FIVE: PREPARATION FOR THE USE OF LECTURES

PREFACE TO THE AMERICAN EDITION

When I first published this book, more than twenty-five years ago, I was astonished at its success. The first edition sold out in ten weeks, and demand has been steady ever since. Seemingly it satisfies a need.

Like musical composition and performance, lecturing is an art. Skill is acquired by practice rather than by reading books. Yet just as the budding composer may wish to study forms of composition known to have been successful, but later disregard them, so new lecturers may think it worthwhile to consider the findings of research into lecturing before developing their own style.

Using a different analogy, Nisbet has suggested three levels of proficiency: the learner driver, the ordinary road user, and the rally driver. The first is learning the rules; the second has everyday skills, and some bad habits; and the third can break many of the elementary rules when racing on a circuit—"a dangerous style, but a delight to the connoisseur" (Nisbet, 1966).

What's the Use of Lectures? was originally written with new lecturers in mind, but it is clear that experienced lecturers have found that it gives them an understanding of what they do (and what they do not!)

Unfortunately, there can be no book of rules for lecturers. There is no more agreement about what is a good lecture than there is about good music. Indeed, inquiries show that individuals want not only different but even conflicting things from a lecture (see for example Falk, 1967). Consequently, since most lectures will be assessed at both extremes of a general rating scale, lecturers will do well if they please more than half their audience.

Therefore it is not the purpose of this book to lay down rules. Some suggestions are offered for consideration, but its chief purpose is to present information that will help lecturers in making their own decisions. The treatment is necessarily general. Inevitably, you the reader are left with the task of selecting what is relevant to your needs.

Many new (and not-so-new) lecturers seek advice. Anyone who has the temerity to offer it lays himself open to criticism whenever he lectures—or if he never does so, since it is often assumed that he should be the embodiment of perfection. I cannot claim to be anything but an ordinary road user who frequently makes errors of judgment, and I am certainly not a virtuoso performer. However, this may be an advantage. When concerned with staff development in higher education, I was more able to help with difficulties with which I myself had struggled as a new lecturer. In skills that came more easily to me, I was less able to appreciate the difficulties of others. Thus I doubt the premise that consultants should be perfect; indeed, I suspect this book is something of a personal confession.

Standards in Discussion

It is the policy of most people engaged in staff development to cooperate with colleagues in the discussion of common problems and to publicize solutions of wider interest so that teachers can make their own decisions on how they will teach. This book may be viewed as a wider part of that discussion. The information it contains is as much to raise, as to settle, issues.

The academic and intellectual standards in those discussions is crucial. When there is a situation in which a large number of people have personal experience of lectures and lecturing but few have much knowledge based on independent measures, the strength with which opinions are held is frequently greater than the strength of their grounds. Because the opinions of students and lecturers do not always correlate with independent measures, I should urge caution in accepting opinions in preference to the results of systematic investigations. Students aiming for careers in medicine, engineering, the social sciences, and indeed every other profession have a right to expect faculty to base their training upon rigorous objective research and scientific facts wherever possible. Universities are dedicated to research employing these standards.

Yet, to my observation, the same standards are not always attempted in university staff development. Double standards exist, albeit often for understandable reasons. I hope this book will be a contribution to pedagogic discipline that raises the standards of educational discussions even though I accept we still know very little of scientific value on many aspects of lecturing.

Revisions and Research

The lecture method may be used in many circumstances both within and outside educational institutions. Readers will appreciate, however, that available evidence may show a bias toward universities, where most of the research has been carried out.

Although I have revised the book extensively for this edition, readers will notice I have retained much of the earlier research because it continues to be relevant and later research is less so. This is particularly true of research into memory, attention, and motivation, covered in Part Two. The development of meta-analyses has not changed my broad conclusions in Chapter One.

The areas that have expanded most are those covered in Part Three. There have been many publications presenting alternatives to lectures, particularly innovations using recent developments in computer technology. They largely confirm my conclusion in Chapter One that there is not much difference in the effectiveness of methods that present information.

There is almost no research on how lecturers should prepare. Consequently, I have made few changes to Part Five.

Language and Style

I must accept that my constant attempts at objective detachment reporting experimental evidence may make my style a bit cold and clinical. The same might be said of textbooks of physiology. But that doesn't mean we should not be caring and compassionate any more than it would mean that for a doctor.

Because there is no consistent vocabulary in education, some explanation may be required on my use of terms. A "lecturer" is one who "lectures," while a "teacher" is one who teaches by any method. I use *lessons* as a general term to cover any complete period of teaching, and *lecture* as a period of more-or-less uninterrupted talk from a teacher. This definition has psychological implications. I am using *lecture* as a period of "output" by the teacher and a period of input or reception or perception by the audience. A *period* is a lesson or part of a lesson. Words such as *seminar* and *tutorial* mean different things in different institutions. The use of these and some other general terms is given in Table 14.1.

Summary of the Book and How to Read It

This book is not a novel, so you are not likely to start at page one and read through to the end. That is not the way to read a book primarily intended to provide information on a method for those new to its use. It has two lines of development, shown in the diagram below. They are lines of argument as well.

The first step is to grasp the logic of the argument, even if you want to disagree with it. See why each part depends upon its predecessors. That's not so obvious in the case of Part Four, which is concerned with alternatives when lecturing is inadequate. The diagram shows that it follows from Parts One and Two. A look at Chapters One and Three will indicate why lectures might be inadequate.

The second step is to check out the table of contents as to why the topic of each chapter fits into that part and not another. If you can answer those questions, you now understand the structure of the book as a whole and why each chapter fits where it does.

In short, you understand the context of each chapter. So now you can turn to any chapter that interests you and adopt the same strategy. (Alternatively, find a specific topic in the Subject Index.) Look at the summary headings at the beginning of the chapter and ask yourself, *How do these subtopics fit into the main topic of the chapter?* and *How do these sub-subtopics fit into the subtopics?* It's all about the context of ideas—seeing how ideas fit together.

After that you are ready to take the plunge and start reading. You may begin at the beginning; but if you understand the context of a topic that interests you elsewhere, you will probably understand it even if you dive into the middle. (Actually, I recommend looking at the pictures first; it's not so painful!) Admittedly, your understanding might be better if you read everything that precedes it, and I don't wish to discourage you from reading all the book, but I'm a realist. Life is too short and too busy for you to read everything that might be helpful. So dip in here and there. In other words, you can use *What's the Use of Lectures?* like a reference book as well as a textbook.

Part One

I start by asking what lectures can achieve, and I get the answers "Lectures teach information" and "They're not as good as discussion for getting students to think or to develop their attitudes, without variations in the usual lecture techniques." That's an important answer. It defines the major use of lecturing. Much of the rest of the book pursues that purpose.

As with any other book of this kind, you can read the Part One at several levels of detail. At the most superficial, if you are happy with that answer you can pass straight on to Part Two. At the next level, you can get the gist by simply reading the main propositions immediately under the chapter title. Then you can get a summary of the supporting evidence by looking at each of the tables in turn. You will have to interpret their data. Finally, the text helps you do just that. Chapter One involves a mass of evidence. (For those who wanted all the detail, previous editions presented appendices summarizing all the original research so that you could look up the original reports with reference to the bibliography. There are now so many reports that it has not been possible to detail them in this edition.)

Part Two

Given that lectures teach information, in Part Two I ask the question, "What factors affect the acquisition of information?" I ask this because it is these factors that lecturers must use to make their lectures effective.

There could be hundreds of these factors, but it seems fairly obvious that factors influencing memory of the information will be important. Remembering is a process; so Chapter Two on memory first describes the process before dealing with factors influencing it.

From the many factors, I have also selected students' attention and motivation for consideration. Lecturers know they are a problem. So in each case I give reasons why I think they are important before describing their influence on the acquisition of information.

Part Three

In Part Three I ask the question, "What lecture techniques apply these factors most effectively?" If we suppose that the objective of lectures is to teach information, as shown in Chapter One, this question can only be answered by applying the psychological factors described in Part Two.

These factors are then used in Part Three to answer such questions as:

- How can information best be organized?
- How do you teach one item of that information? That is, how do you explain a fact?
- How do you find out how well you have taught it—either by feedback at the time or by a more formal evaluation later?
- What's the use of taking notes? Or giving duplicated notes?
- What sort of difficulties are likely to be met, and how can they be overcome?
- If you do have to lecture to stimulate thought or change attitudes, what evidence is there of how to do it?

Part Four

The psychological factors mentioned in Part Two, the limitations of the lecture method, and the fact that teachers have a variety of objectives that cannot all be achieved by lecturing (Chapter One) make it desirable that lectures be combined with other methods. In particular, we see in Chapter One that discussion methods are better than lectures to develop thinking and attitudes. So, as I show in the diagram here, Parts One and Two make it necessary for any lecturer to ask, "How can other methods, particularly discussion methods, be combined with lecturing?"

Some suggestions of ways to do this are made in Part Four.

Part Five

The use of specific lecture techniques (Part Three) and planning particular combinations of teaching methods (Part Four) require a series of decisions to be made in preparing a lecture. So I ask the question "What is needed in preparation?" (Part Five). That is why in the diagram I have shown Parts Three and Four leading to Part Five.

Although the manner of preparation is a matter of taste, some decisions logically have to be made before others. Part Five aims to help you through that sequence.

Acknowledgments

It has been argued in this book that the lack of effective feedback from the audience is a major defect of the lecture method, but the same defect is even more true of books. Feedback from previous editions using a reply-paid questionnaire has been flattering, Parts Two and Four being most favorably received. The respondents are among those who should be thanked for their advice on this volume.

I am also particularly grateful to Laurie Burbridge, who has most generously allowed me to use some of his material in Chapter Eight; to Alan Jenkins for the use of Table 19.1; and to John Richardson for attempting meta-analyses and drawing attention to some errors. Others to be thanked include the late Ruth Beard, Richard Ellis, Anthony Fothergill, Jim Hartley, Masoud Yazdani, and most of all my wife, Barbara. They have all read and commented upon sections of the book. Of course, the responsibility for errors remains mine.

Happy reading!

November 1999   Donald A. Bligh
                                                                      University of Exeter

THE AUTHOR

Donald A. Bligh was a pioneer of university staff development. He trained as a teacher before going to university to study geography and the history of science in the 1950s.

As he taught a wide range of subjects at the college level, he observed what difficulties he had to overcome when teaching and at the same time developed his ideas on the philosophy of science underpinning the training of university teachers.

After graduating in philosophy and psychology in 1967, he became responsible for training teachers of physiotherapy throughout the United Kingdom and Ireland. In this work he observed clinical teaching as well as lectures and small groups, and became convinced that the importance of small group teaching is underrated. His doctoral thesis on university teaching methods devised a new method to test the effectiveness of lectures and other presentations and argued that any period of teaching will be more effective if a variety of teaching methods is used.

In 1970 he joined London University's Teaching Methods Unit, where he wrote *What's the Use of Lectures?* which he published and marketed himself. It was an immediate best-seller throughout the British Commonwealth. A stream of other books followed, including *Research into Teaching Methods,* UNESCO's *Methods and Techniques in Post-secondary Education,* and *Seven Decisions When Teaching Students.*

In 1980 he became chair of the Society for Research into Higher Education. In 1985 he was appointed first professor and director of continuing education at Dundee and in 1989 as assistant principal at Moray House Edinburgh.

He has two other books whose publication is forthcoming: *Understanding Higher Education* (a guide for students visiting Britain) and the twin to this volume, *What's the Point in Discussion?*

Bligh is now an honorary research fellow in the Department of Computer Science at the University of Exeter in the United Kingdom, studying how explanations shift from one type of explanation to another (see Chapter Seven). His e-mail address is d.a.bligh@exeter.ac.uk.

WHAT'S THE USE OF LECTURES?

PART ONE

WHAT OBJECTIVES CAN LECTURES ACHIEVE?

CHAPTER ONE

EVIDENCE OF WHAT LECTURES ACHIEVE

The lecture is as effective as other methods for transmitting information.

Most lectures are not as effective as discussion for promoting thought.

Changing attitudes should not normally be the major objective of a lecture.

1. Lectures are relatively ineffective for teaching values associated with subject matter.

2. Lectures are relatively ineffective for inspiring interest in a subject.

3. Lectures are relatively ineffective for personal and social adjustment.

Lectures are relatively ineffective for teaching behavioral skills.

In the United States lecturing is the most common method when teaching adults. And so it is all over the world. In spite of opportunities for innovation provided by changing technology and educational research, surveys over decades show remarkably little change in the dominant use of lectures (Marris, 1964; Hale, 1964; Saunders and others, 1969; Costin, 1972; Bowles, 1982; Karp, 1983; Nance and Nance, 1990; Gunzburger, 1993; and Lesniak, 1996). With pride architects build terraced lecture halls in colleges and universities equipped with the best projection facilities. They represent a conception of education in which teachers who know give knowledge to students who do not and are therefore supposed to have nothing worth contributing. This is not the conception in this book. Indeed we will look in Part Four at how students can contribute.

The dominance of lecturing is not confined to educational establishments. In commerce and industry the same is true (Glogovsky, 1970). At trade conferences and meetings of professional associations, lectures take pride of place over conferring and meeting with other people. The event typically gets under way with a keystone lecture, periodically reconvenes for large-group lectures, and usually wraps up with a valedictory address.

In politics lectures are called speeches. In churches they are called sermons. Call them what you like; what they are in fact are *more or less continuous expositions by a speaker who wants the audience to learn something.* For our purposes that is a working definition. It implies psychological processes of learning. So in Part Two we must look at those processes. The learning that speakers want their audience to acquire could be of different kinds. There are four logically distinct kinds of objective: (1) the acquisition of information, (2) the promotion of thought, (3) changes in attitudes, and (4) behavioral skills.

I shall argue, with reservations, that on the available evidence:

1. The lecture is as effective as any other method for transmitting information, but not more effective. Programmed learning and PSI—the personalized system of instruction—may be an exception. (See Table 1.1.)
2. Most lectures are not as effective as discussion methods to promote thought.
3. Changing student attitudes should not normally be the major objective of a lecture.
4. Lectures are ineffective to teach behavioral skills.

Therefore the main objective of lectures should be the acquisition of information by the students. Administrative, economic, or other considerations may force their use for the promotion of thought, attitudes, or behavioral skills, but lectures should not be accepted as the normal vehicle to achieve these objectives.

The Lecture Is as Effective as Other Methods for Transmitting Information

When comparing the effectiveness of lectures with any other method, there are three possible conclusions: they are more effective, they are less effective, or there is no significant difference.

Table 1.1 summarizes experimental comparisons of lectures with other teaching methods where acquisition of information is the criterion of effectiveness. With the exception of comparisons with PSI, the majority of comparisons show no significant difference. Those that do show a difference are fairly evenly balanced either way. It is hard to avoid the conclusion that, with the exception of PSI, lectures are as effective as other methods to teach facts, but not more effective.

TABLE 1.1. NUMBER OF EXPERIMENTAL COMPARISONS OF LECTURES WITH OTHER METHODS WHERE ACQUISITION OF INFORMATION IS THE MAIN CRITERION.

Teaching Method	Lectures Less Effective	No Significant Difference	Lectures More Effective
Programmed learning and PSI-related[a]	20	17	8
Discussion (various)	18	54	22
Reading and independent study	10	21	9
Inquiry (e.g., projects)	6	6	3
Other (mostly audio, TV, computer-assisted learning)	27	57	20

Note: Some explanation is needed for the classification of teaching methods used in this and later tables. Teaching methods can vary in a multitude of ways. There is no single dimension on which all can be distinguished.

I regard a lecture as a period of more or less continuous exposition by the teacher. I admit that the phrase "more or less" introduces some vagueness, but that corresponds to the way *lecture* is used. Although necessarily defined in terms of what the teacher does, in practice it sets psychologically what the students are expected to do.

The PSI (personalized system of instruction), sometimes called the Keller Plan, uses five principles, four of them inherited from programmed learning as used in the 1960s: small steps, self-paced active learning, early feedback on performance (from discussion with student proctors), individual support with personal contact, and progress to the next unit of work being conditional on mastery of the previous one. A unit typically involves a week's assignment, including reading and practical work, but no lectures. Lectures are an occasional privilege for students who have reached a stage such that they can understand them. Methods I have classified as related to PSI have at least three of these characteristics and mostly four or all five. My inclusion of individualized instruction under this heading is the most contentious because authors' use of this term is often unclear. I have assumed it adopts at least the middle three principles.

Discussion occurs when students make a spoken contribution and get a response. The criterion would include a student's asking a question in a lecture and getting an answer. That may stretch the definition of *discussion* too much, but Chapter Five shows that such an incident has significant psychological effects on the attention of all students. We simply have to accept that teaching methods are continua. Any attempt to cut a line between them will be arbitrary in some respects.

"Inquiry" assumes that students have to obtain or seek information, but it cannot exclude their being presented with some too. It might be regarded as an element within independent study. It is presented as a separate method here only when experimenters have done so.

"Independent study" could include many psychologically different activities depending on the subject of study. For example, reading a history book is very different from doing mathematical calculations. I have assumed that the dominant activities are reading and writing. This is intended to exclude laboratory work and workshops.

The "Other" category mostly includes other methods of presenting information (for example, audio, television, computers). Strictly, computer-assisted learning is not a single method. Computers are tools that can be used in many ways.

[a]Includes only comparisons reported after 1976. Up to that time Kulik, Kulik, and Smith (1976) reviewed 39 comparisons with lectures; 38 favored PSI, 34 significantly. Ruskin and Hess (1974) reviewed 239 comparisons of PSI with traditional methods and most also favored PSI.

Table 1.1 probably underrepresents insignificant results. This issue has been the subject of more experimental observation in the United States than any other issue in the field of teaching methods in higher education. As long ago as 1963, McKeachie (who is probably better acquainted with the field than anyone else) said that a host of comparisons remain unpublished because there are no significant differences to report. The same is true today. A review of doctoral and masters theses in *Dissertation Abstracts* shows that postgraduate students continue to make similar comparisons (each no doubt with some previously untried variables), but the broad conclusion remains the same: when it comes to acquiring information, there's not much difference between lectures and other methods, except for PSI. I maintain this broad conclusion, but I recognize it is broad. Inevitably, there are reservations within that breadth. But they would cloud my message at this stage.

Dubin and Taveggia (1968) reviewed ninety-one studies comparing two or more teaching methods on one or more "measures" of course content (Table 1.2). Most of these assessments used "objective tests" of the multiple-choice, true-false, or sentence-completion type also used for course examinations. Most of these were tests of factual information, but not every report makes this clear. By using more than one criterion, one study may produce more than one comparison between methods. Thus the sum of the figures in the central column in Table 1.2 may exceed ninety-one. But since the learning of students assessed by more than one measure may be duplicated in these figures, Dubin and Taveggia eliminated this overlap by using only one figure per study. The figures in parentheses give this comparison.

However, it may rightly be objected to both Tables 1.1 and 1.2 that figures giving the total number of studies or comparisons do not prove anything if those favoring one method are highly significant and those favoring the other are not statistically significant at all. Accordingly, where possible, Dubin and Taveggia computed standardized scores from the standard deviations and the numbers of students reported to be involved. In all cases, they found no significant difference in effectiveness between any of the methods listed in Table 1.2.

There were a very large number of studies comparing lectures with television when video cameras first became widely available in the 1960s. I have not included them in Table 1.1, and Dubin and Taveggia did not consider them. Reference can be made to two reviews. Chu and Schramm (1967) summarized 202 comparisons at the college level; 22 favored TV, 152 showed no significant difference, and 28 favored the lecture. With adults, the figures were 7, 24, and 2 respectively. Dubin and Hedley (1969) reviewed 191 comparisons of television with traditional teaching, and although most of the differences were insignificant at the 5 percent level, they thought overall that there was a slight balance in favor of traditional teaching. Table 1.1 includes comparisons published since these early

TABLE 1.2. SUMMARY OF NINETY-ONE STUDIES COMPARING TEACHING METHODS.

Method 1	Percentage Favoring Method 1[a]	Number of Comparisons	Percentage Favoring Method 2[a]	Method 2
Lecture	54.7 (51.1)	201 (88)	44.8 (48.9)	Discussion
Lecture	45.8 (37.5)	59 (8)	51.5 (50)	Lecture and discussion
Lecture and discussion	31.2 (41.7)	16 (12)	50 (41.7)	Discussion
Lecture	52.8 (52)	72 (50)	47.2 (48)	Supervised reading
Lecture and discussion	50 (52.2)	34 (23)	50 (47.8)	Supervised reading
Lecture	40 (40)	20 (20)	60 (60)	Unsupervised reading
Face-to-face instruction[b]	50 (49.4)	116 (81)	50 (50.6)	Supervised reading
Face-to-face instruction[b]	41.9 (40)	31 (25)	58.1 (60)	Unsupervised reading

Note: The figures in parentheses give only one comparison from each experimental group.

[a]Both significantly and insignificantly.

[b]Lectures, discussion, and laboratory teaching.

Source: Dubin and Taveggia (1968).

reviews. They broadly confirm previous comparisons: there is not much difference in the effectiveness of lectures and other methods to teach information.

If there is no difference between the effectiveness of the lecture and other methods on tests of information, it seems reasonable to infer that the lecture is as effective as these methods in transmitting information.

However, if you are a thorough skeptic, you may retort that there is no difference between them because none of them teach anything at all! But there's an answer to that. By comparing results of tests before and after teaching, the experiments provide evidence that lectures and other methods do transmit information. Furthermore, the study by Fodor (1963) and two by Gulo (Gulo and Baron, 1965; Gulo and Nigro, 1966), where lectures were compared with irrelevant activity or no teaching at all, all found lectures to be superior. Moreover, in some comparative studies a control group with no teaching is also tested, and it is clear that lectures result in greater gains. Consequently, available evidence suggests that lectures do teach at least some information.

Therefore, the lecture is one method of achieving the first kind of objective, and its use for this purpose is at least sometimes justifiable. But since the other methods are equally effective, this conclusion does not necessarily justify the frequent heavy reliance on the lecture method.

However, it is not recommended that discussion methods be used primarily to teach information. They are expensive in staff time, and the one significant comparison Dubin and Taveggia did obtain was that unsupervised reading is superior to discussion for the acquisition of information.

Most Lectures Are Not as Effective as Discussion Methods for the Promotion of Thought

Although there is not the same quantity of experimental evidence, I shall argue that the studies that have been made, common sense, and present psychological knowledge give a consistent picture in favor of this proposition; and that if lectures are to be used to promote thought, the technique to be used should be different from the descriptive style traditionally used to "survey an area of knowledge." For example, Corman (1957) found that a knowledge of the principles used in solving problems made no difference to the number of problems students could actually solve, and information on how to approach problems could only be applied by the most intelligent group. Knowledge is not enough. Students need practice in solving problems and applying principles.

It is probably because the construction of questions is relatively difficult that there have been far fewer experimental studies comparing the effectiveness of teaching methods for the promotion of thought. Nevertheless, reference to Table 1.3 gives a very clear impression. Dubin and Taveggia did not compute standardized scores to answer the objection that mere quantity of studies does not prove a case if the minority group displays highly significant results. They didn't need to. I have only found two studies to suggest that lectures stimulate thought better than discussion methods.

Table 1.3 also shows that lectures are ineffective compared with "other methods" to promote thought. This is a surprise. However, most of those other methods involved more student activity than listening to lectures. PSI involves discussion, and it is hard to imagine that teachers using role plays, modeling, simulations, case presentations, and so on do not follow up with discussion of what has been observed by these methods.

TABLE 1.3. NUMBER OF EXPERIMENTAL COMPARISONS OF LECTURES WITH OTHER METHODS WHERE PROMOTION OF THOUGHT IS THE CRITERION.

Teaching Method	Lectures Less Effective	No Significant Difference	Lectures More Effective
Discussion	29	1	2
Reading and independent study	1	3	1
Inquiry	5	1	1
Other methods	12	17	0

I should be the first to accept that this is a broad generalization. To begin, there are many kinds of thinking. Cabral-Pini (1995) evaluated flexibility and creativity. Tillman (1993) was interested in students' seeing issues from many points of view and reserving their judgment. That might be called open-mindedness, although Fielding, Kameenui, and Gersten (1983) wanted students to form their own opinions. Gist (1989) was interested in the quantity and diversity of ideas, Lam (1984–1985) in the depth of questions asked. All these and many more are worthwhile educational objectives that lectures have been comparatively ineffective to teach.

Second, there are many kinds and contexts of discussion among these comparisons. For example, apart from methods simply described as discussion, Mohr (1996), Cabral-Pini (1995) and Smith (1995) used cooperative discussion; Hingorani (1996), Tillman (1993), and Self, Wolinsky, and Baldwin (1989) used case discussion in different contexts. Khoiny (1996) and Jensen (1996) are among those using problem-based discussion, and Sawyer and Sawyer (1981) used microcounseling.

Yet in spite of the variety, with few exceptions discussion is consistently more effective than lectures in getting students to think.

Why is this? Compared with discussion methods, the students' role in lectures is relatively passive. They sit listening; their activity usually consists of selecting information from what is said, possibly translating it into their own words or some form of shorthand, and then writing it down. Bloom (1953) replayed tape recordings of lectures and discussions to students and asked them at intervals to recall the thoughts they had in the original situation. Admittedly, the stimulated student recall was subjective, but the sample was large. It is difficult to suggest a better way of obtaining such data, and Siegel and others (1963) have since found the method "reasonably valid" when compared against independent measures of students' learning. During lectures, 36.8 percent of the time was spent in "passive thoughts about the subject" and "thoughts evidencing simple comprehension," compared with 20.3 percent during discussion. Thirty-one percent of lectures were spent with irrelevant thoughts, compared with 14.5 percent during discussion. During discussions, the students spent 8.3 percent of the time attempting to solve problems and synthesize (interrelate) information, compared with 1.0 percent during lectures. All these comparisons were statistically significant and suggest that during discussion students are more attentive, active, and thoughtful than during lectures.

This has been known for a long time, but too many teachers seem to ignore it. When Hovland and Mandell (1952) demonstrated that students are more likely to accept a conclusion if the lecturer states it at the end of an argument than if all the same evidence is presented with the conclusion left unstated, they showed the inability of students to draw an inference during a lecture. Barnard (1942) and Dawson (1956) found that although a lecture-demonstration was superior for teaching specific information, problem-solving discussions were better on tests of problem solving and scientific attitude. When Asch (1951) and James, Johnson, and Venning (1956) used a nondirective form of discussion, usually known as free-group discussion, students displayed wider thinking and considered more solutions to problems than those who received traditional teaching. This may reflect flexibility and open-mindedness.

In effect, what is being said here is that if students are to learn to think, they must be placed in situations where they have to do so. The situations in which they are obliged to think are those in which they have to answer questions, because questions demand an active mental response. Although it could be modified to do so, the traditional expository lecture does not demand this (Taplin, 1969; Dunn, 1969; Elton, 1970; see Parts Three and Four of this book). The best way to learn to solve problems is to be given problems that have to be solved. The best way to "awaken critical skills" is to practice using the canons of criticism. The best way to develop powers of analysis is to keep analyzing situations and data. If this thesis seems obvious common sense, it should be remembered that some people place faith in their lectures to stimulate thought and expect thinking skills to be absorbed, like some mystical vapors, from an academic atmosphere. Psychologists are likely to wince at the imprecision of such a notion; learning to think is not an absorption process.

The commonsense view finds support from psychologists. Harlow (1949) described "learning to think" as the acquisition of learning sets. Monkeys and children were rewarded for selecting the odd item among three objects. They were trained to make progressively finer and more abstract discriminations and, more important, were able to apply the "odd man out" principle to problems they had never seen before. Similarly, as problems became more complex, they seemed able to apply principles from previously experienced problem situations. Practice with basic simple problems improved, and made possible, the solutions to more complex ones. Gagne (1965) points out that when students are given a problem to solve, they may not only apply principles but also combine them to form new higher-order principles. This ability is essential to the development of a student's powers of thought. (Indeed, Gagne implies that the combination and application of principles is what "thinking" is.)

The important point here is that the essence of learning to think involves practice; that lectures do not normally provide opportunity for this, and still less do they provide an opportunity for the active expression and testing of thoughts.

The Gestalt school described problem solving as a process of achieving "insight" by (1) recognizing the problem, (2) gaining familiarity with its elements, such as the concepts involved, (3) constantly reorganizing the elements, (4) possibly incorporating a considerable period of irrelevant activity or overt inactivity, and (5) culminating in a flash of insight displayed by the sudden demonstration of the solution. For example, children taught to find the area of a rectangle by multiplying its height by its length may try various ways of rearranging a parallelogram before suddenly hitting on the idea of cutting off a right-angled triangle and replacing it on the other end to make a rectangle, so that they may use the rule they already know (Wertheimer, 1945). The first two stages may be achieved in lectures if the lecturer raises problems and discusses them from a variety of perspectives, but in the uninterrupted lecture the remaining stages are neither encouraged nor usually possible. There is little pressure on students to tackle the problems raised themselves. (They depend on the lecturer to do this, and they are rarely disappointed.) Nor are they given time to reorganize the sometimes unfamiliar concepts presented by the lecturer. Furthermore, the whole of a student's experience and expectations of the lecture method favor it as a period of "information input" rather than "information processing." The lecturer who wishes to promote thought by lecturing must overcome the conservatism arising from student experience!

I am not denying that thought may take place during lectures—although Bloom's study (1953) suggests that not much does. Obviously it may. Those students who become lecturers probably think more than most. I am suggesting that the traditional style of continuous exposition does not promote it in such a way as to justify lecturing to achieve this objective. Similarly, I am not denying that lectures can provide the necessary information for students to think about, once they get home; but the teacher must do something to make sure that they do think about it, and this requires something more than the traditional lecture.

Similarly, students will think during lectures, insofar as they have time, if they already have a disposition to do so. The lecturer provides information to think about. But that is different from the lecture method promoting thought. Marton and his disciples (Marton, Hounsell, and Entwistle, 1984) have contrasted students who have "deep" and "surface approaches" to learning. No doubt the former think more in lectures. Others have emphasized the personal context of learning (Ramsden, 1992). Alison King has shown the benefits of instructing students to generate their own questions during a lecture. Ausubel (1968) has argued that having a concept in mind in advance of a presentation (an "advance organizer," to be discussed in Chapter Five) can help students to reorganize the material. But saying that some students are predisposed to think in lectures is quite different from saying that lectures teach them to do so.

Changing Attitudes Should Not Normally Be the Major Objective of a Lecture

The personal nature of attitudes makes this argument more difficult to assert with the same confidence as used regarding information and thought. The assertions are necessarily generalizations. The general argument is that lectures are not as effective as more active methods for changing attitudes and the method should only be used when effective.

The three kinds of attitude objectives specified earlier were (1) the acquisition of values and attitudes associated with subject matter, (2) interest in the subject as a discipline, and (3) changes in personality and social adjustment. These need to be considered separately, because in some subjects there is a much stronger case for using the lecture method to achieve objective 1 than for 2 and 3.

1. Lectures Are Relatively Ineffective for Teaching Values Associated with Subject Matter

Party political speeches and broadcasts are not effective in changing people's voting habits, but they do help to confirm the preferences already held. Sermons rarely convince agnostics, but they give solidarity to the faithful. Similarly, lectures are ineffective in changing people's values, but they may reinforce those that are already accepted.

Elections dominated by television and other media presentations sometimes lead to disenchantment with politicians generally. There is a good reason for this. Presentations can produce doubt by giving negative information that is inconsistent with the values of the audience; but arousing positive enthusiasm requires something quite different. Enthusiasm, and motivation generally, cannot be *given* in presentations such as broadcasts and lectures. Motivation is an inner flame that has to be there already. Passive reception of information will not fan the flame (unless there is an emotionally prepared mind). That requires energy and activity in the mind of the receiver. For example, Dresner (1989–1990) showed that students who already thought politicians can change things were more likely to change their behavior after a lesson on environmental issues.

The greater effectiveness of discussion in changing attitudes and values has been known by psychologists for a long time, and no one now spends much time trying to prove it. (See Table 1.4.) In a now-classic experiment, Lewin (1943) gave exactly the same information on the merits of eating whale meat to groups of housewives in lectures and discussions. The discussion groups were asked to indicate by a show of hands whether they would try the meat. When questioned some time later, 32 percent of the discussion groups had served it, compared with 3 percent of the lecture groups. In a similar study, Lewin (1943) found that group discussion and decision was more effective in persuading mothers to feed orange juice and cod liver oil to their babies than giving the same information individually. The relative importance of discussion in individual decision making has been disputed in the case of students (Bennett, 1955); but Pennington, Haravey, and Bass (1958) and Mitnick and McGinnies (1958) have found that when discussion shows some consensus, it has a greater long-term effect upon attitudes than lectures do. Judging from an experiment by Hovland, Janis, and Kelley (1953) with students as subjects, lecturers' effectiveness in achieving their objectives is more strongly influenced by their personalities than by their academic expertise. Assuming their influence is for the good, it seems reasonable to think that their personalities would be more effective in a teaching method using two-way interaction.

Other experiments are summarized in Table 1.4. Apart from a report by Gerberich and Warner (1936), there appears to be a strong case that discussion methods are more effective than lectures in changing attitudes. It is hardly

TABLE 1.4. NUMBER OF EXPERIMENTAL COMPARISONS OF LECTURES WITH OTHER METHODS WHERE CHANGE IN ATTITUDES AND VALUES ASSOCIATED WITH THE SUBJECT MATTER IS THE CRITERION.

Teaching Method	Lectures Less Effective	No Significant Difference	Lectures More Effective
Discussion	19	11	4
Other	9	13	3

surprising that lectures influence attitudes more than no teaching at all (Kipper and Ben-Ely, 1979). And in debates (Pederson, 1993), there is often pressure to persuade others and not be persuaded oneself. In the study by Benson (1996), the effect of discussion is diluted. The power of social conformity to influence attitudes in group situations (Asch, 1951; Sherif and Sherif, 1956; Cohen, 1964) is well known, and I shall not enlarge on it here. Zimbardo (1960) has shown that "a good group spirit" is an important variable affecting changes in students' attitudes, but in a lecture with minimal student interaction there is hardly a group at all in the accepted sense of the word (Abercrombie, 1978).

Both discussion and decision making involve the activity principle in learning. This may be taken further in simulations and role-play teaching methods. LeBlanc (1996) found that nurses who experienced simulations showed better attitudes toward the elderly in clinical practice eight weeks later, though they did not show significantly better on a questionnaire immediately after teaching. Dresner (1989–1990) found students changed their home heating habits after a simulation, but not after a lecture. Culbertson (1957) has demonstrated that subjects with unfavorable attitudes toward blacks changed most if forced to act the black role. Observer attitudes changed less, and controls changed least.

Similarly, King and Janis (1956) have shown a greater attitude change in students required to present the speech of another student who held the opposite view than those who only heard the speech. These and other experiments summarized in Table 1.4 show that active methods are more effective in producing changes in student attitudes than passive listening. The activity principle is important in many forms of professional training, such as teaching, medicine, and social work, where attitudes are important.

2. Lectures Are Relatively Ineffective for Inspiring Interest in a Subject

The inspirational function of lectures is asserted more often than it merits. Admittedly, most of us can remember a few lectures that stood out and influenced us as students, but they are usually few compared with the total number of lectures received. Also, the same lectures do not inspire everyone because not everyone has a mind prepared in the same way. Furthermore, in many cases the inspiration is short-lived and leads to little further action. For example, Hartley and Cameron (1967) found that only three out of twenty-two students who stated their intention to do further reading after a lecture had in fact done so one month later.

This is not to say that student motivation is not one objective of a lecture. It can and should be. My argument is that, as a generalization, lectures are not effective in generating enthusiasm in a subject and therefore student motivation should not normally be the major objective and purpose of using the method.

Admittedly, there are exceptional lecturers who may enthuse their audience with great regularity late on a Friday afternoon, but ordinary mortals who do not have a distinctive personality cannot achieve this excellence and should not try to copy them. There is another reason why I think this is normally impossible. The excellence of one lecturer often depends on contrast with others. The student's intellectual diet requires a variety of foods for well-rounded development.

Reference to Table 1.5 shows that there have been very few studies comparing lectures with other teaching methods, if we take students' attitudes toward their academic discipline as the criterion of effectiveness. Though the majority suggest that lecturing is less effective than other methods, the alternatives are not consistently of one type. Half involve some interpersonal responsiveness and elicitation of thoughts or feelings from the students, but compared with Table 1.4 a greater proportion are, like lectures, some kind of presentation method.

Consequently, although Table 1.5 supports my contention that the inspirational role of lectures is often grossly overstated, on its own it does not strongly suggest an explanation for this fact. Effective teaching to change attitudes and values is usually best achieved by their elicitation in discussion, followed by their rational consideration. A possible explanation is that the alternative presentation methods had some novelty value compared with lectures; but this assumes that attitudes toward the teaching method influence attitudes toward the subject.

This raises another criterion relevant to the inspirational role of lectures: their popularity (see Table 1.6). It seems unlikely that students will feel inspired and enthusiastic about their subject as a result of the lectures they hear, and at the same time either wish to have fewer lectures or disapprove of the method. "Lectures are interesting; we wish we had fewer of them" seems to be an inconsistent remark. (I admit there could be circumstances in which students might reasonably assert both propositions. Perhaps they are so inspired that they want more private study time to follow the enthusiasm of the moment. But I see little evidence of such all-consuming enthusiasm.)

TABLE 1.5. NUMBER OF EXPERIMENTAL COMPARISONS OF LECTURES WITH OTHER METHODS WHERE INCREASED INTEREST IN SUBJECT MATTER IS THE CRITERION.

Teaching Method	Lectures Less Effective	No Significant Difference	Lectures More Effective
Discussion	5	4	1
Other	11	7	3

TABLE 1.6. NUMBER OF EXPERIMENTAL COMPARISONS OF LECTURES WITH OTHER METHODS WHERE STUDENTS' PREFERENCE FOR THE METHOD IS THE CRITERION.

Teaching Method	Lectures Less Preferred	No Significant Difference	Lectures More Preferred
PSI	12	5	3
Discussion	17	3	1
Other	18	11	10

There can be little doubt about the unpopularity of the lecture system among students. Remembering that PSI includes discussion with student proctors, Table 1.6 shows students' preference for discussion methods. In a survey of eight colleges and universities by students (Saunders and others, 1969), there was a consistent desire for more seminars and fewer lectures (except in art colleges, where students spent thirty hours per week in studio work). In another survey of 1,052 students in twelve teachers' colleges, more than half preferred seminars to lectures and rated them superior for "inspiring ideas" and "developing standards of judgment," while lectures were rated highest for obtaining information (Stones, 1970). McLeish (1970) obtained ratings of teaching methods from ten teachers' colleges and several universities. There was a marked preference for seminars and tutorials, and relative distaste for lectures, in all groups. Interestingly, the students' distaste for lectures was exceeded by all five groups of lecturers who were questioned; one wonders how much enthusiasm for their subject the lecturers engendered in these circumstances. The Hale Report (Hale, 1964) also shows the students' disenchantment with the lecture method, but a more favorable attitude from university teachers. Similarly, in considering seven teaching methods students of English, education, and dentistry ranked lectures seventh for efficiency and fifth for enjoyment, but easily first for their frequency (Flood Page, 1970).

However, it is to be expected that there are differences between groups of students. Observations in adult education together with reports by Reid-Smith (1969) and Gauvain (1968) suggest that this unpopularity may not be true with older students. In an inquiry by Woolford (1969), although in general students were more satisfied the more they were able to participate, those who were more able, less emotionally stable, or less extroverted preferred participation to be restricted. There were no differences between those from different social backgrounds.

Most students in the inquiry by students themselves (Saunders and others, 1969) thought "the acquisition of information" to be the most important kind of objective of lectures, although 41 percent thought lectures should stimulate independent work. (The four most popular objectives were "to impart information," 76 percent; "to provide a framework," 75 percent; "to indicate methods of approaching the subject," 64 percent; and "indicate sources of reference," 47 percent.)

In particular, arts and humanities students seek stimulating ideas. Since lectures are criticized for poor preparation and presentation, or as repetition of standard textbooks, perhaps the lack of stimulation is the fault of the lecturers who commit these errors rather than the lecture method itself. Students desire stimulation, but they do not get it. If that is the case, lecturers must attend to this aspect of their technique, for unless they can surpass their average colleague my conclusion will remain the same: stimulating student interest in a subject might be one objective of a lecture, but it should not normally be the major objective because the method is relatively ineffective for this purpose.

3. Lectures Are Relatively Ineffective for Personal and Social Adjustment

An individual's personality consists of relatively permanent characteristics. Therefore, almost by definition, we should not expect any teaching method to have immediate effects. In particular, lectures are situations in which students are expected to be relatively passive. They are not situations in which students are expected to "socialize" or in which we might expect their personalities to develop by being expressed. The focus of attention is on lecturers and what they say, not on the students. Consequently, to use the lecture method to develop students' personalities, social responsiveness, or self-awareness is to make the same kind of mistake as to expect prisoners to adjust to society by putting them in solitary confinement.

With this in mind, the balance of studies in Table 1.7 might at first seem surprising. We might expect many nonsignificant findings, and none at all in which lectures were more effective than other methods. However, closer inspection of the research reports shows Erlich's finding (1979) is the only real surprise. Nonsignificant findings are often not reported. A few constructive words from a

TABLE 1.7. NUMBER OF EXPERIMENTAL COMPARISONS OF LECTURES WITH OTHER METHODS WHERE PERSONAL AND SOCIAL ADJUSTMENT IS THE CRITERION.

Teaching Method	Lectures Less Effective	No Significant Difference	Lectures More Effective
All methods	14	8	4

lecturer (Tuohimaa, Tamminen, and Fabrin, 1993) before medical students have to dissect their first human corpse are more likely to reduce anxiety than nothing at all. And not only was the lecture in the Yorde and Witmer (1988) study coupled with discussion but the relationship between psychological stress and muscular tension in the face, as measured by their electromyographs (EMGs), is far from established.

More pertinent is the fact that all the methods more effective than the lecture are relatively active and expressive with immediate feedback, usually from peers. Accordingly, I am confident in my conclusion that changes in personality and social adjustment should not normally be the major objective of a lecture. Teachers of clinical medicine, management, social work, education, and other fields where these things are important will need to use other, more active and expressive methods.

Lectures Are Relatively Ineffective for Teaching Behavioral Skills

If you want to teach a behavioral skill, at some stage the student should practice it. If you are training athletes to run 100 meters, at some point in that training they should practice running 100 meters. If you want to teach carpentry, by all means talk about safety in using chisels and demonstrate how to use them; but at some stage it will be necessary to let the students practice using a saw, plane, chisel, and all the other tools. If I am to undergo surgery, I want the surgeons to have practiced the operation before; their being lectured about it is not enough.

You might think this principle is obvious. And so it is, to ordinary people. But it is quite beyond some of the most intelligent people our educational system has produced. They want their students to do well in examinations, but they never give practice in doing them. They want their students to use the library effectively and they lecture them as they show them around, but they don't design practical exercises in using it. A professor who wanted to teach us surveying gave us a lecture; but we never handled the equipment or tried to survey a field. Verbal presentations present words, and words are what students get from them. If you want them to be able to do something, put them in a situation where they practice doing it.

Table 1.8 shows the operation of this principle. Studies only show lectures to be more effective if the other methods compared are presentation methods or no teaching at all. The fact that two studies show lectures and no teaching at all to be equally effective does not inspire confidence in lectures for this purpose. Most of the methods showing no significant difference from lectures are discussion or presentation methods. They don't give relevant skills practice; but most of the methods that are more effective than lectures do.

**TABLE 1.8. NUMBER OF EXPERIMENTAL COMPARISONS
OF LECTURES WITH OTHER METHODS WHERE THE DEVELOPMENT
OF BEHAVIORAL SKILLS IS THE CRITERION.**

Teaching Method	Lectures Less Effective	No Significant Difference	Lectures More Effective
Practice of the skill	13	8	0
Observation (e.g., demos)	5	12	2
Other methods	9	10	5

The truth, it seems, is that the principle is not obvious when the consequences of the behavioral skills are not so physically observable. The criteria in the studies in Table 1.8 are nearly all interpersonal skills. The effects of a chisel, a saw, and a plane are obviously different. Perhaps that is why no one has done experiments to test the effects of lectures on carpentry skills. The effects of lectures, discussions, and role plays are not so obvious—at least not immediately.

However, before we condemn lectures completely for this purpose, it is worth reflecting that most physical skills have an information component. "Knowing how" often includes some "knowing that," and lectures are as effective as other methods for teaching that information. Thus we should expect a presentation (such as a lecture) before behavioral practice to be an effective combination. Most students get lectures before dissecting a cadaver or filling a tooth; but such instruction is not so extensive before learning to swim or drive.

Conclusion with Reservations

I hold that a great deal of evidence supports the four generalizations stated at the beginning of this chapter, provided they are taken for what they are—generalizations. I must admit to several reservations, but I don't think they are sufficient to damage these four broad conclusions.

First, although the categories of the criteria of teaching effectiveness are logically distinct, they are very broad. There are many different kinds of information, thought, attitudes, and behavior.

Furthermore, where experiments use course grades, the criteria are impure. Although research shows that over 70 percent of marks for course grades can be obtained for memory of information even in subjects like medicine and physics (McGuire, 1963; Beard and Pole, 1971; Black, 1968), the remaining marks could influence experimental results.

Third, definitions of teaching methods are not precise. There are innumerable variables. How long does a contribution in discussion have to be before you classify it as a mini-lecture? Each teaching method comprises many techniques, but experimenters give few details about them. To compensate for uncontrolled variables, I have tried to review as much evidence as possible so that random variables even out.

Finally, people who carry comparative experiments are sometimes enthusiasts for one of the methods, and it is not usually the lecture. Could this unfairly bias against the lecture?

Notwithstanding these reservations, I still think the balance of evidence favors the conclusion. *Use lectures to teach information. Do not rely on them to promote thought, change attitudes, or develop behavioral skills if you can help it.*

PART TWO

WHAT FACTORS AFFECT THE ACQUISITION OF INFORMATION?

CHAPTER TWO

FACTORS INFLUENCING MEMORY

Structures and processes.

1. Memory is a sequence of processes.

2. There's evidence for two kinds of memory.

3. But it's not that simple.

4. So, what happens when students listen to a lecture?

Factors causing forgetting.

1. Retroactive and proactive interference.

2. "Trace decay" in the first few seconds.

3. The amount of information.

4. Repressing what you don't want to remember.

Factors aiding memory.

1. Making the lecture meaningful to the students.

2. Whole versus part learning.

3. Organizing the subject.

4. Rehearsing the material.

5. Repetition by the lecturer.

6. Feedback on learning.

7. Arousal.

8. Transfer of learning.

It takes at least two to communicate: a communicator and a receiver. People sometimes talk as if communication is a process of injection by the communicator. It isn't. They talk as if information can be transferred directly from one person's mind to another's. It can't. It requires activity by the receiver.

Whatever our objectives in lecturing, they can only be achieved subject to the physiological and psychological limitations of the students. Lecturers have to work within these limitations. If the acquisition of information is accepted as one of these objectives, it will be useful for lecturers to be able to apply a knowledge of the factors limiting the acquisition of information in lecture situations.

Since the brain has a coordinating function, these factors could include the whole of human psychology. However, Part Two will be limited to a consideration of memory, attention, and motivation with reference to teaching skills.

Structures and Processes

The brain can be thought of as a physical structure within which various processes take place. It is primarily a structure of nerve fibers (neurons); the processes are the stimulation and transmission of impulses along the neurons. Eventually some impulses could be transmitted along these neural pathways to muscles, resulting in observable behavior.

1. Memory Is a Sequence of Processes

If we think of the stimulation and transmission of impulses as information, we can say that previously established pathways "encode" (that is, interpret and organize) incoming information. Interpretations are *constructed* from *selected* information as part of encoding. If "stored" by establishing new pathways, they will influence later interpretations when they are reactivated or "retrieved." Thus memory entails three processes: encoding, storage, and retrieval.

2. There's Evidence for Two Kinds of Memory

Although psychologists now also talk about a sensory memory, it used to be thought that there are only two kinds of memory, a short-term (STM) and a long-term memory (LTM). There were six kinds of evidence for this.

a. Structural Changes in the Brain. First, there was physical evidence. For example, there were experiments in which an animal's brain was frozen and yet it retained skills it had learned before the period of freezing. These suggested that there were structural changes that were preserved in spite of the freezing.

There is also anatomical evidence. For example, structural changes occur at the synapses—the gaps between neurons in the brain—so that subsequent nerve impulses pass more easily from certain neurons to certain others.

b. A Logical Distinction. Second, there is a logical distinction between a process and a structure. The content of memories grouped as STMs are all processes, which is why they are temporary. The retrieval of LTMs may be a process, but their content is determined by neural structures.

c. Electrical Activity and Chemical Stimulation of the Brain. There is physiological evidence for the temporary nature of sensory and short-term memory processes. Electrical activity in the brain seems to die away in a matter of seconds.

Physiological studies using electroconvulsive therapy and chemical stimulation of the brain suggested that the physical consolidation of these memory processes into LTMs may go on for anything up to half an hour (Broadbent, 1970). If Broadbent was correct in emphasizing the importance of retrieving information in the first half hour in order to consolidate memory of it, this may be the maximum time that a lecturer should speak without giving students a task that involves retrieving it.

d. Common Experience. It does not require elaborate physiological evidence to show that there are at least two kinds of memory. It seems to be common sense, as well as common experience, that there is some kind of temporary holding mechanism in the mind as well as a long-term store. For example, if we want to think, we have to hold certain ideas in our mind before we can work on them. That is why Baddeley calls STM "*working memory.*" Since thinking is important for students, the factors that influence it are educationally important.

How are thoughts held longer than three or four seconds? One answer is that, with extra motivational energy, some active neural pathways go around in circles or loops, their impulses activating other areas of the brain as they go. This *spreading activation* is the very essence of creativity, thought, and higher education. In this way, new concepts are associated and distinguished.

e. A Limit to the Number of Items Memorized. It has long been evident that there is a limit to the number of items one can hold in the mind at once. This is clearly not the case in long-term memories.

f. The Methods of Association. There is also some evidence that in short-term memory one associates acoustically, while in long-term memory one associates according to the meanings of words. Thus, there seems to be a difference in the methods of association: the levels of processing.

3. But It's Not That Simple

However, more recent research shows that it is not that simple. If impulses are transmitted along neural pathways, it is clear that there is a sequence of processes over periods of time. The impulses could be initiated by any of the senses, or by the brain itself. Since the brain has a network of neurons, many pathways are possible. Thus many different processes could be involved in memory. Let's consider some of them.

a. Sensory Memories. First, there is a logical difference between STM working with concepts that have previously been stored in LTM, and *sensory memory* as the temporary holding of stimulation or sensations that have just been received through the senses before much encoding takes place. However, in practice there is more of a continuum than this logic might suggest.

A well-known experiment by Sperling is now interpreted in terms of visual sensory memory (iconic memory) and may tell us why students need to glance at a diagram so many times in copying it. Sperling (1960) presented sixteen letters and numbers in a 4 x 4 grid (Table 2.1) for a short period of time and only then told the subjects whether they had to remember all sixteen or just the four in a particular column or row.

The proportion that subjects remembered was twice as great when they only had to remember four than when they had to remember sixteen. This suggested that the subjects possessed more information in the brief moment after exposure than they could give. The memory of some of the items faded while they were remembering others.

b. Temporal Differences. The length of sensory and short-term memories also vary with how much encoding there has been. Sperling's visual images (icons) seemed to be available for only half a second, although this could be extended

TABLE 2.1. TYPE OF STIMULUS GRID USED BY SPERLING.

J	F	8	M
3	Q	W	D
Y	B	K	2
H	5	V	G

Source: Sperling, 1960.

to nearly five seconds if subsequent visual interference was minimized. There is some evidence that if a lecturer's words reach stage 2 in Figure 2.1 (that is, a string of sounds not yet identified as having any meaning), students can remember a sequence up to two seconds long. Whether the words are long or short is irrelevant. By use of a kind of mental echo chamber known as an echoic store, the material can typically be held for up to five seconds.

Yet if I ask you to divide 147 by 19 in your head, you may well hold the numbers longer than that. So the length of these memories differs with how deeply the information has to be processed.

c. Sense Modalities. Third, since there are distinguishable pathways for each of the senses, it is reasonable to talk about separate sensory, short-term, and long-term memories for each. For example, a brain-damaged patient might have impaired *auditory* STM while *visual* STM is unaffected. Our auditory and visual memories can be distinct.

d. Other Distinctive Abilities. Furthermore, there is evidence for several components of STM, each with its own capacity. For example, the *verbal auditory* STM used by students in lectures is distinct from other auditory STMs.

e. Contrasting LTMs. You might also think there are important differences in LTMs: between remembering the way to the train station, how to swim, the date of the attack on Pearl Harbor, and that the product of three times five equals fifteen.

f. Baddeley's Working Memory. This diversity poses a problem. How are these memories coordinated? It is clear that human beings act in a coordinated way most of the time. There has to be some kind of central processor. Baddeley calls it a "central executive." It sounds a bit like a ghost in the machine that does everything wonderful that cannot yet be explained. But Baddeley (1996) believes it is supported by two slave systems, the three together making what he calls "working memory" rather than STM.

One of the slave systems is an articulatory loop and phonological store (traced by arrows 12–10–26–2 in Figure 2.1). Using subvocal speech, this can extend the length of verbal auditory STM from two to three or four seconds. There is some vagueness in Baddeley's conception regarding the level(s) at which it operates. The loop can receive information from LTM as well as directly through stimulation. It is also a holding mechanism that permits thinking. But I have no doubt there are many such feedback systems in the way the brain is wired.

The other slave system is a comparable one for visual information, which he calls a "visuospatial sketch pad." Clearly, a lecture with any visual display uses both systems.

FIGURE 2.1. PROCESSES WHEN LISTENING AND TAKING NOTES IN LECTURES.

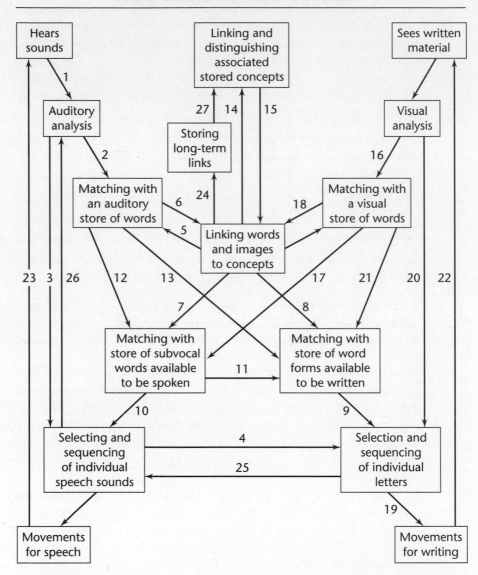

Source: Schema adapted and modified from Ellis and Young (1988).

g. Other Complexities. There are other problems about memory. For example, what pathways tell us that we don't know something? Conversely, it can be shown that we often know things we did not know we knew. This is called implicit memory. It is demonstrable when students solve problems, make decisions, or make judgments using information they cannot explicitly recall. Lecturers depend upon it when this week's lecture builds upon last week's even though students are not sufficiently familiar with last week's to articulate their understanding.

We shall see throughout this book that each of these complexities (a–g) is relevant to lecturing in different ways.

4. So, What Happens When Students Listen to a Lecture?

What happens when students listen to a lecture and take notes? The schema presented in Figure 2.1 adapts and modifies (perhaps controversially) a model proposed by Ellis and Young (1988). Their work is based upon pathways of stimulation (or lack of them) demonstrated among stroke and other brain-damaged patients. It should be noticed that the boxes are not objects. They do not necessarily correspond to identified locations in the brain. They are processes—activities—no doubt *connecting* different parts of the brain. Figure 2.1 represents students' brains as essentially dynamic. Their brains are information processors. One process stimulates another, or at least may do so. Although there are probably more feedback loops than depicted here, the arrows indicate which processes may stimulate which others. Thus they also depict chronological sequences.

a. Auditory Analysis of Sense Data. First, students must hear the noise the lecturer makes, hold it in sensory memory long enough to distinguish it from other noises in the environment, analyze it into individual speech sounds (phonemes), and group the phonemes together to make syllables while ignoring variations in pitch, speed, and accent. See arrow 1 in Figure 2.1.

b. Word Recognition. After auditory analysis, the syllables, either singly or in groups, need to be recognized by (that is, matched with) an auditory store of words (arrow 2). A particular feature of a lecture context is that some words cannot be recognized. They are unfamiliar, new, possibly technical terms. If students want to spell them, they may have to pay attention to the individual phonemes (arrow 3) and associate them with graphic shapes such as uppercase and lowercase letters, numbers, or other visual symbols (arrow 4).

c. Contextual Factors. Some syllables will be identified because of their context in the lecture. This suggests there is some kind of selective facilitation by the part of the brain concerned with concepts (arrow 5).What is significant for note takers, and the lecturers teaching them, is the short and temporary nature of this auditory STM. Though meaningfulness might extend it, we saw that auditory verbal STM for a string of words normally only lasts up to two seconds before the impulses decay. This might explain why people remembered President Reagan's one-liners. It challenges lecturers to make their key points in no more than two seconds each. If they use long words, students can remember fewer at a time.

d. Articulatory Loop. However, we saw that auditory verbal memory can be extended using subvocal speech, what Baddeley (1996) calls an "articulatory loop." He also says articulatory processes can take written material and convert it into subvocal speech so as to become part of the phonological store (16–17–10–26). This suggests students can copy small chunks from the chalkboard with scant knowledge of their meaning.

e. The Construction of Meaning by Encoding. The capacity of sounds and written symbols to arouse concepts is their meaning (arrow 6). Thus the meaning of words is a causal relationship between stimulation of an auditory store of words and a conceptual network (6).

This requires a process of encoding in order to understand. It is a function of short-term memory. Encoding has been described as processes whereby information is transformed by associating, discriminating, chunking, or coding it. Di Vesta and Gray (1972) argue that these processes are necessary when note taking involves extracting, summarizing, and organizing information.

To encode, students must segment the sounds from the lecturer into words; match them with an auditory store; get a preliminary recognition of their meaning, perhaps using probabilities in the context; decipher their syntax; incorporate gestures and other visual information; construct a possible meaning for the whole sentence; test it against context and other long-term knowledge; and try other meanings if it fails the test. All this must happen, much of it unconsciously, before the processes that the lecturers really want can begin, namely, the use of long-term memory and attitudes to apply, analyze, relate, and evaluate what has been said.

According to van Dijk and Kintsch (1978), people in Western cultures learn procedures or patterns for organizing and understanding information. These include cause and effect, compare and contrast, classification, and sequential description. In other words, arrow 15 in Figure 2.1 includes procedures and information processes, not just factual knowledge. Furthermore—and very important—we shall see later (particularly in Chapters Five, Six, Eight, and Nine) that lecturers who give rhetorical cues indicating which organizing procedures to call on achieve much greater clarity, and their students' notes include more information that the lecturers regard as important. (See Kintsch and Yarbrough, 1982.)

f. Thinking. The recognition and thought about what the lecturer is saying could result in a repeated cycle of stimulation (6–14–15–5–6), which interferes with matching the next group of words uttered by the lecturer. In other words, this is what we all know: there is a problem of divided attention if the student spends too long thinking about what the lecturer has just said. Students are under pressure not to think during lectures!

g. Expression or Recording? Once students know the meaning of what a lecturer has said, they may search their minds for ways to express it, either in subvocal speech (arrow 7) or in writing (8). If the latter, they must then select and sequence letters, numbers, or other symbols to write (9). If the former (7), they may subvocally select and sequence speech sounds (10). These may directly stimulate the selection and sequencing of individual letters and other graphic shapes (4). Alternatively, when concepts have stimulated a memory for spoken words (7), the concepts may be directly associated with their written form (11).

   In practice, we all know that as students we tend to write down the same words that the lecturer used. In short, there is some direct stimulation from hearing the words to subvocal expression of them (12) without much understanding of their meaning (6–5–6).

h. Visual Counterparts. It might be reasonable to suppose that there is a corresponding set of processes when students copy written material (16–22).

i. Levels of Processing. In summary, there is reason to think that in lectures there is a succession of processes students must undertake. They are sometimes described as levels of processing. The deepest levels employ the cycle 14–15–14–15, etc., in a variety of ways, while students with a disposition or intention to memorize will emphasize arrow 24. In European research, these two levels are contrasted as deep learning and surface learning, but most researchers and teachers would agree with Craik and Lockhart (1972) that deep processors remember more.

Factors Causing Forgetting

These factors and those aiding memory are fundamental to the lecture techniques discussed in Part Three.

1. Retroactive and Proactive Interference

Interference has long been regarded as the most important cause of forgetting. For example, students may learn certain facts in one lecture and then go on to a second lecture that tends to interfere with their memory of the first one. This is called retroactive interference—it occurs afterwards. Proactive interference is the other way around. What the students learned in the first lecture may interfere with what they learn in the second. Proactive interference occurs when the first lecture interferes; retroactive, when the second lecture interferes. Of the two, retroactive interference is the more powerful, though it is difficult to distinguish it from the effect of recency.

It is well known that facts learned just before going to bed at night are better remembered than those learned at other times. Similarly, it is to be expected that if there is a pause in the middle of a lecture, the facts presented just before the pause will be better remembered than those elsewhere, provided that the pause is not filled by distracting, or interfering, stimulation. This brings out a point that is frequently overlooked. Silence between teachers' remarks is a very important part of a lecture. Silences provide time for consolidation and thought. Their timing requires the skill of an actor. They are useful after rhetorical questions, or when a problem has been posed; provided attention is maintained, they may need to be longer in the third quarter of a lecture, where interference is greatest. Interference is probably the chief cause of forgetting in lectures, particularly when the lecture is too fast.

The more similar their subject matter, the greater the interference. Associative interference is also generally agreed to be the most potent cause of forgetting in long-term memory (Broadbent, 1970). It is for this reason that students are advised to vary their subject of study. This is because when many of the same nerve pathways are involved, there is ambiguity over which should be inhibited. In this instance, spreading activation is a nuisance. One pattern of pathways is not sufficiently distinguished from another.

Interference is particularly potent over short periods, such as a few seconds. That is why, when they say something important, many teachers leave a moment for it to sink in before they go on. When experimental psychologists give subjects a long list of nonsense words to learn, it is often found that the memory of the first and last few words is better than those in the middle. This is known as "the bowing effect" (Figure 2.2). One reason why words in the middle of the list are not remembered so well is that they suffer from both proactive and retroactive interference.

Glanzer and Cunitz have shown that with a slower presentation the effect of trace decay (discussed in the next section), or a longer period of retroactive interference, produces poorer recall of the first items (see Figure 2.2), while the end

FIGURE 2.2. DIAGRAMMATIC
REPRESENTATION OF THE BOWING EFFECT.

Source: Adapted from Glanzer and Cunitz (1966).

of the list is sufficiently recent to remain unaffected. This recency factor is illustrated by the fact that if the time of recall is delayed, recall of items at the end of the list is further impaired, but not recall of those at the beginning (which Glanzer and Cunitz thought had entered the subjects' long-term memories). If, during the delay, the subjects repeat the words to themselves, they can counteract the impairment. In effect, this "rehearsal" keeps the words recent.

Contrary to what many students may believe, most lectures do not consist entirely of nonsense words. Therefore some caution is needed in applying these findings; but if we suppose that a lecturer gives a definition, law, or principle that the students are expected to take down, most of the points I've discussed may be illustrated. If the students start to write before the lecturer has finished enunciating the definition, this act may interfere with their memory of words they have just heard. If they wait until the enunciation is complete, the middle will probably be lost, especially if the definition is long. If the enunciation is slow, repetition will compensate for the consequent impairment of the memory of the opening words, but retention of the middle section will still be poor. Further repetition or slowing of pace may be necessary if a handout or other written source is not available (if the information is important, perhaps it should be offered).

Johnston and Calhoun (1969) have shown that the same thing occurs in short lectures. Facts were not remembered so well when they were presented in the middle of an eight-minute talk. Tannenbaum (1954) found the same with ten-minute presentations. He played twelve tape-recorded news broadcasts, each with the same twelve items but with their positions rotated and found that items at the beginning and end were remembered better than those in the middle (ten minutes after the newscast). After rearranging the order of a twenty-minute tape-recorded lecture, Holen and Oaster (1976) obtained a bowing effect; but unlike the case with Johnston and Calhoun, these students showed better mastery of the beginning of the lecture than the end. All these experiments used presentations of less than twenty-five to thirty minutes, a period related to the consolidation of STMs. I obtained a different result using lectures composed of four rotated ten-minute sections. I found a powerful recency effect; scores for the last twenty minutes were best. Scores for the first ten minutes were worst, presumably because they relied on long-term memories suffering from interference during consolidation (Bligh, 1974). We shall see in the next chapter that there are other reasons for concluding that lectures over twenty-five minutes make extra psychological demands.

It seems likely that the bowing effect can be neutralized by structuring lectures with contrasting approaches, novel points, or surprising facts in the middle. I said the interference by one fact with the memory of another is strongest where the two facts are similar. Statements that are different stand out and are well remembered even when they are in the middle. In a simulated TV news broadcast, Gunter, Berry, and Clifford (1981) compared memory of three similar news items followed by a contrasting topic with four that were all the same. The contrasting item was better recalled both immediately and in a delayed test. Gunter, Berry, and Clifford interpreted this as release from proactive interference, but as we shall see in the next chapter, it could be interpreted in terms of arousal and raised levels of attention. Others have called the item "isolated." Kintsch and Bates (1977) found that extraneous remarks in the middle of a lecture, such as jokes and announcements, were better remembered than key points and details two days and five days later. Holen and Oaster isolated a point by first remarking, "This seems to be an especially significant point." Not surprisingly, it was better remembered than those immediately around it in the lecture sequence. Suffice it to say, effective lecturing is a much more subtle business than many new lecturers may suppose.

2. "Trace Decay" in the First Few Seconds

To avoid distortions from using meaningful material, Peterson (1966) presented three-letter nonsense syllables to subjects and found there was very rapid forgetting in the first six seconds after the presentation (Figure 2.3). He suggests that any trace in the perceptual mechanism quickly fades after presentation. This is consistent with what is known about sensory memory, the early stages of STM, and electrochemical brain processes. The rapid forgetting is sometimes called "trace decay." The amount of forgetting has been shown to increase with the number of items to be remembered (Murdock, 1961). More recent research suggests that interference is probably more responsible than trace decay is for forgetting after five seconds (Baddeley, 1996).

FIGURE 2.3. RECALL OF THREE UNRELATED LETTERS IN RELATION TO THE INTERVAL SINCE PRESENTATION.

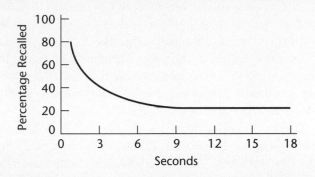

Note: To eliminate rehearsal, subjects were required to count backwards in threes during the interval.
Source: Peterson (1966).

Similarly, it is to be expected that a student's memory when taking notes of what a lecturer has said will also quickly fade, particularly if points are not crystallized by a short key phrase. It is partly for this reason that important points in a lecture should be presented in a brief and semipermanent form on the blackboard, overhead projector, screen, or a handout. We shall see that these provide supplementary holding mechanisms when the lecturer wants students to think about presented information.

3. The Amount of Information

A very common cause of forgetting is trying to learn too much. Katz (1950) has shown that adding to the number of elements in an intellectual task causes confusion and inefficiency after a certain number has been reached. It is a common fault of lecturers with good intentions to try to teach too much. Russell, Hendricson, and Herbert (1984) have shown that students learn more when information density is not too high. When high, retroactive interference is severe (recency effect); and if very high, the middle of the lecture suffers (a bowing effect). Short-term memory has a limited capacity. Miller (1967) says that the average number of items of knowledge that a person can hold in short-term memory is seven plus or minus two. It may be said that, when playing a party game in which a number of articles are presented on a tray and the goal is to remember as many of them as possible when the tray is moved out of sight, one can usually remember more than nine of the small articles on the tray, but this is probably achieved by grouping them in some way—and this, of course, is a way of aiding one's memory.

It is for this reason that I have grouped these twelve factors affecting memory into four concerned with forgetting and eight with aiding the student's memory. You will see that some of the factors could be classified in either subheading. I have found, when presenting these twelve points in a lecture, that student-teachers remember them better if grouped in this way.

Since the capacity of short-term memory is a factor in intelligence, one might expect students to be able to hold more items in their mind at once than the average member of the population; but this is only one factor in intelligence, and students are selected on a wider range of abilities.

There are some students who do not take notes in lectures, and some lecturers who prefer students not to. Although note taking may interfere with students' memories and inhibit their organization of information, it is usually advisable where the lecturer makes more than seven points worth remembering. (See tabulated evidence in Chapter Nine.)

4. Repressing What You Don't Want to Remember

People forget what they do not want to remember. In other words, motivation is an important cause of forgetting. Freud called this "repression." Repression is sometimes thought of as being unhealthy. It may be, if it leads us to be dominated by irrational motives. In most people, it is a very important defense mechanism that prevents us from being mentally disturbed by unpleasant memories. It is important in an academic context to be aware of the temptation to ignore facts that do not fit our interpretations and feelings. One of the functions of discussion, both in teaching and research, is to force us to face facts we prefer to ignore. Of course, motivation can also aid memorization, but this will be dealt with in a separate section.

Factors Aiding Memory

1. Making the Lecture Meaningful to the Students

One of the most important factors affecting memory is the meaningfulness of what is to be remembered. By this I mean how far it fits in with the ideas the person already has. This can be demonstrated quite forcibly by looking at the three lists of words in Table 2.2 for about ten seconds each and then writing down those that can be remembered.

It will probably be found that there are considerable differences in the memory of the three lists, yet each consists of the same thirty letters. But they do not each consist of thirty different items to be learned. In one there are ten words to

TABLE 2.2. "CHUNKING" INFORMATION.

yma	try	the
uyo	can	lid
ont	but	may
teh	you	not
dil	yet	fit
ryt	not	yet
ubt	the	you
nac	may	can
tey	fit	but
tif	lid	try

be learned, and in another, two phrases. Thus the meaning of what has to be learned makes a drastic difference to the quantity. This is why the meaningfulness of what is taught is so important in teaching. By using established pathways, meaningfulness enables information to be grouped into chunks—what is called the chunking of information.

In a lecture containing terms that students do not understand, they are faced with grammatically correct sentences that have no meaning for them. They may take notes with the hope of making sense of them later, or they may refuse to write down what appears to lack meaning. Because, as we have seen, meaning is an important factor affecting long-term memory, the latter strategy is unlikely to produce effective learning. The former relies on the accuracy of short-term memory. But how accurate are students' short-term memories for sentences they do not understand? By taking five "normal sentences," each with five words and the same syntactic form, and systematically exchanging words with the same syntactic functions, Marks and Miller (1964) obtained grammatically correct but meaningless sentences (e.g. "Soapy wildcats give smoky damsels"). By scrambling the word order of the "normal" sentences, they obtained "anagram strings," and "word lists" were formed by scrambling the word order of the "meaningless sentences." Figure 2.4 shows the ability of students to write down the five-word strings in the correct order for each of the four types. The results show an improvement with practice on successive trials, but the important point for us is that short-term recall of so-called normal sentences is two to five times that of meaningless sentences. This difference is likely to be increased with longer sentences.

Although it is difficult to talk about the intelligibility of lectures in quantitative terms, observations such as these suggest that the effect of lecturing in simple language is sufficiently important to justify very careful preparation.

FIGURE 2.4. AVERAGE PERCENTAGE OF FIVE-WORD STRINGS THAT WERE CORRECTLY RECALLED FOR EACH OF FOUR TYPES OF STRING OVER FIVE TRIALS.

Source: Adapted from Marks and Miller (1964).

An important function of active methods of learning, such as writing essays and discussion, is to force students to relate the subject to their own conceptual frameworks. Students can only say what the subject means to them personally. Because the conceptual frameworks of the lecturer and the students are not the same (see Abercrombie, 1960), and the lecture method is largely a one-way process, maximum intelligibility is unlikely to be achieved by the lecture method alone.

Educationalists frequently suggest the need to get down to the students' level and start where they are. This may be trite, but it is nonetheless true. What the lecturer says only has meaning for the students if they can relate it to ideas they already possess.

Consequently, when I am asked, "Should a lecturer cover the ground laid down in the syllabus, even if some students don't understand, or go at a slower pace and get behind?" the answer must be the latter. In either case, some students will not know as much as one would like, but in the latter the lecturer knows what they know and what they do not, while the students have a firm framework around which they may build by reading. In the latter case, students may catch up by systematic study; in the former, neither the lecturer nor the students know the size or place of the gaps in knowledge. Consequently, no systematic, planned build-up is possible and no lecture based on previous parts of the course can be assuredly intelligible to the students. These points apply not only to knowledge but to the "thinking skills" or "patterns of thought" that are normally learned early in a course and that new lecturers can easily overlook as needing to be taught. If lecturers considered their courses in terms of the learning achieved by students rather than as a succession of performances by lecturers, this question would seldom be asked.

2. Whole Versus Part Learning

There is a very debatable question as to whether students learn better by trying to take in everything at once or by splitting a subject into small parts. Psychologists disagree whether learning the whole of something, or only part of it at a time, is better. It is probably better to learn a poem by heart in large sections, because if it is broken into small sections the student also has to learn how to put them together again. This is an extra task. On the other hand, with complicated tasks that must be understood, this is a small price to pay for the greater simplicity that results from dealing with small units. Rote learning and some experimental skills are sequential tasks, like learning the poem; but understanding—for example in the social sciences—can frequently be acquired only by appreciating the component parts of the total social situation first.

3. Organizing the Subject

Organization is involved in both of the previous two factors. If subject matter is arranged in a logical way, it is easier to understand as a whole. Organization of subject matter is particularly important with adults and in academic subjects. This is why the clear statement of the organization of a lecture, the writing of essays, and the tidy summary of a rambling discussion are important for student learning. Chapter Five gives ways to organize lectures.

4. Rehearsing the Material

Many psychologists believe that rehearsal is a very important factor in aiding memory. Rehearsal consists of saying the subject matter to oneself, or in some way going over it after the initial presentation. If Broadbent (1970) is correct that rehearsal, or retrieval, within half an hour of the initial presentation is very important for the consolidation of learning, then the provision of buzz groups, silent revision, or even short tests within the lecture situation are important teaching techniques. Chapters Eighteen and Nineteen give further ideas.

Similarly, it is important that the practice of skills by students should closely follow the theoretical discussion. Indeed, the immediate provision of situations in which the student must apply information, after hearing it in a lecture, is an important and underused teaching strategy. Neurologically, it encourages spreading activation so that connections are made between concepts. It contextualizes the subject matter, gives it meaning, and makes it relevant. McLeish (1968) found that students who averaged 39 percent on a test of factual material immediately following a lecture scored only 3 percent less than a month later when, in the meantime, they had received and discussed the lecture script.

The importance of rehearsal is most strikingly displayed in data reworked by Bassey (1968) from a series of experiments by Jones (1923). Five groups of students (A through E) were given a lecture. Group A was tested immediately, B after one day, C after one week, D after two weeks, and E after three weeks. The results, and those of subsequent tests, are shown in Figure 2.5. It will be seen that even after sixty-three days Group A retained more than B retained after one day. It is inferred that this is the result of A's immediate rehearsal during the immediate test. Thus the immediacy of rehearsal is an important factor in long-term retention. Bassey is probably justified in assuming the comparability of the content and groups across Jones's experiments; and though Jones's data do not justify quite such a smooth graph as Bassey draws, the general argument is valid.

One of the functions of note taking in lectures is to arrest the decay of memory traces by rehearsal of what is written. Reading notes immediately after the lecture will be more effective than "vision" for the first time (hardly *re*vision!) two weeks before the examinations; but rehearsal during the lecture itself would be even more effective. It practices retrieval and the activation of particular neural pathways and loops, thereby making recall and thought more probable. McQueen, Meschino, Pike, and Poelstra (1994) have demonstrated the same point using weekly lecture quizzes. Practice strengthens responses.

It is the responsibility of the lecturer to provide opportunity for this by arranging short buzz discussions between neighbors on issues raised, the provision

FIGURE 2.5. THE VALUE OF REHEARSAL FOLLOWING A LECTURE.

Source: Adapted from Bassey (1968).

of questions, or even short periods of silence specifically to recall notes. (In each case, the purpose of these activities must be explained to the students to ensure their cooperation.)

5. Repetition by the Lecturer

Every teacher knows that repetition consolidates learning, provided there is some initial learning to consolidate. Most teachers have to say a thing a number of times before an acceptable proportion of the class remembers what has been said. Repetition differs from rehearsal in that it is repetition by the teacher. Rehearsal requires an activity by the student.

Following an experiment on learning to associate pairs of stimuli, Rock (1957) concluded that repetition strengthened, or consolidated, associations once they were formed but played no role in their formation. Although Rock's experiment has since been the subject of controversy in the psychology of verbal learning, it makes good sense if applied to a lecture situation. Kiewra and others (1991) presented the same lecture three times. The first time, students noted the most important points. The second and third presentations gave an opportunity to add less important information and build higher-level concepts.

If there is no learning from the first presentation, repetition does not help. Beard (1970) describes an occasion when a lecturer, having been told by the class after half an hour that they had not understood a word, proceeded to repeat the performance in a quarter of an hour. Such repetition is unlikely to be any more effective than the first performance. To take an extreme case, imagine a lecture in a foreign language you don't understand. Your understanding will not be improved however many times you hear it, because no encoding is possible. But if there is some learning on the first occasion, the repetition can have some interactive or consolidating effect; in this case the learning of the first occasion can provide a conceptual framework, a set of neural pathways, to give some meaning to the second (Barnes, MacArthur, and Ballantine, 1983).

6. Feedback on Learning

Students' learning of cognitive and motor skills is normally better if they know how well they are doing. Such knowledge of results, or feedback, can be either rewarding or punishing. The terms *reward* and *punishment* have a wide meaning in this context. A smile, or a checkmark on a student's work, may be rewarding. A sigh, or even silence, can be punishing in some circumstances. In both cases, such knowledge is more effective the sooner it is acquired after testing. Persistent punishment leads to discouragement and a decline in performance of memory tasks, while persistent reward normally gives encouragement and leads to gradual improvement. Both are equally effective at first (Figure 2.6), because students can learn from their mistakes and their successes. It will be seen from this that knowledge of results may be effective in two ways. It can provide information on which the student may act; it may be a regulator of student motivation. Information is most important at first; motivation is more important later.

These principles are important in all contact with students but particularly when handing back written work. The most effective teaching probably consists of selective reward and punishment according to the teacher's objectives and the personalities of the students. Teachers, too, need to have knowledge of their results.

It is important to notice that teachers and students require this knowledge of results as soon as possible if they are to make use of the information it contains. Habits and expectations form quickly. Feedback received after three weeks of a one-year course will have more effect on a teacher's, or a student's, motivation and amount of energy than on how that energy is directed. Even so, the most effective feedback is given before that time. (Three weeks is about 10 percent of a year-long course, 20 percent of a semester.) The results of examinations are too late.

7. Arousal

It is fairly obvious that people remember things better when they are alert than when they are tired (Sherwood, 1965). But since this is dealt with in the section on arousal in the next chapter, no more will be said about it here.

FIGURE 2.6. RELATIVE EFFECTS OF PERSISTENT REWARD AND PUNISHMENT.

8. Transfer of Learning

Finally, something may be easier to learn because it is similar to a previous experience. This is called positive transfer of learning, and the greater the similarity, the stronger the transfer. If memory of the first thing hinders memory of the second, it is called negative transfer of learning. Thus, practice at one skill affects the performance of similar skills. As we cannot hope to teach students everything, positive transfer of learning is a very important principle. Education is impossible without it. To take an elementary example, if a child is taught how to multiply two numbers together, the teacher relies on the child's being able to transfer this skill to other numbers. We rely on the same principle of transfer in tertiary education, with skills such as analytical and critical thinking. It is for this reason that training in study skills is essential for all students.

Conclusion

In this chapter, we have seen that information can be brought to mind either when it is being actively transmitted or by activating such transmissions along pathways determined by neural structures. The transmissions are temporary; the structures are long-term. The job of teachers and students working together is to develop the structures. Factors preventing and aiding this have then been considered in turn.

That may not be the usual way teachers think about their job. At one level, it confirms what you know already: what the lecturer says should be stimulating, well organized, meaningful to all students, and delivered at a speed that all can follow. At another level, it makes possible an analysis of what we do, and what we ought to do, when we lecture. Part Three applies that analysis. But the analysis is not complete. In the rest of Part Two, we need to look at students' attention and motivation and what lecturers can do to maintain and intensify them.

CHAPTER THREE

FACTORS AFFECTING STUDENTS' ATTENTION

The effects of arousal.

Factors affecting student arousal.

1. Variations in stimulation in the learning situation.

2. Students' arousal regimes during periods of teaching.

3. Students' daily work and rest regimes.

4. Students' physical environment and bodily condition.

Although there are many meanings of *attention* (Treisman, 1966), in this context we are concerned with the students' ability to concentrate. The problems for teachers are, first, what factors affect student concentration, and second, how we can use our knowledge of these factors to help them.

There are two broad factors: arousal and motivation. Both refer to the amount of energy a student has. *Arousal* refers to a general level of activity; it is a measure of nonspecific stimulation of a student's cerebral cortex, which facilitates the transmission of nerve impulses from one part of the brain to another. *Motivation* is the energy directed toward a specific kind of activity or goal. (These are intended as nontechnical explanations of the terms, not definitions.) The research into student arousal and motivation is not particularly new, and its findings may seem fairly commonsense if you think about them. The trouble is, many lecturers don't think about them, so I offer no apology for presenting them here.

The Effects of Arousal

At what level of arousal should a teacher aim to keep students? The graph in Figure 3.1 (sometimes known as the "inverted U curve") shows a typical level of

FIGURE 3.1. THE INVERTED U CURVE.

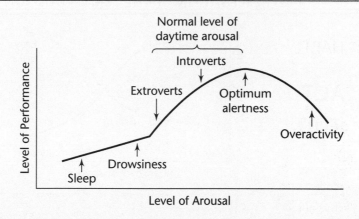

performance in relation to arousal. Students in lectures, it seems, can be conceived as varying from a state of deep coma to berserk anxiety!

It will be seen that at the extremes of relaxation and overactivity, the level of performance at, say, a learning or manual task is poor. But between these extremes there is an optimum level. We live most of our lives on the left-hand side of the optimum level. If we are stimulated, our level of arousal increases. We can be overstimulated, but the more common fault of lecturers is not to be stimulating enough. Arousal varies with personality factors. Extroverts require more stimulation than introverts to reach their optimum level. Using Cattell's 16 Personality Factor Test, Boreham reports that inattention in lectures is related to self-reports of "untroubled adequacy" (Boreham, 1984; Boreham and Lilley, 1978).

So long as they are not too relaxed, students generally perform better at difficult tasks if they start at a lower level of arousal. This is because the effort required raises the level of arousal to the optimum. Conversely, with simple tasks there is a temptation for students to take it too easy, and make silly mistakes. Consequently a higher initial level of arousal favors good performance at easy tasks. This generalization that lower initial arousal produces better performance at difficult tasks, depicted in Figure 3.2, is known as the "Yerkes-Dodson Law." It probably applies within the normal range of wakefulness and aids understanding of experiments such as the work of Thorson and Lang (1992). Using televised talking-head lectures, the insertion of videographics produced an orienting response with increased arousal (measured physiologically). In other words, arousal shifted from left to right in Figures 3.1 and 3.2. The learning of difficult and unfamiliar

FIGURE 3.2. DIAGRAMMATIC
REPRESENTATION OF THE YERKES-DODSON LAW.

material suffered, while retention of easier and more familiar material presented at these times was enhanced.

It may be concluded that a teacher must aim to keep students at the level of arousal appropriate to the task. This usually means finding ways to increase or maintain it.

Factors Affecting Student Arousal

We shall consider these four factors:

1. Variations in stimulation in the learning situation
2. The students' arousal regimes during periods of teaching
3. The students' daily work and rest regimes
4. The students' physical environment and bodily condition

1. Variations in Stimulation in the Learning Situation

Broadly speaking, variations in stimulation increase arousal and hence increase the students' attention. It seems reasonable to expect from this that lectures and audiotapes will be particularly poor teaching methods for maintaining students' attention unless a special effort is made to prevent their minds from wandering. In the lecture situation, the students maintain roughly the same posture, listen to the same human voice, and look at the same visual field.

a. Auditory Stimulation. As a lecturer, you should always ask yourself, *How can I vary my presentation?* One of the unwritten worldwide assumptions about lecturing is that lectures are solo performances. But why should they be? Betts and Walton (1970) provided auditory variation in university physics lectures to nearly four hundred students by alternately presenting differing points of view as a dialogue. One gave the logical organization of the subject, while the other interposed questions and gave illustrations or demonstrations. Comedians have long known that they can hold their audience far longer when there are two of them performing. Television companies know viewers will switch channels if the speaker does not change frequently, even in news programs. The same has been shown in psychological experiments. For example, Gruber (1964) demonstrated that alternation between auditory and visual presentations will raise levels of attention to a vigilance task. The same goes for lecturing; without varied stimulation, students mentally switch off.

Variations in auditory stimulation can also be introduced in lectures if there are frequent opportunities for questions and discussion. Therefore buzz groups and controlled discussion are important techniques for the teacher, especially in large classes where loss of student attention is frequent and can easily go unnoticed. The provision of occasional silence for the rapid revision of notes gives students an opportunity to frame questions in addition to a change in stimulation.

b. Visual Stimulation. Visual illustrations have an arousing effect whether or not they provide necessary information. I have found that students' heart rates will rise ten beats per minute in the six seconds after switching an overhead projector on or off. Human vision has an orienting reflex toward movement, such that some lecturers find they can draw attention to important points by using hand movements. Others overuse such gestures. At the secondary school level, Wyckoff (1973) found that increases in stimulus variation as measured by teacher mobility, gesturing, and pausing increased students' recall of factual information from lectures. The opposite was the case at the elementary school level, where perhaps the pupils were already near optimum arousal.

College decor should also not be ignored on the mistaken assumption that it is irrelevant to student learning. Drab buildings will produce a lower standing level of arousal; the use of color in slides or overhead projector transparencies will be particularly alerting.

c. Posture. Members of an audience will be more alert if their spines are upright. It is difficult for the lecturer to provide variations in postural position for the student, but opportunities to gather around the lecturer's bench for a demonstration, or to move to a short discussion group, should not be rejected as too much trouble if they also can achieve course objectives.

d. Novel Stimulation. The essential requirement is for the teacher to provide novel stimulation (at intervals, if not continuously) throughout a lecture.

This point cannot be emphasized too strongly. The idea that lecturers should use the lecture method and no other for fifty minutes on end is absurd; yet it is quite a common practice. The remarkable tolerance of students for this diet is all the more surprising when one considers that the effect of monotonous stimulation is common knowledge and does not require verification by psychological experiment. MacManaway (1970) reports that 84 percent of his students said twenty to thirty minutes was the maximum length of lecturing to which they could attend.

Television is thought to be a medium that holds attention, but Mills (1966) and Wood and Hedley (1968) found long ago that fifteen to twenty minutes was the optimum viewing time if the material had to be learned. Barrington (1965) reports an optimum of about twenty-five minutes. Smith and Wyllie (1965) found that over half the students benefited when TV and conventional methods were mixed.

Discussion is less prone to lack of concentration partly because of the variety of voices that the student hears, and partly because there is self-stimulation if the students themselves are actively involved. This latter case is more effective than external stimulation.

Many students always occupy the same seats in the library for private study. Superficially, it would seem that if the book to be studied is the only novel item in the environment, the students are likely to concentrate on it. In practice, the monotony of the rest of the environment has a more powerful de-arousing effect. Thus it is better for students to vary their place of work.

e. Intensity of Stimulation. Variations in the intensity of stimulation are also arousing. A sudden loud noise will make a person jump. Similarly, it is a well-known trick that the sudden lowering of a lecturer's voice can emphasize a point because it attracts attention. On the other hand, a continuous or repeated loud noise has a deadening effect. Buck (1963) has shown that a railway accident may be caused by habituation to the loud sound of an alarm bell two feet from the driver's ear if this stimulation is persistent.

2. Students' Arousal Regimes During Periods of Teaching

a. Attention Decrement. Figure 3.3. shows the typical decrement curve for a person's attention to a single task over a period of time. With more difficult tasks, extroverts show a greater decline after the first half hour than introverts (Bakan,

FIGURE 3.3. DECREMENT IN ATTENTION.

1959). This pattern is normally displayed in the level of performance of both students and their teachers in their respective work situations. In addition, it has been suggested (McLeish, 1968; Lloyd, 1968) that student attention takes five minutes to settle down at first, and it rises and falls during the last five or ten minutes of a fifty-five-minute lecture. Lloyd hypothesizes that the lecturer's level of performance conforms to Figure 3.3. Since the effectiveness of a lecture depends on both the lecturer and the students, it will conform to the lower of the two levels shown in Figure 3.4. The lecturer's level is normally higher owing to greater self-stimulation. Lloyd confirmed his hypothesis with reference to the number of notes students took. It may be objected that subject matter is not equally noteworthy throughout a lecture. Perhaps the rise at the end of the lecture would occur if the lecturer said, "To sum up, . . ." and all hitherto somnolent students immediately grabbed their pens to make amends for their earlier indolence.

What is needed is either a measure of arousal independent of the subject matter, or measures of learning in experiments that control for it. Both have been attempted.

Heart rate is one indication of arousal, but it is not a definitive measure of it, nor is the relation to learning a direct one. I took students' heart rates every six seconds throughout lectures and at first found the pattern confirmed Lloyd's hypothesis, including the rise at the end. Indeed, on one occasion when, at the end of normal time, the lecturer asked to continue for an extra ten minutes, there was a double rise in heart rate at the end! There is no obvious explanation for this rise. Even disregarding the student intervention, Figure 3.5 seems to show it in both lecture and discussion (see also Figure 17.1); but it does not always appear (Figure 3.6). Figure 3.6 shows separate regression lines for the first half hour and the second part of four lectures. They suggest that these two periods in lectures are quite distinct.

FIGURE 3.4. LEVEL OF PERFORMANCE DURING A LECTURE.

Source: Adapted from Lloyd (1968).

FIGURE 3.5. STUDENTS' HEART RATES IN CLASS.

FIGURE 3.6. STUDENTS' HEART RATES
IN UNINTERRUPTED LECTURES.

Note: The data are for sixteen students in four lectures with measures taken every five seconds. Thus each dot is the mean of 960 readings in a five-minute period. Heart rates stabilized before teaching began. Each lecture was eighty minutes (longer than most). Separate first-order regressions are presented for the first thirty minutes and the remainder to suggest that the arousal characteristics of the two periods are different. The first six means are as high as, or higher than, any that follow.

Confirming Lloyd's observation using other measures, Scerbo, Warm, Dember, and Grasha (1992) report that students take notes less and less as the lecture proceeds; but immediate recall does not show the same decrement. I have also been unable to confirm the decrement in attention using objective measures of students' learning during periods of lecturing lasting forty minutes. The four quarters of each of four lectures given in four different orders to four groups failed to show a decrement in learning according to their position in the order of presentation. On the contrary, in using an immediate test, learning in the last twenty minutes seemed superior, which suggests the importance of recency when the test is immediately after the lecture. We have already seen that arousal is by no means the only factor influencing learning. In any case, the threat of a test immediately after the lectures may have "concentrated the mind most wonderfully." So this experiment is not sufficient grounds to say that psychological conditions affecting attention are fundamentally different in lecture situations from those studied by psychologists. Furthermore, Giles and others (1982) did find that learning was greatest in the second fifteen minutes of a sixty-minute lecture.

Following Lloyd, Maddox and Hoole (1975) monitored the "information units" noted by students at five-minute intervals through a fifty-minute lecture as a proportion of what the lecturer considered ideal; but the number spoken by the lecturer confirmed Lloyd's pattern. He slowed down. Consequently, the proportion noted by students was relatively constant, while the number decreased. In short, the efficiency of lecturer and students decreased together, much as Lloyd describes.

What can we conclude about the attention decrement? To generalize is difficult. On a subjective level, it is common experience that concentration for a full hour is not easy. There is reason to think that a lecture of twenty to thirty minutes is long enough unless there is varied stimulation. Note taking does decrease during a lecture, but evidence on the temporal pattern of learning during lectures is equivocal as judged by immediate tests. However, the results of immediate tests have a strong short-term memory component. Neither life nor examinations are immediate tests using short-term memory. They use long-term memories. We shall see in Chapter Nine that the opportunity to review notes strongly improves scores on delayed tests. Hence the decrement in note taking will reduce knowledge in the long run, and it is the long run that matters.

b. The Effect of a Short Break. A short break will allow the level of attention to recover, though later decrements will be quicker than the first. Mackworth (1950) has shown that performance on a vigilance task, requiring attention to a dial, will return nearly to its starting level after a short rest period. Adams (1955) found a marked improvement in attention to a manual skill after a brief rest; but improvement was not so great when the rest period was spent watching others do the same thing as when it was a complete change. A change is nearly as good as a rest. Wilkinson (1959) has reported an improvement for up to thirty minutes following a break of twenty-five seconds. If these experimental findings are applicable to teaching, there is a strong case for short breaks and changes in teaching method in each period of teaching (see Figure 3.5).

If Mackworth's, Adams's, and Wilkinson's findings are relevant and are applied to McLeish's and Lloyd's model (Figure 3.4), we may obtain Figure 3.7, which implies a gain as a result of rest. A three-minute buzz group could have a similar effect because it would provide a variation in stimulation. The rate of decrement shown is arbitrary and is steeper with more boring subject matter. Students may be bored because the subject matter is too easy, incomprehensibly difficult, or not personally interesting. The more bored the students, the more frequent the variations in teaching methods should be. Consequently, it is not suggested that the number of rest or buzz periods should always be limited to one.

These ideas are an extrapolation from psychological evidence from specific vigilance situations. They are confirmed by common teaching experience and by controlled experiments in teaching. Notice that the pauses may be quite brief. Weaver and Cotrell (1985) reported more student involvement, understanding,

FIGURE 3.7. HYPOTHESIZED PATTERN OF PERFORMANCE DURING A LECTURE WITH A BREAK.

thought, and feedback as a result of specific mental exercises in the middle of a lecture (for example, "Tear out half a sheet of paper and write your reactions to the lecture so far"). In an important experiment, Ruhl and Suritsky (1995) compared the effectiveness of lectures with three two-minute pauses, the provision of a lecture outline, and a combination of these two procedures. The pause procedure alone resulted in better free recall of lecture ideas and more complete lecture notes. This result could reflect the opportunity to fill in gaps in notes and to revise and rehearse what had been said rather than, or in addition to, superior levels of attention.

Whatever your psychological interpretation, the educational advantages of short breaks remain. Johnstone and Percival (1976) observed students' inattention in ninety fifty-minute chemistry lectures given by twelve lecturers. After initial inattention when settling down, the next lapse typically occurred between ten and eighteen minutes; lapses became more frequent, reaching a point just before the end at which students could not attend for more than three or four minutes at a time. Attention was very much worse in a TV overflow room. Attention varied with the difficulty of the subject, the rate of delivery, the legibility of blackboard writing, and the lecturers' personalities. Yet—a most powerful point—inattention could be postponed, or even eliminated altogether, by short buzz-group discussions.

3. Students' Daily Work and Rest Regimes

The same decrement in attention, with consequent need of variation in teaching methods, occurs through the day as within a lecture. Some people reach their optimum level of performance during the morning, others at midday; but very few people indeed are at their best in the afternoon. In a series of experiments using identical lectures, I found that students scored better on immediate tests at eight cognitive levels after lectures starting at 9:30 A.M. than 11:15 A.M., and better at 11:15 A.M. than 2:00 P.M. (Bligh, 1975). Likewise comparing students with themselves on different occasions, or with each other on the same test items, Holloway (1966) found scores better at 9:00 A.M. than 4:30 P.M.

Similarly, most people are more alert on Monday and Tuesday than on Friday. Yet these facts are commonly ignored by both teachers and those who organize their timetables. Since attention to lectures is more difficult in the afternoon and evening, lectures should be shorter, more varied, and more stimulating, or give way completely to small-group teaching or other active methods of learning, at that time.

After reviewing studies of drivers and others after some hours of activity, Jane Mackworth (1970) concludes that "prolonged performance in a monotonous task may interfere with the ability to make decisions at a fairly high cortical level, but not with automatic activity" (p. 35). This is consistent with the mirthful comment that lectures are periods of time during which the notes of the lecturer are transferred to the notebook of the students without going through the brains of either.

When the level of arousal is lower, either because of the time of day or because of loss of sleep, knowledge of results of the performance arouses the cortex, with consequent improvement (Wilkinson, 1961; Mackworth, 1970). Discussion of problems in small groups provides the student with this knowledge of results in a way that lectures or other presentation methods never can. Therefore, lecturers facing a class on "the morning after the students' night before" or on the day after the "Rag Ball" will be well advised to use discussion methods. Apart from some Russian work, there is little evidence in favor of sleep learning; practice of the art during lectures is not recommended!

Readers of advertisements for a well-known bedtime drink will know that "research has shown that there are many different levels of sleep." The inverted U curve shows that the same might be said of wakefulness.

The important point is that the level of arousal is continuously fluctuating, and even during apparent wakefulness there will be brief moments of sleep, known as "microsleeps" (Oswald, 1966). Contrary to what one might at first expect, students' heart rates fluctuate more toward the end of lectures when students seem more tired. Microsleeps are more frequent among sleep-deprived or tired students, but in between microsleeps normal mental capacity is not greatly impaired. Thus, a student will work more slowly, but not necessarily less profoundly, when tired. The microsleeps are frequently characterized by the dream state of sleep. Thus, we might say that a person's mind wandered for the moment. The overly conscientious or anxious student may often be detected by wary observation of frequent microsleeps during lectures or tutorials. This could be a useful advance warning that gentle student counseling may be necessary.

From the point of view of the student, a lecture is a paced situation, and Wilkinson (1963b) has shown that those suffering sleep deprivation work slower, but not less accurately, at mental tasks. In this case, the lecturers must either lecture at a slower speed and risk being dreary, or place the students in self-paced situations such as discussions or practical work. If they lecture at their normal speed, their students may miss vital information during microsleeps. The work of Pepler (1959) and Wilkinson (1963a, 1963b) suggests that the marked decrease in the speed of work over twenty to thirty minutes can be averted by short breaks every five minutes. Although their subjects were more sleep deprived than most students, the principle of short breaks should not be ignored when the need arises.

Some students claim that they work better against a background of noise. There is some evidence (Wilkinson, 1963b) that sleep-deprived subjects work better where noise has an arousing effect, but this effect wears off after half an hour. Those who have slept normally work better under quiet conditions, but their work will not greatly deteriorate in noisy conditions during the first thirty minutes. These two findings suggest that twenty to thirty minutes' noise is enough. If students have a lower level of arousal later in the day, these findings may be relevant to teaching at that time.

It must be frankly admitted that in this discussion I have taken big steps in reasoning from the precisely specified conditions used by experimental psychologists to the variable and uncontrolled conditions in which teachers work. Only further investigation can show whether the inferences are correct. There is a great deal we simply do not know about normal teaching situations. To some extent, the onus is on my critics to say why teachers and students should be different. The evidence available suggests that when students are tired, when teaching later in the day, or when subject matter is difficult, varied teaching methods, including the use of discussion techniques, are most likely to be effective.

4. Students' Physical Environment and Bodily Condition

The effect upon attention of variations in blood chemistry, especially following the use of drugs, has received much recent publicity and study. But for our purposes concerned with effective teaching, the important physical factors are common knowledge and will therefore be mentioned summarily. A modern, centrally overheated and humid lecture room induces student drowsiness. The fact is well known, but it is easily overlooked when lecturers are more concerned with their subject than their students, or when, being in an active role themselves, the room condition has little effect on them personally. The sharp contrast with the air outside may result in objections if a window is opened more than a little. One solution is to open the door, for moving air may have an arousing effect without lowering the temperature.

The need for varied posture has been mentioned. The distracting effect of uncomfortable chairs in lectures is well known, but it is rare for lecturers to take countermeasures. If the effect is made clear to the students, a break of two minutes during which they are expected to stretch their legs may be unconventional, but it pays dividends. The best position is probably an erect but relaxed spine. The effect of using deep armchairs in small-group teaching is less obvious. The students may contribute as frequently as usual, but owing to their posture they may not note points or references that they otherwise would, and their lower intermittent arousal would not favor memory of the material.

A large lunch and a small quantity of alcohol will increase the somnolent effect, while tea or coffee may overcome it. Hunger may be arousing at first, but then a distraction. For those who are overly studious, the lack of physical exercise that was enforced during earlier schooling may result in a monotonous environment and an increase in weight with a consequent decline in arousal.

Conclusion

In Chapter Two, we saw that consolidation of memories may take up to half an hour. Lectures longer than that are therefore likely to interfere with the consolidation process. In this chapter, we see evidence once again to suppose that lectures should not be longer than twenty to thirty minutes—at least without techniques to vary stimulation.

Admittedly, the evidence is mostly indirect, and more research could be done. But a combination of psychological and physiological studies using a range of criteria, together with common experience, are beginning to form a composite picture that the first twenty to thirty minutes of a lecture are different from the remainder. The remainder is probably less effective and less efficient.

Part Four of this book describes and recommends some ways to vary student activity and maintain attention.

CHAPTER FOUR

MOTIVATING STUDENTS

How can we motivate students?

1. Enthusiasm from the lecturer.

2. Cultivate existing motives.

Common motives of students.

1. "Deep" and "surface" approaches.

2. The desire for relevance.

3. Curiosity.

4. Achievement and fear.

5. Need for social interaction.

6. Activity and esteem.

There is little doubt that student motivation is an important factor affecting the performance of students in their courses. Indeed, there is some evidence that it is more important than intelligence; but in saying this it must be remembered that the range of intelligence of students is smaller than the range in the population as a whole. In one department of engineering, though not in another, Beard, Levy, and Maddox (1964) found a predominantly negative correlation between measures of intellectual ability and first-year examination results. They considered the effects of teaching upon motivation as a possible explanation of the difference. From a long-term study, Himmelweit and Swift (1971) have reported that measures of motivation correlated more highly with achievement in higher education than measures of intelligence or social background. High-drive introverts usually perform better in examinations than low-drive extroverts (Furneaux, 1962; Malleson, 1967; Walton and Drewery, 1967; Entwistle and Entwistle, 1970;

Entwistle and Wilson, 1970). The two studies by Entwistle suggest that the success of high-drive introverts is related to their "good study methods" in that they "work carefully, think ahead, are conscientious and recognize the importance of working conditions."

An alternative or additional explanation is that motivated students work longer, rather than more intensively. This view receives support from Evans (1967), who found that students highly motivated to achieve spent more time on a learning task and were better at it. Thoday (1957) found that students work shorter hours when examinations or other assessments are in the relatively distant future.

If longer study time is the only explanation, we might expect that students with higher intelligence would perform better over a fixed period such as a lecture. There is some evidence for this, particularly when thought is possible or required; but it is by no means always the case (Guetzkow, Kelly, and McKeachie, 1954; Hudelson, 1928; Jamieson, James, and Leytham, 1969). Guilford (1959) has pointed out that the mental processes required of students are often quite different from those used to do intelligence tests. After experiments in programmed learning, Stolurow (1960) observed that achievement is only related to intelligence when the teaching is bad! Corey (1934) has shown that intelligence has less influence on the effectiveness of lectures than on that of reading. In general, previous performance at college and university, rather than school, has better predictive power than standardized tests (Warburton, Butcher, and Forrest, 1963; Halpin, 1968; Nisbet and Welsh, 1966).

We may conclude that the importance of stimulating motivation in lectures lies as much in its long-term effects as in attention and memory during the lecture itself. For example, Baker and Lombardi (1985) showed that motivated students take more notes in lectures and have better learning strategies when using them in private study. Indeed, although it may seem obvious that motivation during a lecture will influence learning at that time, I have to admit that the evidence is decidedly mixed. Blizek, Jackson, and LaVoie (1974) found that highly motivated students performed better in independent learning, while poorly motivated students did better in lectures. Camp (1993) reported that even though measures of motivation were highly correlated, they did not predict grades in math after lectures. Stanton (1994) found the same: only one of fifteen characteristics of motivated students on the Motivated Strategies for Learning Questionnaire showed any relation to achievement (and that was the tendency to elaborate material). Similarly, a program of training to increase the motivation of high-risk students had no effect unless the teaching was particularly good (Menec and others, 1994). Good teaching uses and fosters motivation; bad teaching kills it.

How Can We Motivate Students?

If motivation results in good study methods and is at least as important as intelligence in influencing students' achievements in learning, the practical problem is how to motivate students. We have already seen in Chapter One that discussion is a better motivator than lectures, so the task may not be easy; but this does not mean that it should not be attempted.

1. Enthusiasm from the Lecturer

There's only one thing more contagious than enthusiasm, and that's the lack of it. The way to interest a class is to display interest oneself. This has the support of several experiments. Mastin (1963) instructed lecturers to teach one topic with an "indifferent" attitude and another the following week "enthusiastically." The characteristics of indifference and enthusiasm were vetted by a board of "experts." Nineteen out of twenty classes did better on multiple-choice tests after the enthusiastic lesson. There was no interaction between intelligence and the degree to which students were affected by enthusiasm. Teachers who were apparently enthusiastic influenced the attitudes of their students more strongly and were rated more highly by them. In a similar experiment, Coats and Smidchens (1966) found that 36 percent of the variance in tests of audience recall were attributable to the "dynamism" of the speaker. Dynamism was measured using behaviors such as gestures, eye contact, vocal inflections, and speaking without reading a script. Students take more notes, and taking notes results in more learning, if the lecturer is enthusiastic (Stewart, 1989).

However, there are also some experiments with rather ambiguous results for the effectiveness of enthusiasm. In the Stanford experiments, mentions by observers of enthusiasm, energy, and vitality were positively related to learning for some lectures but not others (Unruh, 1968). In eight out of ten comparisons by McCord (1944), ratings of speech characteristics of enthusiasm correlated more highly with achievement scores than with objective measures of the characteristics themselves. Marsh (1984a) reported that lecturer expressiveness had a large effect on test performance when other sources of motivation were low; but when incentives to learn or to do well in a test were added, the effect of expressiveness was insignificant. At the secondary school level, Wallen found that ratings of "stimulating" correlated with teachers asking questions, giving praise and encouragement, and using hostility and reprimands; but they were unrelated to learning (cited in Rosenshine, 1970).

It is possible that personality characteristics explain these ambiguities. Low-conceptual-level students are better motivated to learn course content by direct instruction; with students capable of higher conceptual levels, motivation is enhanced by indirect methods that allow them to think for themselves (Hancock, 1994). Magnusson and Perry (1989) argue that expressive, enthusiastic teaching can be measured by features such as the amount of a *teacher's movement, eye contact,* and *varied voice intonation.* These increase arousal. Students with an inner locus of control, who can inwardly channel their aroused energy toward their desire to learn, will increase their learning. But those with an external locus of control, who cannot control their inner anxieties or intruding thoughts, need feedback or some other external stimulus before or during the lecture if the lecturer's enthusiasm is to be infectious.

We may conclude that it pays to be enthusiastic and to act as if you are, even when you are not. But don't be too disappointed if you don't enthuse everyone all the time. Interaction with the class will increase the motivation of those whose temperament is not so conducive to enthusiasm.

2. Cultivate Existing Motives

Personally, I have found no other reliable answer to the question, How can we motivate students? Part of the reason for this is that not all students are motivated by the same thing. In this respect, the factors affecting motivation are a little different from those affecting memory or arousal. Second, unlike information, motives cannot be presented by a lecturer to students. The lecturer's task is to cultivate motives the students already possess. They are cultivated by practice in being expressed. That is why lectures are relatively ineffective for this purpose.

Once teachers know what their students' latent motives are, they may first stimulate a need for the motives to be satisfied, and then present their subject as a means of obtaining satisfaction. For example, if a student has chosen to study medicine because of genuine human sympathy, the teacher in anatomy would be wise to show, on some occasions, how the subject can be applied. A caution to observe is that the motive stimulated should be relevant and not overused. When teaching in a college with a large number of unwilling students, a teacher in a nonvocational subject attempted to discuss social relations in the context of sexual motives. It was not long before it became known that students thought him a little odd.

Common Motives of Students

In spite of the differences among students, the lecturer's task will involve using the motives they already have. This raises the question, What motives do they commonly have?

1. "Deep" and "Surface" Approaches

In the past twenty years, there has been extensive research into students' approaches to learning. Typically, students have been interviewed about how they studied a written text, but there is every reason to believe that the dispositions revealed apply equally well in listening to lectures. Students are motivated differently according to their approach.

In "surface" approaches, students' intentions are to store information— in other words, to memorize facts and principles without much thought. They conceive of the learning process as increasing their knowledge and knowing facts, principles, and procedures to be used. They think of the teacher's role as presenting information and the students' role as reproducing it in examinations to demonstrate that they know it.

In contrast, "deep" approaches emphasize thought rather than memory. They integrate new ideas to those already possessed. New knowledge is organized and rearranged in the context of the students' previous knowledge, not the lecturer's. Thus its meaning is different and personal to each individual. Students using a deep approach look for fundamentals. They exercise imagination. They distinguish principles from examples. They look for the overall structure of ideas and relate new ideas widely and to their personal experience.

We may infer from Table 1.3 that a deep approach is not normally achieved in lectures. But the situation is more serious than that. There is reason to believe (Gibbs, 1992) that the lecture system positively encourages a surface approach and discourages the very intellectual skills that higher education claims to foster. The supposition is that students will think about the lectures afterwards, but over-timetabling and excessive course material too often leave little time for that. Methods of assessment using factual objective tests or encouraging regurgitation in examinations make matters worse.

It behooves lecturers to lecture less, convince students of the intellectual aims of their courses, and create opportunities, in lessons and outside, in which thinking can flourish.

2. The Desire for Relevance

Marris (1964) has reported that most of the students he interviewed at four institutions wanted their studies to be at least indirectly relevant to their careers, but they saw that a narrowly specialized course was not likely to be the most useful. In the light of the recent difficulties of even doctoral students in obtaining employment, this judgment appears to be valid. However, only about two-fifths of the students in Marris's survey thought that their studies would be relevant to their later careers.

There is also a connection between vocational relevance and student motivation during specific teaching periods. When I asked student-teachers to assess my lectures, there was a statistically significant correlation between their ratings of "interest" and "relevance to teaching" (but the assumption that students will work harder at things they claim to find interesting requires empirical confirmation).

3. Curiosity

In recent years, there has been less emphasis on developing motivation through manipulating rewards and punishments, and more on how to use students' natural curiosity. In secondary schools, there has been an increase in project work. Universities, too, have increased the role of theses, projects, long essays, and small-scale investigations in undergraduate work. But Table 1.5 shows that lectures are relatively ineffective to stimulate interest in a subject.

So the problem here is how to use lectures to generate curiosity. Berlyne (1960) and Zillmann and Cantor (1973) have found that students' learning and interest were improved if students were asked questions rather than told facts. The most successful questions were those that were least expected, particularly if the subject was already familiar. After numerous experiments, Katona (1940) implies that lectures should begin with stimulating questions. Not any question will do. In an experiment using televised lectures, Creswell and Lin (1989) found that eye contact and inserted questions correlated with student interest and satisfaction but did not seem to have a direct impact upon students' short-term memories. The questions seemed to arouse attention rather than aid memory. McKeachie (1965) has suggested that effective questions are likely to contain a conflict or a paradox that may be resolved during the rest of the lecture; he has concluded that the interplay between the familiar and the novel may be a very important factor in the development of curiosity.

However, the sensitive lecturer will be aware of strong individual differences in response to paradoxes and uncertainty. For example, in one study (Feather, 1969), students who were judged as rigid or "dogmatic" were less interested in novelty and unfamiliar information.

4. Achievement and Fear

Examinations are powerful motivators, whether through fear of failure or through the desire to achieve personal success. Fear of failure evokes the minimum effort to pass. The drive to achieve demands maximum effort for personal satisfaction.

a. Fear of Failure. Fear of failure becomes greater as the examinations, or assignment deadlines, draw closer; but if any inspiration is obtained from a lecture, its power diminishes as the occasion recedes into the past. The deadlines for course assignments create undulating pressures. Correa (1994) claims that as student interest in a subject increases, the optimum number of lectures increases and the number of exams necessary to motivate decreases. When the length of courses increases, to motivate students it will be necessary to increase the number of exams, but not the number of lectures.

Fear, however, is not normally conducive to high student motivation. Janis and Feshbach (1953) gave presentations on dental health to three groups of students and varied the emphasis on the frightening consequences of dental neglect. The use of minimum fear was most effective both in the extent to which they changed their dental habits and in the degree to which they resisted counterarguments. McKeachie (1965) claims that the threat of a test makes students concentrate harder, but an experiment by Coats and Smidchens (1966) to test this hypothesis proved inconclusive. Kuz'mina (1976) found that average students learned more from lectures when they knew they would be tested on it; but knowing this did not affect the performance of good and poor students.

b. Desire for Personal Achievement. Rather than threats, positive encouragement is better. There are enough suicides on campus already. Particularly with students listening to their second language, an empathic lecturer is more effective (Barnes, MacArthur, and Ballantine, 1983). Marsh (1984a) showed that financial incentives improved concentration and test performance, particularly when the information content was dense.

The desire to achieve depends on knowing what to achieve. You might think that if you want students to achieve or strive toward something, they are more likely to do so if they know what it is. That is the usual finding. Yet it is remarkably rare for lecturers to tell their students what they should be able to do by the end of the lecture that they could not do at the beginning. Royer (1977) confirmed that students given instructional objectives before a lecture displayed more intentional learning than others; but in her particular experiment, students given the objectives only at the end of a lecture displayed incidental learning when they were able to retrieve sufficient information and relate it to the objectives.

5. Need for Social Interaction

There is considerable psychological evidence that the desire for interaction with other people is a very strong motive, and this may be particularly true with young people. Yet the lecture method notoriously neglects it, and attention would probably be improved if another method were used to satisfy it during a lecture period.

How far should a teacher bear this motive in mind when selecting a teaching method? Deutsch (1949) showed that students were more attentive, displayed better comprehension, produced more work, and were more favorable to the teaching method when they worked cooperatively in groups than when they competed as individuals. The relative popularity of seminars and tutorials demonstrated in Table 1.6 could also be partly explained by their satisfaction of this motive. Batson and Johnson (1976) designed a course to maximize student motivation by providing a supportive context, challenging students' conceptions of themselves and society, and ensuring they had sufficient background to raise pertinent questions. Students' ratings compared favorably against other courses when there was no final examination; and they preferred discussions led by their peers to those led by graduates. All this suggests that learning should be considered in its social context.

Burke (1955) takes this wider. After a controlled experiment on teaching methods using measures of college marks, social activities, leadership, athletic participation, personal problems, academic adjustment, reading ability, IQ, attendance, age, opinions of courses and teachers, and social and emotional adjustment, Burke concluded that not only teaching methods but also the total college environment may be important for how well first-year students adjust to college life. Loomis and Greene (1947) concluded from a study of mental conflicts in a typical state university that "unhappiness in college is chiefly caused by lack of social acceptance, not sex or poor grades." Yet it is clear that social interaction and acceptance could be adequately achieved outside the teaching situation.

Therefore the importance of using teaching methods that may satisfy the desire for social interaction will probably depend on how well it is satisfied by other means at other times.

6. Activity and Esteem

Achievement and social interaction are associated with students' needs to feel involved and to have the respect of others. All are motives of which the lecture method makes poor use. Patton (1955) found that students were better motivated when asked to share decisions on the running of a course and when teaching methods required greater participation. Those who were more active were also prepared to accept more responsibility. With mature students, Collier (1966) has reported that the involvement required in the syndicate method (see Table 14.1 of that work) stimulated higher motivation than teaching by traditional methods.

One of the most important things for a teacher to learn is to give praise. Because faculty often prefer cautious understatement to enthusiasm, giving praise sometimes requires a conscious effort. Students may learn what they should not do by making mistakes; they learn what they *should* do by the rewards of success.

"Nothing breeds success like success" is a more pertinent dictum than "We learn by trial and error." To develop the drive to achieve, students need to believe that achievement is possible. This may be fostered if they can taste the fruits of success.

In short, positive feedback is a powerful motivator. Therefore to motivate students in this way requires the lecturer to provide the opportunity for feedback that lecturing itself does not give (for ways of doing this, see Part Four and Chapter Eleven in Part Three).

Conclusion

No doubt the readers can think of relevant motives that I have not considered, particularly those that are appropriate to their subject. But there is little objective evidence on the way to motivate students even though motivation is generally recognized as important. It is clear that the teacher has to build on motives that the students already possess, but in some cases these are inappropriate to the lecture method. Therefore alternative methods may sometimes be needed. Consequently, the techniques for the development of student motivation require a conscious decision at the time when teaching is prepared, as well as some spontaneity in abandoning a prepared procedure when motivation appears to flag during a lecture.

PART THREE

WHAT LECTURE TECHNIQUES APPLY THESE FACTORS MOST EFFECTIVELY?

CHAPTER FIVE

LECTURE ORGANIZATION

Common forms of lecture organization.

  1. Hierarchic forms.

  2. Chaining.

  3. Variations and more complex forms.

Making the organization clear.

  1. Introductions: state the organization at the beginning.

  2. For each new point: itemize.

  3. For each new point: use a visual buildup.

  4. For conclusions, take stock and summarize.

Common Forms of Lecture Organization

There are two common forms of organization used by lecturers to structure information they have to teach, but each has variations and may be used in conjunction with the other so that, in practice, lectures do not conform to a very few simple patterns. Nevertheless, knowledge of the basic forms may help the new lecturer organize information when preparing lectures. As we saw in Chapter Two, if the organization is made clear to the students then they may find the lectures easier to follow.

1. Hierarchic Forms

Although the classification hierarchy and the problem-centered lecture form are both hierarchic, in many respects the latter is so distinct that it is not regarded as hierarchic; thus it is the former that we refer to as the hierarchic form.

a. The Classification Hierarchy. The classification hierarchy is the most common basic form. Essentially it consists of a classification, with its criterion as the heading. In other words, different points of information are grouped together with a unifying feature as a heading (Figures 5.1 and 5.2).

FIGURE 5.1. EXAMPLE OF THE CLASSIFICATION HIERARCHY FORM TO SHOW "LINKS."

FIGURE 5.2. SEQUENCE AND PROBABLE BLACKBOARD ORGANIZATION OF A HIERARCHIC LECTURE.

I _____

   1. _ _ _ _ _ _ _ _ _ _ _ _ _ _ _ _ _ _ _

   2. _ _ _ _ _ _ _ _ _ _ _ _ _ _ _ _ _ _ _

       (a) . . . .

       (b) . . . .

   3. _ _ _ _ _ _ _ _ _ _ _ _ _ _ _ _ _ _

II _____

   1. _ _ _ _ _ _ _ _ _ _ _ _ _ _ _ _ _ _ _

       (a) . . . .

       (b) . . . .

       (c) . . . .

   2. _ _ _ _ _ _ _ _ _ _ _ _ _ _ _ _ _ _ _

Assuming that the organization of information requires grouping in some way, this is about the simplest form there can be. Each item of information is linked with only one other idea, so that the grouping aids the memory, while there are a minimum of links to be remembered. Since, for most people, there is a limit to the number of items they can remember under one heading, it is advisable to subdivide them when there are more than nine, and preferably when there are more than five (see Chapter Two and Miller, 1967).

Being simple, the classification hierarchy is ideal for the clear presentation of facts. In other words, it is ideally suited to the main functions of regular lectures: teaching information and surveying an area of knowledge before its study in further detail. For the same reason, it is particularly suitable when first dealing with a difficult topic. When the objective is to give a framework, it provides a few pegs on which students may hang further ideas. Thus at first it is useful where it is intended that students should undertake further reading.

If the subject matter is difficult and subheadings are required, it is advisable to remind the students of the major headings (I and II in Figure 5.2) and the second-order points (1, 2, and 3) before going on to introduce a new level in the hierarchy (a, b, and c). This reminder will be called "taking stock." It is a technique used in programmed learning where the linear form of the program may obscure the overall structure of the information being presented, or where the students need to be reminded of what they should have learned.

A new level in the hierarchy means that a student must keep two kinds of link in mind at once. This, in addition to the facts to be remembered and noted, is an extra load on memory. For this reason, taking stock is a very important technique when the lecture organization is not written in front of the student or when, for some other reason, the student's memory must take the load normally borne by a blackboard or projected summary.

The sequence of presentation is different from the form in which the topic is organized. The order in which points are made requires jumps from one level of the hierarchy to another. It is at these jumps that students easily become lost.

Lectures with a hierarchic organization are the easiest for a new lecturer to give. They require attention to one thing at a time. They do not require much dramatic ability. It is relatively easy to see when the timing of a hierarchic lecture is going wrong, and thus to accelerate or slow down without clouding the major points.

The main disadvantages of the hierarchic lecture form derive from the very simplicity that in some contexts is its virtue. A simple classification of information can produce a rigid way of thinking if students only think of a given fact in one context. For this reason, it is necessary to couple hierarchic lectures with discussion problems or essay topics that require more flexible thinking. Flexibility in thinking may be stimulated by suggesting reading with a variety of sources and points of view. Students will relate a lecture to other contexts if they are given problems in buzz groups that oblige them to do so (see Chapter Eighteen).

The second major disadvantage is possible boredom. Lectures are stimulating and interesting when they link ideas that were not linked before in students' minds; but, as we have seen, part of the simplicity of the hierarchic lecture is obtained by minimizing links between facts.

We may conclude that the hierarchic lecture form is very useful for introducing complex and difficult subject matter, and for the major function of most lectures—the presentation of facts. Like the lecture method itself, it is less suitable for stimulating interest and thought. Consequently, it is more likely to be used with younger and less able students.

b. The Problem-Centered Lecture. In using the problem-centered form, the lecturer asks a question or presents a problem and thereafter gives information, arguments, and hypotheses as possible solutions, so that everything said focuses on the initial problem. For example, the approach may be a telescoped presentation of a scientific investigation.

It is hierarchic in that possible solutions are subsumed under the major problem, while factual evidence and simple inferences are taught with reference to each of these hypotheses (Figure 5.3).

It is distinct in that the relationships between the evidence and the possible solutions, and between the solutions and the problem, are not relationships of classification but rather involve a process of reasoning. This difference is important when considering the kind of objectives that may be achieved by this form of lecture.

Although they only demand limited patterns of thought, problem-centered lectures will be appropriate for promoting thought in those circumstances in which it is not possible to give the problem to the students directly in discussion. It is also suitable for stimulating students' interest if the problem can be made to arouse their curiosity.

Arousing students' motivation in this way involves creating a certain kind of tension, which is not at all easy for the new lecturer. It involves some dramatic skill to convey puzzlement, the use of rhetorical questions, and considerable skill in timing the presentation of the next piece of evidence or when raising objections to the latest hypothesis. Because of the thought demanded from the student, the problem-centered form requires variations in pace that are more subtle than those in a lecture using a classification hierarchy.

When giving a problem-centered lecture, it is essential to get the problem clear at the beginning. If students do not understand what the problem is, the rest of the lecture, consisting of attempts to solve it, will be completely lost on them.

FIGURE 5.3. DIAGRAM TO ILLUSTRATE
THE PROBLEM-CENTERED LECTURE FORM.

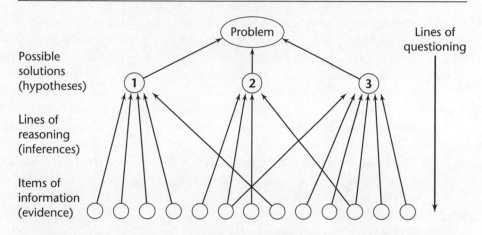

Note: Items of information serve as evidence to support hypotheses by use of reasoning. The hypotheses are directed toward solving a problem. Students are required to follow lines of reasoning by relating ideas. They are also required to understand how the hypotheses are possible solutions. (Although Chapter One of this book is obviously not a lecture, the reader may find some similarities between its organization and this simplified diagram.)

We have already seen the importance of meaning in teaching information, and that it depends on the ability of the student to relate items to one another. In the same way, the evidence presented in the body of a problem-centered lecture has little meaning if it cannot be related to the central problem.

For this reason, it is advisable to keep referring back to the central problem in much the same way that taking stock has been recommended. This may be done each time a possible solution is presented by explaining in an almost elementary way how it solves the problem. It is necessary to explain why each hypothesis is a possible solution, because experiments have shown (Hovland and Mandell, 1952; Bligh, 1974) that students do not make even the most important and simple inferences in lecture situations. Furthermore, it is a very common mistake for lecturers to fail to make allowances for their own assumptions, expertise, intelligence, and familiarity with the problems, and to think that inferences are easier for the students than they are.

The choice of problem requires considerable thought and is best made at the time when the course is planned, not when the lecture is prepared. I find that choosing an appropriate problem and the precise way of posing it are creative tasks, and the steps in achieving them follow the stages described by the Gestalt school of psychologists (see Chapter One), culminating in a new insight into the subject of lecture. Artists and creative scientists have described a similar process (Henri Poincaré, in Vernon [1970]; Stephen Spender, in Ghiselin [1952]). The stages are often spread over several weeks, and if I have a number of courses to prepare, I may be concerned with choosing more than one problem at the same time.

We have seen that the problem should arouse motivation, suit the students' level of attainment, and, if the objectives include the provision of a framework of information, synthesize what is to be taught.

More than other forms of lecture, the problem-centered approach makes assumptions about students' previous knowledge and their ability to handle new concepts.

For all these reasons, the problem-centered lecture is the most difficult to give and to follow, but if given satisfactorily it is also the most rewarding for both the lecturer and the student.

2. Chaining

This form of organization simply consists of a sequence (see Figure 5.4). A story consists of a chain of events; perhaps it is because both our experience and our speech are in sequential form that chaining seems a natural form of exposition.

FIGURE 5.4. DIAGRAM TO ILLUSTRATE THE ORGANIZATION OF A SIX-POINT CHAINING LECTURE WITH A SUMMARY AND TWO PERIODS OF TAKING STOCK.

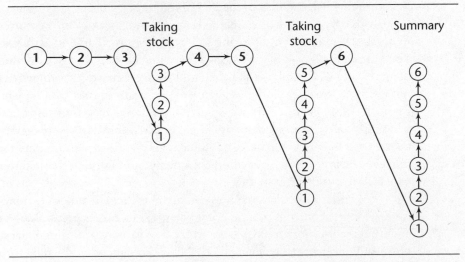

Indeed, Oaks (1996) reports greater recall of instructional content immediately, three weeks, and five weeks after instruction in a storytelling fashion, than after the traditional lecture method.

Not all chains are a simple series in terms of time. As with the hierarchy, the links may involve a reasoning process so that there is a chain of argument. A chain of cause and effect may exist in the time dimension but not be at all simple. Reference to Chapter Twenty, and indeed Part Five as a whole, will show that it has an overall chaining structure (although in detail it is obviously more complex). Introductory textbooks usually show a hierarchic form. Some of the most difficult lectures to follow consist of a chain of ideas each associated with the last, but with no overall dimension. When the Cambridge philosopher Ludwig Wittgenstein lectured, it is said he talked out loud about a problem that concerned him at the time, in between periods of silent thought. Therefore, ostensibly his lectures had a problem-centered form, but in practice the leaps of his creative mind, when considering the chain of argument in one possible solution, were such that the students' main task was to keep track of his thoughts. (This kind of extemporaneous organization is not recommended unless the lecturer has the audience in the palm of his hand, because it requires the students' minds to wander with the lecturer's.) Assuming the links between one stage and the next are easy to follow, chaining is a form of organization that maintains attention very well, as may be evident from the use of stories with children; but if attention is lost, it is difficult for the student to pick up the thread again. Since all students will have microsleeps, in addition to which their minds may either wander or be stimulated to explore some relevant issue, the lecturer who adopts the chaining form must employ tracking devices so that students may mentally return to where they left off.

First, it is particularly important to make it clear when moving from one stage to the next. This may be done by writing the stages on the blackboard or some other continuous display, as one goes along, giving each a number. It is not enough for the lecturer to say "Next . . ." and pass on with scarcely a break. Second, lecturers should take stock of the chain. This should be done with increasing frequency as the lecture progresses because, as we have seen, students' memories have limited short-term capacities, and consolidation by rehearsal or repetition becomes increasingly necessary as the limits are approached (Figure 5.4). A third device with some kinds of subject matter is to state the final stage or goal clearly at the beginning so that students can see where they are being led or what is finally being explained. For example, it can be helpful in a chain of causes and effects in history, or a series of reactions in chemistry, to know the final consequence or product.

In these forms of chaining, once the stages have been written on the board much of the lecturer's energies may be devoted to explaining why each stage follows from the previous one.

3. Variations and More Complex Forms

Because of their clarity, these basic forms are probably the easiest patterns of organization from which to take notes. For this reason, they are suitable for first-year or other students who have yet to learn how to take notes skillfully. The selection and organization of notes requires more skill than many lecturers appreciate, and since, as far as their own lectures are concerned, lecturers have the responsibility to provide training in these skills (although some do not recognize it), more complex patterns should be introduced gradually.

a. Comparison. A common variant of the hierarchic form is the comparison. It is a form of paired classification. The style of blackboard or overhead projector summary shown in Figure 5.5 prevents a load from being placed on the students' short-term memories, because they do not have to recall the two items labeled with the same number simultaneously before making the comparison. (Admittedly, there may still be short-term recognition involved, but this is easier than recall.)

The style may become a little more complex if similarities and differences are distinguished (perhaps when teaching to achieve the same objectives as are assessed by "compare and contrast . . ." examination questions). See Figure 5.6.

A variation with four sections is shown in Chapter One, when comparing lectures and other teaching methods, with reference to one dimension (their relative effectiveness).

b. The Thesis. If one regards a complex argument as the answer to a problem supported by a chain of reasoning, a lecture presenting a thesis is likely to be a combination of the chaining and problem-centered forms (Figure 5.7).

FIGURE 5.5. DIAGRAM TO ILLUSTRATE THE STYLE OF BLACKBOARD SUMMARY FOR AN ANATOMICAL COMPARISON.

Criterion	Upper Limb	Lower Limb
1. Size	1.	1.
2. Strength	2.	2.
3. Dexterity	3.	3.
4. Structure	4.	4.
5. Functions	5.	5.
6. Etc.	6.	6.

FIGURE 5.6. "COMPARE AND CONTRAST . . ."
VARIANT OF FIGURE 5.5.

Criterion of:	Upper Limb	Lower Limb
Contrasts		
1. Size	1.	1.
2. Strength	2.	2.
3. Dexterity	3.	3.
4. Etc.	4.	4.
Similarities		
1. Number of digits	1.	
2. Joints	2.	
3. Etc.	3.	

FIGURE 5.7. THE FORM OF A THESIS LECTURE.

Note: Proposition 4 represents the hypothesis, or solution, to the lecturer's central issue. If the thesis is being argued for, it is likely to be presented in the order 1, 2, 3, 4. If it is being questioned, it is more likely to be presented in the order 4, 3, 2, 1. (See also Figure 5.3.)

The thesis and comparison forms may be combined if both sides of an argument are considered. It should be noticed that arguments against a thesis may consist either of a counterthesis or of objections to statements made in favor of it (Figure 5.8).

When giving a thesis lecture, one may move from one point to another along the links in either direction. If the thesis is an explanatory one, and this is quite usual, then movement is progressively from the raw data toward the thesis proposition that is claimed to explain it. If, on the other hand, one states the thesis proposition and then persistently questions the evidence for it, the broad movement of the lecture will be from the general to the particular. In the first method, one presents data that need to be explained; in the second, one considers a hypothesis by progressively testing it in more detail with observed facts. In practice, thesis lectures do not usually conform to either of these pure styles. The most common style is to select some of the observed data, present the thesis proposition as an explanation, and then fill in the intermediate steps of the argument with reference to raw data when appropriate. In effect, the lecturer says "These are the facts to be explained; this is the explanation; now, how does that explanation fit the facts?"

FIGURE 5.8. DIAGRAM TO ILLUSTRATE THE RELATIONSHIPS BETWEEN POINTS IN A THESIS LECTURE INCLUDING BOTH SIDES OF AN ARGUMENT.

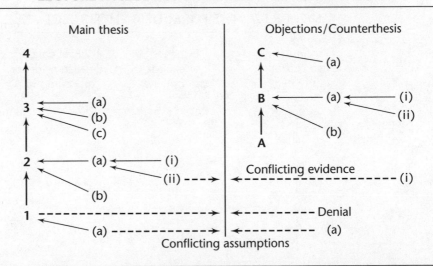

Note: Each number or letter represents a point made by the lecturer. As in Figures 5.3 and 5.7, the arrows represent lines of reasoning (inferences) toward the conclusion. Opposed arrows represent opposing points.

Each of these three approaches has its place, but they are each appropriate for different objectives. Suppose a lecture is to be given on Darwin's theory of evolution. The first approach is suitable to arouse students' curiosity and motivation. The lecturer may ask rhetorically: "How can we explain the fact that the birds on the Galapagos Islands show such extraordinary forms not found elsewhere in the world?" This is a question that Darwin himself must have asked. As the lecturer gives the observations and answers that Darwin made, he attempts to take the students through the same adventure of ideas that excited the scientific investigator. It seems probable that by helping the students to identify with the scientist they may become more appreciative of his difficulties, his methods of investigation, and the historical perspective of the subject; but to my knowledge there are no studies to confirm or deny these possibilities. Nevertheless, if these objectives can be achieved by this approach, it is important.

If one asks different questions about the same subject matter, different patterns of thought will be required to answer them. Therefore it seems reasonable to suppose that the second approach will be appropriate to stimulate critical thinking in large lecture classes or in other situations where critical seminar discussion is not possible. If the lecturer presents Darwin's general conclusion (the principle of natural selection), asks "Why should Darwin have thought that?" and then proceeds to criticize the theory with reference to observations, he may use precisely the same information but achieve a very different result in his students. But again, I know of no controlled experimental evidence either way to verify that lecture organization affects the patterns of students' thought. One advantage of this approach is that widely scattered information may be related to the central thesis and in this way produce stimulating, original, and broadening lectures. For example, a criticism of Darwin's theory could lead to consideration of Mendelian laws of inheritance and modern genetics, so long as the overall organization is not unbalanced.

The third approach may be used to survey a theory without taking students through the rigor of its reasoning. It is used to present information about a point of view. The students are told what Darwin noticed and are given his explanation, but they are not led to appreciate the thoroughness of his observations, the scientific context of the theory, or subsequent modifications of it. There is no pressure on the lecturer or the students to consider the detailed reasoning between Darwin's initial observations and the final production of his theory. Consequently, this approach is used by those with a crammed syllabus, but if the intermediate detail and reasoning are neglected, there comes a point when it ceases to be a thesis lecture. If the observations that produced a problem for Darwin are presented alongside his answer as a pair of facts, there is no challenge to the students' curiosity and no demand for them to follow a line of thought. Thus, although the third approach can be clearer than the other two because the students can see where the chain of reasoning is leading, there is a temptation to skip important links in the argument. If this is taken too far, there ceases to be a thesis, and objectives involving students' thought and motivation are not achieved.

c. Logical Dichotomy. A particularly useful variation of the hierarchic form is the logical dichotomy. Its merit is that is may break down a complex subject without omissions. A social scientist may wish to discuss, say, the advantages and disadvantages for men and women of recent legislation on welfare. In this case, the 2 x 2 grid of Figure 5.9 may make the subject clearer and permit students to concentrate on the subtleties of the law.

The complex increases and decreases in imports and exports during a period of economic change could be broken down in a similar way. In fact, when teaching something that is inevitably difficult, it is a useful tip to lighten the load by making the easy parts very easy.

The presentation of dichotomies as simple grids is obviously not possible if there are more than two sets of variables, but they may be elaborated in other ways. Figure 5.10 shows an attempt to analyze some of the relations between body and mind for medical students with no previous background in philosophy. The visual presentation of this schema with an accompanying explanation produced better comprehension than the same information given only orally. It could have been represented diagrammatically in other ways, as in Figure 5.11.

d. Network. Some subject matter does not lend itself to tidy organization for lecture presentation. Each facet is linked with many others to produce a complex network of interrelationships. But because a lecture necessarily takes place in time, it has a linear form. Lecturers are therefore faced with a double task. First, in their

FIGURE 5.9. VISUAL DISPLAY FOR THE LOGICAL DICHOTOMY.

	Men	Women
Advantages		
Disadvantages		

FIGURE 5.10. EXAMPLE OF VISUAL PRESENTATION OF ABSTRACT IDEAS.

Questions considered:

Do bodies and minds exist?

If they both exist, are they the same or different things?

If they are different things, does one affect the other in some way?

Whether exist	Minds don't exist	Minds exist
Bodies don't exist	(1) Nihilism	(3) Idealism, e.g., phenomenalism solipsism
Bodies exist	(2) Some materialism	

Same thing	Different
(4A) Identity theories, e.g., double aspect	(4B) Dualism

Causal relation	Minds affect bodies	Minds don't affect bodies
Bodies affect minds	(4Ba) Interactionism	(4Bb) Epiphenomenalism
Bodies don't affect minds	(4Bc)	(4Bd) Parallelism, e.g., preestablished harmony and occult intervention

Note: The purpose of this diagram was to relieve the short-term memory load of students not used to abstract thought. Students recognized its limitations and thereby raised questions they would not otherwise have considered (for example, what is it "to exist," "to be the same thing," "to cause something"?). They thought more about the topic because they identified themselves with a particular cell.

FIGURE 5.11. ATTEMPT TO DEPICT DICHOTOMIES IN HIERARCHIC FORM.

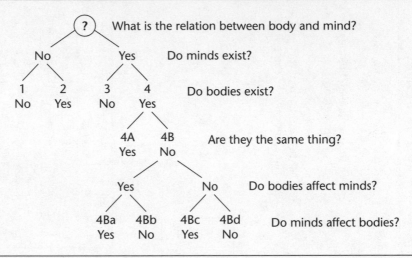

Note: Some students prefer this diagram to Figure 5.10, some the other way around, and others prefer no visual presentation at all.

preparation they must break their subject down into one of the simpler forms by selecting some links and neglecting others. Then, if it is important that all the links be made, those that are at first neglected will need time to be established by going over the subject a second time with a different emphasis and possibly another interpretation. For example, the complex network of interacting factors leading to the location of an industry could be classified by a geographer to form a hierarchic lecture, in various ways emphasizing economic, historical, or physical aspects. This is a fairly gross example, but the network problem also arises within more specialized fields (Figure 5.12). As we have seen, the linear form of lectures and books was too great a restriction on what Wittgenstein wanted to say. This was partly why his lectures had an unusual form and why his book *Philosophical Investigations* consists of separate numbered sections that, each being connected with many others, do not fit into an ordered sequence without distortion of the overall network.

A lecturer in group dynamics was concerned with the question, What is it that makes a number of people a "group"? He wished to consider factors so interrelated that they formed a network. You are invited to construct the pattern of relationships by completing the dashed lines in Figure 5.12 (to form solid ones) wherever you consider that one factor will affect another. You are then invited to

FIGURE 5.12. EXAMPLE OF A NETWORK.

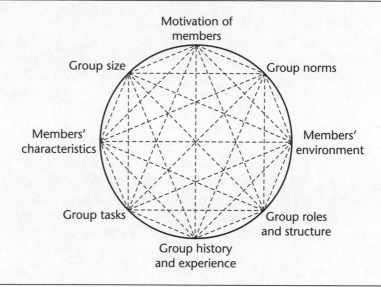

decide the order in which the factors should be introduced to a class of students. (It is appreciated that not all readers are experts in group dynamics, but most will have some knowledge—perhaps more than they realize!)

Making the Organization Clear

It is not my purpose here to assert dogmatically that lecture organization must be made clear in particular ways. What follow are suggestions.

The importance of lecture organization and its connection with the understanding and overall view of the lecture topic has been mentioned in Chapter Two. Yet when Beighley (1954) changed the order of certain paragraphs in a lecture, he found no significant difference in the students' retention of the information. Does this imply that the role of organization is overstated? I think not. It is not simply a question of whether a lecture is organized in a certain way, but whether it is seen by the students to be organized. Beighley does not give this point sufficient weight. A lecture may seem to be well organized in the lecturer's notes but have no apparent pattern when delivered. Ideally, students should be able to state the intended organization, and how one fact is broadly related to the rest, at any time during the lecture—first, because they need to take notes if the amount of information to be retained exceeds the amount they can remember, and second because, as Gage's study (1968) shows, these links are essential to understanding (see Chapter Seven).

Making the organization clear involves giving macro signals about it (sometimes called macro markers). Chaudron and Richards (1986) found they result in better learning. Macro signals are of three kinds: those introducing the lecture, those indicating a move to the next key point, and those signaling the conclusion. Some of these are listed in Table 5.1.

To test the importance of organization, I once conducted an experiment comparing a lecture that made the organization clear with a lecture using the identical words except that certain signals were removed. There wasn't much difference in students' learning. But when I removed all indications of organization, a glaze came over the students' eyes halfway through, and note taking ceased. Instinctively, I began using more nonverbals to maintain attention (thereby destroying experimental control). I then abandoned the experiment on moral grounds. Without links, the lecture simply fell apart. Morally, I could not justify treating students in that way. However, what is pertinent is something I should have realized from the beginning.

Learning from lectures has a tendency toward being all or nothing. To a considerable extent, the key points either hang together or they don't. There are not so many intermediary situations between points being organized on the one hand and being randomly arranged on the other. Although we talk about degrees of understanding (and examination grades often assume a continuum), understanding is not like that. Understanding consists of relating ideas. This necessitates knowing something of both ends of the relation. The Gestalt psychologists got it

TABLE 5.1. COMMON MACRO SIGNALS OF LECTURE ORGANIZATION.

Signal Function	Signal Words Commonly Used
Introductions	What I'm going to talk about is . . . OK . . . All right . . . Last time . . . To begin with . . . Let us begin.
New key point	The next thing is . . . Another development was . . . As you may have heard . . . Firstly . . . You can imagine what happened . . . The problem is . . . The surprising thing is . . . (Display on blackboard or screen)
Conclusions	To sum up . . . In conclusion . . . In this lecture . . . Where does this take us? . . . How does all this answer the question with which we began? . . . Well . . . X, y, and z in this lecture lead us to consider question Q next time.

right (see Chapter One). Understanding involves grasping how the whole thing fits together (Chapter Two). As I said in Chapter Two, for the sentences in a lecture to have meaning they have to relate to ideas the students already have. Organization of a lecture is all about relating. My students could compensate when I removed some relationships; but when I removed the lot, the whole lecture fell apart like a heap of random utterances.

1. Introductions: State the Organization at the Beginning

A lecture is likely to be more effective if its organization is given at the beginning. There are several ways of doing this. It can usually be done very naturally as an explanation of how the lecture's objectives are to be achieved. Most lecturers give the main headings of their lecture, rather like the subheadings in a chapter of a book. Others outline its content.

Susan Thompson (1994) analyzed lecture introductions and concluded they usually have two functions: giving the framework of the lecture and setting its context.

Giving Framework	*Setting Context*
1. Announce lecture topic.	5. Show importance and relevance of topic.
2. Outline the structure.	6. Refer to earlier lectures.
3. Indicate its scope.	7. Relate new topic to given material.
4. Present lecturer's aims.	

Thompson made two pertinent observations. First, lecturers mix and muddle these functions. For example, mentioning 1, 4, 6, 7, 4, 3, 5 in that order was typical. It might be better to follow the order in Table 5.2.

TABLE 5.2. RECOMMENDED SEQUENCE FOR LECTURE INTRODUCTIONS.

Aims	1. Announce lecture topic.
	2. Present educational aims.
	3. Show importance of educational aims.
Context	4. Show relevance of topic to aims.
	5. Refer to earlier lectures.
	6. Relate new topic to intellectual context and resources.
Framework	7. Outline lecture structure.
	8. Indicate scope.

Second, although the majority of students in her survey thought introductions should include background information, they needed to learn how to link ideas using information about a lecture's structure and context. This deficiency needs to be tackled more by faculty as a whole at the beginning of a course, than by individual lectures within it.

Some lecturers may feel that by summarizing all they intend to say at the beginning, they will have "shot their bolt" and have nothing left with which to arouse interest when attention flags. In this case, the overview needs to be given in a way that whets the appetite. The elaboration of points will require interesting details, visual illustration, humor, and an occasional anecdote. Another technique (which does not exactly describe the lecture organization) is to outline the main ideas in the lecture.

A related technique is to give what Ausubel (1968) calls an "advance organizer." Advance organizers are maximally clear concepts at a higher level of abstraction, generality, and inclusiveness than the material in the lecture they precede. They are concepts the audience already possesses that will link and integrate the material that follows. Their function is to bridge the gap between what the students know already and what they need to know. They provide a scaffolding. The difficulty with this technique is to find a concept that satisfies all these criteria. Miller (1996) found that the use of an advance organizer at the beginning of a short lecture improved students' recall strongly but did not facilitate inferences.

2. For Each New Point: Itemize

Itemization has several advantages:

- In the absence of an advance organizer, each item provides a peg on which detail may be hung. Detail is best remembered by association, and the item provides this.
- Although it may be obvious to lecturers whenever they are going on to a fresh point, this is not so obvious to listeners, least of all students who are not already familiar with the topic.
- If students daydream, or have microsleeps, they may easily lose the thread of an argument. If points are itemized, they will know they have lost a point; they might pick it up again more easily and then fill it in with the help of another student later. Much as most people are unaware that they dream three or four times each night (Oswald, 1966), most students are probably unaware how much their minds wander during lectures (Bloom, 1953).
- Itemization is an aid to memory. Revision from notes is more thorough if the students know, say, that "there are five points to be remembered on this topic and seven on the other."

3. For Each New Point: Use a Visual Buildup

The organization of itemized points will be clearer if they are displayed on a blackboard or screen immediately after being mentioned. This has a number of functions:

- With most lecture forms numbering, indenting, and underlining assist clarity by differentiating points and indicating their relative importance.
- Students are more likely to note what is written on the board partly because they believe it must be important if the lecturer has taken the trouble, and partly because they have time to write it when the lecturer stops the steady flow of words to do the same (Hartley and Cameron, 1967).
- For these two reasons, the display is a valuable technique of emphasis.

Lecturers who are not confident of their ability on the blackboard are tempted to neglect it. One way through this difficulty is to use an overhead projector, which may show either normal handwriting done at the time or prepared transparencies perhaps progressively displayed as the lecture develops. Alternatively, a handout containing the main headings, well spaced with blanks in between for the students to add supplementary detail, is useful; and since handouts may be passed on to absentees, they are particularly valuable at the beginning of a course or at other times when it is important to convey the organization of subject matter. Such displays of lecture organization (using the blackboard, overhead projector, handouts, or possibly other methods such as flannel graphs and charts) play a particularly important part in aiding comprehension when a network or other complex form is used because the relations between possibly abstract ideas can be pointed out visually.

If employing a blackboard, it is a helpful convention to use one side for progressively building up the lecture organization as the lecture proceeds, and the other side for more spontaneous and temporary illustration such as the spelling of new terms or names. The latter side may be erased several times in a lecture, while the organization remains permanently displayed and developed. A similar approach can be used with overhead projector transparencies if a lecture theater has two screens. If you only have one overhead projector and are replacing the organization transparency to show others, make sure you place it separately, not in the pile of those you have finished with; otherwise, you will have to go hunting through that pile when you move to the next key point. Using an overhead projector has some advantages over the traditional blackboard for presenting lecture organization:

- The organization can be progressively revealed or shown all at once.
- Black on white is perceived 15 percent more quickly and copied with fewer errors than white on black (Seymour, 1937).
- Color is more pleasing against a white background and color coding can be used to contrast levels in a hierarchy.
- Transparencies provide both a permanent record and continuity from one lecture and the next.
- The overlay facility allows both buildup and breakdown of complex diagrams (as with anatomy or engine parts).

4. For Conclusions, Take Stock and Summarize

It has already been suggested that summaries of a whole lecture both at the beginning and the end are often recommended (Clark and Clark, 1957; Henderson, 1970). The technique of taking stock, which consists of reviewing what has been said up to that time, is valuable for setting the next point in its context. It aids learning by showing how the parts are related to the whole.

New lecturers sometimes think that constant repetition is unnecessary and boring if students have already understood; but we have seen that it is for these students that repetition has value because it reduces the amount of forgetting later. Certainly the dictum "First tell 'em what you're gonna tell 'em; then tell 'em; and then tell 'em what you've told 'em" can usefully be applied to lectures and is particularly appropriate to those who teach a difficult subject or who cannot easily get down to the students' level of understanding.

Conclusion: The Importance of Organization

I argued in the introductory chapter that the major objective of lectures should normally be the teaching of information, and in Part Two that students' memory of information is strongly affected by its organization. It follows that the organization of lecture information normally affects quite strongly the achievement of the major objective of the lecture.

Although there are obviously an infinite number of possible lecture forms, I have tried in this chapter to suggest suitable forms of organization for this objective, and I have tried to show that, even when the major objective is the promotion of thought or the arousal of interest, the appropriate form of organization must be chosen if lectures are to be effective. This in turn suggests the importance of thoughtful lecture preparation in which the organization is carefully related to the lecturer's objectives. Furthermore, in most cases it is not enough that information should be organized; it must be seen by the students to be organized.

CHAPTER SIX

MAKING A POINT

The "general form" of making a point.

1. Concise statement.

2. Display.

3. Reexpression.

4. Elaboration.

5. Feedback.

6. Recapitulation and restatement.

Examples of other forms.

1. Explaining difficult points.

2. Proceeding at the pace of the class.

3. Motivators.

4. Definitions.

It is easy to think that there is no difficulty in making a point in a lecture—that the lecturer simply states it and then proceeds to the next. Such a lecturing style is unlikely to be effective. It is too concentrated and too fast; few students remember or note much of what is said, because important factors influencing memory, such as the roles of word recognition, rehearsal, repetition, and retroactive interference, are ignored. In Chapter Two I explained that to understand what a lecturer says, students must construct meaning by what psychologists call "encoding." I pointed out that it is particularly important for students to place what is said in a context of concepts they already possess. So when a lecturer makes a point, it needs to be placed within a structure of other ideas and language that the students already grasp. Here lies the skill of a lecturer when making a point.

By *point* here I mean a fact, generalization, principle, or concept that is to be taught. It is an item of information. Because there is no uniformity among subjects, lecturers, or their objectives, the term is necessarily vague. Saying the point is to be *taught* assumes that the lecturer intends the student to remember it. A point excludes asides and detail used for arousing interest. Knowledge of the point is assumed to be one of the objectives of the lecture. A list of the information objectives of a lecture will be a list of the points to be made.

Teaching a point in a lecture is quite different from making it on paper. Readers may go at their own pace and reread if they do not understand. The lecture audience can do neither. The audience is committed to the speed of the lecturer and cannot return to a point unless the lecturer does. Thus the presentation of both the lecture as a whole, and each major point within it, requires organization to ease the students' understanding.

However, as with lecture organization, there is obviously no one way to teach a point. It will depend a great deal on its psychological nature (for example, whether it is easy or difficult, abstract or concrete, verbal or aural), the kind of students (their ability, motivation, cooperation, and familiarity with the subject), and many other variables. In an interesting experiment in the teaching of secondary school mathematics, Trown (1970) found that extroverts learned better when an example was presented before a general rule was adduced (the inductive method), while introverts preferred to be given the rule first and then an example of its application (the deductive method). At the university level, Horak and Horak (1982) found a similar difference between internal students (that is, those formally and fully matriculated) and external students (those whose status is less than full time, such as those in night school or continuing education), respectively.

The technique known as the "rule-e.g.-rule" procedure caters to both styles of thinking. As its name suggests, the teacher first states a key point, or rule, then elaborates it, and repeats the rule before moving on to the next point (Table 6.1). This technique is known to be effective in programmed learning.

Contrary to common opinion, the best way to teach a point will not greatly depend on whether the point is classified under chemistry, history, fine arts, or any other subject, except insofar as each subject tends to contain points of a particular psychological nature. The difference in teaching methods for chemistry and history derives from their distinctive psychological requirements, not from the philosophical considerations that define the subject. However, since some subjects have a predominance of one kind of psychological objective, the emphasis in teaching methods may differ qualitatively. Consequently, the suggestions that follow are inevitably generalizations that readers may apply to their own particular circumstances.

TABLE 6.1. "GENERAL FORM" FOR MAKING A POINT IS BASED ON THE "RULE-E.G.-RULE" TECHNIQUE.

Rule	1. Concise statement
	2. Display
	3. Reexpression
E.g.	4. Elaboration
	4a. Detail
	4b. Illustration
	4c. Reasons and explanations
	4d. Analogies
	4e. Asides
	4f. Relating
	4g. Examples
	5. Feedback
Rule	6. Recapitulation

The "General Form" of Making a Point

I shall call the following procedure for making a point the "general form" because it is based on the rule-e.g.-rule pattern yet includes the most common techniques in the order in which they are most likely to be used. But it is not, of course, being suggested that every point a lecturer makes should conform to this pattern.

1. Concise statement

Usually, the first requirement is to state the point as concisely as possible. This may be a simple sentence of seven or eight words with one key word or phrase in it, particularly if the point to be taught is a concept. If it is possible to avoid sentences with strings of modifying clauses, the point will be simpler and more easily remembered because it will have more meaning (Friedman and Johnson, 1968). As we saw from research on echoic memory (Chapter Two), the key point should take less than five seconds to state, and preferably not more than two.

It is not always easy to prepare a lecture with these simple sentences. This is hardly surprising since some subjects cannot be made simple. The choice of key phrases is best made during preparation because lecturers tend to use longer-than-normal sentences. It is a matter of finding what I call the quintessential expression of the key point. Chafe (1982) analyzed spoken discourse into "idea units," which he defined as having a single intonation contour followed by a pause. The average idea unit in lectures was eleven words, and in conversation seven words. This is because lecturers use all manner of qualifying words and phrases that produce syntactic complexity. It may be that the person who knows the subject but cannot teach it fails to devise quintessential expressions during lecture preparation.

2. Display

The lecturer should then display the key word or phrase on the blackboard or screen as part of the progressive buildup of the lecture (which is not to say that the blackboard should not be used at other times). The reasons for this in terms of reducing the load on short-term memory, the ease of students' note taking, the use of rehearsal, the clarity of organization, a method of selective emphasis, and its effect on timing and retroactive interference have already been mentioned. The display of points also facilitates visual memory, which is preferred by some students and permits easy back reference by the teacher later in the same lecture.

If the lecturer then moves away (perhaps in the direction of his or her notes) without saying anything, students taking notes will be able to write it down without their view being blocked and their attention being divided. The lecturer will know when to go on, by looking at the class to see when they are ready. Hence, looking at the class is important at this stage.

3. Reexpression

If the point is then reexpressed another way, the alternative words may have more meaning for those who have not understood, and repetition will aid the memory of those who have.

It is tempting to imagine that once students have understood a point, they understand it in the same way as the lecturer; but the lecturer has a wealth of background knowledge and experience to which the point is related. Understanding is a matter of degree; consequently, reexpression frequently provides students with an opportunity to broaden it by relating the point to their background (Abercrombie, 1960).

4. Elaboration

When the point has been reexpressed—usually in an expanded, and less pithy form—some elaboration is usually necessary. This may take many forms.

a. Detail. Able students may welcome more detail if they have a framework of concepts, or an advance organizer, to make it cohere and coherent. Less able students are less likely to have the framework and are less skilled at relating detail to it. When giving detail, the lecturer must therefore observe the nonverbal reactions of less gifted students.

b. Illustration. Others may want visual illustration. It is not always appreciated that just as it is necessary to state a point in a number of ways, it is sometimes necessary to illustrate it in varying ways. These may be variations in representing information, such as statistical data; differing pictures of the same object from various angles, including cross-sections; or numerous kinds of visual aid. Ideally, two or three simple illustrations are better than one that is complex. But supposing the latter is necessary, the lecturer should proceed from simple to complex aids and then back to the same simple ones again so that each can be related to every other. The role of visual teaching is sometimes undervalued by university lecturers who are selected on the basis of their verbal, rather than spatial, abilities in examinations or publications.

c. Reasons and Explanations. A third feature of the elaboration stage is giving reasons for, and explanations of, the point being made. This is so important that the next chapter is devoted to it; but logically that chapter fits here. In most subjects, reasons and explanations are an essential part of understanding. They are vital if a college education is to consist of anything more than learning isolated facts.

Reasons require thought; therefore it is important to slow down one's speed of delivery. Because thought requires rehearsal without interference, this should be done not by speaking each sentence more slowly but by providing silent pauses at the end of each sentence. These pauses are important "thinking times" for the student. Because reasoning and explaining require relating facts and the student must therefore hold a number of ideas in mind at once, thinking is a more difficult task than holding one fact at a time to write it down as notes, particularly if the points being related are new. Morgan and Puglisi (1982) confirm that pauses at the end of sentences help to overcome this difficulty. Although at first pauses produced no improvement in recognizing verbatim sentences from a lecture, in a second experiment there were small but significant benefits from students' deep and elaborative thought about sentences with pauses, compared with sentences lacking such pauses.

It is important to look at the class to see if they have followed after each stage in a reasoning process. If lecturers wait until the end of a chain of reasoning before seeking feedback, and students have not been able to follow, they then have to find out which link in the chain is broken. They can only do this by going through the whole argument again, one link at a time, as they should have done in the first place. Sometimes students can prevent this repetition by saying what link in the chain they cannot follow and even why they cannot follow it. But this is less common than one is led to think, because students who can say this are usually among the more articulate. They have understood enough to know what they do not understand. Most students who do not understand an explanation cannot say why, and many, not wishing to reveal their ignorance, would not do so if they could. Indeed, in a survey of more than one thousand college of education students, 60 percent said that the presence of a large number of people in the room would deter them from asking questions, even when invited (Stones, 1970).

d. Analogies. Because Jesus taught using parables, for some people teaching by analogy has good credentials. The first problem with analogies is that they usually impose an enormous mental load. Any student with a critical mind (and developing critical minds is the central aim of higher education) will want to check their validity by distinguishing similarities and differences between every element of the analogy and the target subject matter, and to check how far the elements relate in the same way. The number of items of information manipulated in this process depends on how many elements there are; but it is not difficult to see that the number could be far larger than could be dealt with before the lecturer goes on to the next sentence. Thus analogies can leave students more confused than enlightened if the lecturer does not give time to check their validity.

The second limitation of analogies is that though they may explain, they do not justify. They attempt to match a structure of concepts, but they do not give reasons for believing the structure is what the lecturer claims it to be. Notwithstanding that they may help to *explain the reasons* for something, they nonetheless offer explanations, not reasons (Evans, 1988).

To overcome these limitations, Brown and Clement (1989) at the University of Massachusetts Scientific Reasoning Research Institute specify three explanatory factors: choosing a familiar concept for the analogy, explicit description of the analogical connections with what is to be explained, and engaging students actively in the process of analogical reasoning. They warn that presentation methods such as texts or lectures are less suitable than interactive methods for the last of these three.

When analogies are successful, they teach the structure of concepts precisely because it is those relations that the students have to check out. There is empirical evidence for this. Evans and Evans (1989) used posttests to probe whether metaphors helped to assimilate, make concrete, or structure concepts and found that students made general inferences that they could only have made by seeing

how concepts relate. Using the analogy of a factory in a lecture on parts of a biological cell, Bean, Searles, Singer, and Cowen (1990) found that students lectured
with an accompanying pictorial study guide using the analogy did better than
those with the same study guide without the pictures. The advantage of pictures
is that they can show multiple relationships. By relating distant concepts, one
might think that frequent analogies over a long period would foster lateral thinking and creativity; but I know of no evidence for this.

Experimental support for using analogies is weak. For example, Bell (1983)
combined lectures and role play using metaphors in one, both, and neither. Although there was temporary evidence that metaphors improved retention of information, they had no effect upon its acquisition or wider application.

I conclude that the use of analogies in lectures is a risky technique. (I must
leave the reader to judge how far the parables were valid and whether they pur-
ported to justify or to explain.)

e. Asides. The use of asides is sometimes associated with a vague, amorphous
lecturing style. Indeed it might be thought that asides are, by definition, irrelevant
and should not occur in a well-organized lecture. Strodt-Lopez (1991) has shown
this is not so.

Asides have many functions. They are not incidental—even though the lecturer might introduce them with "Incidentally . . ."! They can clarify, consolidate,
and evaluate. Asides can explain by linking ideas. A thorough understanding of a
topic requires links between all its aspects. Owing to the sequential nature of a
lecture, systematic lecture organization inevitably breaks some of these links.
Asides can reinstate them. In this way, asides have an important role in creating
the coherence of a topic. Asides in different parts of a lecture should often be explicitly linked. They can anticipate and refer back. All this is consistent with
McAleese's (1978) finding that asides do not increase vagueness, even though the
density of information (points and examples) in a lecture may be reduced.

Asides can also develop diverse perspectives on a subject and thereby bring
it alive. They allow development of thoughts parallel to the main line of development. They can develop a personal view commenting on the basic information. Strodt-Lopez believes that when another person's theory is being expounded,
this can maintain a professor's credibility. Clearly, asides have a place in a well-
organized lecture.

However, though there is no reason why minor comments and asides should
not be added to any part of the elaboration stage, if they are pertinent criticisms
they will embed, or "nest," as critical key points within other key points. Embed-
ding of this kind is confusing to students. It is a particular danger in the thesis
form (see Figure 5.7). It is clearer to deal with key points positively and then return

to critical points and major qualifiers. In this way, criticisms and reservations are presented at the same level as the points they criticize.

Similarly, asides will confuse if they are not signaled both at the beginning and the end. The entry signal is often a slight lowering of the voice or a straying from the lecturer's notes, rather than a verbal signal. Indeed, the words might not be very different from words that would occur in the main exposition. This can create problems for students if the lecturer does not take special care to give a clear signal. The exit signals (Table 8.1) are often accompanied by a short increase in volume and pace, and the lecturer may reenter the main line of the lecture by repeating the key point, or a key word or phrase from it.

f. Relating. To put a point in its context, it is useful to relate it to general knowledge, other subjects, other parts of the same subject, or what was said two weeks ago. Relating points encourages redeployment of concepts and discernment in their use. Not only is relating ideas often what makes a lecture interesting, but some teachers claim that this is what they expect students to do in their final examinations. If one of the objectives of teaching a topic is that students should be able to relate it to other branches of the discipline, it seems reasonable to expect the lecturer to demonstrate these relationships sometimes.

There are a number of ways of doing so, as in this sequence:

1. Applying lecture information, preferably in interesting ways
2. Specifying the main issues and showing where opinions on one are likely to result in particular opinions on another
3. Posing questions
4. Making comparisons
5. Formulating expectations
6. Evaluating
7. Drawing conclusions
8. Confronting failure

g. Examples. Where possible, examples should be brief, familiar, and in concrete terms. When an example is given, the students have to match it with the major point that has previously been made. Consequently, they must hold the point in mind while the lecturer gives examples. This is not easy if they do not already understand it clearly, because as short-term memory fades, increasing demands are made on long-term memory. But we have seen that long-term memory depends much more upon meaning and therefore assumes the understanding that the example is intended to give. Thus, long examples can defeat their own purpose.

If you remember, as a student, having heard examples in a lecture but have forgotten what they were examples of, it will be clear that holding the general point in one's mind is what proved to be too difficult. The lecturer must therefore employ strategies to avoid this forgetfulness in students. These strategies may consist of a visual aid to memory, writing more than key words on the board, or repeating the general point at the appropriate moment. Lecturers may need to analyze examples so that each element is matched explicitly. To take a simple example, if the general point involves levers, a fulcrum, and weights, and the example is a seesaw with two children on it, the lecturer would need to make it explicit that "the children are the weights . . ." and so on. If the example is simple and brief, forgetting is less likely.

Let humor be natural, not forced. *Humorous examples* have an obvious merit, but the general point is sometimes lost in the laughter. Bryant, Comiski, Cime, and Zillmann (1980) report that humor enhanced students' approval of male lecturers but had the opposite effect with female lecturers—except when their humor was at someone's expense! According to Vogel (1996), nontendentious humor can relieve tension, increase interest, enhance memory, mask embarrassment, and foster group cohesion when giving sex education to adolescents. Humor appears to make no difference to recall immediately after the lecture, but if it is relevant and related to the point being explained, it improves recall later (Javidi and Long, 1989; Downs, Javidi, and Nussbaum, 1988; Kaplan and Pascoe, 1977). Consequently, a pause to give time for the matching to take place, explicitly relating the example to the major point, or the provision of a further example, is usually advisable.

There is some merit in examples disclosing *personal experience*. Nelson (1989, 1992) found that, compared with hypothetical examples, personal examples improved students' attitude toward the teacher, increased their confidence, and increased their recall of lecture material. She interprets these findings in terms of the dictum that increased personal certainty increases personal liking. There may be sex differences: when a male professor used self-disclosing examples on fifteen-minute tape-recorded lectures, McCarthy and Schmeck (1982) found men showed better recall and women rated the professor more attractive and trustworthy.

I find I can never think of good examples at the time of lecturing. They therefore have to be prepared in advance. In fact, it is quite a good idea to carry a small notebook and collect ideas and examples at all times.

5. Feedback

Feedback should be an important and continuous process throughout a lecture, and for this reason a special section is devoted to its techniques later; but it has a particularly important place after the elaboration. Lecturers need to know whether they have gotten their point across before going on to the next, first because later points may depend upon it, and second because the opportunities feedback provides for consolidation of relatively short-term memories by rehearsal cannot be taken later. Furthermore, if ascertaining whether an objective is achieved is so unimportant that one need not bother, one may ask whether the objective was worthwhile in the first place. If it is worthwhile but the lecturer fails, he or she must either make another attempt to achieve it, or assume that the students are capable of achieving on their own what they could not achieve with the lecturer's help. In the first instance, at least, the fresh attempt will be easier before the first explanation is forgotten.

6. Recapitulation and Restatement

Recapitulation and restatement are not the same. They are placed together here because they occur in rapid succession as a kind of summing up, and either may precede the other. Recapitulation is a reminder of examples, explanation, and evidence. Restatement consists of repeating the same words that formed the key statement. It is often helpful at this stage if the same concise statement is used, not simply because the repetition consolidates its learning but because, if further reexpression is used, it has to be related in the students' minds to everything else that has been said on the point. A restatement of the same words requires recognition, rather than recall, by the student, and the former is easier. Furthermore, if the lecturer speaks too fast for the key statement to be fully noted when it is first uttered, and if it is not written on the board, many students wait for its precise restatement.

Examples of Other Forms

There are many variations on the general form, some of which are appropriate for particular objectives.

1. Explaining Difficult Points

A lecturer may have to teach difficult concepts, or principles that are so unfamiliar to the class that the initial concise statement would be unintelligible. Using the concise statement first thing assumes that the point can be made in language the students understand.

If this is not so, it may be appropriate to start with examples or illustrations, followed by observation of students (Table 6.2). Then a slowly reasoned interpretation of the examples is given, before arriving at the concise statement, use of the board, and reexpression. Because students will not remember essential de-

TABLE 6.2. MAKING A DIFFICULT POINT, BASED ON THE GENERAL FORM.

Example	1.	Examples or illustrations
	2.	Observation of students
	3.	Careful analysis and reasoned interpretation of examples
Rule	4.	Concise statement of key point
	5.	Display (on blackboard or OHP screen)
	6.	Reexpression
Rule	7.	Recapitulation
Example	8.	Another example or application showing relevance
Rule	9.	Recapitulation
	10.	Restatement of key point

tails of the examples and reasoning before they know what the lecturer is driving at, a recapitulation may be helpful.

Another example or relation to other aspects of the subject is usually advisable when the topic is difficult, culminating in recapitulation and restatement.

In effect, these ten stages amount to an e.g.-rule-rule-e.g.-rule pattern in which the initial examples are an attempt to make the unfamiliar familiar before giving the concise point.

2. Proceeding at the Pace of the Class

In topics that require thought by the students as the lecturer proceeds, or where, as in a chaining lecture, it is important for the class to follow every stage (namely question, feedback, reasoning, concise statement, display, reexpression, recapitulation, and restatement; see Table 6.3), it is useful to keep the class and lecturer together.

Pacing is achieved by using feedback so that the class appreciates the point just before it is concisely expressed. Without this prior understanding, an e.g.-rule-rule pattern of this kind (in which there is no elaboration after the initial statement of the point) would be unsatisfactory because factors affecting memory, such as rehearsal, meaningfulness, and relation to the whole, are neglected. Repetition is used, but as we saw, this depends on some prior learning.

3. Motivators

To motivate is to change attitudes. We have already seen that the lecture method is not very suitable for that. To motivate is a bit like selling. Every competent salesperson knows that to get a sale, the product must satisfy a personal need. To do

TABLE 6.3. PACING A POINT, BASED ON THE GENERAL FORM.

Example	1.	Question
	2.	Answer; feedback
	3.	Reasoning
Rule	4.	Concise statement of key point
	5.	Display and observe gaze
	6.	Reexpression; observe note taking
Rule	7.	Recapitulation
	8.	Restatement of key point

that, the salesperson must first ascertain what the customers perceive their needs to be. This requires consultation rather than speeches. (If feasible, spend five minutes with every student individually at the beginning of a course; it is a worthwhile investment if it can be used to find out what motivates them.) However, in the context of making a point, I shall assume that this is not possible.

Initial questions can arouse interest. For the reasons just mentioned, immediate feedback is desirable; but even rhetorical questions have some arousing effect (Zillmann and Cantor, 1973). They need to be asked with enthusiasm.

The pattern thus produced (Table 6.4) may be questioning to arouse curiosity, reasoning or feedback to answer it, display of the key phrase, making a concise statement, reexpression, application or relation to other points to provide relevance, recapitulation, feedback to give personal contact and a sense of achievement, and finally restatement of the key point.

In the general form, the features that arouse motivation are found in the elaboration. These are distributed here to prevent the motivation level from falling and to eliminate longer periods in which the key phrase is dryly presented. Similarly, the display can be presented before the concise statement to attract attention, if it is not always done that way.

4. Definitions

Definitions are a specific kind of key point. You might think that because definitions need to be precisely worded, they cannot be reformulated using different words. Flowerdew (1991) has shown this is not so. Representative speech acts can be modified using pragmatic strategies, such as politeness and indirectness. Definitions can even be taught by what he calls "external" modification, using asides, rhetorical questions, and eliciting questions.

Flowerdew (1992) found that although there were big variations between topics and lecturers, definitions were given on average once every one minute fifty-

TABLE 6.4. MOTIVATION FROM A POINT, BASED ON THE GENERAL FORM.

Example	1. Arouse interest: questions for curiosity and personal relevance
	2. Reasoning or feedback to answer
Rule	3. Display
	4. Concise statement of key point
	5. Reexpression
Example	6. Interrelate and apply the point to satisfy motives
Rule	7. Recapitulation
Example	8. Personal interaction: involvement, questions, and feedback
Rule	9. Restatement

five seconds in chemistry and biology lectures when English was the students' second language. Definitions often cluster, but he found no evidence that they occur more at the beginning (though Bramki and Williams, 1984, say that they do).

Definitions have a number of specific forms. Using the word *definition* a little loosely, Flowerdew says there are four kinds of definition: formal, semiformal, substitution, and ostension. Formal definitions commonly take the form $A = B + C$, where B is a class and C is a characteristic or quality of some members of that class; as an example, a puppy is a dog that is young (Trimble, 1985). This could be elaborated using the general form, but that is not always necessary. Semiformal definitions often consist of examples followed by "these are called X"—a simple example-rule format. A combination of semiformal followed by formal is quite effective. Substitutions are typically synonyms, paraphrases, or derivations. Ostensive definitions consist of pointing, either physically with the use of visual aids or by showing how a word is used.

It is advisable to say when you are giving a definition. Too many lecturers do not. Jackson and Bilton (1994) coded 921 definitions in twenty science lectures. Although 52 percent finished with a lecture signal and 12 percent with a comprehension check, 64 percent were introduced without a signal (see Table 8.1). Jackson and Bilton observed that 44 percent had the $A = B + C$ form. Eight percent had one or more reformulations of C, in which D and E were substituted for it one after the other. And in 56 percent of the first formulations, both B and C included technical terms. Reformulations, D and E, were less technical.

More worrisome, 24 percent of the definitions observed involved embedded definitions within the definition. For example the definition of a geological "conglomerate" included explanations of "bonded" and "finer sediments." A definition is a relation of at least three concepts $(A = B + C)$. To hold two definitions in mind and substitute one in the other is too big a load on most students' short-term memories. Consequently the fall-off in comprehension scores is dramatic (Bligh, 1974).

As with all teaching, the art is to keep it as simple as possible.

Conclusion

The purpose of describing these forms is to show that:

- Making a point in a lecture involves a number of elements that may need consideration during preparation
- The effectiveness of lectures may depend upon the way these elements are combined
- The skills in combining them can be learned

It is not intended to stultify all lecturing into a few forms or to inhibit those who have more natural gifts for exposition. The ways of making a point are not formulas to be rigidly applied. Lecturing requires interaction with the audience rather than a predetermined formula. Furthermore, the scientific study of teaching skills (as distinct from teaching methods) has scarcely begun. Yet although a pragmatic approach may therefore be the best, it should nevertheless be well informed. Part of the required information is an understanding of understanding—that is to say, an understanding of the processes of encoding briefly described in Chapter Two.

CHAPTER SEVEN

REASONS AND EXPLANATIONS

The importance of making links.

Reasons as explanations.

1. Regulative explanations.

2. Analytical explanations.

3. Spatial explanations.

4. Temporal explanations.

5. Kinematic explanations.

6. Causal explanations.

7. Functional explanations.

8. Mental (cognitive, value, moral, and purposive) explanations.

L ogically speaking, this chapter fits within the step "reasons and explanations" (4c.) of the general form (Table 6.1). But I think the ideas in this chapter will be clearer if presented separately.

In attempting to explain explanations, this chapter moves to a meta-level. Consequently, it is the most difficult chapter to understand, and the most speculative and forward looking. I also find the chapter difficult to write in that the truth of my assertions is most likely to vary with the reader's academic discipline—areas where a more prudent author would fear to tread.

In experimental studies of learning in lectures, the factors associated with the greatest variations in students' scores are differences in subject matter. In other words, differences in the information students need to know to answer the experimenter's tests have more effect on the scores than anything else. It follows that the greatest gains in lecturing effectiveness will eventually be obtained from analysis of the processes entailed when learning specific items of information.

We might think of information as difficult to learn when it involves a large number of brain cells and relatively few pathways to activate them. When information is familiar, there are well-established pathways. Complex ideas are partly acquired by establishing linking pathways between simple ones. Learning is a process of linking information. The analysis of the best ways to learn information will be a matter of identifying the links.

The Importance of Making Links

It must be frankly admitted that there have been relatively few experimental studies of the most effective way to explain individual points. It has been assumed, no doubt rightly, that the approach will vary with the point in question, the students' background, and variables previously mentioned. But first of all, even these are assumptions that have not been well tested, and second, if they are correct, this fact need not preclude experiment to establish principles of lecturing technique any more than in other disciplines that study interacting variables.

The most thorough experimental studies of micro teaching techniques in lectures are those conducted by Gage and his associates at Stanford University (Gage and others, 1968). But those students were sixteen-year-old pupils in high schools, and the degree to which the results of such findings can be transferred is always a matter of opinion until further studies are conducted. In their first experiment, Fortune, Gage, and Shutes (1966) used forty lectures, sixty pupils, and twenty topics, each based on a "Report" from the *Atlantic*. The lecturettes lasted fifteen minutes and were tested by a ten-item comprehension test. When the test scores were adjusted for the ability of the pupils and the relative difficulty of the topics, it was found that the lecturers were individually consistent in their ability to explain the same topic to different groups on different occasions, but they were not consistent in their ability to teach different topics. Pupils' ratings of the "clarity of presentation" correlated with the lecturers' effectiveness as measured by the test scores. Rosenshine (1968) confirmed that there are consistent and detectable differences in the explaining ability of lecturers. The fact that some lecturers are better than others renders it likely that there are at least some lecturing skills that can be learned.

The task remained to find out what these skills are. Since Gage and Unruh (1967) had demonstrated a high correlation between the estimates of lecture effectiveness by visiting judges and their objective effectiveness as measured by multiple-choice comprehension tests, Gage (1968) concluded that these important lecture skills are at least observable.

Rosenshine (1968) then set to work to find "the cognitive and stylistic correlates of lecture effectiveness." From forty lectures on Yugoslavia, he selected at random five of the ten most effective and five of the ten least effective and subjected the transcripts to content analysis by groups of independent judges who scored them on a host of variables. These included the average length of a sentence, the use of sentence fragments, the number of prepositional phrases per sentence, self-references, aspects of syntax, instructional set, techniques of familiarizing the class with new concepts, the use of previous knowledge, the use of learning sets, devices for focusing attention, organization, emphasis, repetition, redundancy of language, the speed of talking, and so on. The factors that discriminated between the five effective and five ineffective lectures were then cross-validated on the remaining effective and ineffective lectures. The factors that survived this cross-validation were then tried out on the best and worst lectures on Thailand.

The two factors that survived this double screening process were what Rosenshine calls "explaining links" and the degree to which lecturers used the rule-e.g.-rule technique. The latter was dealt with in the last chapter. It should not, of course, be thought that the other factors mentioned above are not important. The fact that they did not survive the double screening procedure shows only that they are not important for all lecturers in all subjects and for all students.

By observing explaining links, Kozoil (1986) analyzed what he called the "kinetic structure" of communications by assessing its continuity and progression of ideas. He said the structure of a lecture can be measured by the extent to which the concepts have some elements in common (a network of links), how concepts progress from one to the next (chaining), how student activities relate one to another, and the extent to which each activity is new. The mathematics lectures he observed scored lower than biology lectures on all these measures. It seems that each problem a mathematics lecturer presented as an example was sufficiently different from the previous one that the students did not make the necessary links.

The importance of explaining links is confirmed by P. E. Johnson (1967), who has shown that the ease with which students associate concepts in Newtonian mechanics is proportional to the frequency with which the words are mentioned, multiplied by the number of ways they are linked together when presented.

It is also confirmed by the fact that experts represent more, and different, links in their minds than novices do (Van Patten, Chao, and Reigeluth, 1986). This is most easily demonstrated in chess, but it also applies to academic disciplines. Expert chess players conceive of sequences and abstract patterns of moves, while novices consider only one or two moves at a time.

Hansen and Jensen (1994) have shown that making links is a particular difficulty for second-language students. Those whose language skills were proficient scored equally well on questions that tested a "global" understanding of a topic as on questions on specific details. Those who were less proficient did less well on both, but much worse on global questions. On specific questions, they relied upon verbatim memory; global questions required them to extract and relate clauses from different sentences and to formulate answers in their own words.

"Extract," "relate," and "formulate" each required a mastery of language they did not possess.

Repeatedly in this book, researchers with different approaches have shown the importance of linking ideas. In Chapter One, I showed that discussion is better than lectures for getting students to think. Why? Because in discussion different contributions relate ideas in different ways. The Gestalt psychologists emphasized insights relating old ideas in new ways. In Figure 2.1, it is pathways 15–5–6–14–15–24–27 that most aid comprehension. With the demonstration of chunking and Table 2.2, I showed that words only have meaning when they can be related easily. Others have talked about the difference between deep and surface processing. The chapters on organization and the various forms for making a point are essentially about structuring concepts. They are all saying the same thing from different perspectives.

This is why a lot of good teaching consists in helping students make links easily.

Reasons as Explanations

We have seen that understanding is enhanced by explaining links because understanding consists of relating new ideas to ideas we already possess.

The question now is, How should lecturers build up explaining links? In most cases there will be no problem. The points lecturers want to teach are in a certain context in their minds. They know what that context is. The course, or the organization of the particular lecture, can usually be prepared so that students know that context. If so, when lecturers make a point, students will see the connection. They will make the links for themselves. The art of teaching is to help students make links.

Difficulties arise either when students don't know the context, or when they don't make the connection, because the context is not uppermost in their minds, even though they know it.

In either case, the lecturer's strategy will be to try to sketch in the context and to show the links being made. Lecturers cannot make links for the students. That is something that has to go on in their heads. All lecturers can do is to show what is in common between the context that explains and the point to be understood. It is a bit like the prosecution's case in a criminal court. When explaining the guilt of the accused, the prosecution must present the context of an offense and try to link it to the defendant. The job of the defense (and of negative academic criticism) is to show that the links are not made.

At this point it looks as if this book cannot help much further. Lecturers' problems lie in their subject matter, of which I have no knowledge. But it is worth drawing attention to the types of explanation. There are at least eleven kinds. They tend to have different contexts. Knowledge of these types may help lecturers in their hunt for gaps in students' knowledge and their failure to make links.

To explain a fact or some other proposition, it normally needs to be linked to at least two other facts or propositions. Only one, and possibly none, will be of the same kind as the fact being explained.

In practice we often only give one fact or proposition as a reason. We assume the listener knows the other; to give it seems like insulting the listener's intelligence. It may be. But too often when lecturing we commit the opposite crime. We assume that everyone knows things that some don't. It is usually better to remind an audience of what you think they know than to try to link new ideas to ignorance. Links with ignorance are not links at all. Most people don't mind being told a few things they know already. It's encouraging; and lectures would be far too intensive if they weren't.

1. Regulative Explanations

Regulative explanations implicitly, if not explicitly, involve a general rule, an instance of that rule, and the application of the rule to that instance. For example:

Most employees pay tax.	(general rule)
Smith is an employee.	(instance: example of an employee)
Therefore Smith probably pays tax.	(application of the general rule)

To show that an instance is indeed an example of a general rule involves showing the elements, or patterns of concepts, in common between the instance and the rule. In this example, it would involve showing that Smith has the defining characteristics of an employee.

When lecturers get feedback that students have not understood the conclusion, there are four possible causes, and they must check out all four. Students might not:

1. Accept or understand the general rule
2. Accept or understand that Smith is an employee
3. Accept or understand that Smith being an employee is an instance of the general rule
4. Be able to reason by applying the rule to the instance in order to draw the conclusion

It is a common error to assume that the students' difficulty lies in one of these four when it lies in another. In that case, lecturers' further attempts at explaining will be ineffective and may create feelings of frustration in both the lecturer and the students. Repeated frustration leads to anger and despair.

It could be argued that every explanation is regulative in one sense, because explaining links are made according to rules—normally some kind of logic. There are some disciplines—notably mathematics, linguistics, law, and logic itself—that study logical and stipulative rules as well as apply them. Most disciplines try to establish empirical generalizations that may then be applied in further study.

Generalizations are often best explained by saying how they were established—the facts and the reasoning that related them to form a generalization. Stipulative rules are best explained by saying who stipulated them, their context, and why. For example, new laws are usually stipulated in a social context.

Another strategy when students have difficulty in understanding regulative explanations is to break down the reasoning into small steps. Each of these steps will also be the application of a rule. This is particularly relevant to mathematical subjects, including physics and engineering. If students cannot see how one line of a calculation is derived from another, it is necessary not only to set out the intermediate steps but also to write words such as "Substituting $x-y$, in equation E we get . . . ," which explain those steps in more detail.

2. Analytical Explanations

An analytical explanation explains something in terms of its constituent parts. By drawing attention to the constituent parts of something, the explanation shows how they fit together. Indeed, in the last paragraph, where I advised breaking reasoning into smaller steps, I was recommending using an analytical explanation to explain a reasoning process. The use of one explanatory type to elucidate another is quite common. Regulative and analytical explanations are fundamental. So they often seem to be elements in other kinds of explanation.

Analytical explanations say that X, Y, and Z are different, and together they make W. The emphasis appears to be on the differences between X, Y, and Z. What is not so obvious, but can be important when clarifying analytical explanations, is that X, Y, and Z are normally distinguished upon one or more dimensions they have in common and that make them part of W. For example, if the human skeleton is analyzed into its constituent bones, despite the differences that distinguish them the bones have characteristics in common. They are made of similar material, have physical similarities, occupy space, and normally have certain spatial relationships to each other. Thus, they may be regarded as having in common that they occupy a spatial dimension; and because the dimension is in common, it is upon this dimension that they can be distinguished. Likewise, blood may be analyzed into red and white cells, plasma, etc., according to their different functions.

In doing so, the analysis recognizes that they each have functions. They have a functional dimension.

Subject matter can often be variously analyzed, using different dimensions. Compared with its spatial analysis, the skeleton might be analyzed, and its parts classified, quite differently according to the functions of the bones (protection, support, mobility, etc.). In this case, the parts will be classified on a functional dimension (most bones being in several categories). We saw something similar with compare-and-contrast lecture forms in Chapter Five. That's not surprising; to compare and contrast requires an analytical method. See Figures 5.5 and 5.6.

A common difficulty with analytical explanations occurs when students cannot see either that the whole is made of the constituents or how the constituent parts fit together to make the whole. Both these difficulties can be overcome if the lecturer recognizes and can represent the dimension on which the parts are distinguished. For example, when analyzing the differences between civil and criminal law, it is not enough to present the two right-hand columns in Table 7.1. It is also necessary to give the first column, the dimensions in common upon which they are distinguished. State the dimension first; then distinguish the parts. It is a matter of asking yourself, *What do X, Y, and Z have in common?* and *What is the conceptual knife that is used to distinguish them as constituent parts of the whole?* In the example in Table 7.1, the law is divided into civil and criminal cases. Each case is brought by someone, aiming to prove something, hoping the court will impose some redress.

3. Spatial Explanations

Obviously, visual aids can be used to explain spatial concepts. Leave some silence immediately after displaying them; otherwise you divide the students' attention. Spatial explanations give understanding by relating distances or by fitting certain shapes, patterns, or structures together. They are common in chemistry, geography, astronomy, biology, architecture, and many other disciplines. How do you apprehend that, of all possible shapes, a sphere has the maximum volume for the

TABLE 7.1. THE ROLE OF DIMENSIONS IN ANALYSIS.

Dimension	Civil Cases	Criminal Cases
Who brings the case	An individual "sues"	The state prosecutes[a]
What the process aims to establish	Loss	Blame, not consequences
What the court "imposes"	"Awards"	"Sentences"
What redress is called	Compensation	Punishment

[a]Private prosecutions are rare.

minimum surface area? No doubt you might prove it using mathematical rules, but originally you probably realized it intuitively when seeing a bubble or some other spatial image. Your understanding initially, and probably even now, was spatial. Lecturers in biology rely on intuitions about shape to explain optimum exchanges of heat, liquids, or gases through membranes. Chemists not only imagine molecular and crystal forms, they represent the periodic table spatially, with regard to the number of electrons in an atom, for ease of understanding.

Figures in Chapter Five illustrate how spatial representations can be used to explain relationships that are not, themselves, spatial. This is a significant point for lecturers. Most faculty partly owe their success to their verbal fluency. Students, too, are commonly selected on the basis of their verbal performance in examinations, but some may be more talented spatially; so it is worthwhile for lecturers to think how they could represent their material spatially.

4. Temporal Explanations

Temporal explanations are a good example of explanations that can be represented spatially. Use visuals to describe temporal relations. They give understanding by temporal comparison of states of affairs or events on a time dimension. Because time is linear, if temporal explanations are difficult they can be represented visually. For example, it is difficult for students to appreciate how enormous the relative lengths of geological periods are without some kind of visual aid.

Temporal explanations also have a logic that can benefit from visual representation. It is not always so simple as A precedes B, and B precedes C, therefore A precedes C. The anthropologist or historian reporting research using radio carbon dating, documentary evidence, and so on, each with margins of error, may need to take the audience through quite complex arguments about probabilities.

5. Kinematic Explanations

When perceptions best fit together by assuming that an object or objects have moved from one place to another over time, the explanation is kinematic. No cause of the movement is given. For example Wegener's theory of continental drift said that continents had drifted apart, but it was forty years before tectonic plate theory suggested possible forces to cause the movement.

Paradoxically, if you want to teach someone how something moves, use two or more *still* images, not moving ones—for example, use slides, not film or TV. If you teach massage or some other manual skill, show where the hands start, where they should finish, and one or two positions in between before demonstrating the movement in full. Moving images are usually too quick and present too much information to remember or copy.

Kinematic explanations require the lecturer to describe and match the circumstances before and after the move. In Wegener's case, this meant matching the shapes of the continents and their geological formations. Similarly, astronomers make intermittent observations of comets and other stellar objects. Some comets are said to come, go, and return many years later. But the only justification for explaining the later appearances as being the same comet that appeared many years before is to match its characteristics on the two (or more) occasions.

If students don't understand or accept that an object has moved, all the lecturer can do to show that the object before and after is the same object is to match its characteristics on the two occasions ever more closely. Ultimately, it is the student's mind that must make the link one way or the other.

6. Causal Explanations

Speaking loosely, a cause is a distribution of forces or objects at one point in time, such that it is followed by another distribution. The first distribution (and its attendant forces) is the cause; the second is its effect.

As with kinematic explanations, the lecturers need to describe the before and after circumstances; but with causal explanations, the forces at work must also be given. These may be psychological (motivations) or physical.

In practice, forces are quite difficult to specify. Consequently, causal explanations are much rarer than many people suppose. For example, when explaining the content of a blood sample someone may say, "The liver purifies the blood"; but that doesn't explain how it does it. Even explanations in scientific journals, purporting to be causal, are often functional.

7. Functional Explanations

Most functional explanations describe what something or somebody regularly does in certain circumstances with certain effects. They are usually generalizations about the circumstances, the something (an agent), and the effects. Being generalizations, they are often supported by statistics.

Functional explanations are very common, particularly in the social and biological sciences. "The liver purifies the blood" describes its function. The theory of evolution largely deals with the functions of organs and organisms. An economist might describe functional relationships between prices and demand. There is an implied cause; but functional explanations give generalizations about effects, not causes. In fact, the precise causes of functional relationships are usually unknown. Furthermore, not all functional relationships are based upon causes. Most philosophers argue that the functions of language, including expressions in mathematics, operate according to rules rather than causes. The relations described are more like correlations than causes, more like correspondences than consequences.

A common error in subjects like economics and engineering is to present the functions only in mathematical form and not in words. Try as many ways as possible.

The lecturer's job is to describe the circumstances, agent, and effects, selecting what is pertinent. Where they are generalizations from repeated observations, selection is necessary; but of course a selective presentation of facts permits bias and distortion.

The fact that the causes of functional relationships are often unknown might make some lecturers feel vulnerable to students' questions; but students accept that not everything is known and that their lecturers don't know everything even in their own subject. There is no harm in admitting it.

8. Mental (Cognitive, Value, Moral, and Purposive) Explanations

Mental explanation is a general name for explanations where what is explained are phenomena obtained by awareness of one's own mind. The method is very common in studying literature, history, social work, and other applied fields of human behavior. The method is self-awareness—introspection. Mental explanations are subjective. Their phenomena include cognitions, value preferences, morals, and purposes. Mental explanations include each of these explanatory types.

Cognitive explanations show the compatibility of information from awareness of one's own memories, knowledge and beliefs, sensations, perceptions, reasons, thoughts, or other cognitive experiences.

Values, morals, and intentions have an emotive component. They are normally explained and justified by a fact of another kind plus a more general value, moral principle, or purpose. When giving these explanations, lecturers need to give both. It is extremely common, particularly in debate, to give only facts and to assume that the values, moral principles, or general intentions are agreed. Both need to be explicit.

Because of their introspective nature, mental explanations require some empathy from the lecturer's audience. Empathy is an attitude. It cannot be injected or presented by the lecturer. The lecturer can only appeal to the better nature of the audience.

Conclusion

The study of explanations is a difficult area and still in its infancy, though it may grow rapidly with developments in artificial intelligence. Effective explanations link what is to be explained to two or more ideas already in the students' minds. If these two ideas are not already in the students' minds, they too will need to be explained. If so, at least one of them will need an explanation of a different type.

If students don't understand, there are two strategies worth adopting. One is to ask yourself, *What does my audience already know about this topic, and how can I use that as a starting point?* The other is to anticipate likely points of difficulty and to work out the premises (explaining links) in greater detail for these trouble spots.

If, when giving the lecture, you notice that some points seem difficult to understand, mark them on your notes. Afterward, work out how they could be better explained by analyzing links and assumptions in your own understanding. If possible, try to remember how and why you understood the point when you first met it or thought of it. Then expand your lecture notes accordingly so that your explanation will be more lucid next time. Don't wait until then. Work out how the explanation could have been better while the topic and lecturing experience are fresh in your mind. That is quicker in the long run. Furthermore, if this is done right away, it may be possible to correct misunderstandings at the beginning of the next lecture.

CHAPTER EIGHT

AIDS TO COMPREHENDING A POINT

Chalkboard.

  1. Advantages.

  2. Disadvantages.

  3. Technique.

Overhead projector.

  1. Advantages.

  2. Disadvantages.

  3. Techniques.

Microsoft PowerPoint.

  1. PowerPoint in general.

  2. Output.

  3. Templates and slide masters.

  4. Creating and projecting slide shows using a personal computer.

  5. Rolling demonstrations.

  6. Quick summary of steps in creating a slide presentation.

A warning about other visual images.

Verbal signals.

Nonverbal signals.

Other factors affecting comprehension of a point.

From the students' point of view, one of the disadvantages of the lecture method is that words fleetingly come and go unless they are captured either in notes or in long-term memory. Chalkboards and overhead projectors reduce this difficulty by allowing a more extended presentation of what the lecturer chooses to display.

I am aware that this book is used in all parts of the world—some where a supply of electricity is unavailable, and others blessed with all the latest technology. So the aids available to students and readers are quite different, and I must beg some tolerance from you if some sections do not seem to fit the context in which you lecture. If you don't have access to Microsoft PowerPoint, for instance, it makes sense to skip that section.

Chalkboard

The chalkboard is perhaps the world's most common teaching aid.

1. Advantages

The advantage of chalkboards is that they are widely available, cheap to maintain, and relatively easy to use. A lecturer can progressively build up a summary of a lecture by displaying its organization of key points on the left, while using the right side for temporarily illustrating aspects of their elaboration. In this way, the lecturer's behavior signals, for each key point, the elements of rule-e.g.-rule, or whatever form is adopted. The temporary displays typically include simple diagrams and the spellings of unfamiliar words.

2. Disadvantages

Unfortunately, chalkboards are messy to use; and erased work cannot be easily re-presented as, for example, a reminder of the organization of the previous lecture. Using a board involves turning away from the audience, so that audience reactions are not so easily gauged. Compared with prepared transparencies for an overhead projector, writing is an extra task that can detract from thinking time and attention to the finer points of lecturing technique. On a blackboard, the use of color is limited to white, yellow, and the lightest shades of other colors. Dark blues, reds, and browns are less visible, particularly in a large room.

For this reason, a white board with felt pens, rather than chalk, is preferable. Furthermore, perception against a white background is both quicker and more accurate (Seymour, 1937; Snowberg, 1973). Some white boards also have magnetic properties so that overhead transparencies, or other thin plastics, can be made to stick with static electricity by placing them on the board and simply rubbing briefly. Alternatively, magnetic bars can be used to pin newsprint or other large sheets of paper for display. Magnetic rubber shapes are also available in several colors and can be slid around on the board to illustrate, for example, the journey taken by blood cells in the heart and lungs.

3. Technique

Some tips may be useful for the new lecturer who has previously only written on paper. Writing on paper uses the wrist and fingers. When writing on a board the movement is more in the elbow and shoulder. To become accustomed to this and the vertical surface of a board, visit the lecture room when it is empty a day or two before your first lecture and practice making large sweeping lines. Notice where your feet need to be, and how horizontals require you to move them. Do this before you attempt to write.

Writing gets worse with age; so set yourself high standards at the beginning. Use script, not cursive (joined) writing. Have in mind three horizontal lines: one under letters that do not have tails, another above lowercase letters, and a third at the top of capitals and tall lowercase letters such as *l, h,* and *k*. Practice making the letters *o, e,* and *c* circular. What position do you need to take to write at the top of the board? How well do you bend your knees when writing at the bottom?

Practice writing at the top of the board and at the bottom. Shoulder movements are difficult at the top. Writing with bent knees and back at the bottom can be tiring. If your line of writing goes up or down, you probably need to move your feet to a more comfortable position. If it goes up, you are probably too close to the board; if it goes down you are probably writing too far to one side of your body.

When you come to lecture, start with a clean board. Clean it systematically with downward strokes so that dust does not go everywhere; and do the next lecturer the courtesy of leaving your board clean when you finish.

If you are right-handed, when you move away from the board, move to one side as if pivoting on your left foot, so that you obstruct no one's view. It is quite a good idea to step right away and look at what you have written from the students' point of view. Check your spelling! Just as you saw, when first learning to type, that the keyboard can't spell, so too beginners embarrassingly misspell words on the chalkboard that they would never misspell on paper.

Overhead Projector

Overhead projectors (OHPs) are now widely available, if not standard equipment, in most lecture rooms.

1. Advantages

Overhead projectors have the advantage that overhead transparencies (OHTs) can be prepared in advance. They can be written in color or smartly produced using word processors in either in black and white or color depending on your printer. There are computer programs purposely designed to produce OHTs, with Microsoft PowerPoint being the one most widely used. Heat copiers can produce black and white OHTs of complex pictures or diagrams most lecturers would have neither the time nor the skill to draw. Although pens can be used for color shading, thin colored translucent film can be cut to shape and will adhere to an OHT by static electricity if smoothed into place. Similarly, silhouettes can be obtained by superimposing paper shapes.

Overlaying OHTs allows a progressive buildup of writing or images and can show spatial relationships of images that are best shown separately at first (say, OHTs of mountain ranges and rainfall distribution; or blood supply and the nervous system).

Diagrams and other visual material can be more detailed and more accurate than most chalkboard work. OHTs can remind students what was said in the previous lecture when explaining a detail or reviewing the whole. In this way they can be important linking devices.

Unlike the chalkboard, OHPs let the lecturer present written material and observe audience reaction. For this reason, it is sometimes said that they permit eye contact to be maintained. For a sensitive lecturer, this is not strictly true. The students' eye gaze goes past the lecturer to the screen behind.

2. Disadvantages

Even experienced lecturers who rely on overhead projectors find it difficult to cope when a bulb blows or there is a sudden malfunction. Some makes of OHP have a spare bulb inside, and it is worth learning how they are replaced.

Where the screen is not perpendicular to the projected light, rectangular images are portrayed as trapezoids. This is known as keystoning. It may not matter much when writing is displayed (indeed, by moving the OHT, a line of small writing can usefully be magnified at the top of the screen), but obviously diagrams are distorted. The distortion can be corrected if the top of the screen can be moved closer to the projector. Some screens have this facility.

The facility to produce OHTs by photocopying tempts lecturers to display far too much written material, often with a print size that is too small and too indistinct. When projected on a screen, thirty-two characters per line is generally regarded as a maximum.

3. Techniques

OHP pens are either water-based or spirit-based. Water-based pens have the advantage that errors can be quickly erased by a damp cloth or a lick on a paper towel; but their "ink" may blotch if you put your sweaty hand on them during the lecture, and the pens don't survive well in hot and humid climates. To avoid blotching when writing with either type of pen, it is advisable to rest your hand on a piece of paper, not directly on the OHT. Spirit-based writing is not easy to correct unless wiped clean at once.

To prevent errors in preparing OHTs ahead of time, it is a good idea to write what you want on paper at the desired size, and then place the paper under the OHT when you write. I use lined computer paper because the lines can guide lowercase letters like *e, a, u,* etc.; the height of *l, h, k,* etc.; and the tails of *y, g, p,* and so on. Practice making the round parts of letters *c, e, p, q, b, d,* etc., truly circular. It is worth practicing a letter *e* so that the hole in the middle is not filled in. Lowercase letters like *e* should not be less than a quarter of an inch high. Not writing large enough is a very common error. Typing and book print are normally far too small.

Use black, blue, red, or green. Yellows and orange do not project well. If you use browns and purple, make sure the lines are thick or else they too will not be visible.

Check the equipment and focus before the lecture begins. When in focus, most unloaded OHPs project an image of fine concentric circles, but some people check focus with a transparency. Check that the size of the image just fits the screen. If the OHP has a fan blowing hot air, make sure it is not blowing at you, or else your mouth will quickly dry out—with uninspiring consequences. The fan can be a problem. Make sure there is a place where you put OHTs once you have used them. It is sometimes a good idea to have a different place for those you know you will show again later in the lecture. Of course, I usually manage to put them where the fan blows them out of sequence, all over the floor, so that I can never find the one I need to use again!

A very lucid technique (the progressive revelation technique) is to have one OHT showing the structure of the lecture with its headings, subheadings, or key points. A sheet of paper is placed over the OHT and progressively withdrawn to display each heading or key point in turn as the lecturer reaches the display stage in making a point. Fold the paper so that it does not fall off as you reach points toward the bottom.

Light pens and laser pointers exist that depict an arrow to point at things to which you want to draw attention. But they are not very effective when pointed at a lighter part of the screen, and if you are nervous, every tremor is magnified for all to see. I prefer to use a propelling pencil (mechanical pencil), or some other fine tip to point at the OHT and thereby cast a slender shadow on the screen.

This has the advantage that I don't turn away from my audience. If my notes are by the projector, it also means I can refer to them, which I can't if I step away pointing directly at the screen.

I call the OHT that shows the lecture structure "the continuo." I return to it over and over again as successive points are reached, interspersed with others dealing with aspects of the elaboration (recall Table 6.1).

In the same way that good chalkboard technique involves using one side of the board to build up the structure of the lecture and the other side for ad hoc illustration, so there is a lot to commend using two OHPs with a screen in each of the corners behind the lecturer. One is for the continuo, the other for elaboration. This enables everything the lecturer says to be contextualized within the lecture's organization. Understanding the context is an important aspect of understanding the meaning of what is said.

Microsoft PowerPoint

PowerPoint is a software package designed to help you produce high-quality, professional-looking presentations in the minimum possible time. This program is available for IBM PC–compatible and Apple Macintosh computers (consult a vendor to determine what equipment and operating system requirements must be met for its use).

1. PowerPoint in General

You can produce slides, handouts, speaker's notes, and outlines in one integrated operation. Microsoft aims to make it as simple as possible to produce a series of slides, OHTs, or screen projections of computer information. The great majority of presentations in the business world are now made with the aid of PowerPoint, and the package has become an industry standard worldwide.

Although I particularly have OHTs in mind here, the increasing availability of PC projection panels and projection systems drives a trend toward using PC-based presentations without printing any transparencies at all. For this reason, the word *slide* is used here (and in PowerPoint itself) to mean an OHT, a 35mm transparency, or a PC projection.

2. Output

Black and white OHT *transparencies* can be created in PowerPoint and then produced directly from a laser or inkjet printer. For color transparencies, you need a color printer. If you want 35mm slides, you can send your PowerPoint file to a service bureau that does such work.

Students increasingly are asking for *handouts* of slides. PowerPoint offers a special facility for creating handouts directly (I deal with handouts in general in Chapter Ten). Handouts are a convenient way of giving your audience copies of your slides. The handouts consist of small versions of the slides; they can be printed two, three, or six slides to a page.

Speaker's notes consist of smaller versions of slides, one on a page, together with a box for explanatory notes relating to each slide. Speaker's notes are also useful as audience handouts.

Outlines give a very useful summary of (as well as a convenient way to enter) all the text contained in your lecture, with the added benefit that the contents (text and graphics) of each slide can be seen at a glance.

3. Templates and Slide Masters

Once you have created one or more slides using PowerPoint, you can change the appearance of all the slides (including slides not yet created) by applying what is known as a design template. Templates control backgrounds, colors, fonts, and other aspects of the slide. PowerPoint comes with a number of ready-to-use templates (some of which are quite tasteful).

Slide masters go one step further than templates. You can add text, logos, slide numbers, and any other objects to all your slides in one operation. The slide master also controls the text fonts and colors of all your slides. (Although a slide master controls all the slides in a given presentation, it is still possible to change the color schemes for individual slides.) Masters can be applied to a presentation at any time. It is a good idea to build up a collection of masters that are particularly relevant to you or to your department.

PowerPoint offers great flexibility not only in creating but also in revising, refining, editing or updating, duplicating, and preparing text and images for output and distribution. In particular, charts, graphs, and other visual depictions of data can be created in a great variety of forms and appearances, which offers the lecturer considerable freedom in choosing modes of presentation appropriate to the data or content.

4. Creating and Projecting Slide Shows Using a Personal Computer

PC projection offers the maximum amount of flexibility. Such presentations can be changed—quite literally—a few minutes before the lecture.

Slide shows are compiled and controlled with a PC (by manipulating the mouse if the lecturer wishes to have control over the pace and progression, backing up, and so on) connected to a data projector or an LCD panel.

Transitions determine with what visual effect one slide replaces another. A complex slide can be "built" by progressively revealing more of its content (perhaps while dimming previously discussed items in a bulleted list). While a slide is on the screen, moving the mouse in any direction will invoke an "annotation" box at the bottom left of the screen; among other things, this allows the mouse pointer to become a pencil with which lines can be drawn (temporarily) on the slide.

5. Rolling Demonstrations

Although seemingly a bit off the subject of conducting a lecture, for events such as open house days and exhibitions it can be helpful to have a number of slides displayed in a continuous loop. But this feature has its uses in a lecture as well—perhaps to show cycles of events in economics or biology.

6. Quick Summary of Steps in Creating a Slide Presentation

Although this is not the place for a detailed look at the use of PowerPoint, here is an overview of the process of creating a slide presentation from scratch:

1. Create a suitable master, using existing design templates with added logos, text, slide numbers, etc.
2. Switching to the outline view, type in the text for each slide.
3. Switch to the slide view, and check the appearance of each slide; adjust font sizes if necessary, and add any diagrams or clip-art.
4. Use the slide show feature to check the appearance of the whole lecture.
5. Add special effects such as transitions and builds.

A Warning About Other Visual Images

There is a danger with using slick visual aids. Dazzling presentations do not necessarily result in learning. The more that technologies allow lecturers to illustrate concepts, or large amounts of information, in ways that students cannot record in their notes or immediately commit to long-term memory, the less efficient lecturing becomes. It may be entertaining for the big occasion; but entertainment is a different objective from learning and educational development.

Notice that films, television, demonstrations, and other moving images are as fleeting as the lecturer's spoken words. Unless an image is held still for two or more seconds information overload is likely (compare Baddeley's visuospatial sketch pad, mentioned in Chapter Two). Slides or other still images illustrating the crucial steps are more memorable. For example, in a demonstration of massage students will copy more accurately if the demonstrator stops still at several positions in the movement so that they register in the students' minds. Students can then move from one position to the next when they massage. Conceiving, remembering, and copying a movement is much more difficult because, in effect, the movement is a very large number of images. The capacity of short-term memory becomes overloaded.

Similarly, although the amount of information that can be conveyed visually in a short space of time is astonishing, visual overload by lecturers who show one colored slide after another in darkened rooms is extremely common. Carousels holding dozens of slides encourage this vice. A few well-chosen slides, with an opportunity to take notes after each, is better. Ten slides an hour is, in most cases, enough. It may be a truism that visual aids are aids to making a point; but too often lecturers confuse them with the points themselves.

Furthermore, as Abercrombie (1960) showed in her classic work, students' interpretations of what they are shown are often varied and inaccurate. The presentation of slides and moving images needs to be followed by perceptual checks in discussion. Lecturers cannot safely assume that their audience has seen what they see.

Verbal Signals

It is no use giving a structured account of a point if the structure is not clear to the students. This clarity is achieved by lecture signals, or what are sometimes called "discourse markers." These signals reduce ambiguity; for example, the reason given for something could be a key point, or it could be part of an explanation. Similarly, a lecturer may itemize key points in the introduction and may also itemize facts, reasons, or causes in the detailed elaboration. Lecture signals can distinguish these contexts. The student who cannot distinguish a lecturer's key point from its detail, its context, the reasons for it, or particular examples of it will have a poor understanding of the lecture and will be poorly equipped to exercise the powers of criticism and judgment that I hold to be the fundamental objectives of higher education. It is customary to blame the student for such shortcomings, but the fault all too often lies with the lecturer who fails to adapt to the abilities of students.

This lays an obligation upon the lecturer to give lecture signals. Lecture signals are all those words phrases or sentences that mark out parts of a lecture as key points, restatements, definitions, examples, comparisons, lists, asides, corrections, reminders, causes and effects, repetitions, summaries, intersentence links, and so on (Wijasuriya, 1971; Young and Fitzgerald, 1982).

There are three levels of signals (though some signals could be regarded as being at different levels in different contexts). First are what DeCarrico and Nattinger (1988) call "global" signals. In particular, topic shifters are used when changing from one topic to another, and summarizers typically come at the end of a lecture, though they could be used at other times.

Second, there are "key point" signals, indicating that a key point is being made. These occur at the beginning and end of the forms described earlier in Chapter Six. Typically, they consist of itemization at the beginning of a point and restatement at the end.

Third, there are "micro" signals, or what DeCarrico and Nattinger call "local signals." They indicate different elements within the rule-e.g.-rule process of the general form or other forms.

DeCarrico and Nattinger list five local signals occurring during the elaboration of a point: exemplifiers, relaters, evaluators, qualifiers, and aside markers. I think they underestimate the variety and subtlety of micro signals. However, their classification (which was written for newly arrived foreign students) draws attention to a possible weakness in the way I have presented the general form. It could be said that I underplay the role of criticisms, reservations, qualifiers, and other evaluations of key points, reasons, and explanations. Arguably, minor qualifiers and asides can be introduced into elaborations at any stage, not just one, provided they do not become so lengthy as to distort the clarity of the key point being made.

Table 8.1 lists common signal words and phrases. There are many more. Obviously signals are very much a matter of personal style. Signals under the three central groups of rule, e.g., and rule in that table can be related to Tables 6.1 to 6.4. For many lecturers, the reexpression glides naturally into giving further details and renders signals unnatural. Most feedback is nonverbal. The important point is that signals must be recognized and understood by the students, particularly when they are trying to take notes.

DeCarrico and Nattinger (1988) recommend that foreign students should learn to recognize not only common lecture signals but also expressions that commonly cause them confusion (such as "as it were" and "as X would have us believe"). They also remark that some expressions, such as "Right," "Now," and "Well," confuse foreign students because they serve as pause fillers as well as signaling a new point or topic.

It is worth mentioning that there can be negative verbal signals, though their effect is more often on the listener's attitude to the speaker than on diminished effectiveness in making a point. In the experiments by Sazar and Kassinove (1991), it was both. Profanities had a negative effect on the acquisition of content and on cooperation during the lecture. Cooperation after the lecture was not affected. The religiosity of the students made no difference.

TABLE 8.1. COMMON VERBAL SIGNALS IN LECTURES.

Signal Function	Signal Words Commonly Used
Topic shifters	Today I'm going to talk about . . . I will tackle this issue from three main perspectives . . . Four main arguments have been proposed. I shall consider each in turn . . . I'm now going to consider . . .

Rule: key point markers

Emphasis	and most important . . . A major development was . . . A compelling argument is . . . A significant factor was . . . considerable . . . maximum . . . great . . . very . . . unbelievably . . . in fact . . . naturally . . .
Itemizing	First . . . Firstly . . . A . . . B . . . etc. . . . Next . . . The following . . . After that . . . In addition . . . Lastly . . . And finally . . . Turning now to my second main point . . . That brings me to my second point . . .
Reexpression	By this I mean . . . To put that another way . . . What I'm saying is . . . In effect this means . . .

e.g.: elaborations, relaters

Detail	Let's consider this . . . If you think about that . . . Let's look at that. You see . . . Enlaring upon that . . .
Logical reasons	Therefore . . . We may conclude that . . . From this we see . . . It follows that . . . It can be seen that . . . The import of this . . . A corollary is . . . The significance of this is . . . Logically . . . In principle . . . So . . . The reason why . . . This means that . . . If x then y.
Causal reasons	Consequently . . . As a result . . . The upshot was . . . The outcome was . . . It influenced . . . A factor was . . . Because . . . Then . . . That was how . . .
Temporal sequence	At the time . . . After that . . . Eventually . . . In due course . . . For the moment . . . What happened was . . .
The same	Furthermore . . . Also . . . Similarly . . . In the same way . . . In addition . . . like . . . akin to . . . The equivalent . . . is tantamount to . . . Comparable . . . By analogy . . . This amounts to . . .
Different	However . . . On the other hand . . . But . . . Compared with . . . In contrast . . . Unlike . . . As distinct from . . . The opposite of that . . . Alternatively . . .

TABLE 8.1. COMMON VERBAL SIGNALS IN LECTURES (cont'd.)

Signal Function	Signal Words Commonly Used
Examples	For example . . . As an illustration of this . . . For instance . . . Applying that principle . . . In particular . . .
Entry to asides	By the way . . . Personally I think . . . This is connected with . . . I might add that . . . As I remarked earlier . . . As I shall mention in a minute . . . To digress for a moment . . .
Exit from asides	Anyway . . . As I was saying . . . To continue . . . To get back to the main point . . . In any event . . . It's interesting that . . .
Feedback or "comprehension check"	Okay? Is that clear? Is everybody with me?
Rule: restatement	
Recapitulation	To sum up . . . In conclusion . . . The point I'm making is . . . What this amounts to is . . .
Summarizers	What I've been arguing in this lecture . . . In this lecture I have . . . Let me summarize what I've been saying . . .

So far, in describing ways to make a point I have described different structures of explanations and the signals that indicate the elements structured. But there is far more to making a point than its structure.

Nonverbal Signals

I am concerned here with nonverbal influences upon the effectiveness of students' learning when a lecturer makes a point. I am not concerned with the lecturer's appearance, dress, posture, body type, or other factors that might affect students' perceptions of the lecturer as a person.

It is clear that nonverbal communications affect verbal learning in a lecture, but not every movement has an effect. When a lecturer (Hood, 1987) used whole-body movements either in or out of synchrony with what was being said, it had no effect upon students' learning (except some loss of credibility!). On the other hand, Coats and Smidchens (1966) compared two ten-minute lectures. One had no gestures, no direct eye contact, minimal vocal inflection, and a lecturer who read the script, albeit with good volume and diction. The other was a lecture delivered from memory with dynamic gestures, eye contact, and vocal inflection. Scores on ten multiple-choice questions were significantly higher after the dynamic lecture.

What is not clear is how nonverbals influence verbal learning. Normal conversation takes place within a range of two to fifteen feet. The tendency for audiences not to sit in the front few rows almost seems like a deliberate attempt to reject nonverbal signals. The difference in angle subtended on a student's retina in the middle of a lecture theater to communicate eye contact with the lecturer rather than a neighbor, is so minute that one wonders whether it is even discernible.

Furthermore:

- Some nonverbals, such scratching, rubbing eyes, and other forms of self grooming ("adaptors"), have nothing to do with lecture content.
- Others that might "regulate" conversation, such as eye signals that one has finished talking and expects a reply, are less appropriate in a lecture.
- There are few gestures that directly substitute for words ("emblems"), and those that do are more likely to be obscene than academic!
- The most informative are "illustrators" in which behavior describes the lecture content in some way—for example, a spiral motion when describing the double helix in biology.
- Probably the most important function of nonverbals is to communicate feelings ("affect displays"). They are more powerful than words. If a lecturer says something pleasant in an unpleasant way, or says something unpleasant in a pleasant way, how it is said is more influential as to how it is perceived (Ekman and Friesen, 1969).

It would be useful for students if there was a glossary of lecturer's nonverbal signals. Interpretation is not always easy. In an attempt to study nonverbal signals Susan English (1985) analyzed video recordings without using the audio track and listed changes in body position, gesture, facial expression, and eye gaze. The audio track was then analyzed for verbal signals, and the transcripts were used to identify the functions of the nonverbal cues. They reflect elements of the general form. When starting a new point, lecturers turned the body, looked down at their notes, and changed physical position. When comparing and contrasting, they turned their heads and shifted their eye gaze, with hand movements indicating first one thing and then the other. Emphasis was made by nodding the head, pointing a finger, or making a striking motion with the hand. Curiously, gestures when exemplifying included leaning on the lectern and turning palms upwards. Counting on the fingers indicated listing or sequencing, while standing behind the lectern to read notes was common when giving a restatement or summary.

For ordinary conversation, Argyle and Henderson (1985) have posited rules of intimacy, friendship, and relationships at work. For example, if one person moves closer, the other might compensate with less eye contact. Compared with conversations, what is unusual about lectures is the emotional distance between the lecturer and the audience. This is reinforced by the lecturer's status, the formal language used, age differences, expertise, the physical distance from the audience, and a defensive position behind a lectern or other furniture. Yet students appreciate lecturers who can break down these emotional barriers. Moving in front of the lectern, using conversational language, engaging eye contact with individuals for longer than a glance, and giving opportunities for audience participation are all ways to decrease emotional distance.

It is possible that gestures have emotional impact upon the audience not only directly but indirectly through self-stimulation of the lecturer. Using a 2 x 2 experimental design, Gauger (1951) compared lectures with and without gestures, and lectures in which the audience could both see and hear the lecturer with those in which he could only be heard. Learning was best from the lectures where gestures could be seen; but even if the gestures could not be seen, students' achievement scores were better than when the lecturer did not use them. Presumably gestures affected the speaker's dynamism (emphasis, inflection, and pacing).

Although the study of nonverbals in lectures is in its infancy, it is clear that they have very varied effects. Gestures notoriously become mannerisms. Used naturally and not self-consciously, and developed with discretion, they can increase a lecturer's impact.

Other Factors Affecting Comprehension of a Point

Comprehension is affected by linguistic factors such as sentence length, ambiguity, the amount of information in a sentence, the extent of redundancy, and its predictability, and by paralinguistic factors such as gesture and facial expression. Foreign students in particular have difficulty with such nonlinguistic factors as speed, manner of delivery, interpretation of rhythm and stress, background noise, and the lecturer's reliance upon nonverbal signals while students have their heads down writing notes. It is quite common for lecturers to speak slowly and simply to nonnative speakers at first, but then to forget and speed up or use ungrammatical idioms. Such pressures upon foreign students prevent the construction of meaning and therefore keep them from building links between ideas—what is sometimes called deep, as opposed to surface, learning.

Comprehension is not a simple one-to-one correspondence between words and meanings. Lecturers cannot personalize what they say for every student.

Students must impose their own context. This is difficult for students from cultural backgrounds other than that of the lecturer. Foreign students, for example, will be baffled by words like "Dickensian" if they have no knowledge of Dickens, his characters, and the nineteenth-century cultures he describes.

Ovaiza (1985) has drawn attention to the difficulties foreign students have with humor, figures of speech, idioms of a discipline, prepositional phrases (such as "put up" for "constructed"), and the differences between written and spoken language. Conversely, Tiffin (1974, cited in Gimson, 1981) has shown that English people understand only 65 percent of the English spoken by Yoruba students from Nigeria.

Conclusion

Like Chapter Seven, this one is a supplement to Chapter Six. It is about things that help an audience understand key points that make up the lecture content, without being the spoken content itself. Except for verbal signals, they are mostly visual.

You will notice it does not include film or television. I regard them as teaching methods in their own right, not aids to lectures (except insofar as any additional method may assist).

If you decide to video-record your own lectures, the first four chapters of Part Three provide a guide on what to observe. Ask yourself:

- How is my lecture organized?
- When I make a point, what form do I use?
- What kind of explanations do I give?
- What techniques do I use to help me make a point?

CHAPTER NINE

NOTE TAKING IN LECTURES

Reasons for taking notes.

1. To aid memory during the lecture.

2. To aid revision.

3. To see the developing structure of a topic.

4. To relate and reorganize during further study.

5. To select what is important.

6. To know what has to be learned.

7. To maintain attention.

8. To provide evidence of attendance.

Helping students take notes.

1. Advice to lecturers.

2. Advice to give students.

3. Teaching note-taking skills.

As I said in Chapter Two, Figure 2.1 represents students' brains as essentially dynamic. They are information processors. One process stimulates another, or at least it may do so. Although there are probably more feedback loops than are depicted in the figure, the arrows represent which processes may stimulate which others. Thus they also depict chronological sequences.

Reasons for Taking Notes

In view of the complexity of these brain processes, lecturers might ask, "Should students take notes in my lectures? If so, how can I help them do so?" The answer to the first question depends on what they are taking notes for. There could be many reasons, as considered in Table 9.1.

Students could take notes to help them during the lecture or for later use. These are sometimes described as encoding and storage, respectively. In either case, note taking might be helpful to aid memory, to understand the organization and structure of the topic, to identify what information is important, or to ensure that attention is paid to what has been said. In this analysis, there are eight possible reasons, as shown in Table 9.1, and we shall consider each in turn. The overwhelming majority of students rightly believe that lecturers expect them to take notes (Hartley and Davies, 1978; Davy and Dunkel, 1989). Lecturers who do not, though, cite alternative sources of information as their reason (Isaacs, 1994).

The question now is what evidence there is to recommend note taking for each of these purposes.

1. To Aid Memory During the Lecture

Note taking aids memory. It fosters encoding, articulation, and rehearsal. There have been a very large number of studies to investigate whether note taking assists memory of lecture content during the lecture itself. In a typical experiment of this kind, half a class takes notes, while the other half is instructed not to do so. To control for individual differences, on another occasion assignment of note takers and nonnote takers is reversed. Tests on memory of the lecture content are given immediately after both lectures, or after a specified delay, and results for note taking and nonnote taking are compared.

These experiments have been criticized on the grounds that their circumstances are unnatural; the lectures are often unusually short; students are sometimes told of the tests in advance; the quantity, efficiency, and style of notes varies

TABLE 9.1. WHY TAKE NOTES?

	Encoding During Lecture	Storage for Later Use
Memory	1. Aids to memory	2. Revision
Understanding a topic and its structure	3. See the development of a topic	4. Reorganize, relate, and study topics
Content	5. Select what is important	6. Know the syllabus covered
Attention	7. Concentrate	8. Evidence of attendance

with the type of test anticipated; the topics are not always relevant to their courses; and individual differences are seldom considered (Trueman and Hartley, 1978; Carrier and Titus, 1981).

Nevertheless, the evidence is overwhelming that note taking during a lecture does aid memory of the lecture. Indeed, Ladas (1980) has cogently argued that experiments, and tabular summaries of them such as in Table 9.2, underestimate the significance of findings. Furthermore, several studies using correlations report that the probability of remembering facts if they are noted is significantly higher than for those not noted (Howe, 1970b; Aiken, Thomas, and Shennum, 1975; Thomas, Aiken, and Shennum, 1975; Fisher and Harris, 1973, 1974a; Crawford, 1925a, 1925b; and Einstein, Morris, and Smith, 1985).

Some personality factors interact with these results. For example students with high-capacity short-term memories are better able to take notes and consequently perform better on follow-up tests (Berliner, 1969), but it does not follow from this that less able students should only listen (Catts, 1987). Dogmatism and intolerance of ambiguity hamper performance on recall tests, perhaps because students with these traits are less able to link facts. These students do better when lectures are explicitly thematic (Di Vesta and Gray, 1972, 1973) or when ideas are explicitly associated in other ways. Surprisingly, by contrast Lacroix (1987) found no connection between students' cognitive style (environmental dependence or independence) and the number of words or information units noted, the efficiency of their notes, their use of chalkboard information, or their scores on immediate and delayed tests of learning.

The reason why note taking aids memory could have something to do with other purposes, namely, maintaining students' attention and the activity of selecting what facts are important. There is no evidence on how these purposes interact. Equally, the reasons might be that the act of noting requires rehearsal and repetition of what has been said; or that in order to select and summarize, note taking forces students to seek the meaning of what has been said (encoding). And we have already seen that attention, retrieval, repetition, and meaningfulness are all factors aiding memory. Indeed, there has been quite a debate about whether rehearsal or encoding is the more important. Whatever the cause, the effect upon memory is clear and justifies note taking in lectures.

2. To Aid Revision

It seems fairly obvious that students who have notes to revise from will do better in examinations than students who don't. Available evidence confirms this; see Table 9.3. Furthermore, nearly all students use notes for this purpose. Surveys by

TABLE 9.2. DOES NOTE TAKING AID MEMORY?

Thirty Studies Favoring Note Taking as an Aid to Memory

Aiken, Thomas, and Shennum (1975)	NT in interval between four-minute lecture segments vs. no NT
Baker, Baker, and Blount (1974)	One study, test of concepts
Baker and Lombardi (1985)	Information in notes related to test performance
Bentley and Blount (1980)	Immediate recall of information
Berliner (1969, 1971, 1972)	Immediate and one-week-delayed matched tests
Brobst (1996)	Free recall
Crawford (1925a, 1925b)	Two studies; immediate and delayed recall (a few days) in essays and quiz
Di Vesta and Gray (1972)	Free recall and MCQ
Di Vesta and Gray (1973)	Two studies; free recall and TF tests
Einstein, Morris, and Smith (1985)	NT students remember more important facts; non-NT less discriminating
Fisher and Harris (1973)	Objective test and free recall; also correlate with quality of notes
Hult (1984)	Immediate test of encoding related to information units noted
Jones (1923)	Immediate and delayed recall (up to eight weeks)
Locke (1977)	NT of lecture information not on blackboard correlates with grades
Maqsud (1980)	Immediate and long-term free recall
McHenry (1969)	Four studies; TF and MCQ comprehension tests
Peper and Mayer (1978)	NT increases attention
Peper and Mayer (1986)	Two studies; NT increases deeper learning
	NT better for applying principles; non-NT for reproduction
Peters and Harris (1970)	MCQ after tape-recorded presentation
Poppleton and Austwick (1964)	Higher test scores for students with lengthy notes
Stewart (1989)	Simple immediate recall
Thomas (1972)	Serial position of recalled material
Trueman and Hartley (1978)	Correlation between NT and men's exams; correlation for women inconsistent
Weiland and Kingsbury (1979)	Immediate and ten-day-delayed quizzes

Eighteen Studies Showing No Significant Difference

Aiken, Thomas, and Shennum (1975)	No NT versus parallel NT
Baker, Baker, and Blount (1974)	One study test of concepts

TABLE 9.2. DOES NOTE TAKING AID MEMORY? (cont'd.)

Carter and Van Matre (1975)	Free recall and sentence-completion tests
Catts (1987)	Immediate and delayed recall and application; immediate comprehension
Crawford (1925a, 1925b)	Three studies; free recall in essays, TF tests and quizzes
Eisner and Rohde (1959)	NT during versus NT after thirty-minute lecture; fifty-item TF test after two and twenty-one days
Fisher and Harris (1974a, 1974b)	Free recall and MCQ correlated with number of information units
Freyberg (1956)	Immediate test
Henk and Stahl (1985)	NT versus non-NT; recall little enhanced
Howe (1970a)	Test delayed fourteen days
Jones (1923)	Two studies; tests of recall delayed three and twelve days
MacManaway (1968)	Unforeseen test after one week
McClendon (1958)	No NT versus normal NT, detailed NT immediately and after delay of five weeks
Milton (1962)	Freshmen exam results
Pauk (1963)	Comprehension

Seven Studies Favoring No Note Taking

Catts (1987)	Comprehension on test delayed one week
Freyberg (1956)	Unexpected test after fourteen days
Maqsud (1980)	Students taking fewer notes better on immediate and long-term free recall
Peper and Mayer (1986)	Problem solving involving some transfer of learning
Peters (1972)	Recall of definitions and MCQ test when presentation is fast
Thomas, Aiken, and Shennum (1975)	Correlation between NT and recall
Van Matre and others (1975)	Free recall and sentence-completion tests

Note: NT = note taking; TF = true-false questions; MCQ = multiple-choice questions.

TABLE 9.3. DOES NOTE TAKING
FOR REVISION IMPROVE PERFORMANCE?

Twenty-two Studies Favoring Note Taking for Revision

Annis and Davis (1977)	Essay and MCQ tests
Bentley and Blount (1980)	Delayed recall
Benton, Kiewra, Whitfill, and Dennison (1993)	Length and organization of essays
Carter and Van Matre (1975)	Free recall and sentence-completion tests
Crawford (1925a, 1925b)	Two studies; free recall in essays and TF tests
Di Vesta and Gray (1972)	Free recall and MCQ
Fisher and Harris (1973)	Two studies; free recall and TF tests
Freyberg (1956)	Expected test after eight weeks
Hartley and Marshall (1974)	Test following review
Howe (1970a)	Test delayed fourteen days
Howe and Godfrey (1977)	Four studies; free recall or objective tests
Kiewra and others (1989)	Recall and recognition of facts
Kiewra and others (1991)	Recall and synthesis of facts
Maqsud (1980)	Delayed free recall of information
Palkovitz and Lore (1980)	Test after opportunities to review notes
Razzell and Weinman (1977)	Factual test
Walbaum (1989)	MCQ and short-answer examinations

Five Studies Showing No Significant Difference

Barrett, Di Vesta, and Rogozinski (1981)	Cued recall in immediate and delayed tests
Fisher and Harris (1974a, 1974b)	Free recall and MCQ
Kiewra and others (1989)	Higher-order thinking
Peters and Harris (1970)	MCQ

No Studies Against Note Taking for Revision

Note: NT = note taking; TF = true-false questions; MCQ = multiple-choice questions.

Hartley and Davies (1978), Davy and Dunkel (1989), Razzell and Weinman (1977), and Isaacs (1994) all attest to the importance of note taking for revision purposes by more than 90 percent of students. Indeed, up to a point the more notes students take, the better they do in examinations (Walbaum, 1989).

Some researchers have asked which is more important: to aid memory during the lecture (by encoding) or to aid revision (by rehearsal). The question is part of the wider debate about the importance of encoding perceptions and rehearsing stored memories.

Kiewra and others (1989, 1991) have shown that for lecturers they are both important. Not surprisingly, students who took notes and reviewed them did better on tests of recall and recognition of information than those who only took notes and those who were only able to review another student's notes.

However, there are significant individual differences in habits of note taking and review. Several studies (for example, Trueman and Hartley, 1978; Razzell and Weinman, 1977; Giles and others, 1982) show women writing more notes than men; and Nye (1978) found that freshmen take more notes than more experienced students. But Howe (1977) says that the most effective notes are those with the largest amount of information in the smallest number of words, and it is possible that men are more efficient in this respect. He reports wide variations between students regarding the number of words written, the use of abbreviations, and the omission of words like *the* and *a* (Howe and Godfrey, 1977). Wilding and Hayes (1992) have shown that these measures of efficiency also vary with students' age, study strategies, and surface learning. Nye found that students who took rough notes, intending to write them up, wrote less and scored less well on final course grades.

The studies reported in Table 9.3 mostly gave an opportunity for revision by using a delayed test. (Significantly, in a 1980 study by Palkovitz and Lore, students who did not take this opportunity performed badly.) But in two studies students wrote notes and revised during pauses of a couple of minutes between lecture segments; this technique proved very effective (Carter and Van Matre, 1975; Bentley and Blount, 1980). Once again, there is evidence for the advantages of breaking the continuous exposition of lectures.

What perhaps is not so obvious is that students who review lecture notes in pairs employ better strategies for extracting and structuring the information than individuals revising on their own (O'Donnell and Dansereau, 1993; Kelly and O'Donnell, 1994). Putting these two findings together, we may surmise that pairs of students revising and restructuring their notes for two minutes between lecture segments would be very effective. In essence, that's a buzz group. I recommend the practice.

3. To See the Developing Structure of a Topic

Whether note taking enables students to see the structure and development of a topic during the lecture itself depends on how they take notes. On the one hand, Peper and Mayer (1986) have argued that insofar as note taking involves encoding, it generates conceptual links in students' minds. On the other hand, if they simply take a sequential record, maybe under headings and subheadings given by the lecturer, the links may be restricted and students will only perceive the organization and development if they take time out to look over what they have written as a whole, or if the lecturer takes time to describe and display the lecture's organization. Both of these take time, albeit a very short time. If lecturers proceed at such a pace that students can hardly keep up with what is being said, students will be under too much pressure to see the topic as a whole.

However, there is a nonsequential method of note taking in which the students build up their own conceptions of the structure of the topic as the lecture proceeds. These are usually called networking, patterned notes, tree diagrams, or concept maps. Anita McClain (1986) calls them "mind maps"; the technique was much publicized by Tony Busan (1974). This method results in a branching or network structure of concepts, as shown in Figure 9.1, rather than a traditional sequential record of specific facts using those concepts and reflecting the organization of the lecture.

Tree diagrams can depict the organization of key points in a lecture, but it is difficult to note details by this method. Research comparing the effectiveness of concept maps and traditional linear notes reflects this fact. Comparisons by Dansereau and others (1979) using prose material suggest that concept maps result in better memory of key ideas but are not so good for remembering detail. Both methods were considerably better than taking no notes at all, but the degree of difference may reflect the fact that Dansereau gave his students five and a half hours' training in taking notes as part of a fifteen-week course in study methods. Concept maps use fewer words, and there is evidence that when the test is immediate and presentation is short, noting only key words is as effective as recording everything (Howe, Ormond, and Singer, 1974). With lectures of normal length, detail is lost.

Ideally, both methods are necessary; but to use both at the pace of a lecture is quite difficult. McClain claims that concept maps liberate students to think, use both sides of the brain, increase comprehension, set up clear graphic structures that allow easy recall, and encourage creative thinking by their open-ended nature. These claims have yet to be justified.

One problem with concept maps is that the lines could have any of several possible meanings. Lambiotte, Skaggs, and Dansereau (1993) taught their students

FIGURE 9.1. TREE DIAGRAM, OR "CONCEPT MAP."

to label arrows with letters according to their meaning (Table 9.4). Arrows tend to point away from the central concepts of the lecture.

Unfortunately, students given concept maps to review a lecture demonstrated less accurate comprehension of concepts than those given word lists. But the idea that relationships between concepts are mostly confined to these ten is interesting and could provide a useful "shorthand" for taking notes in lectures.

A further difficulty is that students cannot anticipate or plan the shape and direction of the map on the page when first putting pen to paper. An effective solution to these difficulties is to give a concept map as a handout, showing the lecture organization as an advance organizer (discussed on page 86 in Chapter Five); the lecturer then lets students note details in their own way (Baggett, 1994). It is also easier to search for information among concept maps than among text (O'Donnell, 1993).

I conclude that if students are to make their own concept maps in lectures instead of traditional note-taking methods, they will need more guidance in how to make them than they usually get; and even then, their effectiveness is uncertain. They may, however, have a role as lecture guides.

4. To Relate and Reorganize During Further Study

Arguably, to take facts and principles and to reorganize them by interrelating and applying them to answer questions and solve problems is an essential part of any academic discipline and of virtually any profession students may enter. If so, to permit further study by interrelating and reorganizing lecture material must be a very important aim in taking lecture notes. Indeed, a vital and much neglected part of private study is to interrelate as many different parts of a discipline as possible, not just the facts that are mentioned in the same lecture. Many essay and examination questions test students' abilities to interrelate in this way.

TABLE 9.4. LAMBIOTTE, SKAGGS, AND DANSEREAU'S SYMBOLS FOR USE IN CONCEPT MAPS.

←t←	is a type of	→d→	definition
←p←	is part of	→a→	is analagous to
←c←	is a characteristic of	←e←	is evidence for
→l→	leads to	→eg→	for example
→i→	influences	→n→	next

In the past twenty years there has been a great deal of research into student note taking in lectures and into students' study methods; but there has been very little on how note taking influences study methods. Nearly all the research assumes that the purpose of note taking is to aid memory rather than to promote thought, further inquiry, or future enthusiasm for the subject.

An important exception is the work of Entwistle and Marton (1994) and their colleagues. They interviewed a small sample of students immediately after their final examinations and asked about their revision procedures. Entwistle and Marton suggest there are five "forms of understanding." Implicitly, they are stages of development, with some students progressing no further at each stage:

1. Absorbing facts, details, and procedures related to exams without considering or changing their organization. In effect, the students revised from a summary of the lecture and scarcely related or reorganized the material at all.
2. Accepting and using only the knowledge and explaining links provided in the lecture notes to form logical organizations of subject matter, such as arguments for and against.
3. Relying mainly on notes to develop summary organizations solely to control exam answers.
4. Developing their own organizations of subject matter from theories and strategic reading to represent personal understanding, but also to control exam answers.
5. Developing organizations of subject matter from wide reading which relate personal understanding and involvement to the nature of the discipline.

Interestingly, students used what I call "visually derived" relationships to reorganize material. Former visual relations of ideas, including notes, were now linked more abstractly. This could strengthen the case for using tree diagrams and for lecturers' making more effort to represent relationships between ideas visually. For example, a matrix like Table 9.1 cross-relates concepts. These are important processes of thought. Kiewra and others (1988) gave notes in the form of a matrix and found that students could transfer the knowledge better than those who had a complete lecture text or summary and reviewed them. In a number of experiments mentioned earlier, Kiewra and his colleagues compared the performance of students who took notes but did not review them (encoding only), students who took notes and reviewed them (encoding plus review), and students who did not attend the lecture but were given another person's notes (review only). Those who took notes and reviewed them wrote longer and better-organized essays (Benton, Kiewra, Whitfill, and Dennison, 1993), and in one case (Kiewra and others, 1991), but not in another (Kiewra and others, 1989), were better able to synthesize the information given. On one occasion, review-only also produced more synthesis than encoding-only.

All this suggests that the cycle of processes 14 and 15 in Figure 2.1 is more likely during review than during a lecture. Little thought can take place in a lecture. The cycle 6 and 5 is not much better when there is a continuing flow of words from the lecturer to be processed. The truth is, despite the labels given by Kiewra, a lot of encoding goes on in the review-only condition, and encoding is actually distracted and inhibited by yet more words arriving to be processed in the so-called encoding-only condition. That's why thinking in lectures is so difficult.

One powerful note-taking technique to encourage thought is to generate questions that require students to relate and reorganize information. Students should be taught to use it. Alison King (1992) found that students trained to generate questions at the end of a lecture retained more information after a week than students trained to summarize the lecture and those who reviewed their notes, though the summarizers did better on an immediate test. In another study (King, 1991), questions generated during a lecture and answered individually or by partners resulted in better learning than reviewing notes, either individually or in pairs both immediately and after ten days. Similarly, Rickards and McCormick (1988) have found that prelecture questions enhance the intellectual quality of students' notes.

Why are self-generated questions so effective? Answers to self-generated questions, and the questions themselves, relate to stored concepts that already have meaning for the student (processes 14 and 15 in Figure 2.1). In other words, self-generated questions and their answers ensure that new information is accommodated within a preconceived organization of ideas. They reorganize the information presented in the lecture.

Reorganizing lecture material is often frustrated because students do not spread out their notes. Consequently, further information obtained by independent study is noted separately, not visually incorporated into a single organized body of notes. With this learning strategy, students are left with sets of notes separated according to their source rather than the relevance of their content. The integration of ideas on the one hand, or their discernment on the other, is thereby made more difficult.

5. To Select What Is Important

There have been several studies investigating how far students are able to select and note what the lecturers themselves deem to be noteworthy in their lectures. Since research shows that students don't remember what they don't note, and it is not possible to note everything, skills in noting what is important become critical.

Several studies show that students lack these skills. It is not so much that their notes contain inaccuracies or errors—though Maddox and Hoole (1975) comment that nearly every senior student in their study made some, and Howe and Godfrey (1977) found that some students omitted negatives! It is that the proportion of important points noted is quite variable. For example, McDonald and Taylor (1980) report that only half their fourth-year students recorded two-thirds of the noteworthy points; and Baker and Lombardi (1985) found that students noted only 50 percent of a lecture's main ideas. Crawford (1925a) reported that students failed to note 47 percent of the important points; Locke (1977) gave a figure of 40 percent, and Hartley and Cameron (1967) 76 percent; while Hartley and Marshall (1974) reported that freshmen noted only 56 information units out of a possible 520.

Jackson and Bilton (1990a, 1990b) showed that students were unaware of lecture signals and had difficulty in extracting key concepts from a lecture exposition, particularly when one explanation or definition was embedded in another. Notes by students who could extract important points showed no standard abbreviations or form of shorthand and displayed poor layout and insufficient relationship between items of information. Hughes and Suritsky (1993) also observed that students with learning disabilities have poor note-taking skills such as paraphrasing, abbreviating, and recognizing lecture signals. Where students have difficulty in following a lecture, they rely almost exclusively on copying from overhead transparencies or the blackboard. Davies (1976) says that oversupply of information leads to confusion when students cannot select appropriately. They cannot cope with individual elements of an argument unless it fits into a wider framework, and these inadequacies can lead to lack of confidence and despondency.

Einstein, Morris, and Smith (1985) reported that both note takers and successful students remembered points of high importance, while nonnote takers and less successful students remembered points of greater and lesser importance equally. Since recall was related to what was noted, these results were interpreted as a failure by nonnote takers and less successful students to select what was important during the lecture.

All these criticisms of students' competence, plus the fact that more senior students take more complete notes, suggest that freshmen need help to learn note-taking skills, particularly skills in selecting what is important. Note taking can become habitual and indiscriminate. There is a legend that if you have a mixed class of freshmen and postgraduates and you want to know which is which, say "Good morning." The freshmen will reply "Good morning"; postgraduates write it down. To select what is noteworthy requires thought and judgment. Consequently, this is where students need most assistance. I will consider this in the next section.

6. To Know What Has to Be Learned

Every discipline is so wide that no one, least of all a student, could be competent in all aspects of it. The content of lectures often indicates which aspects students should select for further study. In this sense, note taking records the syllabus.

This is particularly the case in subjects such as the mathematical sciences and philosophy, which can only be studied by working out problems for oneself. Memory of factual information has a relatively minor role. In these subjects, the function of lectures is often to guide students to the problems they should work on in private study, rather than to dispense factual information. In effect, the syllabus consists of a number of problems. Students do not learn how to solve them by taking lecture notes. They note the syllabus of problems and possible directions to explore them.

7. To Maintain Attention

It is common experience that if one does not take notes in lectures, the mind tends to wander. Peper and Mayer (1978) claim that note taking increases attention and results in greater concentration on the material to be learned. Note taking is an activity that maintains a slightly higher level of arousal because the activity is self-stimulating. Neurologically, there is a feedback mechanism to the brain stem that arouses the brain in general. There is some evidence from tests of immediate recall (Crawford, 1925b; Howe and Godfrey, 1977) that the benefit of note taking is greater when lectures are over thirty minutes. Howe and Godfrey interpret this in terms of note taking maintaining attention after that length of time.

The converse is also true. Enthusiastic, stimulating lectures result in more note taking.

Conversely, over half the students in the surveys by Davy and Dunkel (1989) and Hartley and Davies (1978) reported that note taking sometimes interfered with their understanding of lectures, presumably because their attention was divided. Peper and Mayer (1986) reasoned that since the whole brain should be aroused by note taking, memory and thought should benefit equally. However, contrary to their earlier claim, they found problem solving benefited more than factual memory. The attention hypothesis was thus weakened. Furthermore, the extent to which note taking maintains attention might also be disputed insofar as students take fewer notes as lectures proceed (Lloyd, 1968; Locke, 1977; Scerbo, Warm, Dember, and Grasha, 1992). The intensity of divided attention could well cause fatigue, particularly when noteworthy points are dense or the lecturer's delivery is fast.

It seems likely that note taking maintains, and even improves, attention for a while; but thereafter the benefits may be small or even negative.

8. To Provide Evidence of Attendance

Although in some laboratory subjects students submit reports of practical work as evidence that they have taken the course, to require students to hand in lecture notes as evidence that they have attended lectures is extremely rare. Indeed, Hyde and Flournoy (1986) report that some students with poor attendance achieved outstanding academic results. (However their conclusion that mandatory attendance can harm performance does not follow.)

Helping Students Take Notes

How-to-study books and records of unpublished educational conference papers abound with advice for students on how to take notes, but little of it is supported by solid research. Two exceptions are the work of Hartley and Davies (1978) and Howe (1977). There is even less research on lecturing techniques to assist easy note taking.

1. Advice to Lecturers

This advice can be listed summarily.

*a. **Organization.*** Organize your lectures with key points as described in Chapter Five. Use visual techniques to display the structure of lectures on a blackboard, screen, or handout. Then stick to it; students complain that some lecturers don't (Van Metre, Yokoi, and Pressley, 1994). Several researchers point out that signals of the kind listed in Tables 5.1, 5.2, and 8.1 increase the quality and quantity of students' notes, but they do not seem to increase students' recall of the lecture if they don't review their notes first (see for example Dunkel and Davis, 1994).

*b. **Making a Point.*** Make those points in the ways described in Chapter Six. In particular, use lecture signals described in that chapter. Display the key points on the blackboard or screen, and pause briefly for emphasis after making them.

*c. **Handouts.*** Use handouts to give not only the structure of key points but also bibliographic references, information that needs to be accurate, diagrams, concepts that are complex or difficult, and spellings of technical terms.

*d. **Feedback.*** Observe students noting a point and wait until nearly all have finished before going on to the next. In practice, it is not too difficult to observe what students in the front few rows are writing, even though to the lecturer it is upside down. Occasionally, when getting formal feedback using questionnaires or interviews, include a question about the ease or difficulty of note taking.

e. Separate Listening and Note Taking. Create opportunities to separate students' listening and note taking. Aiken, Thomas, and Shennum (1975) obtained better performance from students when they only took notes between four-minute segments of a lecture than when they either took notes in the normal way ("in parallel") or didn't take them at all. However, this benefit seems to diminish with longer segments, presumably because longer segments give too much to remember and then note. Eisner and Rohde (1959) found no advantage with twenty-minute segments.

In some circumstances, it pays to instruct students not to take notes to begin with, and then go over the material a second time with suitable pauses for students to note what they wish. Obviously, this double presentation takes extra time. It is justified when a topic is conceptually difficult or when the first explanation is so visual (perhaps in a semidarkened room) that students will not understand if they take their eyes away to write.

f. Pauses for Review. Have occasional pauses during lectures when students are instructed to review what they have written. This is particularly advisable when successive concepts and explanations in a lecture build upon each other in what I call a steep conceptual gradient. These pauses also provide opportunities for students to fill in details and personal thoughts that they couldn't note at the time.

g. Question Generation. Having introduced the topic of your lecture, try asking the students in groups of two or three to write down what they think are the most pertinent questions to answer when studying that topic. Get feedback of five or six questions. The best questions may well be the ones you never thought of. Give time during, or at the end of, the lecture for students to answer their own questions.

h. Don't Go Too Fast. Lecturers can enjoy a feeling of satisfaction that they have done their duty once they present information, regardless of whether students receive it. The lecturer who gets behind and then rushes the last part of the lecture to cover ground panders to this feeling. High speed in lecturing is students' major complaint so far as note taking is concerned, particularly when the concepts are unfamiliar (Van Metre, Yokoi, and Pressley, 1994). Peters (1972) presented definitions at 130 and 192 words per minute (wpm) and text at 146 and 202 wpm. The lower speeds are fairly normal. The higher speeds resulted in significantly lower multiple-choice scores and fewer notes.

2. Advice to Give Students

I have written this section as if it were addressed to students. It you are a teacher, it contains the sort of message you will need to pass on.

a. Organization. Familiarize yourself with the way lectures are organized. See Chapter Five.

b. Abbreviations. Develop your own set of abbreviations or shorthand for words and concepts that occur frequently in your subject.

c. Layout. Use layout techniques, and space out your notes so that you can add later detail, personal thoughts, and information and ideas from further study. Use the left-hand page in your notebook for "tree diagrams" or "concept maps." Notes from further study can also go on that page. In this way, notes on the same topic are kept together and are more likely to be connected in your mind. It doesn't pay to save paper. Use broad-lined paper so that you can write in a hurry and still be able to read it in several months' time.

d. Note Questions and Problems. In spite of the emphasis upon memory of facts in this chapter, think of note taking as noting questions and problems rather than facts. The facts are merely ammunition to answer the questions and solve the problems. Note questions and issues that occur to you as soon as you can. If you don't, they often disappear forever. The same applies to criticisms and other thoughts about a topic. Where they are your questions, criticisms, and thoughts, initial them as yours. Otherwise, you might think they are the lecturer's if you only return to your notes after several months.

It is particularly important to note what you don't understand even though— through lack of understanding—these questions are difficult to pose. If you don't note them, you won't know where you are ignorant; that can be fatal in examinations.

e. Keep an Ideas Notebook. Carry a special, small personal notebook with you all the time, to note questions and passing thoughts about your discipline and the world in general. This is particularly important when you have essays, projects, or dissertations to write. Let your ideas notebook include ideas about your private life. It's good to get them down, not to bottle them up. Where appropriate, relate them to your studies.

f. Immediate Review. Review your notes as soon as possible after the end of a lecture, before memory of associated detail is lost. In fact, look them over befo you leave the lecture room. Add in any details, thoughts, questions, and critici that come to mind. Add in cross-references (perhaps opposite on the blank left-hand page) to other courses or parts of the same course.

g. Have a Prepared Mind. Read an elementary text (such as articles from *Scientific American*) on a topic before going to a lecture on it. Familiarize yourself with names and technical terms. The purpose of this is to allow your brain to process information quickly during the lecture. With extra speed, you will get much more from the lecture, instead of spending time trying to work out what was meant. Devise suitable abbreviations that can be written quickly during the lecture. If possible—and it's not always possible in advance of the lecture—identify contrasting schools of thought so that you can quickly relate them to what the lecturer says. A prepared mind is a matter of having what Ausubel (1968) called advance organizers. It is what makes a lecture have meaning.

3. Teaching Note-Taking Skills

Courses on note taking mostly consist of a mixture of precepts of the kind that I have just given and exercises practicing specific skills. They are valuable for second-language students at preenrollment. Although some use live lecturettes, others are packages with audiotapes (Hamp-Lyons, 1982). Videotapes would be better, to teach the interpretation of body language, gestures, and visual signals. Carrier and Titus (1981) used behavioral modification techniques.

Most courses concentrate upon listening skills: focusing attention, responding to "cues" or signals, comprehension, using abbreviations, identifying what is important, paraphrasing, analyzing lecture structures, and summarizing (Hughes and Suritsky, 1993). Relatively few go on to practice critical listening (McKibben, 1982).

Pollio (1990) has demonstrated that instruction in note taking increases the completeness of notes and enhances learning. It is less clear which skills are most important, but noting questions is certainly one of them. We have already seen that students who are questioning perform better than those who review notes and those who summarize them (King, 1992). This finding has been repeated in a whole series of reports by King herself and others. No doubt these results depend upon the test used, but they are striking because reviewing (see Table 9.3) and summarizing are known to be very effective. In another experiment (King, 1989), students using self-questioning techniques significantly improved their lecture comprehension over time. Students using a reciprocal peer-questioning procedure in small cooperative groups achieved higher levels of critical thought (King, 1990). Spires (1993) also reports that instruction in how to take notes combined with self-questioning improved the quality of notes and immediate comprehension among low-achieving college freshmen.

Self-generated questions at the beginning of lectures are very effective because they provide advance organizers related to ideas the student already has. In this way, they give the content of the lecture meaning to which students can relate. They help students interrelate ideas and thereby overcome a basic weakness of the lecture method: that lectures are linear while knowledge and thought require multiple connections.

How can students learn to generate questions for themselves? The process must be in their minds. It cannot be presented by teachers. King (1992, 1994) gave students a list of generic question stems (see Table 15.1) and the thinking process that each was expected to induce. Each student was then expected to bring three questions to class.

Conclusion

We have seen that students' notes are important yet often inadequate, not least because taking notes is a complex activity often required to be done at speed. To overcome these limitations, lecturers increasingly provide summary notes or handouts. It is these we must now consider.

CHAPTER TEN

THE PURPOSE, PREPARATION, AND USE OF HANDOUTS

Purpose.

1. Teaching objectives.

2. Information: as a leveler, to release time, and to reduce pressure.

3. A lecture guide.

4. To save note taking.

5. To stimulate thought.

6. To guide and stimulate reading.

Preparation and use.

1. Stages in preparation.

2. Choice of paper.

3. Layout for easy use.

4. Timing the distribution of handouts.

5. Maintaining their availability.

6. Ensuring their use.

Training in reading.

Judging from the frequency of their questions, this is a subject that worries some new lecturers. How handouts should be used depends on what they are to be used for.

Purpose

Handouts probably have an infinite variety of functions. I shall limit myself here to the ways they are commonly used in conjunction with lectures.

1. Teaching Objectives

If the students have not already received it as part of a syllabus, a very important handout before the first lecture is a list of objectives that the course is intended to achieve, since students usually learn better if they know what they have to learn. Without common aims, students and lecturers will work at cross purposes. A major exception to this rule is the learning of attitudes. If students are told that an objective of a course is to change their attitudes, adverse reactions are likely.

2. Information

a. Leveler. Handouts may be used to give factual information before a lecture. They may be used in this way as a leveler, where the objective is to ensure a common basic background before a topic is further elaborated or developed. Thus, they are a means of teaching more detail than could normally be absorbed in a lecture, and of building complex concepts upon simpler ones that would be unfamiliar without the handout.

b. To Release Time. The presentation of information before a lecture period can release time for discussion and other activity (MacManaway, 1968, 1970) or relieve the pressure of a crammed syllabus. Testing students' analysis, application, and memory of information, Hohn, Gallagher, and Byrne (1990) could find no difference between giving complete and skeletal notes. In both cases students did better when the lectures contained more facts, and it seemed possible that the handouts enabled students to handle more information. However, Russell, Hendricson, and Herbert (1984) obtained contrary results. They varied the information density in lectures and gave the same handout to guide note taking in all cases. When the information density was high, students forgot basic facts given at the beginning. Russell and colleagues believed later information caused retroactive interference, and it seems the handout did not reduce it.

c. To Reduce Pressure. Similarly, as described later, handouts may be used to prepare students for a problem-centered lecture. In this case their function is to relieve students of the psychological pressure of absorbing new information and to free them to think about its application, validity, or relation to other topics.

Since in these cases it is important that the students acquire the information before the lecture, it is essential that the handout be given out about one week in advance. A hierarchic organization of headings and subheadings is usually most suitable, since the students need a basic framework rather than details. Because the information is new to the students, it is essential that the handout be clear.

3. A Lecture Guide

A third kind of handout is used to guide students through a difficult lecture. Lecture guides are particularly appropriate when the topic is complex or the students have learning difficulties (Lazarus, 1988). Since we have already seen in the last chapter that students' own notes are frequently inadequate and often inaccurate, lectures don't have to be very difficult or complex to merit a lecture guide.

It is not essential to distribute a lecture guide a week before, but it is advisable to let the students look it over before beginning to lecture. This enables them to see the whole topic before any one part is considered. It may be given out the previous week if preparatory reading is required, but if it is a difficult topic, references will need to be simple and well chosen in order not to discourage or confuse the students.

a. How Much Detail? The question arises, How much detail should a lecture guide contain? In an experiment by Northcraft and Jernstedt (1975), students with lecture outlines did better than students given either complete notes or lecture scripts. Other findings on this point are inconsistent and unexpected. Morgan, Lilley, and Boreham (1988) found in one experiment (but not in another) that a list of headings was better than headings and a summary of key points.

Possibly, student variables explain the inconsistencies. Lambiotte and Dansereau (1992) projected word lists, outline notes, or concept maps while playing tape-recorded lectures. Though all scores were low, lists of concepts were most effective for students with high preknowledge of the subject. But the opposite was true for students with little preknowledge and for those who were less confident (Lambiotte, Skaggs, and Dansereau, 1993). There are also some indications in experiments by Frank (1984) and Kiewra and Frank (1988) that students more dependent on their environment need fuller handouts than those who are field-independent. There may also be subject differences. It is to be expected that more detailed handouts will be an advantage in subjects such as the physical sciences where accuracy is important. In subjects such as the humanities, where independence of mind is encouraged much earlier, an outline of the lecture structure and key points is sufficient stimulus.

Although the work of Kiewra and others (1988) is an exception, there is evidence (Collingwood and Hughes, 1978; Hohn, Gallagher, and Byrne, 1990; Morgan, Lilley, and Boreham, 1988; Siegel, 1973) that complete notes and even lecture scripts result in more detailed learning when review and revision are made possible before tests. This is hardly surprising, but of course revision is a different purpose for handouts than a lecture guide. Hohn, Gallagher, and Byrne (1990) found that when the test was immediate and there was no opportunity for revision, there was no difference between complete and skeleton handouts in the achievement of knowledge and application of principles. Why? Complete notes are too much to read as a lecture guide, but they allow more thorough revision later.

b. Blank Spaces. The apparent conflict between completeness for revision later and a guide to be followed during the lecture can be reconciled if lecture guides are laid out spaciously, showing the organization of the lecture and having blank spaces between sections for students to add their own notes and comments. In this way, students actively build up their own notes for revision purposes, the lecturer knows that students go away with the essentials, some of the pressure of note taking in lectures is removed, details can be noted that would otherwise be missed, and some of the divided attention between note taking and listening is relieved.

Collingwood and Hughes found this technique more effective than relying wholly on students' notes. However, since copies of the lecturer's detailed notes were better revision for a delayed test, the students' additions may not have been detailed enough. Layout, particularly the amount of blank space, affects how much detail students note. Hartley (1976) found that students with widely spaced handouts took more notes than others.

c. Sentence Completion. Another device is to leave gaps in sentences for students to fill in key words during the lecture. Hartley used a sentence-completion technique and found that students' recall of those particular facts benefited. Recall of other points was not improved. Accordingly, lecturers using this technique should make sure the gaps exercise students' minds on the points they particularly want them to know.

d. Questions. In effect, sentence completion handouts pose questions to students that they must answer by listening to the lecture. Clearly, handouts could be devised with other kinds of questions, in particular the questions the lecturers intend their lectures to answer. Research investigating this technique shows it to be highly effective (Rickards and McCormick, 1988; Chmielewska, 1976; Facinelli, 1982). I shall deal with handout questions to promote thought in the section after next.

e. Advantages. Isaacs (1989) reports that the reason most commonly given by lecturers for handouts is that they outline, summarize, or explain a topic. The advantage of this use of handouts is that even the least able students carry away an accurate record of the major points, whereas Hartley and Cameron (1967) reported that even from a lecture of average difficulty the proportion noted of what the lecturer thought important varied from 21 percent to 73 percent at different times. Further confirmation of this point will be unnecessary for lecturers who find their statements are sometimes distorted in examination answers.

f. Disadvantages. The disadvantage of a lecture guide is that, being openly committed to a certain plan, the lecturer is less free to change the approach during the lecture. Also, as often happens with a difficult topic, when a lecturer needs to go more slowly, there is a temptation to cover the ground set out on the handout rather than to teach it. Paradoxically, it is the experienced lecturer sensitive to nonverbal feedback who is most likely to experience these difficulties. Lecturers who perform rather than teach are less often aware of this kind of problem. One solution is to take the class into one's confidence, describe the difficulty as a teaching problem (not as someone's fault), and explain why (or ask whether) a change of plan is appropriate: "I don't seem able to make this point clear. In view of its importance when we come to deal with [X], do you think I ought to spend longer on it now even though it means I shall not reach [Y] today?"

Taking the class into one's confidence is not only a valuable strategy in many lecturing situations, it is an intrinsic feature of good student rapport. But authoritarian lecturers, and those lacking self-confidence in their knowledge or teaching ability, find it a difficult technique to use.

4. To Save Note Taking

Some lecturers give handouts that summarize their lecture so that students do not need to take notes. In that case, the handouts could serve most of the same functions as note taking (Table 9.1). Handouts are obviously useful in situations where note taking is impossible. These include illustrated lectures in which important information is given in semidarkness, practical demonstrations in which the students are standing, and lectures that for some reason are never delivered. They are also a useful safeguard for bad lecturers (but this remark should not discourage new lecturers from using them). If lecturers teach with a large amount of informal class discussion, or easily get off the point of their own accord, these handouts provide anxious students with some comfort. In some circumstances, they can be used to relieve the pressure of time on the lecturer. They offer freedom to fan the flames of student interest on one point with less worry about the neglect of another.

If understanding is improved by diagrams, lecture time can be saved by including them. (There is an important exception to this: when drawing the diagram is used as an active method of teaching it or when constructing characters in Chinese or Japanese, where stroke order is very important.) This method is quite common and is often especially effective when the diagram is slowly built up from simple elements rather than presented in its complete, and possibly complex, form. Rather surprisingly, Chmielewska (1976) found that handouts consisting of pictures, questions, key points, and headings were most effective in that order. Presumably the importance of pictures is subject-specific.

The advantages and disadvantages of summary handouts are similar to those of a lecture guide, but they raise questions of the extent to which students should take notes for themselves and the value of lectures in which notes cannot, or need not, be taken—questions to which there is no one answer.

Research on the relative advantages of students taking their own notes or being given partial or complete notes is ambiguous; but on balance it pays to give handouts. In Table 10.1, I assume, unless the reports state otherwise, that students were able to take notes in lectures in the normal way.

We have already seen that the study by Northcraft and Jernstedt favored partial handouts. Similarly, Linda Annis (1981) found that students receiving a full set of notes did less well on essay and multiple-choice tests than those taking their own notes or adding to partial notes. There was no interaction with preferred study techniques. She interprets this as showing the benefits of having to encode subject matter during lectures. Students originally preferring to take their own notes or receive full notes switched their preference later to partial notes.

By contrast, Rasor (1980) reports significant correlations between the use of fully prepared notes during lectures and students' course completion rates.

Freyberg (1956) has described an experiment in which some students took no notes, some took them either in full or in outline, and still others were issued a duplicated summary. Both on an immediate test and after two weeks, the first group showed the best retention of information. However, when given the opportunity to revise their notes, those who had them not only performed significantly better than the first group but also obtained higher scores than on the immediate test. Thus, although it is sometimes claimed that note taking aids concentration and learning, in this instance notes were only of benefit if used on a later occasion. Psychologically, we may say that note taking was an aid to memory only when the consequent interference was compensated by rehearsal. In Freyberg's experiment, the group with the handout did best of all after revision—perhaps because their notes were more accurate and contained fewer omissions. If this interpretation is correct, handouts to save note taking could be used selectively for difficult topics.

This kind of handout may be made available only at the end of a lecture, but it is arguable that, like the previous type, students should have the opportunity to make comments and additions. Lectures are clearer if handouts are distributed at the beginning, provided some time is immediately given for students to look them over.

TABLE 10.1. ON BALANCE, IT PAYS TO GIVE HANDOUTS.

Studies Favoring Handouts		
Collingwood and Hughes (1978)	Teacher's detailed notes versus NT Outline notes versus NT	Delayed achievement test
Facinelli (1982)	HO worksheets versus lecture	Five tests in fifteen-week semester
Fisher and Harris (1973)	Lecturer's notes versus NT	Recall delayed three weeks
Kaul (1976)	HO plus discussion versus lecture plus limited discussion	Attitude change
Kiewra (1985)	HO versus NT	Facts learned
Rasor (1980)	Prepared notes versus none	Course completion rates
Rickards and McCormick (1988)	HO of prequestions versus NT; versus no notes	Depth and number of concepts recalled
Smith (1984)	HO versus no notes	Comprehension
Studies Showing No Significant Difference		
Annis (1981)	Partial HO versus NT	Essay and MCQs
Rickards and McCormick (1988)	HO of prequestions versus HO plus NT	Depth and number of concepts recalled
Tucker (1989)	Structured HO versus teacher's notes; versus students' notes	Quiz delayed one week; exam delayed two weeks
White and Chavigny (1975)	Lecture plus audiotape summaries versus lecture	Mid-term and final exams
Studies Favoring Student Note Taking		
Annis (1981)	Full HO versus NT	Essay and MCQs
Fisher and Harris (1973)	Lecturer's notes versus NT	Free recall and MCQs
Henk and Stahl (1985)	HO versus NT	Recall

Note: HO = handout; MCQs = multiple-choice questions; NT = note taking.

5. To Stimulate Thought

Handouts containing questions, tests, or theoretical issues are useful to stimulate thought. Provided the students answer the questions or debate the issues on their own, this kind of handout is particularly useful where it is necessary to give an expository account and there is no lecture time for teaching the important patterns of thought. For this reason, it is sometimes used with large classes with whom little individual or small-group discussion is possible. If given out a week before, students may have the questions in mind (and recollect their initial thoughts about them) during the lecture, and the lecture may have added interest if it allows students to check their answers. The difficulty is to make sure that students think about the questions before the lecture; feedback techniques may provide some check on this, and Elton (1970) has shown that self-tests may be used successfully with first-year undergraduate science courses. I have already mentioned, in the last chapter, King's report (1992) that students posing questions for themselves at the beginning of a lecture learned and remembered more in the long run than students who took their own notes or who were given summary handouts.

The kind of questions asked should depend upon the kind of thought patterns the lecturer wishes to teach. The important point is that not any question will do. The questions may require the application of principles, powers of observation, skills in using books and source material, the analysis of data, the use of judgment, and possibly the need for originality or some other kind of thought process. Therefore, the construction of the question will require some understanding of students' thought processes, and this is not always easy to obtain.

The simplest rule is to give tasks that practice the skills students are intended to learn. In an experiment by Facinelli (1982), one group of students was given bibliographic instruction in lectures; another had additional worksheets containing exercises to find information in dictionaries, manuals, encyclopedias, bibliographies, indexes, biographies, catalogs, and journals. Five pretests and posttests over a fifteen-week semester showed significant benefit to the group with worksheets.

It is frequently difficult to encourage student motivation in large classes. The provision of questions from past examinations may provide an attainable goal and thereby enhance it. Since many examiners give high marks to students who display a breadth of view, it is useful to include hints in the form of supplementary questions that force the students to connect issues which would otherwise remain unrelated in their minds. This is especially true with younger students with whom the objective is to teach new patterns of thought rather than to practice partially established ones.

6. To Guide and Stimulate Reading

Reading lists are among the most common handouts, but they are frequently not carefully thought out. Lecturers may give careful consideration to the presentation of written information on their subject, but when the information is concerned with references the same care is not observed. Yet the amount of student learning at stake may well be greater in the latter case. Indeed, if there is no significant difference in the rate of learning from reading and other presentations (Dubin and Taveggia, 1968), and students spend more time reading recommended references than in any other learning activity (Hale, 1964; Saunders and others, 1969), the preparation of reading lists is worth considerable effort.

It is difficult to generalize for all subjects, but the important functions of reading lists are usually to guide and stimulate the students to read. These are quite unlike the lists at the end of books or journals, which are frequently designed to permit public verification of data and acknowledgment of sources. Consequently, the way they need to be presented is quite different. A long list of references may inform students of what exists (if they bother to look it through), but it is more likely to discourage. If the reading for a whole course is given at the beginning, in the belief that students will welcome the freedom to plan their work, the students' reaction is often to delay getting down to work, or to seek the security of a standard text and neglect journals and other original work. This may lead to concentration on understanding facts at the expense of a spirit of inquiry, criticism, the excitement of originality, and other "higher level" objectives.

Therefore, while not rejecting the use of a short initial reading list to inform students of "books to buy," "reference books," or "basic books" (for those who have forgotten required basic knowledge), it may help if it is short enough to make its guidance practical, if the function of the recommendations is made explicit, and if it is supplemented with more stimulating references through the course when their novelty will be attractive.

Many lecturers give guidance on the relative importance of references by using a system of asterisks; it is also helpful, but less common, to suggest the degree of difficulty or the order in which they should be read. Where a knowledge of technical terms would save reading time, the provision of a glossary handout is useful, particularly if recommended authors use the same term with different meanings, or different terms for the same thing. These confusions can cause the student endless frustration, whereas lecturers, being familiar with their subject, can sort them out relatively easily if they look through their recommendations as the list is made.

A second cause of student frustration is the inability to find the recommended sources. This may sometimes be avoided by giving the classification used in the college library, since librarians do not always classify volumes in the way that others expect, and the books associated with some subjects may be dispersed. Time can be saved if availability of reading is assured. Most college libraries will now stock photocopies of articles in heavy demand when requested, and others will temporarily classify popular volumes as "for reference only." In the long run, these precautions make the lecturer's job easier, because well-read students understand better and are easier to teach.

Students' understanding is frequently better if they have read a variety of viewpoints, but until they know the subject, they cannot guide their own reading in this respect. The lecturer can give this guidance and stimulate considerable interest if comments or questions are added to each recommendation. These may draw attention to bias or important points.

It may be objected that, in the interests of scholarship, lecturers should let their students make their own judgments on what they read, and that they should learn to select what is important for themselves. I agree with this but do not think it is a serious objection. The guidance suggested in the previous paragraph applies to the beginning of the course and is to help students guide themselves later. It is arguable that students will be able to make better-informed and more difficult judgments by the end of a course, if the results of early spadework can be achieved in less time. The objection is rooted in the belief that students who are spoon-fed never learn to use a knife and fork, but this is not necessarily so. The reverse may be true, if the food they are given (knowledge) is the basis on which later skills depend, and the development of academic skills has a particularly interactive character of this kind.

Preparation and Use

Although the preparation and use of handouts depends on their purpose, there are some considerations that are nearly always applicable.

1. Stages in Preparation

Consider six stages in the preparation of a handout.

a. Envision the Effect in Context. Handouts are an integral part of the teaching methods used during a period of teaching. They are not, or should not be, an adjunct. So, the first step is to envision the period of teaching as a whole. What are its objectives? What part will handouts play in achieving them? In other words, what will be the effect of the handout in its context?

b. Decide When It Should Be Used. Considering how a handout is to achieve certain objectives will answer the next question: How and when should it be used? If it is an advance organizer (see page 86 in Chapter Five), it will need to be given either before the lecture or at its beginning. If the latter, time must be given for students to read it before the lecture starts.

If the handout is to help students follow the lecture, it will also need to be given before the beginning of the lecture and referred to as the lecture proceeds. If it is only given at the beginning, without students' having the opportunity to read it before the lecturer starts speaking, they will listen and read with divided attention. That is a recipe for ineffective lecturing.

Some lecturers give a summary handout at the end of a lecture in the belief that it gives opportunity for repetition and rehearsal. In practice, this creates a dilemma for students. Should they take detailed notes during the lecture, knowing that essentials will be duplicated more accurately in the handout to come? Or should they take no notes, rely on the handout, and listen to the lecture, avoiding the usual conflict between noting one point and listening to the next? Much depends on how detailed the follow-up handout is. Only the lecturer knows that. So, if lecturers insist on delaying distribution until the end of the lecture, to remove this dilemma they should give advice on the students' best strategy.

When a handout, such as a diagram, relates only to part of a lecture, it may be given during the lesson. You might think this would be a disruption. It can be, if the distribution is not well organized with a little forethought, but we have seen that there are advantages in lecture breaks.

c. Decide Its Structure. The organization of a lecture handout will normally correspond to the organization of the lecture itself. Anything else might be confusing. However, I should not be too dogmatic on this point. Prelecture handouts as levelers may introduce concepts without covering the ground of the lecture; postlecture handouts might be used to show that a topic could be viewed in quite a different way.

d. Pilot a Draft. Prepare a draft and check it out with a colleague. Piloting on a sample of students is a good idea unless the handout can only be understood in the context of a lecture they have not heard.

e. Revise, Produce, and Distribute. Revise the handout in the light of feedback. Check it for errors, not least word-processing errors. Produce a few more than you should need—somehow they are always needed. Make sure you file a copy with your own lecture notes and overhead transparencies. Plan how you intend to distribute them (for instance, put a small number at the end of each row of students).

f. Evaluate. It is not normally necessary to make a formal evaluation, but it is useful to get some feedback from the students. It is also a good idea to write evaluative comments on the file copy so that changes can be made before the handout is used another time.

2. Choice of Paper

It is usually intended that students should keep handouts; therefore it is necessary to produce them on paper to fit their files. If various kinds of "handout" are used (such as lecture summaries, instructions for practical work, bibliographical references, or question sheets), photocopy paper in various colors will facilitate quick and easy reference for students.

3. Layout for Easy Use

The layout of handouts requires careful thought. A blank wall of prose is normally to be avoided (unless, of course, its purpose is to present literary quotations rather than notes). Sufficient space for students' additions and comments often helps them think because the two sets of ideas can be related more easily when set out together.

In an investigation by MacDonald and Romano (1983), lecturers underestimated the value of layout and summaries. Female students were particularly inclined to neglect poorly presented handouts; and MacDonald and Romano say if they are not well presented lecturers should work through them in class.

4. Timing the Distribution of Handouts

When should handouts be distributed? A clear conception of their purpose largely answers this question. Handouts as a leveler need to be given a week before the lecture. Those to state objectives, save note taking, or act as a lecture guide must be presented at the beginning of the lecture at the very latest. Those to stimulate thought and reading could be collected by students at the end. McDougall, Gray, and McNichol (1972) found that students given a handout before a lecture outperformed others on a test immediately afterwards but were not significantly better in an examination seven weeks after the end of the course. Once again, the revision function of notes and handouts compensated for the immediate disadvantages of poor teaching technique (not receiving the handout earlier).

5. Maintaining Their Availability

There are always some students who fail to receive a copy at the same time as the others. Therefore, it is usually advisable to duplicate more than one per student, to ensure the availability of copies (perhaps from a departmental secretary) during the following weeks, to retain at least one copy (with errors boldly corrected in red) for one's own use, and—if future reduplication is likely—to make sure the master copy is not destroyed.

6. Ensuring Their Use

Handouts are more likely to be read if they are an integral part of a course than if they seem to be addenda. This may be achieved by the addition of relevant examination questions, the inclusion of one or two essential references, and their use during teaching periods, especially practicals.

MacDonald and Romano (1983) found that students don't read handouts unless there is intrinsic motivation to do so. Freshmen and part-time students tend to leave them until revision for examinations, and then they rely on them heavily. The higher the level of student, the less reliance they place upon handouts. Older students are more likely to read long handouts but are more discriminating about what they read. The researchers found that most students preferred handouts that gave some scope for activity.

Training in Reading

Although it is not the purpose of this book to discuss students' reading skills, they are relevant to the extent that students' learning is frequently the product of an interaction between lectures and their reading. Second, lecturers expect students to supplement their lectures by this means. Furthermore, when training in reading skills is given as part of a college course, it is often conducted in a lecture situation.

The failure of most colleges to provide training in reading to learn is, in my opinion, little short of a disgrace. Although it is probably true that some commercial training courses have made exaggerated claims for increases in speeds and comprehension using their methods, the average gains far outweigh the costs. Reading speeds over 1,000 wpm after training are frequently reported, but after looking at data from many institutions Poulton (1961) found that the average reading speed was 160–280 wpm before training and 340–500 wpm afterwards. These figures represented increases of 40–130 percent. If we assume a mean of 85 percent interacting with a mean improvement of 10 percent in comprehension scores (MacMillan, 1965), the gain in efficiency is just over 100 percent. However, this figure may be optimistic. There is evidence of some regression after the completion of such courses except when motivation is high (where there are even some reports of further improvements; see for example Berry, 1965). A practice effect may operate on the postreading tests used, and there may be other imponderables.

Suppose we therefore arbitrarily reduce the improvement rate to 50 percent; this would mean that one-third of the time spent in reading could be saved. To put it another way, if we suppose students are on a three-year course, their training course in reading would have to exceed the whole of one year's reading time in reaching a 50 percent improvement before one could say that the training was not worthwhile.

If we imagine students on a three-year course who read for one thousand hours (that is, roughly eleven hours per week during two fifteen-week semesters but never during vacations or at any other time in the rest of their life), they would need to make less than 3 percent improvement in reading efficiency after thirty hours' tuition before we could say that the time spent training them to read faster was not saved by increased efficiency.

These calculations ignore the special requirements of reading specific subjects. Eighty-one percent of the students in a university psychology department claimed that instruction in how to read experimental reports would have been helpful. It seems reasonable to expect that specialist literature should require specialist training, yet few university departments see such training as an intrinsic part of the development of their subject.

Efficient reading is not simply a matter of speed. The training should include familiarization with a technical vocabulary, reading to get the main idea of a passage, the extraction of details, the application of principles, the testing of inferences, and reading to evaluate. Techniques for skimming and identifying the structure of a passage are of vital importance. The earlier these skills are taught before the establishment of bad habits, the better. When detailed handouts are given, annotation by underlining key words is quicker than written notes, and quick to review later. Ayer and Milson (1993) found it no less effective, though Howe and Godfrey (1977) did, possibly because selecting words to highlight was more of a distraction than an aid to memory in the short time allowed.

The present inefficiency in reading is a luxury we do not want and cannot afford. Short courses in conjunction with subject departments need not subtract any time from the specialist disciplines. They could ease teaching, raise academic standards, and help students, but until the will is present, the necessary staff will not be appointed.

Conclusion

A theme running through this section has been the need to prepare the design and manner of distribution of handouts according to their purpose. To ask the purpose of a handout seems a fairly obvious step before its preparation, yet in practice it is easily overlooked.

The need to teach study techniques such as reading skills is an extension of the same principle. If students arrive at college after careful coaching but with little experience of independent work, they will require training to work efficiently on their own.

CHAPTER ELEVEN

LECTURE STYLES

Stylistic descriptions and their limitations.

1. What style is.

2. The paucity of research.

3. Personal factors as dimensions of styles.

4. Traditional styles among disciplines.

Dimensions of description.

1. Management of information.

2. Familiarity and clarity of language.

3. Styles reflecting the relative certainty of subject matter.

4. Educational values as determinants of style.

B ooks like this too easily leave the impression that there is only one right way of lecturing. There may be a few wrong ways, but there are many right ways. If everyone lectured the same way, students' academic diet would be very monotonous. Idiosyncratic styles are to be welcomed provided they are effective. Much of this book describes what makes a lecture effective.

Stylistic Descriptions and Their Limitations

A question for you as a lecturer to ask yourself is, "What is my usual style?" It is a question of self-awareness so that the perceptions and reactions of audiences can be understood. Answering this question is a step toward a mature self-evaluation.

1. What Style Is

Lecturers' styles consist of the characteristics and frequency of the techniques they employ and the way those techniques are combined. For example, lecturers may write on a blackboard frequently or not at all. Obviously, it is a matter of frequency. They may also write clearly, or quickly, in block capitals, with yellow chalk, and so on. These are characteristics or "qualities" of their writing technique. They may combine this technique with other techniques, such as making a key point, giving examples, explaining, lowering the voice, and observing the audience, each of which has its own frequency and characteristics. It will be evident that whereas all the characteristics of any technique could be enumerated with difficulty, the number of techniques is great, and the number of their possible combinations into styles is astronomic.

It follows that any description of lecturing styles first involves selecting both techniques and particular characteristics of them. Just as important, it involves not selecting a million others. Since neither techniques nor their characteristics are sharply defined, there is then a process of classification.

The selection is usually arbitrary. Every chapter of this book mentions techniques and their qualities that could be relevant.

Any description of a lecturing style is wholly constrained by this selection. The data are typically gathered through questionnaires. Researchers may use a principal components analysis or factor analysis to detect factors underlying responses, and then a cluster analysis to group together individuals for whom each of the factors is of similar importance. It is said of computer data entry "garbage in, garbage out." The same might be said of factor and cluster analyses, or indeed any statistical treatment of data. The choice of observations or data collected wholly determines the techniques and their characteristics that constitute a description of style.

Given the limitations, there are two broad approaches. One is to attempt global descriptions by gathering as much information as possible on whatever seems important, and then analyzing it statistically. The other is to restrict data to particular techniques and characteristics so that the resultant styles are explicitly linguistic, traditional, subject-centered, value-driven, or whatever the particular restriction is. The relevance of such selective descriptions depends upon what they are used for. Self-enlightenment, improvement, evaluation, and adjustment to particular audiences are all possible purposes.

2. The Paucity of Research

The study of lecturing styles is in its infancy. There is no generally agreed classification. There are studies of students' learning styles, and research into styles of teaching in general, such as student-centered and subject-centered teaching; but there has been very little research into specific styles of lecturing. What there is is largely dependent on the subjective opinions of students in questionnaire studies. There are very few objective studies using direct observation by trained observers. With the exception of a study by Bakhtar and Brown (1988), the range of observations in these studies is very restricted.

Dudley-Evans and Johns (1981) thought there are three lecture styles: reading, rhetorical, and conversational. They pointed out that these styles involve quite different lecture signals. Although the rhetorical style might be more appropriate in arts subjects, the choice of these styles probably reflects personal preferences.

3. Personal Factors as Dimensions of Styles

It might be thought that personality factors would be determinants of lecture style. Surely, for example, the confident and the timid will have different approaches. Maybe they do; but there is remarkably little confirmation from research. Indeed, there is very little research on this point, and what there is does not paint a consistent picture. Possibly the number of relevant variables is so great that no one factor, or group of factors, shows up strongly.

Another possible reason for inconsistencies is that even if the personal characteristics of lecturers determine their styles, it is the interaction with those of the students that will determine any measurable outcomes; and since students differ, they will not all interact the same way. Arguably, different students will flourish with different styles. Katz (1990) found that students with a reflective learning style did better on problem-solving tasks following lectures; those with a more active learning style needed discussion or more involvement than passive listening. However, Cavanagh, Hogan, and Ramgopal (1995) showed no advantage for students with a reflective learning style, though their recommendation that lecturers should cater for a variety of styles, and therefore involve the students in a variety of ways, is a repeated message in this book.

In one study (Winocur and others, 1989), regardless of their sex, lecturers with a friendly style were perceived by students as more effective, confident, professional, and approachable. Whether they were in fact more effective was not reported. Indeed, "educational seduction" is a well-recognized phenomenon (Chapter Fifteen); there is some confirmation of it from Kelly and Kelly (1982). They interviewed nine professors who had won teaching awards and found that on the whole they were older, came from nonaffluent families, had a strong academic preparation and motivation for a teaching career, and questioned the priority of research in salary and promotion criteria. Their styles were characterized by enjoyment, enthusiasm for the subject, humor, theatrical performance, a good command of language and its delivery, and involvement of students through questions and discussion.

4. Traditional Styles Among Disciplines

The relative privacy of lectures means that the only role models that many faculty have are those who lectured to them in their student days—perhaps some years ago. Not only does this produce a very conservative profession but the inbreeding within subject disciplines means that teaching styles are characteristic of academic subjects. Indeed, anyone who has observed lectures on a range of disciplines across several continents can testify that there is more in common stylistically between, say, biochemistry lectures in Indian, European, and American medical schools, than with biochemistry lectures in the chemistry departments of the same universities.

These conservative stylistic traditions within disciplines still need to be researched. They are not always a function of the subject matter. Nor are they based upon objective evidence of what is effective. For example, philosophers want students to consider specific propositions, but it is remarkably rare for philosophy lecturers to display the propositions on an overhead projector or chalkboard, or to stop lecturing and let the students consider them either individually or in groups. The convention is that the philosopher keeps tight control by responding immediately to any contribution a student makes. This inhibits thought in a discipline that—almost above all others—aims to promote it.

Dimensions of Description

We have seen that the number of dimensions could be infinite. In seeking awareness of their own style, lecturers might choose any of them. What follows is confined to published studies and is not intended to restrict the scope of lecturers' self-awareness.

1. Management of Information

The best and most global study of lecturing styles was carried out by Bakhtar and Brown (1988). To choose their data, they noted similarities and differences of style and discussed them with a few faculty. After piloting a questionnaire asking faculty what is important when lecturing, they got a 65 percent return rate and responses from more than fifty subject specializations, which they classified into humanities, social science, science and engineering, and biomedical. The questionnaire included self-reports and open-ended questions on good and bad lecture techniques. Although wide ranging, most of their items were concerned with how lecturers manage the information content of their lectures—its preparation, organization, language, sources, presentation, assessment, and so on. Factor analysis revealed six aspects of lecturing: information giving, structuring, a sense of purpose, visual techniques, self-doubt or self-confidence, and attention to presentation techniques such as asking questions, quoting, and using repetitions.

The factors clustered into five lecturing styles, which they labeled exemplary (26 percent), amorphous (23 percent), oral (18 percent), visual (26 percent), and eclectic (9 percent). Bakhtar and Brown found no relation between group membership and either seniority or length of experience. If this implies that lecturers do not change and develop their techniques throughout their working lives, it lays stress upon the importance of initial training. You are invited to consider whether your own and others' lecturing styles fit any of these groups.

Exemplary lecturers appeared to follow the advice given by the majority of respondents. Around one-third of lecturers in humanities, social sciences, and biomedical sciences were in this cluster. They are confident, well organized, use a variety of oral and visual techniques, structure their lectures and lecture notes clearly with headings and subheadings, and inform students of their objectives and future topics. Less significantly, they recapitulate and link previous lectures, outline the organization of the present one, raise questions at the beginning and end of lectures, use visuals and quotations to illustrate points, and provide handouts and advice on note taking. Overall they strive to promote thought and understanding, not just factual information.

The amorphous group are the most distinctive. They are confident, but vague and poorly prepared. They are the least likely to tell students their objectives, lecture organization, future topics, examination topics, or how to take notes. They approve of lecturer training but don't think they personally need it. Around 30 percent of scientists and engineers in Bakhtar and Brown's sample were in this cluster.

As their name suggests, oral lecturers scarcely use the chalkboard, overhead projector, or any other visual aid. They are to be found (particularly among scholars in arts and humanities—34 percent) using and possibly quoting several sources, and relying almost exclusively on their own verbal fluency to expound them. Accordingly, they don't prepare in detail on paper; headings, subheadings, and brief notes are all they require.

Visual lecturers are strongly represented in science and engineering subjects (43 percent). They are most inclined to rely on one text, prepare full notes, and spend much of the lecture writing (calculations and proofs) on the chalkboard or overhead projector. More than other groups, they are inclined to give more information than students can absorb at the time. They may summarize on completing a topic, but because topics do not fit neatly into fifty-minute lectures, these summaries are often in the middle of a lesson.

Last, the eclectic group was the smallest in Bakhtar and Brown's survey (9 percent). They use a variety of techniques but lack confidence in using them. Indeed, in an earlier research paper (Brown, Bakhtar, and Youngman, 1984) they were called "self-doubters." They don't write their objectives down, but like all the other groups except the amorphous lecturers they claim to think about them.

In a more restricted inquiry, Bakhtar and Brown (rightly in my view) place some emphasis on the organization of lectures when discussing styles. They briefly described the classification-hierarchy, problem-centered, chaining, comparison, and thesis lecture forms and then asked lecturers which they used most often. With the exception of humanities (48 percent), all used the classification hierarchy around 60 percent of the time. Problem-centered (20 percent) and chaining (18 percent) were each the second most used by about a third of the lecturers. Comparison and thesis lecture forms were said to be used very little.

Two other studies have focused on how lecturers manage their information. Rather than investigate lecture styles and then see which is most effective, Albanese, Schuldt, Case, and Brown (1991) asked students which lecturers they rated high and low; they then compared the styles. Differences in student involvement and the clarity of introductions and organization emerged as most important. Clarity, organization, and student involvement also emerged as the important stylistic factors for students, regardless of their age and sex, in a study by Ross (1989). These two studies tend to confirm Bakhtar and Brown's emphasis upon organization.

2. Familiarity and Clarity of Language

Lecturers differ in linguistic style. Lectures are more difficult to understand when the style of language is unfamiliar. Bernstein has shown that lower social groups are relatively disadvantaged because they speak with much simpler sentence constructions than their teachers. Even lectures in American sign language show different styles in their syntax, lexical choice, speech rate, pausing, and intonation (Shaw, 1987). Linn (1973) describes several varieties of English: the "frozen style" of written documents, the academic or "formal style" that faculty expect students to write, the "casual style" between friends and acquaintances, and the "intimate style" between friends and lovers. He says the language of black Americans lies somewhere between the last two and is characterized by ellipsis, jargon, and slang. The typical linguistic style of lecturers is "formal" and maintains a social distance too great for a fully supportive climate to develop. On the other hand, if lecturers try to use a linguistic style that is not their own, they are quickly perceived as insincere and not genuine.

Familiarity is one important aspect of a lecturer's language. Clarity is another. Land (1981) used three videotaped lectures of twenty minutes with the same information but varying in the number of vague expressions and uninformative phrases. Students' learning and ratings of clarity were both related to the lecturer's accuracy of language. In a later experiment (Land and Combs, 1982), Land varied the amount of unexplained content in fifteen-minute videotaped lectures. When there was "none," the lecturer was perceived as clearer in explaining, more confident, serious, better prepared, less nervous, and more knowledgeable in the subject.

Hiller, Fisher, and Kaess (1969) found that a lecturer's vagueness and students' acquisition of knowledge correlated negatively (−0.48 and −0.59). He therefore confined a later study (Hiller, 1971) to the spoken indications of conceptual vagueness and concluded that if lecturers lack knowledge they suffer stress and adopt stylistic behaviors to defend themselves. These relationships are represented in Figure 11.1.

In general, both lecturers' emotions and their knowledge of the subject influence lecture techniques, particularly the clarity or vagueness of language. The techniques, or their consequences, may also affect feelings such that a spiral effect

FIGURE 11.1. THE IMPACT OF IGNORANCE AND EMOTION UPON VAGUENESS.

Note: Arrows indicate direction of cause to effect.

Source: Adapted from Hiller, 1971.

is created. In particular, where lecturers lack knowledge (because they have insufficient knowledge, are confused, are uncertain, or can't remember) they are afraid to express themselves. The resulting defensiveness, anxiety, and low self-esteem may make the confusion, uncertainty, and information retrieval far worse. Fear of expressing oneself leads to a variety of linguistic techniques described as nonspecific equivocation, such as excessive cautiousness or simplified statements (Hiller, 1971). Similarly, Carlsen (1993) found that scientists teaching unfamiliar topics in schools tended to talk for longer periods and ask rather low-level questions.

3. Styles Reflecting the Relative Certainty of Subject Matter

The influence of conservative traditions and lecture content could result in lecture styles varying with subject disciplines. The styles of explanation could be different. Influenced by Bakhtar and Brown, Behr (1988) also obtained responses from lecturers. He classified the results into four styles (Table 11.1): information providers and three types of presenters (dramatic, structured, and visual). With the exception of engineers, the majority of every subject group saw themselves as structured presenters. One wonders whether their students would see them the same way.

Although Behr's sample was not large, his data show a tendency for subject disciplines to stand in a certain order with regard to lecturing styles. According to Schachter (Schachter, Christenfeld, Ravina, and Bilous, 1991; Schachter, Rauscher, Christenfeld, and Crone, 1994), lecturers in natural sciences, social sci-

TABLE 11.1. TENDENCIES TOWARD STYLES FOR SUBJECT DISCIPLINES.

	Percentage of Respondents			
	Structured Presenter	**Dramatic Presenter**	**Information Provider**	**Visual Presenter**
Engineering	20	–	–	80
Science	47	8	–	45
Health	40	10	15	35
Commerce and law	45	21	17	17
Humanities (social sciences)	50	20	17	13
Arts and languages	61	22	7	10

Source: Behr, 1988.

ences, and the humanities, in that order, are increasingly likely to fill pauses with the likes of *uh, er,* and *um,* because humanists have a wider vocabulary and therefore more words to choose from and more possibilities of what the next word should be. Language in the natural sciences is more precise, so there are fewer options for the lecturer and less hesitation is needed. A similar order appears on many other apparently different measures: as examples, what students expect from lectures (Smithers, 1970a, 1970b); numerical-verbal emphasis within disciplines; the vocational orientation of students (with the possible exception of scientists); and personality dimensions such as authoritarianism-independence of mind, dogmatism-open mindedness, convergent-divergent thinking, and anxious introversion-stable extroversion. Ramsden (1992) shows the same sequence with regard to evaluation data.

Much more study is needed, but so far it looks as if the certainty of the subject matter taught is more definitive of teaching style than a concern for teaching itself. Though different, these measures all reflect the degree of certainty in the disciplines. They reflect a discipline orientation.

4. Educational Values as Determinants of Style

The order as associated with an educational orientation is not quite the same. Ratings by people of different disciplines of educational values, an interest in educational research, or expertise in teaching commonly show a slightly different order: health, engineering, physical sciences, commerce and law, social sciences, languages, and arts (in decreasing order) (Ramsden, 1992). However, using a different questionnaire, Falchikov (1993) did obtain five factors having to do with teaching: qualities necessary in a lecturer, a positive attitude to teaching, a negative attitude to teaching, responsibility for students, and beliefs about the best way to teach and learn. On the basis of these factors, Falchikov identified seven groups of faculty:

1. *A group favoring student autonomy with a student focus,* believing students should take responsibility for their own learning and teachers should turn them into thinkers.
2. *Traditionalists,* who think their job is important and satisfying and is to communicate, impart knowledge, and help students pass exams.
3. *The pro-student-autonomy group with a faculty focus,* who believe their job is satisfying and is to develop students and to be enthusiastic.
4. *A group under pressure* thinks students learn by finding out, solving problems, taking responsibility for their own learning, and going to the library. Faculty need to communicate, have more time to prepare, and create a supportive environment. They find their job stressful.

5. *Senior faculty* like course development and think there is no best way to teach; they also think students should take responsibility for their own learning, and they have an open outlook.
6. *Professionals* contribute to their discipline, want promotion, and want to be a team member.
7. *Defensive traditionalists* are subject-centered and keep abreast of their subject. They think there is too much emphasis on research and that their job is to impart knowledge and maintain standards of discipline.

Innovators tended to be among groups (1) and (5). Scientists tended to be traditionalists, with less emphasis upon higher levels of intellectual and ethical development (Perry, 1970).

Conclusion

Lecturing styles is an area ripe for research. Millions of people have observed and discussed differences in lecturers' styles, yet remarkably little is known about them with objective detachment. What is known seems to indicate the importance of organization and language.

CHAPTER TWELVE

WAYS OF OBTAINING FEEDBACK

Nonverbal communication.

1. Arrival of students.

2. Seating position.

3. Students' reactions.

4. Styles of note taking.

Verbal feedback.

1. Questioning technique.

2. Mechanical means of response.

3. Help with individual work.

4. Buzz groups.

5. Submitted work.

6. Step-by-step lecture.

7. Record of answers in a problem-based course.

8. Prepared answers.

9. Interpolated questions from students.

10. Questions from groups.

One of the most serious criticisms of the lecture method is that the lecturer has no feedback on his or her performance, and students have no knowledge of the amount and accuracy of their learning. Beard (1967) has drawn an analogy with two kinds of evaluation in industry. The first consists in assessment by inspection of completed work, while the second monitors the production process in order that continuous improvements may be made in its efficiency. In manufacturing processes the second is regarded as the more important, but in education great emphasis is placed on the final examination and less on the process of teaching and learning. What is required is for the effectiveness of a lecture to be evident at the time so that corrections can be made if necessary. This is the importance of feedback.

This is confirmed by psychologists who have shown the importance of feedback for learning and the performance of other tasks (Annett, 1969). The lecture is a form of one-way verbal communication such that neither the lecturer nor the audience has adequate knowledge of what they are doing.

There are three broad solutions. Lecturers may rely on nonverbal communication from the students. They may abandon the exclusive use of the lecture method by obtaining verbal feedback. Or they may evaluate their effectiveness after the lecture either from the opinions of students and other observers or from indicators of students' learning. Evaluations after the lecture, whether from direct observations or students' learning, will be considered in the next chapter. This chapter is concerned with feedback during the lesson itself.

Nonverbal Communication

The observation and interpretation of the nonverbal behavior of students in the lecture situation is an essential skill for good teaching. The new lecturer cannot expect to acquire it fully in his first three years; some probably never do, and remain oblivious of missing anything. It is essentially learned by practice. Observation of students during other people's lectures by sitting to one side near the front may provide practice without the additional need to concentrate on the lecturer's subject matter.

The first task is to make informed "guesses" about the students' emotions and attitudes. (I say *guesses* because one can never know what they are for certain. Many students have learned the art of maintaining a fixed expression that hides their thoughts and feelings.)

1. Arrival of Students

Do the students arrive as a group, or dribble in by ones and twos? This may give an indication of the relationships among the class and therefore reflect the degree of cohesiveness in the group as a whole. If the teaching methods require work in groups for discussion or practical activities, the social structure of the group may be important.

Do they arrive on time? Are notebooks opened, ready for the lecture, or are they reluctantly pulled out of a bag with an "Oh well, I suppose we had better . . ." attitude once the lecture has started?

2. Seating Position

Where do students sit? Sitting at the back may indicate a distant relationship between the students and the lecturer so that two-way communication is more difficult. This will affect the willingness of students to ask questions when they do not understand, and the ease with which the lecturer can obtain responses or contributions from the class. Thus, these relationships impose limitations on the teaching techniques that can be used. How has the lecturer's manner affected these relationships? Obviously, if the lecturer is aggressive or pinpoints individuals with questions, the students are likely to retreat; but usually, student-lecturer relationships are more subtle than this so that individuals react differently and the sensitivity of the lecturer to the reactions of individuals needs to be acute.

It is very useful to observe differences between students and groups of students. Who is independent in judgment, and who looks sideways for the support and agreement of others? Are there individuals who indicate the general mood of the class? If so, it is useful to recognize these barometers early in a course.

Look at Figure 12.1. Student A has come not only to listen to the lecture but also to watch everyone else. If he is a student, not an inspector or an academic colleague, he may be a bit of a loner.

B is what used to be called "a swot" (a person who studies hard). She is intent on doing well academically to the exclusion of her wider education, the development of her social skills, and what else the university can offer. (In tests with a score of 10 maximum, Giles and others, 1982, found that students in the front, middle, and back rows scored 8.00, 7.16, and 6.81 respectively.) In Section 4 on page 177, I recommend observing the note taking of typical students near the front, to judge the pacing of the lecture and the clarity of its organization. B is not a good one to observe for this purpose.

C represents a courting couple. They seem a bit wrapped up in each other. If they have shared their tasks for private study and have only one set of notes between them, they will be in difficulties if they quarrel and split up before the examinations.

The students around D and E form a group. It is difficult for a lecturer to observe every student when there are more than thirty in a class. The reactions of students in the group will be strongly influenced by the group leader. But which is the group leader? It is likely to be either D or E. Other group members will sit where they can observe the leader and take their cue from him. Thus the leader won't be in the row behind; nor is he likely to be at the end of the group in the row in front. So, for this group of seven students, the lecturer can get feedback most efficiently by observing either D or E. Another way to identify the leader is to observe this group when they arrive. Others will observe and follow wherever

FIGURE 12.1. SEATING POSITIONS IN A LECTURE THEATER.

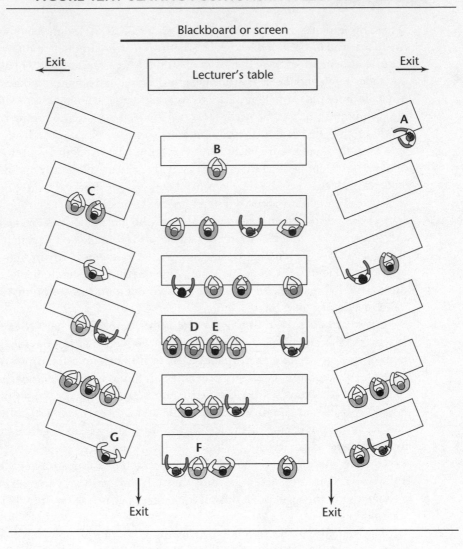

the leader intends to sit. For this reason, he may well be the second or third member to come through the door.

Many students who want to enjoy other things think they are least likely to be observed if they sit in the back row. This is a mistake. They are much less noticeable if lost in the crowd. Experienced lecturers use eye contact to engage the attention of students in the back row.

Finally, we may notice that G has taken a seat near the back door because she wants to get away fast and be first in the lunch queue or borrow the only library copy of the book you have just recommended. If you want her to hear administrative announcements, make them at the beginning of the lecture.

These examples are, of course, anecdotal, but they should give the beginning lecturer some feedback about students from their choice of seating position.

3. Students' Reactions

How alert and responsive are the students? The speed of their reactions reflects their interest and speed of comprehension. How far do the emotions of the students reflect the emotions of the lecturer? Because humor is an expression of the emotions, reactions to the lecturer's jokes are a particularly sensitive indicator of the lecturer-student relationship. A very wide range of emotions and relationships can be expressed in laughter. These are frequently signs of the limits of student tolerance. Is the reaction appreciative? Is it spontaneous? If there is no reaction, communication is minimal.

What reactions are shown on the students' faces? Are they attentive, tired, sullen, rebellious . . . ? Do they meet or avoid the lecturer's gaze? Do they look for nonverbal communication from the lecturer? If this kind of feedback is difficult to obtain from some students because they never look up from their notes, pointing to visual aids at the front of the class and using such words as *this, these, here,* and *now watch* will force the students to look up. The lecturer may slow the pace momentarily to give students time to look up, thus affording time to observe their leftover facial expressions, which often gives a sign of their recent feelings. Subsequent pauses give the students "thinking time" and the lecturer time to see how they use it.

4. Styles of Note Taking

Attention should be paid to what students note. Students who always write too much may be lacking in self-confidence, which should be boosted in tutorials or group discussion. Noting everything frequently indicates an inability to select what is important. This may have many causes: lack of background knowledge, poor critical ability, or lack of clear organization by the lecturer. The first requires a carefully planned course of reading; the second, practice in applying knowledge and solving problems in written work, discussion, or private study; and the third, itemization of points under headings on the blackboard or screen as the lecture progresses.

It is worth noticing—by looking for the spacing of headings and the presence of numbers in the margin or inset from it—how far the students' notes reflect the organization of the lecture. (This is not to say that they always should. The best students may reorganize the lecturer's information in their own way; or they may know the facts already and only note their reactions. It is for the failure to grasp any organization at all that the lecturer should be vigilant.) If these observations are related to a student's written work, it is possible to get some understanding of how a student deals with information, thought processes, and possibly general study habits.

These observations are also essential to the timing within a lecture. If you want the students to listen with undivided attention, you should wait until students have finished noting one point before going on to the next. Yet it is quite common for lecturers to proceed apace, regardless of what the students are doing. This may easily happen if you are a new lecturer and nervous; but if you can get a firm grip on yourself and pause (which may not be easy), the pause can be used to steady yourself.

Verbal Feedback

About 5 percent of the students interviewed by Marris (1964) complained of lecturers who resented or evaded questions. If lecturers want immediate verbal feedback from the students, they must stop their own exposition to obtain it. Once students have begun to give and receive feedback, the lecturer's job is relatively easy. The difficult task is breaking the ice both with the class as a whole and with particular individuals. The suggestions that follow are neither exhaustive nor infallible. They are techniques that some lecturers have found useful. Much depends on the personal feelings of those involved.

1. Questioning Technique

Because questioning is the form of language that requires a response, lecturers requiring feedback are likely to use a questioning technique. But it must also be remembered that questions are threatening stimuli. They produce a fear reaction.

Using pulsemeters, I have found that the heart rate of students in a tutorial group increased by five to ten beats per minute in the first thirty seconds after a tutor asked a question. The heart rate of students who spoke increased by ten to seventy beats per minute. It seems reasonable to think that answering questions in the presence of a lecture audience would be an even more stressful situation. This awaits further investigation, but it is interesting that in both group tutorials and lectures, I have found that students' heart rates rise appreciably when their neighbors speak.

Two tentative conclusions may be drawn: the questions and the ways in which they are asked should produce minimal psychological stress; and to obtain feedback from those students for whom a public response would be too stressful, the lecturer will need to adopt a less direct technique. Questions requiring personal reactions, personal opinions, or application of personal experience such that the answers are unlikely to be wrong are, paradoxically, the least incriminating. They are also useful in that they easily permit supplementary questions leading to the development of the topic. Psychologically speaking, if student feedback is to be encouraged, their responses need to be rewarded. Consequently the lecturer's manner is of vital importance. Therefore the relevance of a lecturer's first question is less important than its emotional climate.

2. Mechanical Means of Response

Some teachers have developed techniques to obtain feedback in private, so to speak. Lecture theaters can be wired for electrical responses to a display panel that only the lecturer sees. Such panels have been used on television host shows. They may give individual or collective responses on a visual display unit like a television screen.

Lecture theaters with networked computer terminals for each student allow much more sophisticated presentations and responses. Significantly, they allow sophisticated analysis of individual students' responses such that follow-up tuition and counseling can be personally directed more than in the past.

Using a much less costly device, Taplin (1969) supplied U.S. Air Force trainees with two-and-a-half-inch cubes with differently colored faces so that answers to multiple-choice questions could be shown privately by students, each holding a cube in cupped hands so that only the lecturer could see the color selected to correspond with the answer. Dunn (1969) has used colored cards more cheaply for the same purpose with medical students. Harden, Wayne, and Donald (1968) devised "an audience response card" with five colors covered by paper flaps, which could be shown in fourteen combinations, permitting relatively complex multiple-choice questions to be answered.

For example, during a lecture on goiter the following question was asked:

Iodine deficiency:

1. May result in goiter
2. Results in hypothyroidism
3. Is commoner in the winter
4. Is associated with low urine iodine excretion
5. Results from a deficiency of meat in the diet

The correct answers are 1 and 4. When a significant proportion of the class answered 2, the lecturer realized that his lecture had not sufficiently stressed that in most countries iodine deficiency is rarely severe enough to cause hypothyroidism. Harden, Wayne, and Donald (1968) found that the preparation of questions and the organization of the lecture took more time, but that the result was more interesting and more effective teaching. Taplin, too (1969), found that the preparation of questions took time, but that without this feedback he would have assumed more understanding from his students than was justified. This assumption is more common than to underestimate students' knowledge.

3. Help with Individual Work

It is, of course, possible to set problems for students to solve individually in the lecture situation while the lecturer goes round to help those having difficulty. This useful technique can promote thought and help the lecturer to know the students, as well as provide feedback on students' understanding, but it can cause resentment if students come expecting only to listen, if they think the lecturer is not doing her job, or if they do not appreciate the value of immediately applying the principles they have just learned. Consequently, as with all techniques that break the long-established habits of teaching, its purpose must first be explained to obtain student assent.

4. Buzz Groups

An alternative feedback technique is to give the problems to small buzz groups of two to six members, to discuss for two to five minutes before reporting their answers (see Chapter Eighteen).

5. Submitted Work

Some lecturers set problems to be solved before the next lecture or tutorial group. But as we have seen, rehearsal and feedback are not as effective when delayed as when given immediately, during the lecture itself (Chapter Two). Furthermore, motivation frequently wanes during the ensuing week unless the obligation to complete the work is reinforced strongly.

6. Step-by-Step Lecture

What I call the step-by-step lecture method consists of three to ten short periods of exposition by the lecturer each followed by class discussion under the lecturer's general control. The student activity, frequent feedback, opportunities for rehearsal, the periodic relaxation from concentrated listening, and the consequent reduction of retroactive interference make this a very useful method with classes up to thirty and with difficult subject matter that is best built up in stages.

Koo, Wong, and Tam (1993) compared traditional lectures and lectures based upon a handout with spaces and problems. Interaction with the lecturer was monitored every five seconds. Students spent 13 percent of the time on the problems at intervals through the lectures and 33 percent in discussion with the teacher immediately thereafter. There was no difference in their learning as measured by an objective test of factual information after three weeks; but the researchers might have found a difference if they had tested more thought. Students strongly favored the interactive method.

7. Record of Answers in a Problem-Based Course

McCarthy (1970) used a variation of this method by basing his course around problems that were each projected on a screen, attempted by the students, and discussed by the teacher before proceeding to the next. The questions were also supplied on a handout with space for students' notes so that a complete record of the course could be maintained. There was little formal lecturing. The method was quite popular with the students, but like Taplin (1969), the teacher overestimated students' knowledge and had to slow his pace considerably.

8. Prepared Answers

Elton (1970) provided a first-year physical sciences course with full lecture notes and space for additions together with self-tests. Possession of the notes did not discourage attendance at lectures, which became occasions for feedback on test performance rather than the reception of information for the first time. Almost half the students did the tests either "always" or "frequently," while only 7 percent "never" did.

Instead of lecturing, MacManaway (1970) circulated complete lecture scripts together with questions and assignments designed to extend thinking and comprehension in sociology. Feedback was obtained by contact with seven or eight discussion groups during the first half hour and then by general discussion following group reports. This method was appreciated by the majority of students; only 13 percent would have preferred some form of lecture.

9. Interpolated Questions from Students

It is quite a common practice for lecturers to deliver their lecture and ask if there are any questions only at the end. However, it will already be clear from what has been said about reducing retroactive interference, the provision of opportunity for rehearsal, the immediacy of feedback for motivation, and the effect of a change of stimulation or change of activity on the decline in students' attention that it is better to avoid long periods of uninterrupted exposition. Furthermore, students may be embarrassed to ask questions about the early part of a lecture if doing so implies they have not understood the rest, while if the later part of a lecture is to be understood it is the lecturer's duty to ensure these questions are answered before that point is reached. In any case, the effect of retroactive interference in a paced situation is sufficiently strong that students frequently forget questions they would have liked to ask. Delaying the opportunity for questions fails to take advantage of the temporary initial interest in a point. Asking "Are there any questions?" at the end frequently means the same as "If there aren't any questions we can all go"; at some times of day it takes a strong-willed student to respond. Consequently, questions are often asked only by the more able and dedicated students, while feedback is required more from those with difficulties. It may be controversial, but in my view few periods of exposition by a lecturer should exceed twenty minutes to half an hour without some feedback or other variation in method.

If the lecturer wishes to elicit questions and contributions from a class, it is usually not a good idea to give the student carte blanche by asking "Are there any questions?" It is usually better to direct questions to an important issue on which feedback is desired. If there are still no questions, it is useful for the lecturer to have supplementary open questions ("Did you find Smith's explanation convincing?" or "Do you think this fact is surprising?"). When a student answers this sort of question, it is possible to ask "Why?" and elicit a full explanation that gives valuable feedback on understanding.

10. Questions from Groups

A useful way to obtain feedback is to instruct buzz groups (Chapter Eighteen) to ask at least one question each. This has the advantages that foolish and time-wasting questions are eliminated by fellow students who answer them; students who are too shy to speak in a lecture class may be willing to pose a question in a small group; and many students are willing to ask a question if they discover they are not the only ones who do not understand, or who disagree with, a particular point.

If further anonymity is required, the questions may be written on paper and either passed forward to the lecturer or collected when visiting each discussion. In either case, it saves time and leads to a more orderly presentation if the questions can be grouped appropriately. Because a number of buzz groups usually ask similar questions, this technique is useful for lecturers to find out which part of a topic is most difficult and thus requires most careful explanation. (See the conclusion of Chapter Seven.)

Conclusion

Some of the techniques that require greatest skill in obtaining feedback are derived from a lecturer's observation of his class. The sensitive lecturer notices the slight frown, the hesitation for thought, the smallest expression of puzzlement and a student's stare at notes that is longer than usual. These often signify thoughts about the lecture; if the lecturer can tactfully elicit them, it may be possible to develop the lecture topic in a way that is particularly meaningful to the class. Thus, it is the combination of techniques that leads to good teaching, not their use in isolation.

CHAPTER THIRTEEN

EVALUATION OF LECTURES

The debate about what approach to take.

Make a preliminary inquiry.

Get professional help to observe and describe.

1. Who are the professionals?

2. Difficulty in facing oneself.

3. Procedures and principles of consultation.

Students' opinions.

1. Reasons for obtaining students' opinions.

2. Devising the questionnaire.

3. What should be evaluated?

4. The potent variable in students' opinions.

5. Students' opinions are reliable.

6. The validity of students' opinions is modest and inconsistent.

7. Conclusion on students' opinions.

Assessment of learning objectives achieved.

1. Recognition of a key point.

2. Memory of a simple stated relationship.

3. Making simple inferences.

4. Application.

5. Analytical thought.

6. Synthesis.

7. Evaluation.

8. Attitudes.

9. Conclusion on assessment of objectives.

The logic of this chapter is slightly different from that of the others. In other chapters, I have tried to combine research, common sense, and experience to paint a picture of generalizations lecturers can apply in their own teaching. In this chapter, the aim is to suggest generalizations about particulars—that is to say, how to find out characteristics of a particular lecture or lecturer in order to improve them.

The Debate About What Approach to Take

What methods should be used? There are any number, and the answer depends upon your paradigm of inquiry. Among educationalists, this has been a matter of debate. Being a debate, too often a method, or sequence of methods, has been presented as opposed to others, rather than recognizing that they all have their merits depending on what you want to find out.

In a traditional approach, a lecture is evaluated by testing the students' learning to see how far the lecturer's objectives have been achieved. Students' learning is a fundamental indicator of the lecturer's success. This is sometimes described as a scientific paradigm, as if it used experimental testing of a hypothesis to increase confidence in a generalization. It is nothing of the kind. First, that is not the way generalizations are made about teaching. Second, as I've just said, establishing generalizations is not what these evaluations are for anyway.

The assessment of learning can have some objectivity, but it has its limitations. It does not evaluate whether the objectives were sufficient or worthwhile. The criteria are sometimes imposed by the evaluator, not negotiated with those evaluated. They take no account of the students' aims. A lecture might teach all the knowledge and so on that the lecturer intended but have such disastrous side effects—for example on students' motivation—as to render the lecture a failure in a wider context. There are always subsidiary aims and standards of this kind that normally go unspoken. Furthermore, the assessment of students alone does not tell the lecturer where or what improvements are needed, or what to do about them. Some critics will go further and say that a lecture should be conceived as a social event governed by all kinds of unacknowledged rules and rituals. A lecturer's and students' intentions and values can only be understood in a social context.

Accordingly, it is argued that a lecture cannot be evaluated in an objective way detached from its context, but only *interpreted* from within a subculture. In this view, a lecturer's behavior, and the students' response, can only be interpreted in light of their intentions, perceptions, and the whole background of their knowledge and assumptions. Hence these interpretations are necessarily subjective. An independent evaluator cannot observe them. All the evaluator can do is to help the lecturer and students *reflect* on what they did, why they did it, and what they would want to do differently on another occasion. Helping others reflect may involve some *negotiation*. Alternatively, by working to clarify their assumptions, rules, understanding, and values, the evaluator may behave more like a counselor than a researcher. Such an inquiry will go wider than what happens in the lecture room. For example, it will include reflection on administrative processes and how knowledge is organized in their minds.

There are several variants of these subjective approaches. Their critics will point out that we all have coherent and consistent self-deceptions and illusions about ourselves, what we do, our reasons for doing it, and out social perceptions. You don't have to study Freud to know that because lecturers feel exposed, they have all manner of defense mechanisms that only full-blown psychoanalysis will reveal.

It will be clear that both objective and subjective methods have their limitations. The things that can be evaluated are legion and complex in their interactions. Subjective methods can range more widely than objective assessments. So it probably pays to start with the more subjective approaches and use them diagnostically to *progressively focus* on particular areas for improvement. My advice is keep it simple:

1. *Preliminary inquiry.* First of all, carry out a preliminary inquiry. Let this be descriptive and potentially diagnostic, like the open-ended questionnaire presented just below. Very likely, it will tell you as much as you need to know.
2. *Consultation.* If it doesn't, and you want to inquire in more detail on more specific points, then wherever possible consult someone professionally engaged in evaluation work. A deeper inquiry is a research task. If educational evaluation is not your field, no one should expect you to be expert at it. Depending on what you want to know, the consultant could use any of many research techniques. To describe them would take another book. This chapter can only sample two of them:
3. *Students' reflections and opinions.* Questionnaires are by far the most researched and commonly used methods.
4. *The assessment of learning objectives achieved.* Although there are several kinds of objective test, truth-functional tests (about which more later in this chapter) were specifically designed for assessing the effectiveness of lectures.

Make a Preliminary Inquiry

First, it is necessary to decide what is to be evaluated. There are so many aspects of lecturing and what goes on in lecture rooms that it is impossible to evaluate everything simultaneously. Even if one could, the evaluation process would so disturb the lecture itself as to render the evaluation invalid. Any evaluation is partial. Inevitably there is a selection process. Being preliminary to any objective evaluation, the selection is necessarily impressionistic. Consequently, right at the beginning there is a loss of objectivity in all evaluations, quite apart from whether the data and their interpretation are subjective. The subjective selection of what to evaluate runs the risk that unimportant aspects will be given undue weight and important aspects will be omitted.

One way to reduce this risk is to give students a preliminary, open-ended, free-response questionnaire of the kind shown in Figure 13.1. Covering only one side of the sheet of paper, it is quick to produce and administer. It needs no professional evaluator.

The first question seeks an overall judgment that helps to interpret later responses. However, there is a trap to be avoided in its interpretation. Lectures are multifaceted. Different students will use different criteria. Therefore responses should be treated individually, not averaged or rendered statistically in other ways. Up to a point, this caution goes for any rating scale; the more specific the scale, the more objective it can be. This scale is particularly general. The comments may indicate an individual's criteria.

If the lecturer and the students are trying to achieve different things, they will get nowhere working in conflict. Question 2 checks this out.

Questions 3 and 4 are diagnostic. Question 4 elicits details for self-improvement or further investigation. More important, Question 3 shows the strengths that can be built upon and that should not normally be restricted by changes for improvement. Demanding itemized points encourages thought and brevity. I often ask for three of each, but not more. With responses from a whole class, it is usually clear where I need to improve, and what the good points are that I should not remove when doing so.

Question 5 is designed to encourage constructive responses and can be the springboard for discussion later.

As I said, this form can be administered by the lecturer and is usually sufficient. If further inquiry is required, it is generally best to get professional advice.

Get Professional Help to Observe and Describe

To some people, seeking help may feel like an admission of failure. Not a bit of it. It is a sign of strength, honesty, and commitment.

1. Who Are the Professionals?

The question arises as to whom should you consult. That is, who are the professionals? In institutions where someone is appointed for staff development, there should be an established facility.

FIGURE 13.1. FORM FOR A PRELIMINARY INQUIRY.

Lecture Evaluation

In order to help me to improve my lectures, please complete the form below. Your response will be treated as strictly confidential and anonymous. Please do not put your name on the paper.

1. What is your overall opinion of this lecture compared with lectures generally?
   Place an X in the appropriate box. Please comment.

   Poor   Good

2. State your objectives in attending this lecture. To what extent have they been achieved?

3. Give two things you liked about the lecture:

   A.

   B.

4. Give two things you disliked about the lecture:

   A.

   B.

5. If I were to teach this topic again, what changes would you recommend I make?

Yet few people are expert in lecture observation. Even college of education tutors who are called upon to help student teachers frequently have little preparation for the task. Their assessments are known to correlate badly with estimates by students' first head teachers, subsequent head teachers, and vocational promotion (Wiseman and Start, 1965). Presumably some experience of teaching is an advantage, but it is also possible to have too much, so that the experience of learning to teach is remote. Similarly, being a good lecturer could easily be a handicap in appreciating the difficulties of others, just as being good at mathematics does not necessarily enable one to teach it. An athletics coach need not be better than the athletes at athletics but needs to be good as a coach. Being able to do something is different from knowing what to do and getting others to do it.

Relying on subjective experience is not enough. Aspects of experts' personalities will affect their judgments. For example, Cicirelli (1969) has shown that supervisors with differing scores on tests of creativity observed and used various features of student-teachers' behavior. Their diagnoses and assessments consequently differed. Less creative supervisors tended to give specific recommendations on how teaching could be improved, while creative supervisors were more concerned with overall objectives, planning, and organization.

Consultants should have a good knowledge of lecture research and have tested and trained their subjective impressions against independent objective criteria. Too few staff developers have undergone this discipline. One exception is Cartmell (1971), who was able to observe fourteen behaviors that correlated highly with his judgment of a good teacher. He videotaped the behavior of sixty trainee lecturers and correlated twenty-three aspects of their performances with subjective judgments of their merit on a numerical scale, course marks, Eysenck's Personality Inventory, the Occupational Interest Questionnaire, and other tests. Trainees rated in the top 30 percent tended to be younger, stable extroverts who were interested both in people and the job. Those in the middle 40 percent were not so extroverted, and the lowest 30 percent were not so interested in teaching. There was a significant correlation between overall course marks and the observations of the videotaped teaching; but whether this is best explained by the halo effect, trainee motivation, or some other common cause is difficult to say.

2. Difficulty in Facing Oneself

It is still relatively rare in colleges and universities for lecturers to invite educationalists or other colleagues to their lectures. In the long run, it seems doubtful whether this isolation benefits anyone. Discussion of techniques and difficulties is most practical when there are observations in common.

Lecturers may hesitate to invite colleagues because they fear being judged by others. Most faculty are sensitive about their reputations. But confidentiality and reciprocal observations could be conditions of the invitation. In any case, it is better to have a reputation based on careful observation than on casual remarks and hearsay gossip.

However, the fear of observation is not as simple as this. Few lecturers take the opportunity to make audio or video recordings of their lectures privately, confidentially, and available to themselves alone (Beard, 1970). Yet in most institutions the opportunity exists. Thus the fear of visitors comes partly from difficulty in facing oneself. Once this difficulty has been overcome, it is easier on later occasions provided the delay is not too long.

If you do videotape yourself, encourage six to ten students from the class to take time out and view it with you. My experience is that in the informal situation students not only comment on lecture technique but ask a lot of questions about lecture content that help them and show the lecturers in detail where the lectures could improve. More important, the cooperative relationship thus fostered lasts until and beyond the students' graduation. Why? Because the lecturer and the student have trusted one another where they feel vulnerable: their incompetence and their ignorance, respectively.

3. Procedures and Principles of Consultation

In my work as a consultant, there are typically eleven steps in the evaluation process (Figure 13.2).

a. Lecturer Approaches Consultant. First, I am approached by a lecturer, usually in casual conversation and often more by a hint rather than direct invitation. It is not I who makes the first move, nor will I respond to requests by the department head or other administrators to "inspect" one of their staff. Trust is of the essence. The lecturers' consent or willingness is not enough; they must actively want the available support. Since the casual context is generally unsuitable to take the conversation further, I usually arrange a time and place where we can meet privately.

b. Progressive Focus on Information Required. At that meeting, my task is to narrow the investigation down to exactly what the lecturer wants and needs. Essentially what I hope to provide is information. It might be about any of the things mentioned in this book—for example, how the lecturer uses handouts or lecture signals, how key points are presented, lecture speed, what techniques are used to maintain attention, and so on. To provide information about conceptual vagueness is tricky because that information is close to the lecture content, of which I

FIGURE 13.2. TYPICAL SEQUENCE OF PROFESSIONAL EVALUATION.

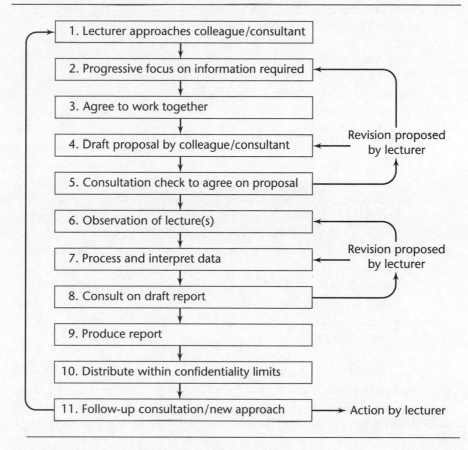

am ignorant. Lecturing is so complex I cannot undertake to evaluate, or even observe, everything. If what lecturers want and my perception of their needs differ, I may have to use some counseling skills. In particular, I shall need to empathize with their feelings and clarify the problems if there are any, without controlling them. Teaching situations are conflict situations. Part of the clarification process is to recognize the conflicts the lecturers must face. I am not seeking to change their styles, but I may create opportunities for lecturers to consider changes for themselves. The conversations are often also an educational process for us both.

c. Agreement to Work Together. I need to employ some negotiation skills. Essentially we are working toward a "contract." As any consultant would, I may need to recognize that I am not the best person to help. But if we agree to work together (and it is a joint undertaking, not a one-sided operation), we usually finish with my promising to draft a proposal within a week for the lecturer's approval.

d. Draft Proposal. The draft proposal is like a miniresearch proposal. Indeed, that is its ethos. So far as possible (and in many respects it is not possible), the evaluation should be a scientific investigation. Its aims, procedures, observation instrument(s), and methods of data processing and interpretation are briefly specified. By *scientific* I don't necessarily mean the narrow sense of hypothesis testing. On the contrary, what I usually attempt is a description, first that the lecturers will accept as reasonably objective (in the sense that others, including the lecturers, would make the same observations), and second that the lecturers will be able to interpret for themselves. Lecturers are more likely to act upon their own interpretations.

Very often, the proposals are to confirm or quantify some behavior reported in the preliminary survey. Recording will enable the lecturer to confirm my observations. Providing the lecturers are willing for me to attend, I make paper-and-pencil notes against either the precise time or the counter number on the recorder.

The most common instruments are the student rating questionnaire and some more direct and objective assessment of student learning. These are dealt with in the next two sections of this chapter.

e. Consultation Check to Agree on Proposal. There is a consultation to make sure all involved agree on what is to be done, including who else, if anyone, will receive copies of the eventual report. As Figure 13.2 shows, if changes are agreed, certain steps in the consultation process are recycled.

f. Observation of Lecture(s). Once agreement is reached, the observation instrument will be produced and used in the lecture(s) agreed. The instrument is not necessarily anything very sophisticated. Usually it is a list of behaviors to observe. When observing teaching, I try to remember the principle that different lecturers are good in different ways; so consultants and colleagues should look for talents that can be developed, rather than faults to be corrected.

Observing the behaviors of students is more difficult partly because lecture theaters are not designed to observe the audience, and partly because pertinent behaviors come and go so quickly that there is no time to focus cameras or even scribble a note.

g. Process and Interpret Data. As in any investigation, once the data have been gathered, the consultant, as the researcher, will process and interpret them.

h. Consult on Draft Report. As a professional consultant, I reckon to produce a written report. A lecturer's colleagues would probably not do so. They would go straight to step k.

I invite lecturers to correct any factual errors and suggest revisions. Very infrequently, the lecturer has wanted something changed because, if it got into the hands of Professor X or Dr. Y in another context, it would be interpreted quite differently. In practice, most lecturers see it as a matter of integrity not to change what I have written; but if they do, we jointly go over the data and my interpretations of them.

Whenever I think lecturers are very sensitive, I consult them on interpretations of observed facts before I write these matters into the report. In other words, I write the report up to and including the results section, but we talk about the discussion section before I write the results.

I also need to check at this stage that my recommendations are feasible and acceptable. To some extent my recommendations are negotiated. I am conscious of the principle that there is no one right way to give a lecture and that variety, not a model, is to be encouraged. So I try to elicit from lecturers what they see as their talents—or, if modesty forbids them, at least find out the techniques with which they would feel most comfortable. These are the abilities that need to be extended and developed into new techniques to overcome, or compensate for, any difficulties. For example, it is no use trying to develop powers of oratory for a lecturer who is shy and sensitive. Far better to develop that sensitivity into an attribute of a caring and meticulous teacher. Then both kinds of lecturer can be valued for their distinctive contribution.

i. Produce Report. Once agreed, the final report is produced.

j. Distribute Report (Within Limits of Confidentiality). It is distributed or made available on request only as previously agreed. When other people have contributed to the research (and that may include students), I operate a convention that copies should be available to the contributors; but this must have been agreed at step e.

k. Follow-up Consultation; New Approach. Follow-up consultations are very important. Have the lecturers implemented the recommendations? Do they want any help in doing so? Would they like a follow-up investigation to monitor changes?

Even before I ask these questions, a most constructive follow-up is to enlist the support of students in a three-way meeting among the students, the lecturer, and the consultant. Theoretically the consultant chairs the meeting, but such meetings are always most constructive if they are very informal and afford a free interchange of ideas among students and the lecturer.

Students' Opinions

It is hard to think of an area of educational inquiry that has been more heavily researched than this one. There are literally thousands of studies. Though most are concerned with teaching in general rather than lectures in particular, it is impossible to give here all the lessons to be learned from them.

1. Reasons for Obtaining Students' Opinions

Gathering students' opinions is by far the most common method to evaluate lectures. Yet there is a curious logic about seeking them. In most consumer surveys, researchers use questionnaires and interviews to find out something about the consumers, not the product. The qualities of the soap powder, or whatever the product is, can be studied by more scientific methods. But in the case of teaching, it is assumed that student surveys tell us something not about the students but about the teaching. It depends on the question asked. Yet it is hard to see any difference in principle from the methods used to find out about consumers. The truth is, there are lecturers, students, and interactions between them. Students' opinions will reflect all three. Surely the corresponding way to study the qualities of a lecture is to observe, classify, experiment, interpret, or do whatever else scientists do.

So, why seek students' opinions?

a. The Argument That Customers Are Always Right. It is said that the customers are always right. Except that we all know they often are not. This view has been most forcibly expressed by J. A. Johnson (1967): "It is often the individual student who knows best whether or not he is learning. It is the student who knows best when he cannot understand or already knows what is being discussed. It is the student who knows whether a course is stimulating him to learn more about a subject or whether it is boring him to death. . . . It is the student who can best evaluate when he is beginning to integrate the process of learning with the problems he continually confronts in life" (pp. 289–290). We shall see later that each of these four claims is highly contentious. I shall argue that although students' opinions of specific lectures are reliable in the sense that they are consistent, and although they are undoubtedly the authority on some matters, on others the validity of their opinions as measured against objective tests remains uncertain. Nevertheless, they are useful impressions to obtain. Students' evaluations of lecturers and courses are statistically reliable, but evidence of their validity is also at present inconclusive.

b. Complex Judgments Are Possible. It can be argued that objective tests of lecture effectiveness are highly selective, but the human mind is wonderful. It makes countless complex evaluations every day. The range of factors unconsciously considered in any one such judgment is much greater than could be listed in any reasonably sized objective test. The factors and their interactions in the lecture situation should be given weight according to circumstances. Objective tests are not flexible in this way, and the most sophisticated statistical techniques cannot do justice to complex interactions in a classroom.

c. *Superficially, Subjective Opinions Are Easily Gathered.* Questionnaires with rating scales are quick to administer to a captive audience at the end of a lecture. They neither arouse the opposition of students nor the anxiety that they personally are being tested. The data are numerical, giving the false impression that it represents quantities, rather than qualities and value judgments. With that impression go a collection of statistical assumptions when the data are processed by readily available computer programs. Numerical data also give the impression that they can be used to compare lecturer X with lecturer Y, even if they teach different subjects to different students. Opinions are not measures. They are pointers to areas that could benefit from further study.

d. *The Observer Effect Is Removed.* The presence of observers or the knowledge that one is being tested may interfere with the teaching situation itself. Arguably, students' opinions are less open to this kind of uncertainty principle.

e. *Valid Opinions, or Are They?* Insofar as ratings by students are indications of their opinions, they are necessarily valid. (Whether they are valid indications of lecture effectiveness is a question we must consider later.) A lecturer cannot afford to neglect student reactions, for even if students are at first incorrect in believing that Professor Y's lectures are of little value, the consequent decline in motivation will make their judgment a self-fulfilling one, especially if their disenchantment results in absenteeism.

In my opinion, it is knowing students' reactions, valid or not, that is the strongest justification for collecting students' opinions. This information contributes to a constructive dialogue of mutual cooperation between lecturer and students each to assist the other. It is not a matter of praise, blame, or passing judgment. Compared with the lecturer's subjective impressions, the use of questionnaires is more systematic than chance verbal or nonverbal feedback. It also obtains data from a larger proportion of the students.

For constructive dialogue, it is advisable to obtain some knowledge of students' reactions after about one-tenth of the course has been completed. Because courses are so varied, the figure of one-tenth may require modification, but the third week in a one-year course, or the end of the second week of a fifteen-week semester, is a suitable time. It should be borne in mind that the purpose of student evaluation is to modify a course to suit the students' needs. Thus, to leave it until much later allows little time to compensate for weaknesses and makes established habits and routines difficult to break. Because the end of one course and before the beginning of another is frequently a time for replanning, there should normally be a further evaluation at the end of the course. Whether intermediate ones are used will depend on whether they can serve a useful purpose for the students.

2. Devising the Questionnaire

Accepting, therefore, that lecturers should adopt some form of evaluation by students, what method should be used? Interviews are time consuming. The preliminary inquiry uses open, free-response, and fairly comprehensive questions. That may discourage their further use. Rating scales are by far the most common method.

The use of rating scales will not make the judgments objective; they merely substitute a number of subjective judgments for more comprehensive ones. But they may ensure that students consider a range of criteria and provide quasi-numerical estimates on which it is thought that a more general opinion should be based. Even so, the halo effect is likely to operate. (This is a distortion such that an opinion on one issue influences ratings on other items.) For example, Rugg found that ratings of army officers showed less variation when the instructors were previously known to the judges (Rugg, 1921, 1922). This suggests that lecturers are more likely to obtain guidance on specific features of their teaching techniques if they invite relative strangers to assist them.

There are other factors to consider when devising the questionnaire. Students who are not used to rating scales are sometimes inclined to opt for the middle positions, especially if there are only three from which to choose. For this reason, I prefer a 6-point, or even an 8-point, scale, but this is not the usual practice. Also, anonymity is essential, and if follow-up comparisons are to be made later, pseudonyms can be used to match responses. It is important to ensure that the evaluation is completed by all students; otherwise the personality factors affecting the selectivity of response would probably give an unbalanced impression. I therefore recommend that questionnaires be completed during class time. It is also advisable that space be left for free comments and time made available for follow-up discussion if the full meaning of the ratings is to be apparent.

3. What Should Be Evaluated?

The choice should be guided by the purpose of the evaluation. These might be (1) to improve lectures; (2) to assess the lecturer, possibly to inform personnel decisions; or (3) in some cases to help students choose courses. In this book I am primarily concerned with improvement. Improvement is only possible if the lecturer is so motivated, if the evaluation provides relevant information, and if alternative lecturer behavior is possible.

The preliminary inquiry should indicate what areas may need further study. In other words, it is best if student evaluations are purposely designed to throw light upon particular problems experienced by a specific lecturer or group of students.

However, all too often evaluators take or adapt a questionnaire designed by someone else. An implicit assumption of this approach is that there is a standardized set of model criteria to which the lecturer should conform. With a little thought, most people would regard this assumption as false. Students and universities need variety, not conformity.

Where did the set of model criteria come from? Very often, out of the original evaluators' heads. Typically, a very long list is prepared on a 5-point rating scale and given to a very large sample of students to evaluate a large number of lecturers. Numerical values are given to each point on the scales and a factor analysis to identify the factors underlying students' judgments is carried out. Items contributing strongly to the main factors are then included in a shortened questionnaire, though typically even this questionnaire is long. Factor analysis assumes (possibly correctly) that students' opinions are based on relatively few underlying factors. The exclusion of any item not associated with any of the main factors assumes that it is not important, or at least not important for students in their opinion. But some poorly associated items could be very important (for example, audibility). Because it only takes one element of a lecture to vitiate the whole, a similar problem could arise if a crucial item is absorbed within a factor. Again, my advice is to keep it simple. Statistics can mislead.

Two broad factors constantly recur in published reports. One concerns clarity of subject matter; the other is rapport in personal relationships. With this in mind (notwithstanding my cautions that evaluations should be purpose designed and simple), where an evaluation is general rather than focusing on specific aspects of lecturing, intending evaluators would be wise to include items related to these two factors—or at least have reasons for not doing so. As you will see below, they relate to almost everything of importance in lecturing.

a. Clarity of Subject Matter. This factor might include items on lecture organization, its speed, the clarity of its purpose, visual aids, summaries, effective use of time, lecturers' knowledge of the subject, and care in preparation. Items contributing to this factor are typically related to issues discussed principally in Chapter Two and Parts One, Three, and Five of this book.

b. Rapport. Rapport includes a wide range of items dealing with the interaction between lecturers and their audience. The items have more to do with feelings than subject matter (stimulating interest being both). They include personal style, questioning techniques, opportunities for discussion, inspiring interest, responsiveness to the audience, and general personal characteristics. In this book, Chapters Three, Four, Eleven, Twelve, Thirteen, Fourteen, and Sixteen and Part Four are particularly relevant.

Most researchers find more than two factors, depending on the balance of items included, but they can usually be classified under these two headings. For example, Feldman (1976) reviewed a large number of studies and concluded that students are consistently concerned with eight factors:

1. Clarity
2. Enthusiasm
3. Stimulation of interest
4. Friendliness
5. Preparation
6. Helpfulness
7. Knowledge of subject matter
8. Openness to others' opinions

How would you classify them?

c. Global Value Judgments. A small number of researchers (see Cranton and Smith, 1990) have also found a factor consisting of global value judgments—for example, ratings on how much was learned, the significance of the content, lecture effectiveness, interest generated, and overall value.

Of course, the factors obtained are only as good as the original list. It is strangely rare for lecturers to consult their students about items that might be included in student evaluation questionnaires (though the preliminary inquiry does). To do so would foster a spirit of mutual help. Hodgson and McConnell (1985) used personal construct theory to elicit areas of concern to students rather than the preconceptions of lecturers. Students were asked in what way two lecturers were alike but different from a third. The criteria thus elicited were students' mental constructs. When classified, the nine most important were:

Criterion Construct	*Number of Times Mentioned*
Content of lecture	61
Lecturer's attitude to students	59
Structure and organization of lecture	51
Stimulation and maintenance of interest	46
Lecturer's enthusiasm for subject	32

Encourages student participation	32
Pace of lecture	27
Lecturer's knowledge of subject	20
Lecturer's ability to put subject over	14

A second stage of the project elicited further criteria:

- Students' general attitude to the lecturer
- Students' perceptions of the lecturer
- Ease of note taking
- Use of audiovisual aids
- Clarity of explanations

Though Hodgson and McConnell's sample was heavily weighted toward the social sciences, in the present context their study has the advantage that it focused specifically on lectures, not other teaching methods.

4. The Potent Variable in Students' Opinions

I suggested earlier that students' opinions of lectures may reflect characteristics of the students as much as the characteristics of the lecture or lecturer. There is not much evidence to suggest that the age or sex of students is related to their ratings; nor is the sex of the lecturer. Ratings tend to be more favorable if students have an interest in the subject, have opted to attend the lectures or take the course, and found them a challenge. There is a slight tendency for ratings to be higher if they are anonymous, if the purpose of the evaluation is known, when the lecturer is present, and if the lecturer has a distinguished reputation for research. Inconsistent findings have been obtained to show higher ratings for more senior professors, when students expect or have obtained good grades, and for lecturers in arts and humanities compared with sciences and engineering. There is some reason to think that small classes and very large ones are preferred to classes around forty or fifty.

Caution should be observed when interpreting these generalizations. They are partly based upon ratings of courses of which lectures were only a part. Still, it could be argued that this is reasonable because opinions of lectures cannot be separated from their social and institutional context. The large number of students involved results in low correlations being statistically significant even when the variable has little if any effect upon the rating. In any case, correlations do not imply causes; so it does not necessarily follow that ratings of lectures are biased by these student characteristics. Even if they were so biased, the bias would be reasonable if the students' characteristics genuinely influenced their learning.

This catalog might lead you to think that evaluators can ignore the characteristics of students who express opinions about their teachers. Needless to say, this is not true.

The question is, What characteristics are important, and what if anything do lecturers need to do about them? Look at Table 13.1. Students expect a variety of things from their lecturers, but except for the "Enjoys lecturing" and "Likes students" (in Part A), there is a common dimension underlying the differences. Some students crave certainty: they want facts, clear objectives, a full set of notes, and attainable standards. Others tolerate uncertainties, controversies, and ambiguities; they welcome a framework but want to explore ideas and do their own thinking.

Similar contrasts, but with different labels, can be found in the work of other researchers. Marton and his disciples (1984) have described as having a "surface level approach" students who want lectures to cover the ground, who concentrate on memorizing detail, and who expect to find the "right" answer to questions. These contrast with students adopting a deep approach, who are concerned with a lecture's central point, what lies behind the argument, what it boils down to, the logic of the argument, getting the whole picture, and challenging the conclusions. Parlett (1970) described "syllabus bound" students, who only study what they are required to study, want the lecturer to give clear instructions, do not often question things they hear from professors in lectures, and are more focused on exams than interested in their discipline. "Syllabus free" students, by contrast, explore ideas not mentioned in lectures, try to think of a better way of doing something than what is described in a lecture, and generally display independence of mind. Perry (1970) also describes freshmen starting their university careers believing it is the job of lecturers to dispense truths, and finishing regarding lecturers' knowledge and values as contextual and relative. Feldman and Newcomb (1973) cite more than thirty studies showing students becoming less authoritarian, less dogmatic, less ethnocentric, and less prejudiced during their time at college.

Two implications are of interest. First, in most disciplines it is the duty of faculty to try to wean students away from craving dogma and toward rational independence of thought. This will best be achieved by placing students in small groups, where their own ideas are tested and where they must confront the views of others. In the lecture room, this is best achieved by using buzz groups, not by lecturing (Chapter Eighteen).

Second, though I accept that the variable I have described is multidimensional, its relationship to students' evaluations of lectures (or indeed of lecturers and courses) has been curiously neglected. The personalities of lecturers have not. Yet all this research suggests that craving for certainty may be the most potent

TABLE 13.1. PERCENTAGE OF STUDENTS RATING
LECTURERS' CHARACTERISTICS AS "ESSENTIAL" OR "DESIRABLE."

Part A

	Engineering	Life Sciences	Physical Sciences	Arts and Social Sciences
Speaks slowly enough for full notes to be taken	87*	82*	66**	62**
Talks around brief notes	19*	27	25	35**
Provides essentials as a framework	46*	70**	56*	81**
Takes distinctive line on unresolved problems	20*	37	38**	47**
Gives references	81*	89	90	92**
Enjoys lecturing	78*	82*	61**	66**
Likes students	76*	70	61**	57**

Part B

	Extroverts	Introverts
Is entertaining	71*	53**
Appears confident	87*	70**

Part C

	Unstable	Stable
Stimulates independent thought	82*	97**
Presents all sides of a controversy noncommittally	50*	68**
Speaks slowly enough for full notes to be taken	80*	65**
Sets attainable standard	74*	56**

Part D

	Unstable Introverts	Other Students
Reads out notes relevant to the exams	71*	44**
Allows exercise of the imagination	53*	79**
Takes a distinctive line on controversy	24*	48**
Explores ideas not in the textbooks	59*	77**

Part E

	High Dogmatism	Low Dogmatism
Sets clear objectives	85*	64**
Sets attainable standard	83*	51**
Gives summary handout	57*	38**
Prepares thoroughly	93*	77**
Keeps to the point	76*	57**
Links with other work	91*	64**
Uses appropriate visual aids	49*	25**
Shows clear blackboard organization	70*	49**

Note: * is significantly different from ** at the 5 percent level.

Source: Smithers, 1970a, 1970b.

variable. It could also be a variable that might invalidate students' evaluations because—if too many students are seeking the wrong thing from lectures, namely, the certainty of indubitable knowledge—the criteria for their evaluations would be inappropriate.

5. Students' Opinions Are Reliable

There is no doubt that students' evaluations of teaching are highly reliable in the sense that they are consistent. This has been found repeatedly in research for more than seventy years (Remmers, 1934; Heilman and Armentrout, 1936; Guthrie, 1954; Lovell and Haner, 1955; Remmers's review, 1963; Spencer and Aleamoni, 1970; Harvey and Barker, 1970; Costin, Greenough, and Menges's review, 1971; the series of articles by Feldman, 1976–1989; Abrami, Perry, and Leventhal, 1982; Marsh, 1984b; and Murray, Rushton, and Paunonen, 1990; to name but a few). The reliability coefficients are consistently in the range 0.7 to 0.9, whether the same students rate a lecturer more than once, or different students rate the same lecturer.

In fact, the consistency can be galling. One lecturer obtained ratings on forty-four criteria and then, using this detailed information, spent two years working hard to improve his lectures. When he gave the same rating scale to a later cohort, he was dismayed to find that the ratings hardly changed at all. The correlation would only have occurred by chance once in two thousand times (Foy, 1969).

6. The Validity of Students' Opinions Is Modest and Inconsistent

The validity of students' ratings of lectures is far more doubtful. No account would be complete without mentioning studies in educational seduction. An actress was introduced to a class of education and health professionals as "the distinguished educator Dr. Myron Fox." She gave a lecture almost devoid of content on an unfamiliar topic, but in an enthusiastic and expressive manner using eye contact and every conceivable nonverbal skill. The lecturer was rated highly not only for personal expressive qualities but also for the lecture content (Natfulin, Ware, and Donnelly, 1973)!

Though the study was criticized for having no control group, a poor evaluation instrument, and a rather brief lecture, confidence in the validity of students' opinions has never been quite the same ever since. Replications have adopted a standard 3 x 2 design with three levels of lecture content and two of expressiveness; they have also assessed students' learning and opinions. Their broad conclusions are that expressiveness affects students' opinions and has a small effect upon learning, while the content affects learning with only a small effect upon students' opinions (e.g. a meta-analysis by Abrami, Leventhal, and Perry, 1982). As mentioned in Chapter Four, expressiveness increases student motivation; but if other incentives are introduced, particularly before the lecture, overall motivation is not further enhanced (Marsh, 1984a).

The validity of students' judgments will depend upon what they are judging. There are some matters on which they are the authority. If students tell me they cannot hear what I say or cannot read what is projected on the screen, I should not normally doubt them. If they tell me they don't understand the point I'm making, I believe them. But when they tell me they do, experience has made me more skeptical. I reckon I'm a better authority on whether they understood!

Ratings are much more likely to be valid with reference to variables to which they are logically or theoretically related. For example, we might expect responses to the item "The lecturer is inspiring" to be valid with reference to students choosing further courses with that lecturer, but much less valid for example with reference to how often the lecturer gives handouts as a lecture guide. This is why ratings should be specific. Specific ratings also give more direction for lecturers seeking to improve their techniques.

In other words, the question "Are students' opinions valid?" begs the question "Valid for what purpose?" The most obvious way to test the validity of students' opinions of lectures is to argue that the purpose of lectures is student learning and to correlate students' ratings of their learning with objective tests of their learning. But things are not that simple.

The results of that procedure give remarkably inconsistent and contradictory results. Consider "Professor Smith's" lectures. Most of his topics are moderately difficult. The more gifted students gain satisfaction by responding to the challenge. The less gifted struggle, know they are struggling, and get a little frustrated. Consequently the gifted students rate "I learned a lot from this lecture" favorably and score well on an objective test. Less gifted students rate that item unfavorably and score badly on the test. The result? A positive correlation between ratings and test scores. The following week's lecture is on an easy topic. The gifted students say "I knew all that already," rate it low and score highly on the test. Less able students say "Thank God, at last I've understood something" and rate the lecture highly, but they still score much lower than their peers on the test. The result? A negative correlation. Clearly, the invalidity here (Figure 13.3) results from variables among individual students.

However, multisection studies using class averages, rather than scores for individual students, are not vulnerable to this criticism, provided differences between class sections are controlled and the size of class sections is sufficiently large for individual variables to even out. Most multisection studies evaluate courses rather than lectures specifically; but these, too, give inconsistent results. Abrami (Abrami, Cohen, and d'Apollonia, 1988; Abrami, d'Apollonia, and Cohen, 1990) found

FIGURE 13.3. ONE EXPLANATION
FOR INCONSISTENT VALIDITY STUDIES.

more than forty such studies, together with six reviews of them. The reviews came to markedly different conclusions. For example, Cohen (1981) said "the present meta-analysis provides strong support for the validity of student ratings as measures of teaching effectiveness. Teachers whose students do well on achievement measures receive higher instructional ratings than teachers who do poorly." By contrast, seeing widely varying validity coefficients, Dowell and Neal (1982, 1983) said "the literature can be seen as yielding unimpressive estimates of the validity of student ratings." In their later paper, they said student ratings are "indicators of student satisfaction rather than teaching effectiveness."

Abrami, d'Apollonia, and Cohen (1990) reworked Cohen's data. Cohen (1981) had classified the validity coefficients relative to student achievement from studies he reviewed into ten categories—two general (course and instructor) and eight rather more specific (Figure 13.4).

Not only did Abrami and colleagues now regard these average validity coefficients as modest, but as Figure 13.4 shows, the coefficients were very wide ranging. They therefore concluded it was premature to say that students' evaluations of teaching are valid (Table 13.2). They also concluded that because the correlations between the ten sets of validity coefficients were low, it is both conceptually and empirically reasonable to analyze these factors separately. This reinforces my advice not to try to evaluate everything at once.

The validity of students' opinions can also be tested against criteria other than student learning. For example, the invalidity of students' opinions has also been found with respect to their judgments of lecture speed. A tape-recorded forty-five-minute lecture in three parts was played to three groups of students such that each group heard parts spoken at different speeds. Half the students perceived no vari-

FIGURE 13.4. THE UNRELIABILITY OF VALIDITY COEFFICIENTS.

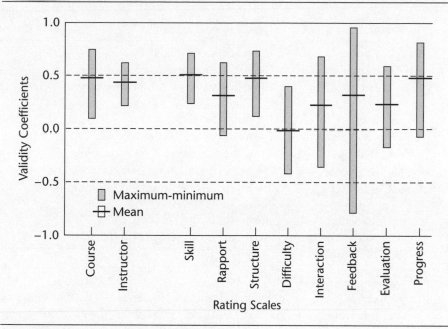

Source: Data from Cohen, 1981; see Table 13.2 below.

ation in speed—although the fastest was twice the speed of the slowest—and only 10 percent placed the three parts in the correct order of speed (Bligh, 1974). In another experiment, expressed intention to read more about a lecture topic had no bearing on whether they actually did read about it, even though it may have indicated the degree of initial interest aroused by the lecture.

7. Conclusion on Students' Opinions

It will be seen from the evidence cited that the chief correlates of students' opinions of lecturers are features of their own personalities, courses, and learning strategies. It is always dangerous to step from correlation to causation, but if we assume that their personalities and course interests affect their judgments, this would explain their highly significant reliability but modest and varied validity where other independent measures have been obtained. In other words, students' opinions of their lectures may reflect the nature of the students as much as that of the lectures.

It does not follow from this that lecturers need not bother to seek students' opinions. Quite the contrary, if students' personalities are unlikely to change very quickly, it is lecturers who may have to change their techniques, because it is the

TABLE 13.2. FACTORS IN COHEN'S META-ANALYSIS.

Factor	Typical Item	Average Validity Coefficient
1. Course	This is an excellent course	.47
2. Instructor	The instructor is an excellent teacher	.43
3. Skill	The instructor has a good command of subject matter	.50
4. Rapport	The instructor is friendly	.31
5. Course structure	The instructor uses time well	.47
6. Difficulty	The instructor assigns difficult reading	−.02
7. Interaction	The instructor facilitates class discussion	.22
8. Feedback	The instructor keeps students informed of their progress	.31
9. Evaluation	The examinations are fair	.23
10. Student progress	I have learned a great deal in this course	.47

lecturer who initially controls the teaching situation. To do this appropriately, the lecturer will need to know students' reactions. Thus the chief purpose of ascertaining students' opinions of a lecture is to help the lecturer help the students, not to pass judgment on the lecturer. It is for this reason that they are useful early in a course and when planning the next.

Assessment of Learning Objectives Achieved

If the opinions of students are rejected as invalid, the most satisfactory way to evaluate a lecture's effectiveness will be to test the students' learning directly. This may be done by one-word answer tests of the key points or multiple-choice questions. But the first may produce a reaction of "We're being treated like school children" and the second takes a considerable time to prepare if the "distractors" (the false answers) are to be suitably plausible and if a variety of objectives are to be tested. The first may be avoided if the purpose is carefully explained; then the students too can obtain feedback by marking their own answers (which also saves the lecturer's time) and anonymity is preserved by handing in answer sheets en masse. (If questions are given on a handout, it is advisable to duplicate a few spares, as there are usually some students who wish to take a copy away with them.)

Before going any further, you are asked to imagine that Chapter Two has been presented to you as a lecture. I now invite you to fill in the questionnaire in Figure 13.5.

FIGURE 13.5. AN EXAMPLE OF A "TRUTH-FUNCTIONAL TEST."

If you have read Chapter Two you are invited to attempt the following question-naire. All the questions consist of a statement. You are asked to say whether you agree, disagree, or don't know. Please work briskly. If you do not know, it is quicker to say so. If you have some idea but are not certain, it is better to guess.

Place an X through the circle of your choice.

	Agree	Don't Know	Disagree
1. Repetition consolidates learning	O	O	O
2. One reason why words in the middle of a list suffer from proactive and retroactive interference is that they are not remembered so well	O	O	O
3. The capacities of long-term and working memories provide evidence that they are different in kind	O	O	O
4. If you practice playing table tennis with your right hand, your left-hand game will improve	O	O	O
5. All evidence for there being two kinds of memory has been obtained by psychologists observing other people and animals	O	O	O

6. A and B are matched groups:

Group A	(1) Memory task	(2)	(3) Test of memory task
Group B	(1) Memory task	(2) Undemanding dissimilar task	(3) Test of memory task

	Agree	Don't Know	Disagree
The results of the above experimental design could reasonably be claimed to demonstrate the effects of rehearsal	O	O	O
7. No experiment on forgetting can rule out the effects of retroactive interference	O	O	O
8. Lecturers' understanding of short-term memory should enhance their empathy for students taking notes in lectures	O	O	O

Thank you.

Note: The preferred answers appear at the end of this chapter.

This test design, devised as a research tool to study the relative effectiveness of presentations such as lectures and lecture scripts, is called a truth-functional test because in principle the statements may be constructed so that they have a particular relationship in truth-functional logic to statements given in the presentation (Bligh, 1970b, 1974). This means that not only may it be objectively marked, but unlike most other tests it is objective in its construction. Furthermore, the logical relationship can be varied to test different kinds of thought; it rebuts the criticism often made of objective tests that they don't.

1. Recognition of a Key Point

Question 1 of Figure 13.5 tests recognition of one key phrase. In other words, it tests the memory of a "key point" that was made. It only tests one idea.

2. Memory of a Simple Stated Relationship

Question 2 tests recognition of a reason that was presented (see Figure 13.6). That is, it tests memory of a relationship between two ideas—the fact that one is the reason for the other. It will be seen that the cause and the effect have been reversed in the question. This kind of inversion is one of the most common errors in reasoning by students who find it difficult to distinguish between the truth of statements and the validity of the reasons for them. The strongest variable in these tests is the subject matter. Using a question like this immediately after a lecture, only 41 percent got it right when correction had been made for guessing (Bligh, 1974).

(This particular question also assumes some knowledge of how the terms *proactive* and *retroactive interference* are used, but since a person could confuse them and still get this question correct, it does not require a knowledge of their precise meaning.)

FIGURE 13.6. RECOGNITION OF REASON
PRESENTED IN QUESTION 2 OF FIGURE 13.5.

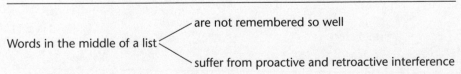

3. Making Simple Inferences

Question 3 of Figure 13.5 tests the ability to make a relatively simple inference and remember it:

1. There is a limit to the number of items one can hold in working memory at once.
2. There does not appear to be a limit to the number of ideas in long-term memory.

One is then expected to assume that:

3. The difference between there being a limit and no limit is a difference in kind.

and infer that:

4. Working and long-term memories are different in kind.

It should be noticed that truth-functional tests require students to relate meanings of presented propositions, not their precise words. Just as Question 2 tested more than recognition, Question 3 tests more than memory of a relationship. It tests simple comprehension because it requires the ability to manipulate presented information in certain simple ways. Immediately after a lecture using the words of Chapter Two, 37 percent were judged to have answered a question like this correctly (once corrections for guessing were made).

4. Application

Question 4 tests the ability to apply the information that has been acquired. Thus it requires more than relating ideas that were given; it requires the student to relate examples that were not presented, to general principles that were. In this case, the principle given was summed up in the phrase "practice of one skill affects the performance of similar skills." The student has to select the principle as relevant, and then apply it. Questions to test application essentially consist of supplying an instance of a generalization that was presented. In tests given to students, 85 percent got this question right after corrections for guessing. (However, this item illustrates a problem. The pretest score was positive and therefore had to be subtracted to assess learning.)

5. Analytical Thought

Logically, questions like number five in Figure 13.5 require that the students check whether "all A is B." Question 5 requires the student to check through the five kinds of evidence presented and ask of each kind, "Is it obtained by observing other people and animals?" It therefore assumes that students will remember all instances of A (that is, the kinds of evidence). It is an analytical mental process because the student must consider a characteristic (that is, B) of all instances of A. Because the characteristic in this instance is a methodological one, it is more abstract than many analytical questions and could be said to require some judgment in addition to analytic thought. In addition to "all A is B," statements of the forms

Some A is not B.

Some A is B.

No A is B.

will test analytic thought.

Because critical thinking often requires checking all the instances of a concept, these analytical questions are very useful in training students in critical thought, as well as being an indication of the thought processes permitted by lectures.

6. Synthesis

To answer Question 6, students must ask themselves, *If I want to demonstrate the effects of rehearsal, what experimental design will I need?* To answer this, they will require a creative act (by which I do not mean "original" except in the sense of being original to the individual). It is a constructive process of making a decision or proposal. In this sense, it may be described as "synthetic." If they come to the conclusion *I must have two matched groups, one that can rehearse and one that cannot, and then compare results,* they will first need to analyze the design given in the question to see if it fits their requirements, and then check whether necessary controls are observed.

This type of question is difficult because it requires analytical thinking in addition to the synthetic process. It is also difficult to set because highly critical students may see weaknesses in the proposed design and therefore reject it. Although this kind of student will compensate on the analytic and judgmental questions, it may seem unfair to penalize them for this virtue here. In some respects, it is true to life that the critical mind is uncreative, and if this is so, perhaps one should not be too apologetic for the weakness. But it is a weakness nonetheless, and this is inevitable since creativity cannot be well tested by any question that admits only one correct answer.

Nevertheless, the frequent use of this kind of question may help to detect students with potential research ability more easily than by using projects that, when time permits only one or two in a course, are less reliable. The essential feature of these questions is to relate one's own ideas to ideas given in the presentation. This is difficult to do during a lecture. In fact, after adjustments for guessing, virtually no student got this item right after a lecture. This illustrates once again that thinking in lectures is either difficult or rare, or both. It also lends support to truth-functional tests as a research tool less vulnerable to the criticism that the thought takes place during the test rather than during the period assessed.

7. Evaluation

Question 7 requires different kinds of analyses and generalizations. For example, it requires a conceptual analysis of retroactive interference to appreciate that:

1. It refers to psychological events that follow the memory task.
2. Testing will follow the memory task.

After considering experimental situations, a further generalization is necessary to infer that:

3. Retroactive interference will always occur before testing in experiments on forgetting.

Having inferred that

4. Retroactive interference takes place in all experiments on forgetting.

the statement in the question will then be judged incorrect.

8. Attitudes

Question 8 is a test of attitude, yet it poses as a question of fact. Clearly, this book has failed if the reader is unsympathetic to this attitude. The important point here is that attitudes and values may be tested alongside cognitive skills, and this may produce a more genuine result if students are not conscious that their values are being examined.

The purpose of describing these eight types of question is to show that feedback on a variety of lecture objectives may be directly obtained by a form that is apparently uniform in design. The types here correspond with levels of thinking in Bloom's taxonomy of educational objectives (1956), but there is, in principle, a far wider range that could be assessed. Practice is required in designing questions of different types because most lecturers are not used to thinking in these terms. They are easy to mark and quick to administer. The test is amenable to marking by computer if required.

The provision of a "don't know" category and a marking scheme such that 2, 1, and 0 are awarded for answers of correct, don't know, and incorrect respectively can help to decrease guessing. In any case, the proportion of incorrect answers to don't-knows will give an indication of how far a student risks a guess (a caution-risk factor).

Although in general the more complex thought processes are more difficult, this is by no means always true. The familiarity and abstractness of the concepts involved are important variables here. Because students tend to agree with the statements given, questionnaires of this kind should have an equal number of preferred agreements and disagreements with each type of question.

9. Conclusion on Assessment of Objectives

The truth-functional test provides a method of testing a wide range of objectives directly. As with all such checks on lecture effectiveness, the cooperation of students should be sought. The tests also have a worthwhile teaching function by practicing students' thought in a variety of patterns, and there is room for much further development of the technique for this purpose.

Conclusion

The evaluation of teaching is probably the most heavily researched and controversial area in the study of education. Obviously, not all is about lecturing; even so, I am conscious that I cannot do justice to the controversies within the scope of this book. There are many relevant principles. Here are some underlying this chapter:

- Involvement: let lecturers initiate and be involved and consulted throughout.
- Purpose: be explicit about the purpose of the evaluation.
- Priorities: let improvement take priority over personnel and funding decisions.
- Competence: get expert advice.
- Relevance: tailor the evaluation to achieve that purpose, not something else.

- Individualization: don't use prepackaged evaluations; satisfy the individual's needs.
- Sampling: evaluate over time and courses.
- Multiple methods: use several methods.
- Criteria: use some open-ended questions.
- Objectivity: be cautious about opinions.
- Timing: early evaluation allows time to put things right.

Preferred Answers to Questions in Figure 13.5

1. Agree
2. Disagree
3. Agree
4. Disagree
5. Disagree
6. Agree
7. Disagree
8. Agree

CHAPTER FOURTEEN

OVERCOMING COMMON DIFFICULTIES

The use of inappropriate teaching methods.

  1. Diagnosing the difficulty.

  2. A possible solution.

Teaching at the students' level.

  1. Diagnosing the difficulty.

  2. Possible solutions.

Nerves.

  1. Consequences of the difficulty.

  2. Possible solutions.

Speed.

  1. The consequences of going too fast.

  2. Possible solutions.

The problem of large audiences.

  1. Diagnosing the difficulty.

  2. Diminishing the difficulty.

Lecturing skills can be learned.

It is easy to find fault with lecturers. Because lecturing is an art, no one style suits everyone, and probably no conscientious lecturer is ever wholly satisfied with his or her teaching. What is required is an understanding and diagnosis of the lecturer's difficulties coupled with constructive suggestions to overcome them or to make the best of them.

The purpose of this chapter is to diagnose and suggest, with reference to common difficulties of new lecturers not touched on elsewhere. However, since difficulties are frequently personal, the suggestions made here are necessarily a little hit-and-miss for the needs of the individual reader.

The Use of Inappropriate Teaching Methods

One of the most common mistakes by lecturers is to use the lecture method at all. For objectives classified as "the presentation of information," we have seen that the lecture method is no better than any other, and it is less effective for the promotion of thought and for changing attitudes.

Broadly speaking, available evidence suggests that reading, tape recordings, videotapes, summary handouts, programmed texts, and discussion methods are all as effective as lectures in teaching information—and, if self-paced, may be more effective with classes of mixed ability.

1. Diagnosing the Difficulty

Yet one must appreciate lecturers' difficulties. Because they have no other model or experience from which to draw, they are likely to conceive of their role in terms of the kind of behavior exhibited by their own teachers. The architecture of many lecture theaters makes the use of any other teaching methods extremely difficult. (Heads of expanding colleges are frequently blissfully unaware that they commit their teaching staffs to decades of inappropriate teaching methods when they accept an architect's plans.) Students' expectations and other social factors pressure lecturers to lecture. There are psychological constraints to play it safe because unknown methods are accompanied by fears of unforeseeable problems with unknown solutions. The choice of appropriate teaching methods is not difficult for those who have had some training for the task, but few lecturers have done more than attend a course for a few days. (Even the training for teaching in schools experienced by most college of education lecturers gives little guidance in recently developed methods in the teaching of adults.)

In short, the diagnosis of this difficulty is lack of professional training. Once the complex combination of skills required by a lecturer is appreciated, few will dispute that it is needed. Unfortunately, it is often not appreciated. (This book only touches on one teaching method of a possible thirty that a lecturer might need to use. Apart from knowledge of teaching methods, most lecturers require knowledge of how to specify objectives, student selection techniques, the selection and use of assessment techniques, and possibly some knowledge of administration and student counseling.)

2. A Possible Solution

The selection of the appropriate teaching method requires, first, analysis of the teaching objectives in terms of the psychological change required of the students; second, matching a method to the objectives; and third, the ability to carry out the method. This requires knowledge of psychology, especially occupational psychology, that few lecturers possess. Yet since most new lecturers are more than busy preparing the subject matter of their courses, even fewer are placed in a position to spend time on further study.

Although this book cannot provide professional training, Table 14.1 lists a number of teaching methods currently in use in continuing education and higher education together with the objectives they are said to achieve. If you say, as some others have when shown this list, "I've never heard of some of these teaching methods," perhaps this is further evidence in support of the diagnosis.

Teaching at the Students' Level

The second major difficulty of new lecturers is to get down to the students' level of understanding.

1. Diagnosing the Difficulty

Feeling a little unsure of their knowledge, some new lecturers overcompensate by a display of erudition. Others conscientiously feel that it will benefit the students if they are told everything they need to know. Thus the problem is one of both level and quantity.

This is the problem of trying to teach too much. However you measure it, studies show that students learn less than half of what a lecturer says (McLeish, 1968). McKeachie (1963) has shown that, up to a point, if you try to teach less, students learn more. It is a particular problem for lecturers who have recently been students themselves. Having usually been good students, they modestly fail to appreciate that the average student does not find the subject as easy or as interesting as they did. A characteristic of good students in examinations is that they are able to display a lot of knowledge and thought in very few words. This compact style is an excellent skill for timed examinations to be read by professors familiar with the subject; but it is almost the opposite of what is required when teaching. New lecturers may be tempted to think that they know what it is like to be a student because they have recently been one; whereas they only know what it is like to be a *good* student. They have read widely and become so immersed in their subject that they are aware of neither their assumptions nor the fact that the concepts

TABLE 14.1. SOME COMMON TEACHING METHODS AND APPROPRIATE OBJECTIVES.

Teaching Method	Commentary	Category of Primary Objectives
Audiotapes	These may be played to a whole class or individually	Guide practical work Variation of presentation method Knowledge of information Self-awareness Demonstration (e.g., of social interaction)
Brainstorming	An intensive discussion situation in which spontaneous suggestions as solutions to a problem are received uncritically	New ideas (creativity) Problem solving Decision making
Buzz groups	Groups of two to six members who discuss issues or problems for a short period, or periods, within a lesson	Encourage reticent students Group cohesion Feedback Consolidate memory by rehearsal of facts Learn terminology by use Thought (at all levels) Arousal Training in discussion techniques
Case discussion	Real or simulated complex problems are analyzed in detail for students to suggest their own solutions or decisions	Understand complex interrelationships Application of principles
Closed-circuit television (CCTV)		Knowledge of information and skills Self-awareness
Computer-assisted instruction or learning (CAI or CAL)	Not strictly a single method; computers may be used in many ways to present information, set tasks, and obtain feedback	Knowledge of facts Computing skills Thinking and problem-solving skills Feedback to student and lecturer
Controlled discussion	Teaching in which students may raise questions or comment, but the general direction is under the teacher's strict control; this is normally used after a presentation method with a class, not a group	Knowledge of facts Understanding (including "revision") Feedback
Counseling	Students voluntarily consult a trained tutor, doctor, or welfare officer about their private or academic problems	Quite varied Student welfare

TABLE 14.1. SOME COMMON TEACHING
METHODS AND APPROPRIATE OBJECTIVES (cont'd.)

Teaching Method	Commentary	Category of Primary Objectives
Demonstrations	The teacher performs some operation exemplifying a phenomenon or skill while the students watch (A presentation or reception method)	Observation skills Knowledge of principles Knowledge of physical skills
Films		Knowledge of information and skills Development of attitudes
Free-group discussion (FGD)	A learning situation in which the topic and direction are controlled by the student group; the teacher observes and facilitates only when necessary	Observation Change in attitudes, feelings, human relations Self-awareness Willing to receive and consider new ideas
Group tutorial	A period of teaching devoted to a single student	Individual development of student thought, especially at higher levels Ask questions Give reasons Feel for others
Horseshoe groups	Groups (normally four to twelve members) with a specific task that is discussed	Evaluation Decision making Analytical thinking Know how to apply principles
Individual task	Usually a problem to work out in class, but it could consist of other activities performed by each individual separately	Active learning Involvement by all Problem solving
Lecture	A period of more or less uninterrupted talk by the teacher (not necessarily a complete lesson); in effect, "lecture" is defined here in terms of the psychological conditions it implies	Knowledge of information Obtain general background of a topic
"Practicals" and laboratory work		Observation Manual skills "Scientific thinking"
Programmed learning (various)	Usually a text containing questions each of which must be answered before proceeding	Knowledge of information Simple problem solving

TABLE 14.1. SOME COMMON TEACHING
METHODS AND APPROPRIATE OBJECTIVES (cont'd.)

Teaching Method	Commentary	Category of Primary Objectives
Projects	Quite varied, but commonly an exercise submitted on paper as a result of practical skills connected with the subject	Information skills (knowledge of, how to seek, application of, organization of, illustration of information) Skills of presentation
Reading		Knowledge of information Some thinking Ability to seek and select information
Role play or "sociodrama"	Students are given certain social roles and freely dramatize them in a group, i.e., they act out their specified role	Empathy Work off tensions Self-awareness Attitude change
Seminar	Group discussion introduced by the presentation of an essay or other work	"Critical" thinking Ability to present an argument Thought at all levels
Simulation and games	Teaching in which a real situation is duplicated in its essential features perhaps in the form of a game or a problem; the participants adopt an appropriate role or status, if possible	Empathy Work off tensions Self-awareness Attitude change Vocational skills
Step-by-step discussion	Teaching by a carefully prepared sequence of issues and questions to draw out the required information from students	Knowledge of facts Understanding (especially logical argument or developmental sequence)
Step-by-step lecture	A lecture organized around three to ten topics, each of which is talked about for a few minutes followed by discussion or other activity	Knowledge of information Routine problem solving
Syndicate method	Teaching where the class is divided into groups of about six members who work on the same or related problems with intermittent teacher contact and who write a joint report for the critical appraisal of the whole class	Skills in seeking and organizing information Develop teamwork and committee skills Interdisciplinary application Decision making Presentation skills

TABLE 14.1. SOME COMMON TEACHING
METHODS AND APPROPRIATE OBJECTIVES (cont'd.)

Teaching Method	Commentary	Category of Primary Objectives
Synectics	A development of brain-storming in which special techniques, such as choosing group members from diverse backgrounds, are used to produce a creative solution to the problem	Creativity, including creative problem solving and decision making
Tape and slides (various)	As with audiotapes, except that the attached projector or viewer is used for visual teaching	Knowledge of information, especially visual information Observation
Television		Knowledge of information and skills Development of attitudes
T-group method	A method of teaching self-awareness and interpersonal relations based on therapeutic group techniques in which individual members discuss their relationships with each other	Sensitivity in human relations Self-awareness, especially of feelings, motives

they use every day are unfamiliar and complex to their students. More especially, they are unaware of the time it takes for these concepts to be built up.

Consequently, it is a common mistake of new lecturers to demand too great a conceptual development from their students in one lecture. Using truth-functional tests after lectures, I have found that students score around 80 percent on tests of new concepts (Level B in Table 14.2) that were defined in terms of already familiar ones (Level A), but only about 20 percent on tests of new concepts described in terms of other ones new that day (Level C). Notice that understanding a new concept is not an all-or-nothing process. If it were, we might expect students to score around 64 percent on Level C concepts (that is, 80 percent of 80 percent). A thorough understanding involves linking the concept to many others.

2. Possible Solutions

As we saw in Chapter Seven, a lecturer cannot make all possible links for students. Students must make them for themselves. They can do very little for themselves while the lecturer is bombarding them with more information. The solution is for the lecturer to stop lecturing and give students an opportunity to make links.

TABLE 14.2. THREE LEVELS OF CONCEPTS USED IN LECTURES.

Level A	Level B	Level C
Familiar concepts	New concepts defined in terms of level A	New concepts defined in terms of level B
100 percent	80 percent	20 percent

The students can do this if they are allowed to use level B concepts in discussion or problem solving so that Level B language moves toward assimilation with that of level A. If assimilation in the lesson were 100 percent possible (which of course is most unlikely), Level B concepts would become Level A and Level C concepts would become Level B, with scores around 80 percent, not 20 percent.

Thus, the use of discussion in small groups (four people at the most) between short periods of lecturing may partly overcome this difficulty. If the lecturer moves among the class, the level of students' understanding can be gauged and misconceptions corrected as soon as the lecture is resumed. In this way, lectures build upon discussion.

The temptation to teach too much was mentioned in Chapter Two. McKeachie (in Gage, 1963) and Erskine and O'Morchoe (1961) have reported that students learned more when told less. Gane (1969) and Taplin (1969) found that the use of questions to obtain feedback after each stage of a lecture prevented them as lecturers from racing ahead of the class. Indeed, it is to be expected that all feedback techniques will be possible solutions for this reason.

New lecturers who transfer the compact examination style of their student days to their lectures need to learn how to elaborate a point as described in Chapter Six. They will find it easiest to practice the general form first because its elaboration phase is explicit and the timing of the lecture (frequently an underlying anxiety) is easiest with this form.

Nerves

Lecturing causes teachers more anxiety than any other part of their job (King, 1973).

1. Consequences of the Difficulty

From measures of heart rate, cortisol excretion, and subjective anxiety, Houtman and Bakker (1987, 1991a, and 1991b) concluded that lecturing is ego threatening and imposes both psychological and physiological stress, particularly at the beginning. It was greater in simulated lectures than during the real thing. Although the symptoms decreased over a three-month period in which the lecturers gave at least twenty lectures, the rank order between them hardly changed.

Although they may have other causes, a large number of lecturers' common difficulties originate in early lack of confidence. The bad habits resulting from nerves become embedded in their style long after beginners' nervousness has disappeared. Consequently it is advisable to face these difficulties in the first few weeks of teaching. Some hide self-consciously behind a hand in front of the face, others mumble for fear of embarrassment at what they say, and most (of us) have mannerisms. Because fear of the class prevents some lecturers from looking at the students, they continuously look down at their notes or sideways out of the window. Others, for fear of being tongue-tied, write out their whole lecture and usually read it with a monotonous voice, which is also the result of the same nervous tension. Unfortunately, when the eyes-down manner of reading results in inflexible and inappropriate remarks, or when the consequent failure to observe students' reactions results in a more evident adverse response, the lecturer retreats yet further into the security of overprepared notes, or builds a defensive mental barrier between himself and the class, so that the problem is only exacerbated. Some people blame the students when they don't understand; others show false bravado. Marris (1964) suggests that the failure to invite questions is sometimes based on the mistaken belief that lecturers should never admit their ignorance, or the mistaken fear that their prestige will suffer if they display any lack of knowledge. Speaking too fast is also sometimes caused by nerves, but this difficulty is so common that a special section will be devoted to it.

2. Possible Solutions

These consequences seem like a list of students' criticism of their lecturers. Yet we have seen that a critical attitude only makes matters worse. Criticism is inappropriate. What is needed is an appreciation of the difficulty. Correction of faults too often implies that there is only one way of giving a lecture. Nervous lecturers need reinforcement of their good points with suggestions on how these strengths can be used to achieve the teaching objectives. This is possible because nervousness is, itself, a good sign. It shows that the lecturer is concerned about students' reactions.

Most university lecturers overcome the adverse effects of nervousness in their first few months of teaching. Indeed, we saw in Chapter Eleven that amorphous lecturers become complacent. Two research groups have developed confidence-building techniques for those who are less fortunate. Weaver and Cotrell (1985) describe "imaging" as a process whereby a picture of the self is imagined and "scanned," rather like reviewing experience of an event. This produces a series of self-revealing images. After deciding what self-image the lecturer would like to project, images are selectively sensitized. Weaver and Cotrell say that neural impulses, bodily movements, and lecture problems associated with fear are reduced.

In a series of articles, Stanton (1978, 1979) reports using relaxation training, positive suggestion, and success visualization with a total of fifty-eight lecturers as well as student teachers. More than 75 percent reported increasing self-confidence and were rated as such by students, while controls showed little improvement and even some deterioration. Success visualization involved lecturers' "seeing" themselves performing in the way they would like to perform. Positive suggestion improved physical and mental health and increased energy levels, the ability to cope, calmness, and concentration, as well as feelings of contentment, well-being, and self-confidence.

The second ingredient of early nervousness is usually lack of information on what the student reaction is. It is fear of the unknown. Therefore, one solution is to find out by obtaining feedback in one or more of the techniques previously suggested. If a case of nerves derives from feeling inadequate, it is unwise to pretend to be more adequate than one is. Students appreciate an honest and open person.

Nervous tensions normally require an outlet. Surgeons reputedly obtain this by expressions of bad temper, and schoolteachers by supposedly confident displays of aggression toward their pupils; but neither of these would be acceptable in lecturing. If this energy can be displaced into enthusiasm for the subject, or the vigorous exposition of a theory, the lecturer will have the support of a good proportion of the students surveyed by Marris (1964), Smithers (1970a, 1970b), and the NUS (National Union of Students) Commission (Saunders and others, 1969), especially arts students.

A common cause of nervousness is simply that some lecturers do not like to be the center of attention. They can avoid this for some of the time in a lecture, and have an opportunity to gather their composure, if they use buzz groups or other forms of small-group teaching within the lecture situation. Thus the use of alternative teaching methods can give some relief (Part Four).

Speed

Going too fast is a common difficulty, one to which new lecturers are particularly prone. In fact it is very rare for students to complain that a lecturer is going too slowly. For example, when Geller, Chaffee, and Farris (1975) manipulated lecture speeds and asked students to press electric feedback buttons when they were too fast or too slow, students hardly ever indicated that the speed was slow.

1. The Consequences of Going Too Fast

Empirical evidence on the effects of listening speeds is occasionally ambiguous, yet the model depicted in Figure 14.1 may reconcile apparent conflicts. This model supposes that lecture speeds may be increased up to a certain point without serious losses in effectiveness, but after this point there is a rapid decline. The critical speed is hypothesized to depend on the cognitive difficulty of the lecture and the tests used.

According to this model, less able students and lectures requiring thought will show a decrement in test scores at slower speeds than will intelligent students and lectures with easy subject matter.

Actually, this model applies to other lecture variables too. For example, if you gradually remove techniques of clear explanation (lecture signals, itemization, blackboard buildup, etc.) there will be little effect at first. But then test scores for the least able students will suddenly fall. Then scores for average students will plummet. Finally, once your lecture organization is poor and your explanations abysmal, even your best student won't understand.

Why do their scores decrease suddenly? The answer, once again, is that understanding consists of linking ideas. When students understand one idea, it is linked to others, and so they understand the others too. But when the links are not made, the ideas at either end of the links are not so easily retrieved from mem-

FIGURE 14.1. MODEL TO DEPICT
THE EFFECTS OF INCREASING LECTURE SPEEDS.

Note: Curves A through F are for tests of increasing cognitive difficulty.

ory, even if they were stored in the first place. Why? Because memory tends to be by association of ideas. Retrieval uses the links. Teaching and learning are all about making links, not storing facts in isolation.

Orr (1968) has suggested that the critical presentation speed is about 275–300 wpm. This is two or three times faster than normal lecture speeds, but Orr's generalization is probably based on experiments using situations cognitively easier than lectures. Furthermore, these speeds are obtained by mechanical compression of tape-recorded speech. (In most cases measures to correct the change of pitch were taken.) But comparisons of virtually identical lectures given live and on tape suggest that the critical speed of live lectures for answering questions requiring thought may be at nearly half the speed of tape-recorded speech (Bligh, 1970a). Using eighty university students, Reid (1968) found the decrement occurred after 325 wpm, that comprehension was superior when grammatically simple speech was used, and that grammatical complexity interacts with subject matter. Certain generalizations may be inferred from his experiment. If you wish to lecture fast, it is better not to use unnecessary words; to use the active, rather than the passive, voice; to put *if-when-because* clauses at the beginning of sentences; and to keep sentences short. If it is always desirable to maximize comprehension, this advice is probably applicable to all lectures.

Grobe and Pettibone (1975) varied the speed of lectures from 102 to 145 syllables per minute (spm). Even though none of these speeds is high, they found that attention increased, and disruptive behavior decreased, at the higher speeds. Curiously, Pettibone and Martin (1973) reported that noise levels in university classrooms were lowest at the mean speed of 134 spm, greater at slower speeds, and greatest at higher speeds. Aiken, Thomas, and Shennum (1975) showed that higher speeds (240 wpm compared with 120 wpm) result in a "terse" note-taking style that does not favor memory. At higher speeds, the time taken to note a point interferes with more information. Recall was best when no notes were taken and the lecture was given twice at 240 wpm. The first lecture probably acted as an advance organizer for the second.

Other variables have been demonstrated by Friedman and Johnson (1968), Sticht (1968), and Woodcock and Clark (1968), all of whom showed that intelligence, especially verbal ability, is an important variable. Orr (1968) demonstrated the role of practice routines in learning to comprehend speeded-up speech, and motivation may have been an important factor in Barabasz's (1968) finding no effect on recall and retention scores when lectures were speeded from twenty-one to fourteen minutes. (However, the critical point may not have been reached.) The changes in speed required for variations in lecture objectives have already been mentioned (Bligh, 1970a, 1974)—if you want students to think, go slower.

2. Possible Solutions

These research findings still leave some ambiguity. Why should students complain so persistently that lectures are too fast when experimental work suggests that they may be speeded considerably without loss of comprehension?

a. Use Short Periods of Lecturing.   One obvious point is that most experiments did not describe situations in which the listener took notes. Another is that, with the possible exception of Barabasz's, the passages used were very much shorter than a typical lecture and concentration may be possible for short intensive periods. Indeed, initially slight increases in retention following moderate compression of speech have also been interpreted as the result of less trace decay owing to the shorter time taken for delivery. Therefore, if lecturers who tend to go too fast use only short periods of lecturing interspersed with student rehearsal, some consolidation of memory may be achieved to produce a very intensive—but effective— learning situation. Ideally, throughout a period of an hour, the sections of lecturing should be progressively shorter, whereas periods of rehearsal should lengthen.

b. Maintain the Length of Pauses.   A further clue to resolve this ambiguity may be found in the work of Miron and Brown (1968). Instead of using mechanical speech compressors, they read passages at three different speeds and compared the proportion of time spent in phonation (actually speaking) and in pauses between words and at the end of sentences. They found that as speakers speed their delivery, they disproportionately decrease the total pause time. Slower speeds with longer pauses permitted superior comprehension. If we bear in mind the role of interference of a memory trace (Chapter Two) and the need for rehearsal, it would seem that if lecturers wish to increase their speed of speech they should take care to maintain the length of pauses at the end of sentences and especially after major points. Thus the variation in speed and the timing of pauses are significant factors affecting the comprehension of lectures.

c. The General Form.   The use of the general form for making a point is recommended for new lecturers because by using repetition it lengthens the time spent on each point.

d. The Lecture Guide.   The use of lecture summary handouts with headings, essential points, and space for additions is useful for lecturers who cannot slow themselves. Reference to this technique has already been made (see Chapter Ten, pp. 150–152).

e. Feedback Techniques. Finally, if lecturers do talk too fast, amends can only be made if they first find out the points that were lost and then fill in the gaps. For this reason, feedback techniques are essential for the rapid lecturer.

The Problem of Large Audiences

As pressures upon teachers grow, the problem of large classes is becoming a major difficulty.

1. Diagnosing the Difficulty

There is a belief that large classes are less effective than small ones. A recent study (Gibbs, Lucas, and Simonite, 1996) seems to confirm this with regard to enrollments on courses. But when the criterion is the amount of information learned in lectures, there is a large amount of evidence that this belief is false. For example, Hudelson (1928) has reported fifty-nine comparisons of learning in small and large lecture classes. Although most of the results showed no significant difference, forty-six of the fifty-nine favored the larger classes, and so did the majority that were significant. This finding has since been repeated many times with substantially the same results (Rohrer, 1957; Camorosano and Santapolo, 1958; Nelson, 1959; Macomber and Siegel, 1960; de Cecco, 1964). In most of these studies, small classes ranged from twenty to thirty students, while large ones were over sixty. Two-thirds of the lecturers in the Dorward and Wiedemann study (1977) thought the maximum size for efficient teaching is forty.

McKeachie (1963) and Meredith and Ogasawara (1982a) have claimed that large lectures tend to be inferior when the criteria used are more concerned with thinking and attitudes. Since management of personal interaction is more difficult in large classes and small classes are presumably more intimate, this is probably true; but so far I have found very little empirical confirmation. It is true that Siegel, Adams, and Macomber (1960) found fairly consistent differences favoring smaller classes when the criteria included thinking, problem solving, and changes in attitude, but the differences were slight and for none of these criteria was there a consistent significant difference. Smith (1996) found the same when teaching the application of simultaneous equations in economics.

In contrast, there have been many studies of the effects of class size at secondary school level. After a meta-analysis, Glass (1987) concluded there is not much difference between the outcomes of classes over thirty; but with classes smaller than thirty the advantages are greater, the smaller the class. More important, the effects are cumulative with more hours of instruction. The same broad conclusions may not apply to nonstop lectures, but if they do not apply to varied teaching methods at college level, one might ask why.

The expectation of a difference arises if one only considers the lecturer's task. If the two situations are considered from the point of view of the individual student, the lack of difference is hardly surprising. When listening to a speaker, the fact that a certain number of other people are doing the same thing does not greatly change the student's mental activity. Consequently, the kind of psychological objectives that can be achieved remain the same.

It is the teacher's role that is changed by increases in class size; the changes in the students' role are relatively slight. Some research by de Cecco (1964) throws an interesting light on this. When he asked students and lecturers directly whether they preferred large or small lecture classes, they both claimed to prefer the smaller ones. But when students answered a questionnaire containing a large number of items about particular classes not apparently related to their size, the students showed no preference for one or the other. Meredith and Ogasawara (1982b) and Marsh, Overall, and Kesler (1979) also report that size is only weakly related, if at all, to perceived educational outcomes and satisfaction with the lecturer.

If large and small classes are equally effective, does the difficulty lie in the fact that lecturers do not like teaching large ones? Startup (1977) reported that lecturers who valued informal feedback from students were more satisfied with small classes. Some saw themselves as thinking out loud and were indifferent to class size! Certainly, (1) the range of teaching methods that can be combined with lecturing is progressively restricted with increases in size; consequently, (2) the compensating demands upon lecturing technique are greater if the problems of attention and motivation are to be overcome.

2. Diminishing the Difficulty

The way to diminish the difficulty consists of asking oneself, "What is it I can do with a small class that I cannot do with a large one?" The answer might be, "Get feedback," "Observe and react to individuals," "Maintain attention," and so on. Then consider alternative techniques to compensate.

a. Use Buzz Groups. The demands upon technique mostly derive from the difficulty of obtaining both verbal and nonverbal feedback. Obviously, with larger classes there are more people to observe, a smaller proportion can speak, and fewer will have the courage to do so (Stones, 1970). Of the methods suggested in Chapter Eighteen, only buzz groups give a satisfactory sample of feedback when students number more than one hundred; and even this method may be restricted.

b. Personal Projection. There are also less obvious difficulties. The greater the distance of members of the audience from the speaker, the more difficult it is to establish eye contact. This in turn affects timing, humor, facial communication, and many conversational cues of which we are seldom conscious.

To overcome this, it is necessary for speakers to project their personalities. This may require some confidence and dramatic ability, particularly at the beginning. A certain amount of lightheartedness can release the tension, make the lecturer more relaxed so that her personality is displayed, and let the audience feel free to react. By contrast, large lectures tend to be more formal, and students expect them to be. Consequently attempts to break the formality by flippancy or casualness are risky tactics that can bring disrespect and poor attention if not handled with care.

c. Sentential Pauses. A useful tip is to pause a little longer at the end of sentences than you might with a smaller class. Use the opportunity of the pause to look around the class, gauge reaction and, where possible, get eye contact. If you see a furrowed brow at the back, ask the student by name whether he has understood, and reexplain or otherwise have a brief exchange of conversation. This sends a message to all students that they are not lost in the crowd and that their nonverbal behavior is noticed. It keeps a personal touch, and it breaks the formality of the lecture acceptably.

d. Maintaining Attention. It is more difficult for students to concentrate in a large lecture. A periodic review (or taking stock) of the lecture thus far helps students grasp the overall structure of the lecture and fill in gaps where their attention lapsed. Since we saw in Chapter Three that attention declines in the middle of lectures and the lecturers cannot be sure how well they have been understood, it is sometimes suggested that the density of information should be less at that time. As we also saw in Chapter Three, a buzz group or some other change of activity helps to maintain attention. Warning the class at the beginning that you intend to introduce an activity also creates pressure to concentrate. The activity could be very brief, such as completing a line in a calculation.

Inviting a colleague to form a duo and share the lecture is another way to introduce variety (see Betts and Walton, 1970).

e. Inviting Questions. Because students are less likely to ask questions or interrupt in a large lecture, members of buzz groups can be given the task of answering each other's questions. Those that cannot be answered by group members should be written on a sheet of paper and passed to the front for the lecturer to deal with. This avoids any embarrassment of students' expressing ignorance to a large audience, and it enables the lecturer to deal with similar problems at the same time. Obviously, it is also useful feedback.

f. ***Slower on Key Points.*** Another tip is to speak slower on key points. The different routes by which sound rebounds in a larger room result in it being less distinct. Ideally, the vowel sounds in words need to be a little longer and the consonants more distinct, but it is difficult to do this consciously without speech training. If, however, every sentence is spoken slower, attention in a large class is much more difficult to maintain.

Lecturing Skills Can Be Learned

It is sometimes said that good lecturers are born, not made. Don't despair. There is now good evidence that this is not true. No doubt as in other fields of human endeavor, some people are more gifted than others, but lecturing skills can be learned.

Some skills are more easily learned than others. Sixty-five lecturers gave pairs of videotaped explanations on the same topic (the second after some training). Trained independent observers rated them without knowing which were given first and which second (Daines and Brown, 1983). All skills showed improvement, particularly openings, organization, the use of audiovisual aids, creating interest, and global ratings. Lecturers were less successful in improving their endings and in taking account of their audience. Linguistic analysis showed significant improvements in signposting and linking; there was also some improvement in focusing attention; being aware of the audience; and reducing stumbles, hesitations, and incomplete sentences.

The skills most easily acquired included the use of examples, appropriate vocabulary, diagrams, audiovisual, and other materials; summarizing; selecting appropriate content; focusing attention on important points; setting the stage for the explanation; and repeating main points. The least learnable features were changes in the lecturers' style; verbal fluency; the elimination of digressions; the use of metaphors and explaining links; and displays of enthusiasm, flexibility, and interest.

The most difficult skills relate to affect (feelings, attitudes, and motivation). Using reflection-based decision making in a teaching laboratory, Klinzing (1988) was concerned not only with lecturers developing clarity, interest, and a social climate but also with four skills of nonverbal expressiveness that communicate affect: gestures, voice delivery, facial expression (including eye expression and eye gaze), and posture and movement (including movement in the room). The training consisted of preparing, giving, and discussing a lecture in a group of seven;

hearing a lecture on theory and research on nonverbal behavior; practicing and imitating each of the four skills; discriminating emotions shown in pictures; and finally a repeat lecture in the group of seven. Ratings on adjective scales showed improvement in all domains.

King (1973) found that new university teachers were more anxious about lecturing than anything else. Fox (1980) found their principal concerns were to do with assessing their own teaching and development. Either way, we cannot be surprised that 75 percent of lecturers are apprehensive before video feedback sessions intended to improve their lecturing (Cryer, 1988), even though these sessions are always the ones most highly rated afterward. Cryer recommends that participants be reassured by first seeing others lecturing on video, and watching themselves in videotaped discussion. I always give lecturers the first opportunity to criticize themselves and establish a convention that favorable comments should always precede any adverse criticisms. From observing lecturers for many years, I am acutely aware that behaviors to overcome difficulties in their first three lectures become habits that last a lifetime. I therefore strongly recommend that lecturers get help right at the start of their careers, even if they think they don't need it.

Conclusion

The problems of lecturing covered in this chapter are ones that most lecturers share at some stage in their career. There is no use pretending that these problems have ultimate solutions. All that lecturers can do is make the best of a bad job. I hope these suggestions are helpful, but I suspect some of them are easier to make than to carry out.

CHAPTER FIFTEEN

LECTURES FOR THE PROMOTION OF THOUGHT

Stimulating thought.

  1. Choose a suitable lecture form.

  2. The use of questions.

Making thinking easier.

  1. Visual display.

  2. Use handouts.

  3. Recommend prereading.

  4. Watch your speed.

I have argued in Chapter One that the typical descriptive lecture is unsuitable for the promotion of student thought. The argument was based first on experimental findings that "thought objectives" are not achieved, and second on the psychological grounds that lectures do not provide a situation in which much thought may take place.

However, when making suggestions for new lecturers, the practical situation in which they are frequently placed must be faced. It is no good blaming principals, professors, or department heads. The new lecturer may have to face the immediate problem of taking on large classes for a course with no follow-up seminars and in which it would be irresponsible not to have objectives including student thought.

Stimulating Thought

The question must be posed, How can you promote student thought in large classes? The answers should take account of the psychology of thinking. Presumably, this will involve either a lecturing technique other than those used in the experimental studies or the inclusion of discussion techniques (Part Four).

1. Choose a Suitable Lecture Form

A "descriptive" lecture mostly consists of the presentation of information and is likely to adopt the hierarchic form of classification, a chain of narrative, or some combination of the two. But we have seen that in a problem-centered lecture, a chain of argument, or the presentation of a thesis, the student is required to think in order to follow the reasoning. Since thinking is learned by practice, if lecturers are in situations in which they must lecture rather than arrange student discussion or other active learning, it is these forms that should be used for the promotion of thought.

In other words, if the objective is to teach students to think, the provision of information—though necessary—is not enough. In teaching students to solve problems, Corman has shown that knowledge of how to go about them is more important than knowledge of the principles to be used. This is a pertinent study because it is often assumed that if students are told about the principles of a subject, they will know how to use them. Corman (1957) tested students on their ability to solve problems after he had systematically varied the amount of information they were given. The information was of two kinds. One was about the principles to be applied; the other was concerned with the methods students should use to apply the principles and to discover the solutions.

Application and discovery require thought. For most students, the ability to solve problems varied directly with the amount of information they were given on the method of approach. Students who had scored highly on intelligence tests were better able to apply knowledge of the principles and did less well than others without it. Less able students managed only to cope with a limited amount of information about the method, and whether they were told about the principles made no difference to the number of problems they could solve. This experiment illustrates the maxim "teach students what they need to know, not something different." Students who were given guidance in methods of thinking were better at thinking. It sounds obvious, but it cannot be done if the lecturer does not have clear objectives.

2. The Use of Questions

The most common device to promote thought is to ask questions. This may be done in a number of ways. Where students are supplied with networked computer terminals, lecturers can monitor individual and group responses. Questions in lectures may be rhetorical, and although these do not compel activity from the student it is the nature of our language that they stimulate it, particularly if followed by a brief silence. We are conditioned to try to answer questions that are asked even if we have been trained not to shout the answer. In a well-controlled experiment, Sime and Boyce (1969) inferred that questions raised the level of attention because the learning of concepts, including concepts about which no questions were asked, showed greater improvement in classes with questions than in classes with no questions at all.

In general, questions should be those that require the specific kind of thought stated in the teacher's objectives. Hunkins (1967, 1968) asked only analytical and evaluative questions of one class and only factual questions of another. Subsequent tests showed no difference in the groups' abilities in questions requiring knowledge, simple comprehension, application, and synthesis of facts, but significant differences in the predicted direction in the students' abilities to analyze and evaluate.

Testing (or apparently testing) students' factual knowledge in public will almost invariably provoke an undesirable reaction, for no one likes to be placed in a position that might display ignorance. Students will not be discouraged, though, if they are asked for their personal opinions or personal reactions, first because their answers cannot be wrong and second because they feel respected if their opinions are considered worth hearing. Supplementary questions to elicit clarification of an individual's viewpoint are often necessary for the rest of the class, but so long as answers are accepted for consideration there need be no feeling of intimidation. Intimidation should normally be avoided at all costs; because of the manner of some secondary school teachers, fear reactions are more common among students than lecturers might expect. In my opinion, acute sensitivity to slight changes in students' emotive reactions is essential to good teaching.

Provided lecturers know precisely what they are trying to do, it is not difficult to use student replies to open up and develop a lecture topic. No matter what students reply, if lecturers can relate it to their objectives, their objectives can in turn be related to what is already in the students' minds (that is, the students can "understand").

Less personal questions can be set as essay titles, as discussion topics, or for individual answers on handouts (Elton, 1970). Uren (1968) has described a technique of raising a question for discussion before the lecturer expounds upon it. He found that, by thinking, the class was able to suggest most of the important points the lecturer would have raised. As a result, students' thought was encouraged and the lecturer was able to synthesize the suggestions and develop the topic further than would otherwise have been possible.

A variation on this technique is to ask each student to work individually on a problem before resuming a class discussion approach or formal lecturing. Obviously, two of the benefits of attending lectures are to listen to experts and to meet fellow students, and both these are denied if individual work is overused. But the technique can maintain student attention, afford a change of activity, direct student thought, and provide welcome feedback for both student and teacher when the answer is explained.

The use of buzz groups is described in Chapter Eighteen. They may provoke thought in a specific direction, provided their task is carefully thought out and the purpose made clear to the students.

A most important technique has been developed by King. She created a set of question stems with gaps, to be used as a guide for students to generate questions:

- How are _____ and _____ alike?
- What is the main idea of _____?
- What would happen if _____?
- What are the strengths and weaknesses of _____?
- In what way is _____ related to _____?
- What values are assumed by _____?
- How does _____ affect _____?
- What is the function of _____?
- What principle is applied when _____?
- Compare _____ and _____ with regard to _____.
- What causes _____?
- How does _____ tie in with what we learned before?
- Which one is the best _____, and why?
- What are the possible solutions for the problem of _____?
- Who are the major authorities in this field? What are their central propositions?
- Do I agree or disagree with the statement _____? Why?
- What do I still not understand about _____? (adapted from King, 1991)

Each student was required to generate three questions by inserting appropriate concepts or lecture content in the gaps. This technique not only provided a degree of learner autonomy but also demanded critical thinking and thought at a meta level with reference to the topic of a lecture. King (1989, 1991) compared the comprehension scores for students who answered each other's questions ("1" in Table 15.1) and their own in buzz groups of three members, only answered their own questions (group "2"), reviewed a topic in a buzz-group discussion (group "3"), and reviewed the topic individually ("4"). Students working on questions (groups 1 and 2) outperformed those reviewing the material (3 and 4). She also compared 1 and 3 with a group like 1, except that the students could not use a guide (such as the list just above) to generate the questions (King, 1990). Although this group did better than group 3, group 1 displayed more critical thinking. A further report (King, 1994) showed that students who generated and

TABLE 15.1. THE CONDITIONS OF KING'S EXPERIMENTS.

	Worked Individually	Worked in Buzz Groups
Answered student-generated questions	2	1
Reviewed lecture material	4	3

answered their own questions performed better than those who answered the same questions generated by others.

Making Thinking Easier

Thinking involves holding in the mind more than one idea at a time in order to relate or distinguish them. These processes employ short-term memory. But we have seen that short-term memories have limited capacity. Therefore, one way to make thought possible is to reduce the load on the students' short-term memories.

It is because thinking imposes an extra load that the conditions required to promote thought are more exacting than those that allow students to remember and take notes on information. Consequently, in addition to trying to stimulate thought, much of the lecturer's task will consist of making thinking easier. Both are necessary. (Some lecturers call this spoon-feeding—an emotive expression—but there is no point in expecting students to do what numerous studies have shown they cannot normally achieve, without attempting to make the task easier.)

1. Visual Display

We have already seen that relatively permanent visual display of information, using the blackboard, overhead projector, or slides, is one way of doing this.

2. Use Handouts

Another method already mentioned is the use of handouts that not only contain the necessary information (perhaps in summary form) but arrange it appropriately together with the problem(s) being discussed. When used in this way, the handout functions to provide a substitute for student note taking and to redirect attention to the issue that requires thought. It was suggested that if the handout is distributed a week before the lecture, the students could become familiar with the basic information and thus lecture time could be saved; but in this case the lecturer must rely on the novelty of the problem, rather than the newness of the subject, to arouse interest. Also, with difficult subject matter prior distribution may not always be advisable, although it has the advantage that student attention is less likely to be distracted from the lecturer to the handout at the wrong time.

3. Recommend Prereading

A further suggestion is to set reading the week before; but if this is adopted certain precautions should normally be observed. The lecture will fail if the students do not do the reading unless the lecturer has plans for this contingency. Therefore, these contingency plans must be made in addition to the intended lecture. (It is not enough to say "If I do my bit, I expect the students to do theirs." This attitude does not face the reality that not all students act in their own best interests. Consequently, teachers have a managerial role. They are not simply someone who produces information for the students to assemble in their minds; they need to have a view of the whole learning process. This includes anticipating difficulties, in the same way an industrial manager may anticipate human problems affecting the production process.) But to do this alone is defeatist. Students will read as required if they want to, and if they can. Thus the task is partly to arouse motivation. One way to do this is to read short extracts as "trailers" that arouse interest, summarize the major points, or stimulate humor. Another way is to make it clear that full benefit from next week's lecture cannot be obtained without preparation, and when the time comes, explicit reference to the prescribed texts will provide psychological reinforcement of their preparatory behavior.

The references must be available, easy, and short. If they are not easily available, the lecturer may put the books on reserve in the library or ensure the provision of a suitable number of photocopies (perhaps also placed on reserve in the library).

The readings need to be in sufficiently easy language not to require an introductory lecture. Articles and books with summaries are useful. If the reading is longer than six to twenty pages (obviously this varies tremendously with the subject, size of page, and so on), a substantial proportion of the class will not have read it by the following week. This should be avoided. Like the breaking of New Year resolutions, once students fail to live up to their intentions they will find it difficult to keep good study habits. It is better to set too little, and to lecture to a class with a known uniform background, than to set too much. If students fail to read, there is little a lecturer can do to make them. It is better to make sure that they never fail in the first place.

A useful compromise is to summarize the reading at the beginning of the lecture, selecting what is relevant to the central problem to be considered and without implying that the summary is complete, or indeed that it is a summary. (If students come to believe that the summary is complete, they may not do the required reading.)

The summary may also be used as a framework by students who found the reading difficult; consequently, close observation of individual class members at this time (such as checking whether they take notes) is a useful way to discover the lazy and less able. Assuming the required reading was a key reference, rereading and borrowing of photocopies available in class may be advised, particularly when combined with horseshoe groups (Chapter Eighteen).

4. Watch Your Speed

It has already been mentioned that a very important factor affecting the amount of student thought that can take place in a lecture is its speed. In an experiment, I gave the same lectures at three different speeds to three groups and then tested the students not only on their gain in knowledge and simple comprehension of the subjects but also on their ability to analyze, resynthesize, evaluate, and use the information to solve problems. Although there was no difference between the groups in their ability to recall information and display simple comprehension of it, students who heard a lecture at its slowest speed did significantly better on questions requiring more thought (Bligh, 1974). Since students require time to think, especially when presented with new information, this result may not seem surprising, but it is nonetheless important if the promotion of thought is one of the lecturer's objectives.

Conclusion

Lectures are not usually effective in teaching students to think; this objective is better achieved by using lectures in conjunction with other methods, as suggested in Chapter Eighteen. If these are not possible, a problem-centered lecture form, a chain of argument, and the presentation of a thesis are suitable alternative forms of organization. Thought may also be encouraged by the use of questions and techniques to reduce the load on students' short-term memories.

CHAPTER SIXTEEN

LECTURES TO TEACH ATTITUDES

The lecturer's task in teaching attitudes.

1. Acquisition of attitudes.

2. Change of attitudes.

Strategies in the presentation of information.

1. Students' initial attitudes.

2. Stating possible conclusions.

3. Previous education.

4. Order of presentation.

5. Credibility of lecturer.

6. The amount of attitude change advocated.

7. Personality of the student.

Summary of strategies.

I t is the purpose of this chapter to suggest some ways in which attitudes may be taught by lectures. It is not concerned with philosophical questions of what attitudes ought to be taught or whether we ought to teach them at all. In many vocational subjects, such as law, medicine, education, and business studies, certain professional attitudes and values are assumed to be necessary. Therefore, if students do not possess these when they enroll, they will need to be taught; and although it has already been argued that lectures are not the best method for these objectives, teachers are sometimes forced to use the method.

There is a second class of attitude objectives in which one is concerned not so much that the students possess a specific attitude, but that they do have an attitude toward a particular thing and that they can justify it rationally. For example, whatever attitude students have toward Sartre's plays or the theory of continental drift, they may be required to support one or the other by argument.

The Lecturer's Task in Teaching Attitudes

There is a fundamental difficulty in the teaching of attitudes, which does not arise in the teaching of information and which as a consequence normally demands a different approach. Factual information is usually absorbed following some kind of presentation, but attitudes are not something external to the student; they are based on emotions and therefore cannot be absorbed from outside. They are predispositions for dealing with information that is presented; they cannot, themselves, be presented by a lecturer. They are a kind of internal coding system. Thus a change in attitudes must originate from the student. In this sense, attitudes cannot be taught; it is the teacher's task to engineer the situation so that the students will acquire or change them for themselves. Information alone is not likely to change attitudes. The lecturer must appeal to some emotion the students already possess.

1. Acquisition of Attitudes

Engineering this situation commonly has two stages. The teacher may first make the student aware of a need, and then provide the means of satisfying it. This pattern is familiar in advertising, except that the lecturer's audience is often captive while an advertisement must first attract attention. This latter feat is frequently achieved by means of some device quite irrelevant to the product, but thereafter the pattern is recognizable. Motives such as maternal affection, social status, and sexual attraction are aroused, and a product is offered that may satisfy them.

This process may be thought of as objectionable in the educational field, although it is a normal feature of human conversation. But it seems to me to be acceptable provided it is not coupled with deliberately restricted information. It is the restriction of information that is antithetical to education, not the appeal to students' motives. To teach students to seek information and to teach them to express opinions are important educational objectives. Thus at the beginning of a lecture in medicine or education the lecturer may point out the needs of the patient or child to arouse certain motives in the student. Attitudes may be formed when these motives are associated with the information and techniques taught.

2. Change of Attitudes

Attitudes may be changed if they are inadequate to deal with information presented. The inadequacy may be of three kinds.

a. Change Resulting from Inadequate Information. The students may have no relevant attitude or system for coding presented information. If they have never read any of Sartre's plays and know little or nothing about them from other sources, they will look for any attitude that makes sense of the new information. This may be, say, irrelevant prejudice against the French, or irrational respect for the lecturer. Students are likely to agree with their friends or people they admire even though the source of their admiration and friendship may be quite irrelevant to the issue for agreement (Tannenbaum, 1953). The ignorant are more suggestible than the knowledgeable.

b. Change Resulting from Conflicting Information. If new information cannot be reconciled to two attitudes, a person may change one or both. For example, if a student holds favorable attitudes toward labor unions and the Republican party but is told that many people in the Republican party support what he believes to be antiunion legislation, his favorable attitudes toward one or both may change. Complete rejection of a previous attitude is unlikely. The student is likely to take up an in-between position, which may be nearer the unions or the Republican party according to the relative strengths of his previous attitudes; he may attach reservations to these principles, or establish a higher-order principle to deal with the conflict. Thus attitudes may develop and become more complex by successive modification. It is this process for which free-group discussions are particularly suitable (Barnett, 1958; Abercrombie, 1960).

Because it is difficult for people to face up to conflicts in their own ideas, it is necessary in the lecture situation (where individuals do not have to explain their inconsistencies) to state issues very clearly so that they cannot easily be repressed. Yet, if the clarification is achieved by oversimplification, the students' reconciliation of attitudes may easily be naïve. The consequent need for both clarity and detail makes it very difficult to achieve a change of students' attitudes by lecturing.

This second situation—change resulting from conflicting information—is more common in student learning and everyday life; but the first—change from inadequate information—has particular importance here, both because students are constantly having to cope with new areas of knowledge and because lectures are essentially situations in which information is presented.

c. Change Resulting from Threatening Information. The effects of threatening presentations are ambiguous. The information that smoking will result in a slow and lingering death has had remarkably little effect upon people from all walks of life and all levels of intelligence. The consequence is delayed. The threat of one or ten years' imprisonment will make little difference to the incidence of crime. The consequence is delayed and uncertain. In a now-classic experiment, three groups of students heard lectures varying in accounts of the dire consequences of dental neglect and what they should do to prevent it. Those who heard the most severe lecture expressed most anxiety immediately afterwards but took least remedial action later. Those with the least threat acted upon it most (Janis and Feshbach, 1953).

It seems that severe threats don't bear contemplation. We put up defenses to prevent being disturbed by the message. However, there is reason to believe that strong appeals will have an effect if they threaten our loved ones, if the topics are relatively unfamiliar, if the individuals have high self-esteem or low vulnerability, and if the source is credible.

Strategies in the Presentation of Information

The degree to which students' attitudes will change following the presentation of information will vary with their initial attitudes, their previous education, the order in which the information is given, whether both sides of an issue are presented and are considered, the credibility of the lecturer, the amount of change advocated, the personality of the student, and no doubt many other factors.

1. Students' Initial Attitudes

If students' initial positions are unfavorable to the lecturer's arguments, they will change their attitudes more if both sides of an argument are given; but if their initial positions are favorable, these attitudes will only be strengthened by the presentation of their point of view alone. When favorable students heard arguments on both sides of a question, no signs of change were observed. Presentations of information alone did not result in permanent changes unless coupled with a decision the students had taken for themselves (Hovland, Lumsdaine, and Sheffield, 1949).

These findings suggest the need to be aware of students' initial attitudes. This may be obtained by the use of discussion methods at the beginning of a lecture, but if that knowledge is obtained by requiring an expression of their opinion, the act of commitment may result in a less open mind. When it is remembered that adults have subtle ways of concealing their attitudes, it will be realized that the lecturer must show considerable sensitivity to the feelings of students by means of nonverbal means of feedback during the initial class discussion. This can sometimes be done by getting the class to raise issues rather than give answers. The lecturer will frequently sense the initial attitudes by the way issues are raised and selected. If the questions are translated into neutral language as they are written on the board, commitment is avoided.

2. Stating Possible Conclusions

The importance of decision making in the formation of attitudes may lead one to suppose that students will acquire appropriate professional attitudes if the lecturer states facts and then leaves students to draw their own conclusions. This may be true of able students, but where subject matter is difficult or unfamiliar, a statement of the conclusion produces the necessary comprehension for attitude change. Hovland and Mandell (1952) presented identical arguments favoring currency devaluation to two groups, except that the argument's conclusion was omitted for the second group. Devaluation is a complex subject, and they found twice the number of people changed their attitude in the favored direction in the group that heard the conclusion. Since students in lectures are required to understand difficult and unfamiliar information that they cannot easily relate, it is probably better for lecturers to state the conclusions that can be inferred from their lectures.

Some lecturers (not to mention some newspapers) claim that it is their duty to present "facts" rather than to state a conclusion, and thus to leave the students to make up their own minds. The validity of this claim will vary with the lecturer's objectives, but the facts and the words in which they are expressed are necessarily selected; we shall see that attitudes are learned as much from a teacher's personality as from the conclusions stated. Therefore, paradoxically, if lecturers wish to be impartial it is sometimes necessary for them to state their point of view.

3. Previous Education

If complete impartiality is impossible and it is more effective to make possible inferences explicit, should both sides of issues be considered? The answer to this question seems to depend on the extent to which previous education has taught people to look at both sides before making a judgment. Because students in higher education are capable of some critical thinking (which is usually to be encouraged), it seems reasonable to expect lecturers to present both sides of an argument. During World War II, Hovland, Lumsdaine, and Sheffield (1949) found that although less educated soldiers were persuaded by a one-sided argument (on the probable length of the war against Japan), those with more education took balanced arguments more seriously.

Lumsdaine and Janis (1953) found that those who had previously heard both sides of a question were more resistant to change in later group discussion. This may be relevant to a current problem in the training of teachers. There is a tendency for teachers to become more authoritarian and less child-centered in their first year after training, although their lecturers in the colleges think that this is a retrograde change. The lecturers may, therefore, need to take steps to face their student teachers with the difficulties and arguments against the approaches they advocate. Indeed, students may react unfavorably if well-known contrary arguments are not considered. The failure of a lecturer to consider contrary arguments arises from the fear that the arguments may be convincing. But students are more likely to react unfavorably if such arguments are familiar but remain unmentioned than they are to be convinced by arguments presented by one who does not believe them.

4. Order of Presentation

Granted that it is usually better to consider pro and con arguments in a lecture, in which order should they be considered? This is known as the *primacy-recency question*. Provided the student is not warned about the fallibility of first impressions (Cohen, 1964), the argument presented first is more likely to be convincing if the students have no previous knowledge and it fixes their orientation to the subject, or if, unlike later presentations, it does not compete with previously formed ideas. However, the most recently presented ideas may be more convincing if they interfere with the memory of earlier ones, or students are wavering between two equal arguments.

Not surprisingly, the first of two equal arguments is more effective if the audience is tired or not very interested. Janis (1957) found that the first argument presented for or against participation in civil defense was more persuasive as measured by the listeners' readiness to volunteer. Miller and Campbell (1959) found that the first-presented argument was highly effective when both are presented on the same occasion, whether students were given a posttest immediately or after one week. But if the two sides of an argument are presented one week apart and immediately tested on the second week, recency is stronger than primacy.

With people already possessing an opinion, McGuire (1963) has shown that attitudes change more if points they favor are presented first. If nonfavored points are presented first, the students seem to listen with *but . . .* on their minds. They seem to resist contrary points until their own have been expressed. Because the students are emotionally involved, and attitudes are partly the product of emotions, this is a more powerful factor than those previously considered. Since it is difficult to know the range of students' views in one class, it may often be advisable to start a period with class discussion after raising a question, and only then go on to lecture (if necessary for complete treatment of the question) rather than start with a lecture that produces resistance.

Cohen (1964) reports that if, after hearing only one side of a controversial issue, listeners make a response that publicly indicates their position on an issue, they are less likely to change their minds. This effect does not operate if they anonymously fill in a questionnaire. This is worth bearing in mind when dealing with student protest or other forms of negotiation. (Politicians, too, sometimes find it difficult to change their minds in public.) On one occasion when I sought the cooperation of a class for introducing an innovation in teaching, one vocal member at once declared dogmatically that he would not cooperate. The reasons for his impulsive reaction need not concern us, but it was necessary during ensuing discussion to make him feel there would be no loss of face by withdrawing from his publicly stated position. It was necessary to make it clear that he was not regarded as finally committed and that no one would notice if he changed his mind (for example, first "the door had to be kept open," and second, it was necessary to draw attention away from the individual by dissociating viewpoints and personalities).

5. Credibility of the Lecturer

The persuasiveness of a lecture will vary with the credibility of the lecturer, and Hovland, Janis, and Kelley (1953) have shown that the credibility of "communicators" (not necessarily in a lecture situation) is the result of their expertise, trustworthiness, fairness, and intentions as perceived by listeners. Of these, fairness was found to be more important than expertise and intent. Aspects of the person that were irrelevant to the subject, such as appearance, prestige, prowess in sport, and membership of a minority group, were also found to be influential. Tanner (1968) has shown that a lecturer's influence is enhanced by the support of a student confidant or an expert. In short, lecturers are more likely to be believed if they are perceived as a good guy by their students. Academic expertise is not the only factor, or even the most influential one; the effectiveness of lecturers in achieving attitudinal objectives is strongly influenced by their relationship with their class.

6. The Amount of Attitude Change Advocated

Up to a certain point, the degree of attitude change will increase the greater the change required. But beyond that point, at first little, and then no change, is obtained (Cohen, 1964). It is as if there are limits to individuals' credulity, and when the limit is reached they refuse to yield an inch.

This implies that if lecturers require a big change in the attitudes of their audience, they will have to design their programs in small steps. Since not all their audience will change by the same amount, the size of the steps will need to be progressively smaller.

Cohen reports that the limits of credulity vary with the credibility of the source of information. With respected and credible teachers, the greater the discrepancy between the students' views and those presented, the greater will be the shift in attitudes. With doubtful or less credible lecturers, the degree of resistance increases as the discrepancy increases. Aronson, Turner, and Carlsmith (1963) demonstrated this by giving students reviews of a literary work that were attributed to either T. S. Eliot or a fellow student; the reviews had been carefully graded with regard to their estimates of the value of a literary work. As the praise said to be given by Eliot increased, so the estimates of the work's value increasingly exceeded those expressed in a pretest. When the same praise was said to have come from the fellow student, changes in attitude increased up to a point but then decreased. It should be noticed that, as in a lecture situation in which students can make no contribution, the opinion of the "information source" could not be changed or further elaborated. The reverse is true when attitudes are expressed in student tutorials or group discussion.

However, Cohen has suggested that the advantage of high credibility is nil after three weeks. He explains this in terms of dissociation of information from its source, or the interaction of experimental subjects in discussion. This is not to say that there is no attitude change at all, but that those who record big changes revert to their original position in time.

7. Personality of the Student

The degree of attitude change in students also depends on their degree of "persuasibility." Hovland and Janis (1959) have suggested this as a personality trait with seven characteristics.

> *Low Self-Esteem.* Students who hold themselves and their opinions in low esteem are more likely to change their attitudes by persuasion. Positive correlations were obtained between measures of attitude change and scales based on self-rating questionnaires administered by Janis and Field (1959).
>
> *Perceptual Dependence.* Witkin (1962) has shown that some students tend to perceive themselves with reference to their physical environment more than others who perceive themselves and relations between objects independently. These differences correlated with Rorschach and other personality tests. Students who are dependent on the environment are more easily persuaded.
>
> *Other-Directedness.* People who are inner-directed, in that they have strong personal motives and goals, are less easily persuaded than those who are weak-willed.

Social Isolation. Cohen (1964) argues that people who are isolated seek social contact and are therefore more suggestible. This is consistent with the work of Asch (1951) and others on the power of group pressures for conformity.

Authoritarianism. Some psychologists have suggested there is an authoritarian-democratic dimension in our personality that is capable of measurement. People at the authoritarian end of this scale not only give orders to their inferiors but more willingly accept them from their superiors than do those with democratic attitudes. Cohen suggests that they accept presented attitudes more readily than "democrats" in the way that they more readily accept orders. Since lectures, when compared with discussions, are authoritarian situations, this is consistent with Smithers's finding (1970a) that dogmatic students (as measured by the Rokeach Dogmatism Test) prefer to be given very direct guidance.

Richness of Fantasy. People with good imagination are most easily convinced.

Sex. Hovland and Janis (1959) suggested that the acquiescent social role of women makes them more persuasible than men, who display more variable changes in attitude; but whether this generalization is applicable forty years later is more doubtful.

The small but positive correlations between personality tests and changeability of attitudes may be explained by a combination of three processes: fear of social disapproval, feelings of inadequacy, and motivated gullibility. The first could be described in terms of group pressure or conditioning. For example, the desire for approval can be rewarded, and attitudes strengthened, by saying "good" (Hildum and Brown, 1956; Singer, 1961). The role of conditioning and group pressure is also confirmed by Scott's finding (1957) that students proposing the opposite view to the one they actually believed showed greater attitude change if their side won the debate. But the implicit principle of learning-through-activity suggests that this process is not very applicable in lectures.

The effect of feeling inadequate is illustrated above in discussion of the characteristics perceptual dependence, other-directedness, social isolation, and authoritarianism. Motivated gullibility is related to the characteristics of low self-esteem and richness of fantasy. Students also have a need to impose meaning and organization on experience. Cohen (1964) has demonstrated that students with a high need for cognitive clarity, who are sometimes called "sharpeners," may change their attitudes to achieve it. Paradoxically, therefore, with this particular kind of student increasing ambiguity and lack of clarity in a lecture could force the student to change attitudes more than a clear lecture would—provided that the lecture was not so obscure that nothing could be sharpened. Obviously, though, in view of the difficulty of obtaining this balance and the fact that not all students are sharpeners, vague lectures are not to be recommended. The important point is that students who work hard to reconcile opposing views display greater attitude change than others. Lectures themselves do not provide time for this work, but they may provide the viewpoints.

Summary of Strategies

In Chapter One, it was argued on the basis of experiments in teaching that the lecture method is relatively inappropriate to teach values or to change attitudes. The more analytical findings of psychologists referred to in this chapter confirm, and to some extent explain, this relative unsuitability. If, however, teachers are obliged to use the lecture method, there is some evidence that they will be more effective if they are fair-minded, present more than one point of view, consider the students' viewpoints first (perhaps by asking their opinions), present their own conclusion first if the students do not already have one, and require some reconsideration of the issues within three weeks at the most.

PART FOUR

ALTERNATIVES WHEN LECTURING IS INADEQUATE

CHAPTER SEVENTEEN

THE LECTURE METHOD ALONE IS RARELY ADEQUATE

Psychological reasons.

1. Give feedback to students and lecturers and get feedback from them.

2. Use rehearsal.

3. Avoid interference and negative transfer.

4. Encourage deep processing.

5. Reduce the intensity with self-pacing.

6. Favor active learning.

7. Maintain high levels of attention.

8. Foster motivation by activity.

9. Accept and use human nature.

10. Teach thought and feeling by discussion.

11. Use a mix of methods to teach information too.

12. Match the mix of learning styles.

A general educational argument.

1. Different kinds of objectives are best achieved by different methods.

2. Teachers usually have different kinds of objectives in any one lesson.

3. Therefore the objectives of any one lesson are usually best achieved by different methods.

Chapter One showed that there are many methods just as effective as lectures. In principle, any of them could replace lectures. But this book is not about other methods. They have their defects too. Part Four is about combining other methods with lectures to compensate where lectures are inadequate.

Using evidence already presented, I shall argue in Part Four that the inherent defects of the lecture method mean that, on its own, it is rarely adequate. Therefore, if not replaced, it will need to be combined with other methods in some way.

Accordingly, in this chapter I shall first review the reasons why the lecture method alone is rarely adequate. In Chapter Eighteen, I shall describe a number of teaching methods that can be used with lectures; then, in Chapter Nineteen, I shall briefly suggest some ways in which they may be combined.

It must be emphasized that the statement "the lecture method alone is rarely adequate" does not imply (as is sometime misconstrued) that the lecture method is rarely appropriate. The lecture has a place, but the place it is given is often too prominent. Surveys show that lecturing is still the dominant teaching method, yet lecturers themselves yearn for more variety (Strasser and Ozgur, 1995). My point is that the heavy reliance placed upon lecturing and its frequent use as an all-purpose method are unjustified in the light of evidence as to what it can achieve (Part One) and the psychological limitations of students (Part Two).

Psychological Reasons

Much of the information given in the early chapters of this book comes together in this short chapter. We have seen, particularly in Chapters One, Two, and Three, that there are strong psychological reasons for supposing that the sole use of the lecture method for fifty minutes or an hour is ineffective. The following reasons for using a variety of teaching methods in the same period of teaching are not in any particular order, but I believe they add up to a powerful case for variety in each lesson.

1. Give Feedback to Students and Lecturers and Get Feedback from Them

The importance of feedback in learning, and in pacing the teacher, has been stressed (see in particular Chapter Twelve); but verbal feedback is not obtained unless a lecturer stops lecturing and permits some form of response from the students. Weaver and Cotrell (1985) have described what they call "mental aerobics." During a lecture students are asked to take half a sheet of paper and write their reactions to the lecture thus far. This technique encourages feedback, expression, involvement, criticism, insight, and higher levels of thinking. The buzz-group and horseshoe-group methods are also particularly effective for two-way feedback (see Chapter Eighteen).

2. Use Rehearsal

A lecture without pause or interruption does not permit students to rehearse what they have learned. Quite the opposite; one part of a lecture may interfere with memory of another. Rehearsal is important to consolidate students' memory traces, to develop concepts by their use, to relate different items of information, and to obtain a view of the whole topic being considered. (See "Rehearsing the Material" in Chapter Two and "The Effect of a Short Break" in Chapter Three.) After the lecture is too late. Furthermore, as Kelly and O'Donnell (1994) among others have shown, students who review lecture notes in pairs or small groups adopt a more comprehensive approach than individuals do. They extract, elaborate, and restructure the information better. That being so, when is rehearsal better for short, small-group reviews than during the lecture period itself?

3. Avoid Interference and Negative Transfer

Furthermore, because the concepts used in a lecture are likely to be similar, "negative transfer" (see page 43) is more likely to cause confusion than if opportunity is provided for students to clarify what they have heard. The longer you lecture without a break, the longer will be the period damaged by retroactive interference.

4. Encourage Deep Processing

Thus an early opportunity to reconsider and organize the information before it is forgotten will make it mean something in terms of the students' background knowledge, and thereby reduce the amount to be remembered (Chapter Two). Without an opportunity to digest what has been said, there is information overload, information is lost, and deep processing is impossible.

One way to reduce information overload and facilitate reorganization of material is to use an advance organizer. This could be a short buzz group to consider a problem before you lecture on it. Brant, Hooper, and Sugrue (1991) found that students using a computer simulation as a framework for understanding before formal instruction did better than those who used it as a synthesis afterward. They understood the lecture better.

Browne, Hoag, and Berilla (1995) complain of a disparity between faculty intent and practice in their failure to promote critical thought at the graduate level. They recommend interrupting lectures by asking questions, introducing controversy, devising test instruments, and integrating knowledge across the curriculum.

5. Reduce the Intensity with Self-Pacing

The tendency for many lecturers to go too fast results in psychological interference, while the interspersed use of self-paced teaching methods such as short periods of discussion may reduce the intensity of learning demanded.

6. Favor Active Learning

It has long been known that active methods of learning are more effective than passive ones. Indeed, conference papers demonstrating the fact no longer reach the research journals (Collard, 1994; Drew, 1990; Troisi, 1983). It's no longer news. Although the amount of activity involved in listening to lectures is a relative question and can be considerably increased if students are trained in how to listen, the method remains a relatively passive form of learning. As long ago as 1925, experiments by Bane and others showed that retention of information presented in lectures is worse in delayed tests of recall than when the same information is taught by more active methods such as discussion. This was not the case on immediate tests.

One technique is to give students a photocopied extract from a research journal to criticize during a lecture pause. Most lectures consist of secondary material, not the lecturer's own research. Most textbooks are the same. Too many university students rely solely on these secondary sources. In addition to demanding active thought and judgment, this technique can initiate students' use of the research journals (Pennington, 1992).

Bonwell and Eison (1991) recommend pauses in lectures for brief demonstrations, ungraded written exercises as precursors to discussion, feedback, debates, role playing, and problem solving, and for students to consolidate their notes.

7. Maintain High Levels of Attention

The lecture method is relatively poor for maintaining attention. Compared with the uninterrupted lecture, variations in teaching methods will usually provide greater novelty, more arousing auditory stimuli, changes in posture, and opportunities to take occasional microsleeps without serious loss in efficiency. The importance of novelty in teaching methods was demonstrated when Little (1964) found that lectures supplemented by periods of programmed learning were popular with students for the first three weeks of a course but not thereafter, because programmed learning demands even more concentration than lectures. Several times after significant points were made in a lecture, Hollingsworth (1995) instructed students to discuss for two minutes what they thought was most important. Compared with a control group, these students listened more attentively, and although their advantage was insignificant on a delayed test, they scored significantly higher on an immediate posttest.

There is no one measure of arousal that is entirely satisfactory, but heart rate gives some indication and is relatively easy to obtain with the use of pulsemeters. Figure 17.1 shows the heart rate for four military personnel aged about forty-five, in a group of twelve during two lessons. During the lecture there was a relatively smooth decline in a curve remarkably like that suggested by Lloyd (1968; see Figure 3.4 in this book). Three weeks later, the teacher used a variety of methods; after a relatively stressful situation in which each student spoke to the rest of the class, there was no general decline. Indeed, the group as a whole was probably as alert during buzz groups after sixty-five minutes as they had been for most of the previous hour.

FIGURE 17.1. MEAN HEART RATES DURING TWO TEACHING PERIODS.

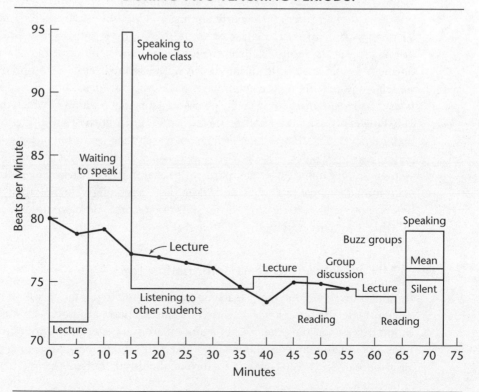

8. Foster Motivation by Activity

In contrast to the performance of a solitary lecturer, the provision of problems and ways of involving the students fosters motivation. Involvement motivates; passive listening does not. Furthermore, naturalistic studies (Hertz-Lazarowitz and others, 1981) show that although social interactions between students do occur in lectures, lecturers do not use this social motivation constructively to enhance learning.

9. Accept and Use Human Nature

Small-group discussions are natural; lectures are not. It is human nature to talk and to socialize. The lecture method stifles the desire for self-expression instead of using it, and it disregards the natural desire for social interaction, especially with one's peers.

10. Teach Thought and Feeling by Discussion

We saw in Chapter One that thought and feeling are best encouraged by methods other than lectures, particularly discussion. Cognitive skills, such as the ability to apply principles, to analyze or synthesize complex data, to make decisions or fine judgments, require active learning before the memory of detail received during a short period of lecturing dies away. Thus intellectual development in a subject requires mixing the cognitive processes involved. Unless special care is taken, the lecture method normally places students in a position in which they are only concerned with one process: the acquisition of information. But education is about developing thought and feeling, not just stuffing heads full of facts. Galotti (1995) instructed pairs of students to develop an argument about how many kinds of thought they observed in their partner (for example, geometric analogies, moral dilemmas, deductive reasoning, and "everyday" reasoning). He then used a combination of lectures, small groups, and class discussion to develop students' critical thinking, creativity, and models of thought.

11. Use a Mix of Methods to Teach Information Too

By definition, using numerous teaching methods entails greater variety of stimuli than a single one does. Because varied stimuli maintain arousal levels, we might expect diverse teaching methods to maintain arousal better than unremitting lectures. I compared three teaching methods (lecture, audiotape, and reading forms), all using identical words, with a mixture of the three. Students scored better on truth-functional tests after the mixture, and the scores for reading and audiotape showed the attention decrement (see Chapter Three). I must admit the lectures did not, perhaps because I unconsciously used nonverbals to maintain attention (Bligh, 1974).

12. Match the Mix of Learning Styles

If students differ in the methods by which they learn best, and teachers should adapt their methods to maximize their effectiveness, it seems reasonable to think that teachers should use a variety of methods to cater to the differences between students. This is not easy to do systematically because of the difficulty of knowing specific students' needs; but it is a further reason for adopting a general policy of using a variety of methods.

Over the past seventy-five years, there has been surprisingly little research directly focusing on how lecture effectiveness relates to personality differences. There is reason to believe that anxious introverts, students with a more favorable disposition toward authority, and students who are reflective and theorist rather than activist and pragmatic prefer lectures to more participative methods. But the relative strength of their preference is not reliably matched with greater learning from lectures compared with other students.

With reference to reading and independent study, Marton and others have distinguished students with a disposition to memorize facts from those who are more thoughtful. It might be thought that the former would feel more comfortable in lectures than some other methods, but whether teachers should give them the diet they prefer is another matter.

A General Educational Argument

Apart from the specific inadequacies of lectures, which may be compensated by combining them with other methods, there is a general educational argument for the use of varied teaching methods within a period of teaching. Briefly summarized, this argument is that:

1. Different kinds of objectives are best achieved by different methods.
2. Teachers usually have a number of different kinds of objectives in any one lesson.
3. Therefore, the objectives of any one lesson are usually best achieved by different methods.

1. Different Kinds of Objectives Are Best Achieved by Different Methods

Much of the argument to establish this proposition depends upon the premise that students learn best by active methods involving the desired behavior. In other words, the best way to teach people to analyze data is to place them in situations where they have to analyze it; the best way to teach students to put their thoughts in words is to use methods that require them to express themselves; the best way to teach them how to apply their knowledge is to let them apply it; and so on.

The truth of this principle is particularly evident in practical skills. The details of a lecture demonstration are soon forgotten unless rehearsal is followed by practice. Similarly, though it may be true that to learn facts they must first be presented, if understanding and thinking involve actively relating one fact to another then students will need to be given a task that has been consciously planned to include this activity. Again, although some suggestions have been made for when a lecture method has to be used, attitudes cannot easily be taught by any form of presentation method. What the teacher has to do is provide situations in which students will consciously consider and apply their attitudes. It is only when they express their attitudes in relation to others that many students become aware of what their attitudes are, so that they may begin to consider them more objectively. This may require problem-solving or decision-making situations, but the lecture is essentially a method that inhibits expression by the students. (Free-group discussion, role play, T-groups, and counseling are also suitable for achieving attitude objectives but cannot be used so easily in a lecture room.)

In one way, this premise may be thought so obvious that it requires no argument. Insofar as one lecture is like another, it seems reasonable to expect that they will produce similar effects. To expect to teach practical skills from one lecture and attitude change from another using the same basic techniques seems unduly optimistic; yet the reliance on the lecture method in some institutions makes this kind of assumption.

2. Teachers Usually Have Different Kinds of Objectives in Any One Lesson

It cannot be proved that teachers usually have a number of different kinds of objectives in any one lesson, because one cannot know what most teachers' objectives are. I can only appeal to you the reader, if you are a teacher, to consider your own objectives for yourself. There would be something odd about saying "I want the students to know these facts, but I'm not bothered at the moment whether they understand them or see how they are related to things I've said in other lectures," or "I want them to be able to conduct this experiment, but I won't worry about their scientific attitude." It seems obvious that one must teach these things on the same occasion. Similarly, in many subjects it would be educationally unsound to separate considerations of theory from practical application.

3. Therefore the Objectives of Any One Lesson Are Usually Best Achieved by Different Methods

If premises 1 and 2 are accepted, it seems to follow logically that the objectives of any one lesson are usually best achieved by different methods.

It will be seen from both the psychological reasons and the educational argument that discussion methods provide important combinations when used with lectures. Therefore, in the next chapter particular attention will be paid to discussion methods, with special reference to the objectives they may achieve.

Conclusion

Taken altogether, the arguments are very strong for mixing lectures with other methods within the same period of teaching. This is not just theory. There are a host of unpublished documents available through ERIC (the Educational Resources Information Center) that attest to the importance of variety (Zacharakis-Jutz, 1983, and Couch, 1983, on guided design; Osterman and others, 1985, on feedback; Drew, 1990, on peer teaching; Bonwell and Eison, 1991, on pauses, demonstrations, and ungraded exercises; Browne, Hoag, and Berilla, 1995, on critical thinking; Campbell and Lison, 1995, on simulations; Ransdell, 1992, on computer activities; Collard, 1994, on role playing, games, debates, and lectures based on students' questions; and Fontenot, 1996, on cooperative learning techniques in science and mathematics lectures, to name only a few).

There are others, outside the scope of this book, where the alternatives involve no lecturing at all (for example, Hubbard, 1990, on tertiary mathematics). These will increasingly use computer disseminations.

In short, not only the dominance of lecturing but also the presumption that teachers and visiting speakers will lecture must cease. The alternatives are practical, and it is some of those practicalities we must now consider.

CHAPTER EIGHTEEN

TEACHING METHODS TO USE WITH LECTURES

Buzz groups.

   1. Possible methods.

   2. Possible objectives.

Horseshoe groups.

   1. Method.

   2. Possible objectives.

Controlled discussion.

Lecture-discussion method.

The case-study method (case discussion).

Short talks by students.

Reading, audiotapes, and videotapes.

Computer facilities in lecture rooms.

In this chapter, I shall suggest a number of teaching methods that can be used in a lecture room, though they probably cannot all be used in any lecture room or with any students. Therefore you will need to select those that are practicable in your circumstances. Nonetheless, it is hoped these methods will suggest new ones and new combinations of them and that you will jot down your ideas as they come to mind. (If left until later, they may be forgotten because the rest of the chapter, being similar information, may induce retroactive interference.)

Jot down ideas here:

_____

_____

_____

_____

_____

Buzz Groups

Buzz groups are seldom used in college teaching. My purpose here is to encourage lecturers to consider using them more often, and to suggest when they are appropriate. To this end there are two broad themes: the use of buzz groups is possible in a wide range of circumstances, and they may be used to achieve a variety of objectives.

1. Possible Methods

Buzz groups are groups of two to six members who discuss issues or problems for a short period, or periods, within a lesson. Used within a lecture situation, the most common method is to ask students in alternating rows to turn around to face those in the row behind (Figure 18.1). This may be difficult in a steeply terraced lecture theater or where high-backed chairs are fixed tightly together in rows. In this case, the groups may consist of two or three members in the same row (Figure 18.2). Notice it may be necessary to ask one or two students to move to a group.

In either situation there should not normally be more than three in the same row if those at the ends are to be able to see and hear each other with ease. Another reason for moving around is that to keep the overall noise level down it is advisable where possible to ensure that the maximum distance between any two members of the same group is less than the distance between groups.

If it is desirable to vary the composition of the groups, those who did not turn round the first time may do so the second, while part of the front row moves across to form a group with the rest (Figure 18.1). If the seating position is uncomfortable, the length of a "buzz" period should be short.

If the problem set is one where students may have highly individual viewpoints (as is frequently the case in philosophy and literature), smaller groups will offer individual students a better opportunity to develop their own thinking and have it considered by others.

FIGURE 18.1. BUZZ GROUPS IN A TYPICAL CLASSROOM.

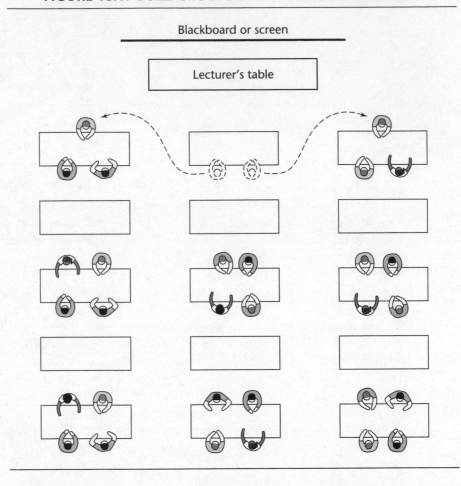

To ensure that every individual has something to contribute to a group and that it has no idle passengers (sometimes call "social loafers"), the task can first be set individually. As soon as the first students seem to have finished, or even sooner, suggest that they compare their answers with their neighbors'. Then encourage others to do so, sooner rather than later. In this way, buzz groups are introduced without being proclaimed as a new teaching method—a useful technique if it is thought that some students might resist the method.

Tasks should be focused and specific ("List three reasons for . . . ," not, "Why do you think . . . ?"). Listing tasks has the advantage that the teacher can see the

FIGURE 18.2. BUZZ GROUPS
IN A STEEPLY TERRACED LECTURE THEATER.

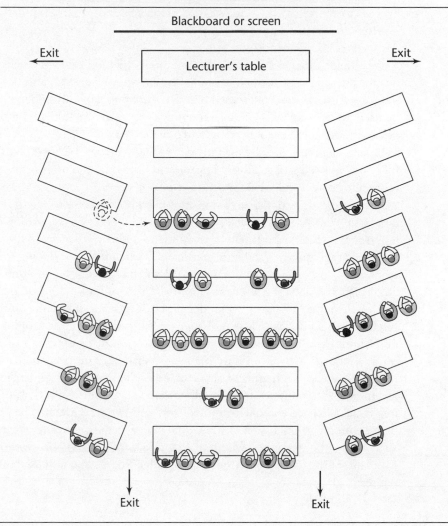

length of lists from a distance without invading and disturbing groups. Break down big tasks into smaller steps. This requires the teacher to analyze the thought processes expected of the students. It is usually, but not necessarily, better if they involve concrete and familiar examples from which the lecturer can then go on to draw general or more abstract principles (Jenkins, 1992).

Although discussion techniques are among the most difficult teaching methods for a teacher to learn, buzz groups are among the easiest, and they may be the basis for developing other methods. They are popular with students, they may be used in either formal or informal settings with 6 to 360 students, and they are flexible in that they do not necessarily require elaborate preparation and may take as little as half a minute of class time depending on their objective. Consequently, they may be used in a relatively impromptu fashion if the need arises. Furthermore, they may be adapted for a variety of objectives.

It is important to realize that groups need not buzz for a long time. Even a task lasting thirty seconds, such as writing the next line of a calculation or jotting a personal opinion, is sufficient to rearouse an audience (Figure 3.7).

In fact it is quite a good idea, particularly when first introducing the method to students, to pressure them by saying, "I will only give you two minutes to discuss this" and then say after one minute, "You've had half your time." This teaches them that activity is demanded and that a businesslike and committed approach is required. Your classes are no place for students to hang around. Di Vesta and Smith (1979) compared giving three two-minute pauses (in a twenty-one-minute lecture) with six-minute pauses either before or after the lecture. The pauses were filled with group discussion, individual review, or an irrelevant puzzle. Interspersed pauses with group discussion was the most effective as judged by free recall and cued recall tests immediately and two weeks later. The postlecture pause with group discussion or individual review came next. The irrelevant puzzles before, or interspersed within, the lecture interfered with learning. (See also Ruhl and Suritsky, 1995, referred to in Chapter Three, who also used two-minute pauses to great effect.)

2. Possible Objectives

The objectives of clarification, feedback, consolidation of understanding, and using concepts and terminology concern the acquisition of information. The objectives of practicing specific types of thought and teaching relevance have to do with the promotion of thought. And the objectives of releasing tensions, respite for anxious lecturers, confidence for reticent students, and building supportive relationships cultivate attitudes and feelings.

a. Clarification. Lecturers who think they may not have gotten their point across may set a problem or task for the students to work at in twos or threes. The problem should be simple but require knowledge of the point in question. The objective here is clarification. It may be achieved either by the students' teaching each other—which they may be able to do more simply than the lecturer who is an expert—or by the lecturer as the solution is demonstrated afterward.

b. Feedback. Lecturers will obtain feedback on the effectiveness of their teaching if, in the same situation, they visit those groups that seem to be having difficulty or receive suggested solutions from the class before demonstrating their own. By choosing a suitable task, feedback on the whole lesson can be obtained quite quickly.

c. Consolidation of Understanding. "I understood it at the time, but I don't now" is not an uncommon remark from students writing up experimental work or doing revision. What was required was some consolidation of the learning and understanding that took place. Almost any discussion situation could provide this, because all provide an active learning situation and use of the information taught. But buzz groups have a particularly important role because they may take place immediately following the initial learning situation such as a lecture, and before substantial forgetting takes place (Chapter Two). Since the students in this case understand the information, the task should be more difficult than for "clarification." It may require the student to relate different parts of a lecture to one another or to common experience.

d. To Use Concepts and Terminology. The same kind of tasks will teach new concepts and terminology provided the students can only perform the tasks by using the concepts. We saw in Chapter Two that the articulation and rehearsal of information assist its memory. The ineffectiveness of presentation methods alone for learning terminology may be demonstrated if you read three pages of a dictionary and then test yourself to find the proportion of meanings you can remember only one day later.

There is another powerful reason for using buzz groups to teach terminology. We saw in Table 14.2 that on an immediate postlecture test, students typically score 100 percent for (A) terms in the student's everyday language, 80 percent for (B) new terms defined in everyday language, and 20 percent for (C) words defined with other new terms. As students use B words in a buzz group, the words shift to become more like A; that is, they become part of the student's everyday language. Consequently, words that were on level C shift toward level B. Their comprehension shifts from

20 percent toward 80 percent. As a result, lecturers will be far more effective if, before using C-level words, they initiate buzz groups that will use B-level words.

e. Practice Specific Types of Thought. The ability to think is best acquired by practice. It is part of the job of the teacher to provide the opportunity. This requires the design of situations in which the student must apply, analyze, and evaluate information. Buzz groups provide one such situation, although horseshoe groups, seminars, and group tutorials probably allow more thorough thought if there is more time and greater diversity of opinion. Problem-solving situations may teach the application of information. Questions such as "What is the difference between . . .?" and "In what way are . . . and . . . similar?" require analytical thinking. Discussion of evaluative statements or simply listing the merits and demerits of a theory may teach evaluative thinking. (The question "What are the merits of . . . ?" is sometimes neglected in favor of a more destructive form of critical thinking. Both have their place in education. The former may be important for developing an appreciation of research and its difficulties.)

If we suppose that Chapter Two is an account of a lecture (although the way points are made would be unsuitable if spoken), the lecturer has only described brain processes and presented a list of factors causing forgetting and factors aiding memory, together with some applications to teaching students. The audience has not been made to think about these factors or use the concepts, nor has any attempt been made to consolidate their learning of them. When students can be made to analyze the concepts for themselves, all these objectives may be achieved. For example a lecturer may form buzz groups and give them a task: "If you think about the concept of 'motivation' as it affects memory, you will realize that I could have classified it as a factor aiding memory just as easily as a factor causing forgetting. 'Interference', on the other hand, could only be classified as a hindrance to memory. Look at each of the other factors I mentioned and decide which is like motivation in this respect, and which is like interference."

f. Teaching Relevance. Relevance may be encouraged by providing a task that has definite criteria of completion. Problem-solving tasks are usually suitable. A handout, placed in the middle of each group, with a succession of short problems each with space for an answer will provide a physical focus of attention and criteria of relevance. However, irrelevance may spark off creative and original solutions. If creativity is one of the course objectives, perhaps the students will first need to be taught to distinguish between problems that have definite solutions and those that do not.

g. ***Release Tensions.*** Just as individual tutorials and counseling provide a confidential situation between a member of staff and a student, buzz groups provide a confidential situation among a small number of students. Yet, unlike the college dining hall or the student union bar, they are within the total teaching situation. They provide the immediate reaction of students to the teacher, and teacher-student interaction is immanent. Consequently, they possess unique properties in their group dynamics that the teacher can use. Buzz groups may be used to release tensions because everyone has the opportunity to express them. The discipline of listening to lectures prevents the release of these tensions; the energy needs to be constructively channeled. Thus the use of buzz groups is a particularly valuable technique for bad lecturers! They may be used to work off examination nerves that prevent attention to any kind of class teaching, but horseshoe groups are usually even better.

h. ***Respite for Anxious Lecturers.*** Buzz groups may also be used to give the flustered teacher breathing space. No doubt in the best of all possible worlds the teacher is never flustered; but some new teachers in universities, thinking that they must lecture all the time, find that if a lecture starts badly they are unable to recover the situation. It is sensitive lecturers who easily go from bad to worse in this way. The use of buzz groups can give them time to think and recover their composure. Furthermore, group work is precisely the kind of teaching in which their sensitivity is an asset.

When buzz groups are used in this way, the objective is an immediate one in terms of class management. It is only indirectly related to the long-term objectives of the course, but such secondary objectives are nonetheless important in the long run too.

i. ***Confidence for Reticent Students.*** The same confidentiality and release of tension may encourage reticent students to put their ideas into words. They are therefore more likely to be listened to, heeded, and accepted by a small group. Each of these gives encouragement. With the prior agreement of their group, they are more likely to risk a contribution to the whole class at the reporting-back stage or in a larger group. Since most forms of student assessment and selection place heavy emphasis on verbal ability, and the ability to express oneself is an important objective of most teaching, buzz groups have an important role with sensitive students. Since patterns of college behavior (which may be quite different from their behavior at home) are probably established in their first semester, buzz groups may be particularly important at that time.

j. Building Supportive Relationships. This conclusion is reinforced if buzz groups are used to foster a cohesive class spirit. Although few people make a large number of friendships quickly, a buzz group places up to six students on speaking terms with each of the others in quite a short time. The observant teacher will be able to notice if these relationships continue outside the classroom. Assuming students do not always sit in the same seats, the network of relationships may be broadened by frequently using the method. The speed with which it establishes friendships is important for short and sandwich courses. It is useful for evening classes and nonvocational courses where students frequently come for the social contact as much as the social culture, and where student numbers are important. Early friendships are also important for the full-time student away from home for the first time. Signs of homesickness are difficult for the teacher to observe, but the work of student medical officers suggests that it is more frequent than many teachers suppose.

Thus it is important to see teaching methods in their social and emotional roles, as well as their academic context. Buzz groups can satisfy the need for social interaction. They may not be possible in all circumstances, but they are in a great many. Most teachers will have some of the objectives I've described at some time, and buzz groups are an appropriate method of achieving them. It therefore seems probable that most teachers should at some time consider using them.

Horseshoe Groups

"Horseshoe groups" is my term for this method. I have not seen it described by anyone else.

1. Method

A horseshoe group may be an amalgamation of two buzz groups, varying in size from four to twelve members. The larger the group, the shorter the time it will take to answer problems that demand special knowledge, skills, or particular procedures, because the necessary expertise is more likely to be found in the groups. If the answer to the problem is a matter of opinion, consensus will on average be obtained more quickly in a small group, as there will be less variation of opinion to be reconciled (Klein, 1961). In most cases, a group of six is very convenient. Groups larger than this may break into smaller conversation groups for short periods of time at first, and then longer periods—unless there is a leader, the problem supplies a sense of common purpose, or the seating arrangement creates a tightly knit group.

By definition, a discussion group is arranged so that each member may interact face-to-face with every other member (Abercrombie, 1978). Obviously, in these groups the seating arrangement is in the shape of a horseshoe (Figure 18.3). Chairs are normally arranged in a C or U shape with the opening facing either the center or the front of the room. The central opening enables the teacher to stand in the middle of the class, listen to the progress of each of the groups, and unobtrusively join each group to give help as needed. This is made easier if there is a vacant chair in position at the opening ("+" in Figure 18.3) so that the teacher closes the circle, making it more intimate, when joining the group. The arrival of the teacher can easily kill discussion. To avoid this, enter the group at the students' eye level. Do not stand towering above them. Crouch if necessary. And avert your gaze, avoiding eye contact for two or three exchanges of conversation after joining a group. If you do not, their eyes will invite you to take over and dominate rather than listen as an equal in the group. It is as if they say, "The professor has arrived. He will tell us all the right answers, and we won't have to think for ourselves."

FIGURE 18.3. THE ARRANGEMENT OF FURNITURE FOR HORSESHOE GROUPS.

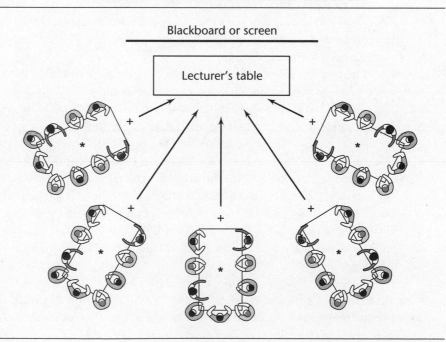

The front-facing openings, as in Figure 18.3, can be used in a similar way and have the additional advantage that the teacher may stop the discussions to explain a difficult point from the front with the use of the blackboard or other visual aids. It is a useful arrangement for alternating formal teaching with group work; and if the problems are written on the board rather than separately for each group, the students may refer to them as they go along. Provided there is a table in the center of the C for specimens and notes, the flexibility in teaching method offered by this seating arrangement is very convenient for any teacher who possesses a variety of teaching skills, and who is sufficiently sensitive to student reaction to know when to change method and what method to use. The horseshoe-group method is a particularly good one for getting to know the students when the size of the class is less then forty and is never taught in small groups at any other time.

One caution should perhaps be observed: the teacher should make sure that the sides of the C are not long and straight so that those at one end cannot see those at the other. As with buzz groups, three per straight side is the maximum because it is possible to lean forward to see past one's neighbor, but not past two people.

It should be noticed that this method requires careful planning. Thought must be given to the arrangement of the furniture. Time must be allowed for introducing the problems, visiting each group (preferably more than once), and pooling the findings of the class at the end if necessary. "Introducing," "visiting," and "pooling" each require different teaching skills (for example, clear, succinct and interesting statement of a problem; sensitivity to both individual and group reactions; astute chairmanship).

The preparation of the problems often requires considerable thought if they are to develop student thinking in a specified direction. Table 18.1 presents a series of problems given to student teachers of physical medicine. The objective was to make them aware of philosophical assumptions in the treatment of patients. Formal lectures and group tutorials had not achieved this with previous students who failed to see the relevance of philosophy. Horseshoe groups succeeded. You are invited to place yourself in the position of these student teachers, answer the questions, compare your answers with those of another person, and find the reasons for any disagreements there may be. These reasons may either be assumptions themselves or point to assumptions. If assumptions were not made explicit in the discussions, it was the teacher's role to elicit them in visiting and during pooling.

Notice the technique of focusing thought. Most of the questions require very short answers, even one word; but taken together, they raise big issues. A series of precise questions help students focus on their dilemmas or exact points of disagreement. Judging from an experiment by Hinkle and Hinkle (1990), this is more

TABLE 18.1. A SERIES OF PROBLEMS FOR PHYSIOTHERAPISTS SEATED IN A HORSESHOE GROUP.

1. Is it true that you (students, patients) can sometimes choose to do one action rather than another?
2. Does choosing involve selection from various possibilities?
3. Is it a scientific assumption (an assumption made by scientists) that all physical events in the universe are completely caused (by what has happened before)?
4. Is this assumption valid?
5. If some process or events are completely caused and some are not, which are not?
6. Are all human actions physical processes?
7. Is all neural activity some kind of physical process?
8. Are all human actions completely caused?
9. If you answered no to Question 8:
    A. Which is not?
    B. Is it possible to have physiological theories?
    C. Is physiotherapy possible?
10. If you answered yes to Question 8:
    A. Is there a possibility of a person not doing what he or she in fact does?
    B. Can a person choose to do one thing rather than another?
11. Does having "professional or moral" standards or principles assume it is possible to choose one action rather than another?
12. If you answered yes to Question 11:
    A. Is there a conflict between having professional or moral standards or principles and believing scientific evidence?

effective than setting an essay on the lecture topic (and it certainly takes less grading time). They compared "focused freewriting" with "focused thought." Both improved comprehension, but the focused thought group was superior on a test one week later.

2. Possible Objectives

The major objective of teaching using horseshoe groups is that the students should think. Whether the precise kind of thinking is analytical, creative, evaluative, or applying general principles depends on the problem given.

A second objective is to provide an opportunity for feedback from the class to the teacher.

There are five kinds of problems that can be set to a horseshoe group. It is easier if these are introduced, broadly speaking, in the order presented here.

a. Seeking Information. There is the task to search for information, including an element of selection and organization of the information that is found. This may be set with the objective of teaching facts and their organization, but it may also be set with the objective of teaching how to find facts and how to use the available literature of the subject. This second objective is very important for students at the beginning of a course, and it may be that this task is suitable for buzz groups whose members know each other fairly well. In this latter case, the groups should feel free to go to the library and use other sources of reference during the period, and come back at a certain time to report their findings. I shall call this type of horseshoe group a "minisyndicate" since it only requires part of one lesson and no formal written report is needed. A lively method to acquaint up to thirty students with relevant literature available in the college library is to borrow about one hundred books for the duration of the lesson, arrange them about the room, and set problems that may be answered by using specific references given on the problem sheet. If reporting back is delayed until the following week and the books have to be returned at once to the library shelves before the students have finished their task, they usually use the library catalogs to complete it. This method is more effective than giving a bibliographical handout for an essay because their appetite is whetted, they know what they are looking for, and there is allegiance to the group to finish the job. The syndicate method may also be introduced by this means. (See Table 14.1.)

If one has a larger group and is more concerned with the first objective—especially the organization of facts—it saves class time to set specific reading before the lesson so that the students are expected to arrive having both read and selected appropriately. Much of the lesson is then concerned with organization and the consequent understanding of facts from different viewpoints.

It may be that not many lessons need to be spent on this kind of objective at the university level since these students have often learned these skills in secondary school. These skills are essential to any other kind of independent work on which so many courses and professions depend.

b. Convergent Thinking. The groups may be asked to work out a problem that has a correct answer. The term *problem* should be interpreted very widely here. It may consist of interpreting facts or identifying the cause of some phenomenon of the specific subject of which students have some previous knowledge from lecturers or prereading. Hence this kind of horseshoe group is normally used in conjunction with other teaching methods. It requires knowledge of facts and use of the general principles of the specific subject.

The usual objectives of this kind of discussion are to consolidate the knowledge of general principles, teach how to apply them, and teach students how to relate their knowledge of facts to principles. These three objectives are relevant to all levels of higher education.

Using more than two hundred subjects, Gore (1962) formed two experimental classes to compare the effectiveness of lectures and horseshoe groups of three or four students each given job sheets. In addition to the usual sources of information, films and visual aids were available for the horseshoe groups on request. Changes in group membership were permitted. The job sheets were also given to the students in lecture classes, but they had to be done outside lecture time. The performance of the horseshoe groups was significantly superior on tests at the end of the course, on delayed tests of retention of information, and on the answers to the job sheets themselves.

c. Divergent Thinking. One may also ask the groups to work on a problem with a number of possible answers. For example, there may be a number of possible interpretations, causes, or explanations of a given set of facts. In many ways, this kind of discussion has the same objectives as those mentioned under convergent thinking. But since there are a number of possible answers, it has the additional objective that students should be aware of, and understand, different points of view. Because of this, the form of the discussion often varies significantly from that in which where there is a correct answer. Where there is a correct answer, the form of the discussion will converge toward that answer. Anything that does not do so many be eliminated by the participants as irrelevant or incorrect. Where there are a number of possible answers, the discussion will have a number of possible strands running at the same time. Consequently, the task of the group will be much more difficult. If the students do not do so, the teacher must relate the alternative answers either when the groups are visited or when students report their conclusions at the end. The teacher must try to preserve a balance between the different answers that are put forward. This requires an open, clear, and flexible mind. The teacher must make sure that the alternative answers are laid out clearly, side by side, either on paper or on the blackboard so that the differences and similarities can be understood easily. Flipcharts or poster paper can be used for this, though I often get students to itemize their points on overhead projector transparencies.

d. Judgment, Discernment, and Criticism. A fourth kind of problem may require the students to make an act of judgment. Once a number of possible answers are laid out before the students, they can then decide which is the best. For example, students may be asked to evaluate a theory. In these cases, there may be a judgment commonly accepted by the experts in the field, which the teacher wishes the students to infer by the same reasoning.

Insofar as there is an accepted answer, the discussion techniques here may be similar to that in convergent thinking, although the criteria for the judgment are much wider because they will often involve the use of principles, such as the principles of scientific method, which are outside the empirical science. These principles are frequently not those that can be looked up in a textbook before the lesson. They are principles of reasoning that the teacher cannot necessarily expect the students to have learned from lectures or reading before they come to the class. Therefore they often require a questioning technique to make the students think behind their everyday judgments. This technique involves posing a number of questions that crystallize and polarize the central issues so that the students' answers will form a closely reasoned argument. The best questions are those with yes-no answers, but these take a lot of thoughtful preparation (see examples given in Table 18.1). In this respect, the technique is more subtle than in convergent thinking.

e. Revision and Planning Exam Answers. Horseshoe groups have a very useful function in revision and in preparing students for essay examinations. They provide an outlet for preexamination nerves that seems relevant to the student, whereas the presentation of yet more information in lectures only provides more to be anxious about. The urgency of the preexamination situation enables horseshoe groups to be used with larger classes than at other times. The limitation in size is usually dictated by the furniture, space, and general physical provision rather than the number of students. The problems set require the group to plan answers to examination questions in about fifteen minutes each. The teacher may present a specimen plan, conduct a brief period of pooling the groups' ideas, or, if there is time and the groups have been given different questions, visit each group to improve its "model answers." Used in this way, horseshoe groups are particularly good for helping students see the breadth and possible interpretations of questions, and to suggest ways of organizing the answers. They provide a suitable opportunity to discuss examination technique.

Teaching with horseshoe groups is a useful technique, but the problems, their answers, and the general organization of the class require thoughtful preparation and a variety of teaching skills.

Controlled Discussion

Most teachers practice controlled discussion (sometimes called "class discussion"), in which points or questions are raised from the lecture floor. The usual objectives of this method of teaching are clarification on matters of fact and the development of lines of thought and interest that have been stimulated. Smeltzer and Watson (1983) showed that students listen more closely if they know there is going to be class discussion on what a lecturer is saying. Most teachers use this form of discussion after periods of lecturing, but it can easily fall flat if the lecture was not stimulating.

In my opinion, controlled discussion is not at all easy, and it is made all the more difficult by the fact that its defects are not always apparent. Although it involves some feedback, not every member of the class is able to contribute; consequently, there is always the possibility that serious misunderstandings and interesting viewpoints are not revealed. This may be exacerbated by the fact that those who have understood the lecture least are least likely to ask questions or expose their misunderstandings to correction. There is also a tendency for particular personality types to be vocal, and for others to be silent. It can be difficult to ensure that the points raised permit balanced consideration of the subject. In some cases, it is difficult to get the discussion started. As suggested elsewhere (when discussing verbal feedback; Chapter Twelve), this can often be achieved by asking questions requiring personal reactions or other relevant information about which the audience, not the lecturer, has special knowledge. These questions do not have wrong answers to be corrected by the lecturer, and class members need not fear correction or serious contradiction.

Although it is common practice, I think it is nearly always unwise to go straight from lecturing to controlled discussion. Even in public meetings, it is far better first to give a few moments for silent reflection and review, or buzz-group consideration of what points to raise. These moments for consideration remove factual misunderstandings and raise the level of discussion.

A genuine atmosphere of discussion is more likely to develop if the teacher takes opportunities not to reply to points raised but gestures to accept further contributions from the audience.

Lecture-Discussion Method

This method essentially consists of obtaining the key points from the class and the teacher providing further elaboration, technical reexpression, and necessary detail. The teacher raises general questions before any lecturing and writes the students' key points on the blackboard or overhead projector to give a summary as they go along. As each point is raised, the lecturer adds or seeks detail. For example, if we imagine that the sections on memory, attention, or handouts in this book are each to be the subject of a lesson using the lecture-discussion method, most of the major points could be provided by the collective contributions of a class in answer to such questions as "When do you find it easy to remember things?" "What things keep you alert?" or "When do you think handouts are most useful?" As the discussion proceeds, the teacher may change the wording of the questions to give different emphases and elicit different points ("When do you find you can concentrate most?" "What keeps you that way?" "Are there some situations in which you are always drowsier than in others?" "Why is that?") and then gradually reexpress the questions in more general, abstract, and technical language if this is necessary ("What general factors affect alertness?" "What are the variables of arousal?"). In this way, a class can find itself involved in a conversation using technical language which the students did not know when they walked into the room.

The key points may be written on the board in the order in which they come, but if there is a preferred or logical order they may be written up as they come though suitably spaced for later insertions.

This is a very effective method of teaching, for a number of reasons:

- It makes the students think.
- It forces them to relate the subject to their personal experience, background knowledge, and practical examples if suitable questions are asked.
- The teacher can be relatively sure they understand because the key points are expressed in the students' words.
- Students are encouraged when their points are accepted.
- It forces the teacher to proceed at the pace of the class and to go slower on more difficult points.
- It maintains attention very well by using class involvement and various voices.

The method may be used without so much elaboration by the teacher when findings of buzz groups or horseshoe groups are reported back to the whole class (that is, when they are pooled).

Because not all groups will organize their reports in the same way, it is usually better for the teacher to have a checklist of points to be brought out and to write them on the board (or overhead projector) in their most logical order.

Another variation is to elicit as many points as possible from the class first without much elaboration and then proceed to give a prepared lecture that draws them all together. This is useful where the topic is difficult and lecturers want to be able to relate what they say to the students' background knowledge and their ways of expressing it, as much as possible. It is therefore useful for developing a subject or going a little deeper. If another teacher has lectured on a closely related topic and it is difficult to know exactly what was said, what slant was taken, and what was neglected, this variation can help to relate the two topics. In the same way, it is useful before a practical to revise theoretical work covered a long time ago.

The Case-Study Method (Case Discussion)

This method has some similarities with the horseshoe group except that it is not always conducted as a group method. Essentially it consists of a detailed study of a particular example (what it is an example *of* obviously depends on the subject), It usually involves consideration of an actual example requiring the synthesis of a large amount of information of various sorts, and the making of recommendations or decisions. It is applicable in law, medicine, education, business studies, politics, English, or any subject that studies the making of decisions. Because it is appropriate for the study of complex interactions of principles, it could be used by teachers in almost any subject. It is useful for demonstrating the application of principles and for practicing the analysis of complex situations (Kletz, 1970).

If we consider political decisions, or examples of medical or architectural recommendations, it also has value in showing students what they do not know—and in some cases what they cannot know. In this way, it may teach students to reserve their judgment and recognize the need to seek further information. Provided the cases are well chosen so that students must select certain items of information and use them to make particular inferences, the case-study method can have some impact on students who display superficial thought or easily jump to conclusions.

Lecturers sometimes fear that if discussion groups are formed without the presence of a subject expert, mistakes will be learned and go uncorrected. This is not so, provided the task or problem is designed with sufficient focus (Davis and others, 1994). Davis and colleagues found no difference in students' tests scores and satisfaction between groups led by experts and nonexperts. Indeed, experts tend to dominate groups, and students then wait for the experts to give the answers rather than thinking for themselves. Consequently, teachers and other leaders are a nuisance; they get in the way and prevent intellectual development.

The skills of task design at the micro level are insufficiently understood by many teachers. Many present problems that are too big. The technique of presenting a sequence of smaller problems that together make up a larger one can direct the focus. To use this technique, the lecturer needs to analyze the larger problem into a series of smaller steps. Table 18.1 gives an example; it is quite different from saying "Discuss the problem of free will and determinism."

To use case studies in this way requires very careful preparation. If the case is not a genuine one, it is easy either to overlook important details or to include some that are inconsistent. It is impossible to generalize for all subjects, but very commonly the kind of information given includes a history of the case and a description of the conditions that exist at the time the decision has to be taken. Whether these conditions are physical, emotional, economic, social, or of any other kind will obviously depend upon the subject and the kind of case. The way in which the information is provided may be made as similar to the practical situation as possible. In medicine, education, or law they may consist of the patient's notes, the child's records, or a client's file. The students may be given these together with a problem to be discussed in groups before general class discussion; or the teacher may distribute the information for individual perusal for, say, three minutes, and then conduct an inquiry by the lecture-discussion method. In either method, it is useful to obtain photocopies of the documents ahead of time and transfer them to transparencies so that they may be shown using the overhead projector. (If there is no one illustration that all may see and to which the lecturer may point, the lecturer is liable to spend many minutes saying, "You will see this is mentioned two-thirds the way down the third page. Have you all got that? No? Well it's . . ." Once students have found the place and are looking down at the text, the lecturer can obtain no eye contact by which to make discussion flow.)

Because a case study requires students to use a large amount of information, if conducted in small-group discussion it is useful from the teacher's point of view for students to keep a record of their discussion so that the teacher can check which items of information have been considered.

Short Talks by Students

The use of student talks has been recommended for use in engineering and medical faculties (Henderson, 1970), but it is equally useful in training for any profession requiring oral skills (education, law, management, social work, and so on) or where oral examinations form part of the system of assessment.

Once the method is accepted by the students, it is usually fairly successful, but it requires cautious introduction and it can flop badly if the innovation is made without consulting the students first. Students expect lecturers to lecture; any sudden attempt to reverse the roles without an explanation of how they benefit requires some psychological adjustment. Even after tacit acceptance, students' failure to turn up when it is their turn may indicate a submerged mild "trauma." The difficulty of adjustment can be minimized by not requiring more than ten minutes' exposition (they frequently overprepare and speak for too long) and by making the occasions informal.

The teacher needs skills in working for an emotional climate in which the audience is appreciative and wants to learn from what is said. The choice of topics is therefore crucial.

Each talk requires follow-up class discussion in which the good points of the talk are reinforced. If criticism of the content is necessary, this may be done after dissociating the point from the speaker. Occasionally, a student will abuse the occasion, but—provided class members as a whole accept the method—they will deal with the abuse more effectively than the teacher.

Reading, Audiotapes, and Videotapes

It may be objected that all these methods take too long compared with the lecture, but this objection as it stands is incomplete. One may say "They take too long to achieve X, Y, and Z compared with the lecture," but as soon as the objection is clearly stated in terms of objectives achieved, its inapplicability becomes obvious if the lecture method cannot achieve X, Y, and Z. This is the case with the alternative methods so far suggested.

However, the problem remains of how to achieve all the course objectives in the time available. Since we have seen in Chapter One that other presentation methods, such as audiotapes, videotapes, and reading, are equally effective for retention and comprehension of information (Bligh, 1970a; Frank and Lesher, 1971; Greene, 1934; Joyce and Weatherall, 1957), class time could be saved by making these available at other times. The provision of handouts and reading has been mentioned elsewhere. They are widely used, but the provision of audio and videotapes in college libraries has received scant attention and finance. If audiotapes are accompanied by a slide viewer and earphone attachments, they may provide illustrated lectures at any time, as often as necessary and at the students' preferred pace. They are suitable for revision, the method is cheap, and if well used it is thorough. They are invaluable for foreign students with language difficulties.

Apart from problems of copyright, the chief difficulty with audio and video presentations in lectures lies in their overuse. When overused, attention is generally poor, caused at least in part by lack of interpersonal interaction. Used with discretion, they have an important place. Videos can repeatedly illustrate and demonstrate processes that cannot be shown in a lecture theater (a surgical operation, interviewing techniques, contact with deep-sea fish, high-temperature and pressure reactions, etc.).

Videotaped lectures are not normally popular with students (Firstman, 1983), but they are acceptable when mixed with other methods. As ever, the secret is variety. When Sox, Marton, Higgins, and Hickam (1984) interrupted videotaped lectures for questions and discussion, the mixture proved more popular with students than uninterrupted traditional lectures. Sox and colleagues recommend the technique whenever expert lecturers are not available. Smeltzer and Watson (1983) found that a group viewing video demonstrations during lectures asked more questions and wrote better lecture summaries than students receiving a traditional, uninterrupted lecture. The latter took more notes.

Lectures introducing practical work are frequently ineffective because students have to remember everything in advance. Audiotapes in the science laboratory may be used for repeated instruction. Goodhue (1969) reports that not only could students using tapes and slides dissect a rat in one hour when it previously took three, but they made fewer errors. Carré (1969) thought students accepted responsibility for their own learning when placed in a self-paced situation. Harris (1971) used an audio tutorial supplement in engineering and found no difference from instruction supplemented with written scripts. Able students preferred the tapes, and less able students, the scripts.

There is some evidence that audiotapes are more effective if accompanied by questions (the same is also true of live lectures), and they are more popular if a variety of voices are used (Frank and Lesher, 1971). Most lecturers find that if they record their lecture they need to prepare it more thoroughly, but this may be a comment on the lecture method as much as the use of audiotapes.

Computer Facilities in Lecture Rooms

Computer facilities are increasingly available in lecture rooms. Where an LCD (liquid crystal display) is placed on an overhead projector, the lecturer can show the result of calculations or other computer processes. In principle, this is another technique to present information. It is a useful visual aid. It is not an alternative to the lecture method and is not likely to teach more than information. Accordingly, no more will be said about its use here.

Computers offer a different teaching method, one that may achieve higher cognitive objectives if students have networked terminals and are set problems or other tasks that demand thought. As with other methods considered in this chapter, the kind of thought taught depends upon the task designed. As with some other methods of presenting problems, there is some evidence that learning is better if the problems are tackled in pairs, or first individually and then in pairs.

Where computer-equipped lecture rooms differ is in their opportunities for feedback both to the lecturer and to the student. Consider a class in statistics in which the lecturer has taught a particular technique and then sets an example for the students to work out. The teacher can monitor each student's (or student pair's) terminal to check their progress and, by implication, get feedback on the effectiveness of the lecture. The teacher may also get feedback on the percentage of students giving the same answer to a question. This could be coupled with an audio facility, as in a language laboratory, by which the teacher can guide individual students (or pairs) over their difficulties. In contrast, Nager (1983) has described a computer-assisted feedback system using electronic index cards to interact with students' ideas in answer to subjective examination questions. Campbell and Lison (1995) have devised computer simulations to reflect the real-world complexity of even interpersonal skills, and to provide rapid self-assessments to students on their performance.

It is a short step to adapt this facility for interaction over the World Wide Web and combine it with distance methods of presentation such as audio or television. As we saw in Chapter One, hitherto the disadvantage of distance methods of lecture presentation has been their inability to teach thought and affect. Computer-supported lecture theaters make distance teaching of higher cognitive skills much more possible. The teaching of affect remains difficult, however.

Conclusion

Lectures are inadequate because they do not teach thought or affect well, and for many students they hold attention poorly after about twenty-five minutes. The alternatives in this chapter attempt to solve these problems. The art in using them lies in how they are combined with lecturing. We must now consider this.

CHAPTER NINETEEN

SOME COMBINATIONS OF TEACHING METHODS

Lecture—Buzz groups—Horseshoe groups—Controlled discussion.

Buzz groups or horseshoe groups—Lecture.

Brainstorming—Lecture.

Lecture—Buzz groups—Practical—Buzz groups.

Lecture—Unsuccessful class discussion—Buzz groups.

Lecture—Buzz groups—Brain trust.

Step-by-step lecture (alternating lecture-discussion).

Lecture—Individual problem solving—Reading.

Minisyndicates—Debates.

Lecture—Audiotape alternately.

Lecture—Audiotape—Group tutorial.

In theory, there are an infinite number of ways in which these teaching methods may be combined. The task facing new lecturers is to decide and invent combinations suitable for their purposes. This chapter seeks to liberate them from the pressures of conformity and tradition by giving examples of some combinations and the objectives they may achieve.

Lecture—Buzz Groups— Horseshoe Groups—Controlled Discussion

Have you ever been to conferences where no one confers? They spend all their time listening to lectures. The audiences do not engage with the enthusiasms of the speakers because they are given no opportunity to do so. The chairpersons conceive of discussion only as opportunities to respond to the speakers, not as opportunities for people to discuss among themselves. They have not heard of buzz groups and would be afraid of losing control if they used them. The result is that the mixing of minds is not as thorough as it might be. Strangers don't get to know each other so well as they might.

The sequence suggested in this heading elicits immediate reactions to the lecture and produces a much more lively controlled discussion. Maybe the terraced lecture theater does not permit genuine horseshoe groups; but the essential technique, where the architecture allows, is to merge or reconstitute pairs of buzz groups, thus widening the circle of contacts for conference members.

If you want a lively conference, then chairpersons must be trained, attendees should be forewarned of the technique, and timetables must allow for it.

Buzz Groups or Horseshoe Groups—Lecture

The most common way of using buzz groups or horseshoe groups is first to lecture and then to set up discussion groups, on the assumption that the lecture has provided some stimulus and information. But, as with controlled or class discussion, where the objectives are to make students think and to relate a subject to their previous background, it is often a good idea to present the central issue of a lecture to the students first so that they try to solve the problem using their background knowledge. After a period of pooling in which the students' suggestions are written on the board (or overhead projector), the teacher may give the prepared lecture, making sure to relate it to the students' suggestions wherever appropriate. Bearing in mind that the objectives include the promotion of thought, which normally requires a slower speed of delivery, this combination allows a subject to be covered relatively quickly. There are several reasons for this. The students have turned their mind to the problem; the pooling has provided a common background; and the lecturer does not have to remind them of the basic groundwork, since not only has the discussion done this but feedback enables the lecturer to start at the students' level of understanding. Thus, in spite of the belief that discussion groups take a long time and that lectures can cover the ground more quickly, in terms of these objectives this combination is a time-saver.

Brainstorming—Lecture

A variation on this combination, when the intention is to teach creative problem solving and open-mindedness, is to use a brainstorming technique during the initial discussion. This consists of introducing some time pressure by allowing only a few minutes, and instructing students to concentrate on making as many suggestions as possible, however implausible, and not to view them critically at this stage. The theory behind this is to throw together as many ideas as possible so that a chance association that produces the creative solution is more probable. However, although the ideas produced by the group in this way may be more original and creative than those by other methods, there is conflicting evidence on how far a sustained course using brainstorming techniques results in greater individual creativity (Taylor, Berry, and Block, 1958; Parnes and Meadow, 1959).

The use of time pressure when a group is introduced to group techniques in lecture situations is valuable to instill a businesslike approach. Because students like to feel they have achieved a lot in a short space of time, this approach is important to the success of innovations.

Lecture—Buzz Groups—Practical—Buzz Groups

Buzz groups in practical classes can be useful to clarify the students' task. If the period begins with lecturing to provide information and is followed by horseshoe groups or buzz groups to plan an activity or experiment, the organizational crisis that often occurs when practical work begins can be avoided because the groups will be ready to start at different times. The groups may reassemble at the end of the period to evaluate and coordinate their results before writing them out.

Lecture—Unsuccessful Class Discussion—Buzz Groups

Buzz groups can also be used after a lecture to get the teacher out of difficulties in the subsequent class discussion. The opportunity provided for reticent students has been mentioned, but these groups also provide an opportunity for everyone to have their say if too many wish to speak. They may also be used to cool things down if personal acrimonies intrude, by separating the contestants. They may be used in the same way if there is a conflict as to which topic should be discussed.

Lecture—Buzz Groups—Brain Trust

If subject matter is noncontroversial and does not raise issues that can easily be discussed, or if students are unwilling to express their difficulties in class discussion, buzz groups may be instructed to agree on a question they wish the lecturer to answer and to write it on a sheet of paper and pass it anonymously to the front. If some of the questions show lack of understanding on the same point, this technique provides useful feedback on the teacher's effectiveness in addition to clarification of the lecture. Instead of the teacher, it is sometimes possible to have a small panel of students, lecturers, or research students answer the questions.

This technique is also useful in an industrial context, whenever new proposals are considered. By contrast, in a mass meeting the individual worker is a spectator rather than a participant and cannot put critical questions to management anonymously. Furthermore, individual opinions are less likely to be distorted if passed directly to the panel than if presented by a representative in meetings at successive levels of the industrial hierarchy.

Step-by-Step Lecture (Alternating Lecture-Discussion)

Alternating short periods of lecture and discussion (any of the kinds mentioned) may be used to regulate the pace of a difficult chaining lecture or one that requires particularly close reasoning such that the next step must not be taken until the previous one is fully understood.

A variant of this approach by Jenkins (1992) is shown in Table 19.1. Students' attention and active participation were maintained for three hours with a twenty-minute break. Notice that time was taken to explain and justify the methods being used. Tasks are tightly focused while allowing individuality. Initial doubters later recognized that they had been made to work and think intensively, and they had learned to think more independently and critically. Having experienced this class, students were not likely to ignore the instructions to prepare for the next class.

Lecture—Individual Problem Solving—Reading

When tutorials are not possible, one way of facilitating personal development in a subject is to present a problem sheet of the kind shown in Table 18.1 coupled with a detailed set of references (giving precise page numbers) that the students may consult in the lecture room in the way that was described for minisyndicates (except that students may work individually). For example, a lecturer could begin by outlining the theoretical positions that may be taken on a certain topic (for example, the theories of light, the origins of matter, an aesthetic judgment) and then present a sheet of questions of either the multiple-choice type or the kind with distinct alternative answers, as shown in Table 18.1. Students are required to read certain passages according to their responses to the individual questions. Thus

TABLE 19.1. ANALYSIS OF A THREE-HOUR STRUCTURED LECTURE.

Minutes	Lecturer or Student Activity
0–10	Task on OHP directs students as they enter to pick up course guide and a nine-page lecture handout, and to arrange the seating so they can sit in groups of two or three and get to know each other.
10–15	Task requires student groups to interpret graphs showing decline of student attention in a conventional lecture and the impact on student attention of the structured lecture used in the course.
15–25	Lecturer gives his interpretation of the graph and uses it to explain how the course will be taught and what he expects them to do during class sessions.
25–35	Task requires groups to interpret a quote from Wittgenstein and explain its relevance to geography.
35–45	Lecturer analyzes quote and shows its relevance to the course themes, which are set out in the course guide.
45–55	Task requires individuals to write answers to questions on the lecture handout. The questions require them to draw upon their commonsense knowledge of Britain's changing geography.
55–65	Task requires individuals to compare answers.
65–80	Lecturer draws upon what he has overheard, but his analysis takes it beyond commonsense knowledge. Using student's statements, he shows that it is possible to give very different interpretations of Britain's geography.
80–90	Task to write the quote from Wittgenstein in the student's own language and explain its relevance to the course. They are warned that the lecturer will not go over this task, and the course guide shows that it was on last year's exam.
90–110	Students and lecturer take a break.
110–120	Task requires students to analyze a set of quotes that give contrasting definitions of geography as a discipline and emphasize very different processes as explaining geographic patterns.
120–130	Lecturer interprets these quotes and links back to the quote from Wittgenstein.
130–140	Task. Lecture handout includes part of the introduction to the course textbook. Task requires students to analyze the author's view of geography, which processes they will emphasize, and which they will neglect.
140–150	Lecturer reiterates the text's central viewpoint and introduces alternative perspectives.
150–160	Task to analyze a brief extract from a book with a contrasting interpretation.
160–170	Task that requires students to write a summary of the whole session.
170–180	Lecturer emphasizes the role of the textbook in the course and introduces a task that requires students to work outside class to answer questions relating to the first chapter. They are told next week's session will be based on the answers.

Source: Jenkins, 1992.

each student follows an individual path of reading as if on a branching program, so that competition for specific texts decreases when there is diversity of opinion.

However, although this combination may achieve very worthwhile objectives in difficult circumstances, it requires a great deal of careful preparation and the teacher must know the subject very thoroughly. Furthermore, because of its branching nature, it is difficult to pull together all the strands or use them as the basis of further teaching. It is therefore most appropriate at the end of a series of lectures. Alternatively, this combination may be used to make horseshoe groups go deeper into a subject by using reference books.

Minisyndicates—Debates

Student speeches can be combined with horseshoe groups if one member of a group is asked to give a fairly formal report on its decisions. If two groups are mini-syndicates with the task of finding evidence for or against a proposition or hypothesis, the reporting back can be turned into a kind of debate. But because this requires students to look at only one point of view, it is educationally questionable unless some other method is used to preserve a balance. For example, some compensation is obtained if each group is required to sum up the other's case.

Lecture—Audiotape Alternately

The technique of using more than one lecturer, as a form of team teaching employed by Betts and Walton (1970), has already been discussed (under "Auditory Stimulation" in Chapter Three). If staff timetables do not permit this form of cooperation, the use of tape-recorded voices to provide alternative viewpoints and varied auditory stimulation can sharpen distinctions and maintain attention; but this technique can easily be overused.

Lecture—Audiotape—Group Tutorial

Assuming two rooms are available, classes of up to twenty-four can be divided after a fifteen-to-twenty-minute lecture so that one half may have a group tutorial with the lecturer on what they have heard, while the other group, in another room, hears a tape-recorded lecture for another fifteen to twenty minutes. After this time the tape recorder and lecturer change rooms. This combination permits feedback on learning to both the students and the lecturer, while in view of the normal decrement in attention in a uniform situation it is possible that the total amount of information conveyed by the lecture and tape recording would be no less than for a fifty-five-minute lecture.

Conclusion

The purpose of Part Four has been to persuade the reader that it is usually better to use a variety of teaching methods in a so-called lecture period.

All the combinations of teaching methods suggested have been successfully used, but whether they are applicable to other situations can only be decided by the teacher concerned. Factors that may influence this decision are considered in the next chapter, but it must be emphasized that their effectiveness, like that of any single method, depends on the goodwill of the students. Although it is possible to prepare the students' minds the week before, goodwill is established over a longer period of time.

PART FIVE

PREPARATION FOR
THE USE OF LECTURES

CHAPTER TWENTY

THINKING THE LECTURE THROUGH

The sequence of decisions.

1. Ask questions about the college and departmental organization.

2. Decide on or modify objectives.

3. Decide on suitable teaching methods.

4. Select the most suitable teaching methods.

5. Decide on the key points and organization of subject matter.

6. Decide how the teaching time is to be organized.

7. Decide on student preparation and follow-up.

8. Decide on detailed teaching techniques.

H ow should a lecturer with no previous experience prepare to use the lecturing techniques that have been discussed? This is not easy. There is plenty of room within the suggested techniques for variations in style. Different people prefer to prepare in different ways, and different subjects may require different approaches.

The Sequence of Decisions

Following is a checklist for a series of decisions about lecture preparation. The items may have to be varied selectively in the light of each reader's particular needs and approach.

1. Ask Questions About the College and Departmental Organization

It will be assumed here that the course has already been planned, at least in broad outline. In practice, what most new lecturers have to teach is more or less imposed on them either directly by the department head or indirectly by an examining board (or vocational needs). Visiting lecturers are frequently given a topic. New lecturers soon discover, if it is not immediately obvious, that many of the most important decisions about their courses have been made without consulting them.

It is not the purpose of this book to discuss overall course design and course objectives, but the new lecturer may find it helpful to answer certain questions. What are the limits of the constraints imposed? In what area does the lecturer have freedom to make decisions? These may include selecting specific topics from a wide syllabus and deciding the order in which they should be tackled.

Frequently there are less tangible constraints, involving the customary organization of teaching, that are not formally binding and may easily be accepted without thinking but that should at least be recognized, if not questioned.

New lecturers may also consider which decisions will need the cooperation of their students.

In other words, the new lecturer normally has to ask: "What is the system in which I am to work, and what is going to be my role in it?"

2. Decide on or Modify Objectives

Assuming the course objectives and syllabus have been decided, the teacher's first task with reference to a specific period of teaching is to select the objectives to be achieved at that time. They should be expressed in terms of what the students should be able to do at the end of the period (that is, their achievement should be testable in principle). It is a good idea to jot them down in rough form because nearly all other stages depend on these decisions. (When I give an unsatisfactory lecture—which is more often than I sometimes care to admit—the root of the trouble is frequently inadequate preparation at this stage because these decisions take time for careful thought. I cannot be sure that others make the same mistake, but they may whenever time is short.)

Although in principle course objectives should not require modification, in practice they usually do. In fact, courses and teaching usually seem to go better if they are constantly being modified to suit particular circumstances—provided an overall view is maintained.

3. Decide on Suitable Teaching Methods

If the teaching methods that could achieve these objectives are written down, the teacher may avoid assuming that one particular method must be used. Referring to Table 14.1 helps guide this decision.

We have seen, especially in Parts Two and Four, that a variety of methods are probably needed.

4. Select the Most Suitable Teaching Methods

There are three sets of factors that may influence these decisions: the limitations of the teacher, the students, and the physical conditions.

Obviously, teachers should choose methods that they have a reasonable chance of being able to use satisfactorily (where the criterion of satisfaction is the achievement of the objectives). Like most social skills, learning to teach involves using the talents one has, rather than trying to be what one is not. No teacher will teach equally well by all methods, and most of us would consider ourselves unskilled in the majority of them. The skills and personality traits required by different teaching methods make conflicting demands. For example, the extrovert lecturer who commands the attention of the audience by occasional showmanship may have difficulty in finding the empathy required of a counseling tutor.

This is not to say that teachers should stick with a few methods. It is to say that they may need to plan a course of self-development in the use of all appropriate methods. Because five to ten years is a realistic time for such a program, department heads have an important role in planning the opportunities given to their staff.

The limitations of the students are imposed by their expectations and previous experience. New lecturers cannot know what these are for a few weeks, until they have used feedback techniques (Chapter Twelve). Because part of the teacher's job is to train students in new learning skills, teachers will need to plan a program of development for them too. This responsibility is not always appreciated by teachers in universities and colleges. Thus the selection of a teaching method may be partly influenced by its place in a sequence of teaching designed (among other things) to train students how to study, listen, and learn.

Finally, because the physical conditions impose limitations upon the teaching methods that can be used, it is helpful to look at the room allocated and check on the timetable for feasible room changes that could overcome these limitations if necessary. For example, the unsuitability of a steeply terraced lecture theater for the flexible use of horseshoe groups might be overcome with a simple room change. (The tendency for administration to dictate the educational process should, in my opinion, be vigilantly restrained.)

A second reason for looking at the room is that preparation is easier and more practically oriented when teachers can imagine themselves in the room with the facilities it offers.

Check the size and surface of the blackboard. See if there are available screens; if so, do they obstruct the board so that they cannot both be seen at once? A look at the lighting and blackout facilities may save later embarrassment if any kind of projectors are to be used. Not knowing where the light switches are can be disturbing for an inexperienced lecturer. In particular, if a dimmer is provided so that notes may be taken, it will affect the speed at which slides may be shown and the silences that are necessary. If unavailable, a longer and more careful recapitulation is necessary for each illustrated point, and the number of slides that may be shown at one time is restricted. Thus important features of timing are affected.

What teaching aids are available? How long are the power cords? Where are the outlets? Where should the overhead projector be placed, to avoid obscuring anyone's vision? How great is its magnification? This will affect the size of letters and density of colors on prepared transparencies.

What is the shape of the room? Can the furniture in it be rearranged if desired? Will you be in a raised position? Will you be behind a large bench such that there is a barrier between you and the class? These things affect rapport and the amount of spoken and nonverbal feedback that can easily be obtained. These in turn affect the use of class discussion, questioning, and the selection of other techniques.

Will you be seen by all the class? Will you see what all members of the class are doing? (The latter question is concerned with more than being able to see them.)

5. Decide on the Key Points and Organization of Subject Matter

Let us now assume that having considered these factors the teacher has decided to use the lecture method either on its own, or with other methods. (Hence I shall now refer more to the lecturer, lecture, and audience than the teacher, period, and class.)

Whether the key points or the lecture organization is decided first will depend on the lecturer's objectives. If the objectives consist of teaching information, it is probable that the most important items (key points) will be decided first so that they can then be organized in a simple way.

This is not always the case, however, because there are some instances where the requirements of a latter part of the course make it advisable that information should be arranged in a particular way. (Again we see a need for an overall view of the course.) To take an overly simple example, if the objective is for students of geography to compare two regions, it may be easier to describe them under similar headings. The example is more pertinent if applied to comparing the merits of various methods of bridge construction, or the similar initial symptoms of subsequently contrasting diseases. Otherwise, if the objective is to encourage varied patterns of thinking, perhaps the geographical descriptions should be fundamentally different in approach.

Where the objectives require a chaining structure, this usually imposes itself so that the lecturer is left with the task of deciding the key stages to be emphasized.

Similarly, when the objective is to stimulate thought during the lecture period, a step-by-step lecture form with questions (see Chapter Nineteen and Table 19.1) or a problem-centered lecture organization usually imposes itself, so that the selection of key questions or key points in the problem's solution is usually the second group of decisions.

Where the major objective is a change or development of certain attitudes, the key points will be decided during preparation and the order of presentation will only be decided during the teaching itself, once the knowledge and initial attitudes of the students become clear during an opening period of class discussion. Thus, where attitude change is the major objective, the lecture organization is probably left flexible and only brought together in a predetermined way in the final lecture summary.

Whatever the form of lecture organization, it is useful to jot down the proposed arrangement of key points as soon as these decisions are taken, in order to clarify the overall plan.

6. Decide How the Teaching Time Is to Be Organized

This involves a host of decisions depending upon the organization of subject matter. We have seen that it is advisable to use a variety of teaching methods; what is to be the timing of them, and how are they to be organized (Chapter Five)?

Active learning is more efficient than passive learning; what activity will the students undertake and how will they become involved in it? "What are the students going to do?" is a more crucial question for the lecturer than "What am I going to do?" Consider, for example, Chapters Nine, Ten, Eighteen, and Nineteen.

The importance of immediate rehearsal and feedback has been emphasized; how are they to be facilitated?

How is student attention to be maintained? What inherent motivation is there in the subject? If little or none, what interest can appropriately be aroused?

7. Decide on Student Preparation and Follow-up

What previous knowledge is required? If the lecturer assumes some knowledge, then what preparation, such as prereading, is expected of the students? How is it to be organized?

If it is not possible to teach all that is necessary during a lecture, what follow-up will be required? Are there the available resources for all students to do what is required?

Will either the preparation or follow-up require questions, essays, or other tasks to be set? How are the preparation, the lecture itself, and the follow-up related to seminars or other teaching?

In short, what is the total activity required from the students to achieve the objectives associated with a particular lecture?

8. Decide on Detailed Teaching Techniques

Many teaching techniques (as distinct from methods) cannot be prepared because they are the spontaneous expression of the lecturer's personality. Nevertheless, it is particularly important for the new lecturer to attempt to cultivate an ideal as near to perfection as possible because early standards of technique quickly become habitual. It is quite possible for the first few lectures to influence subsequent teaching style for the rest of a teacher's life. Consequently, careful thought and sound guidance are invaluable at this stage. Part Two of this book attempts to raise the issues that the new lecturer should think about.

How is the lecture to be introduced? Some people like to write down their introductory statement verbatim. Since it should not be read, I myself find this inhibiting, inflexible, and unnatural when the time comes, but I sometimes note the germ of an idea. The introduction usually serves to suggest an attitude or background against which later information is set (see Table 5.2).

How is the lecture to be organized? In particular, think through any points that may be difficult to explain (Chapters Five, Six, and Seven). When it is difficult to think of examples illustrating the key points, some lecturers write them down whenever they come to mind, on a small jotting pad with tear-off sheets that can be placed in the appropriate places in their lecture files. Because in some subjects examples can turn a dull lecture into an interesting one, this habit can avoid latent difficulties.

How is the blackboard or other visual work to be arranged? It is sometimes useful to leave one part for ad lib explanations. How is other visual apparatus to be used? (See Chapter Eight.)

How is students' critical thought about the subject to be generated? What exam questions could be based on the lecture topic? If the lecturer sets no assignments, exam questions can guide students' thinking, especially if the lecturer uses class discussion to elicit the range of relevant information and how it may be applied.

Conclusion

Much of what this chapter tries to develop is the lecturer's self-image. An essential part of lecture preparation is to imagine oneself doing the job. Answering the many questions in this chapter will help to achieve that.

CHAPTER TWENTY-ONE

WRITING THE NOTES

When?

Key points.

Objectives and introduction.

Elaboration.

References.

Reminders about procedure.

Task design.

Equipment required.

Handouts.

Preparing the conclusion.

H aving thought the lecture through and made some rough notes, you face the next step: preparing the notes for use as necessary during the lecture. How this is done is largely a matter of personal taste, and you will usually develop your own style. Therefore I shall describe a method I have used, which you may adopt, modify, or reject according to how far it suits your particular lecturing style.

When I need detailed notes, I usually still write them with a four-color pen. Somehow it's more personal.

The advantage of having your notes on a word processor is that you can make additions and alterations for when you lecture on the same topic another time. But there's a trap to avoid when reusing notes (which I will mention in the next chapter).

On one-time speaking engagements, my notes are usually the same as my slides or overhead transparencies. The advantage of this is that I look at them together with my audience; it enables me to move toward the audience, away from where my notes would otherwise have been, while maintaining better eye contact.

When?

Contrary to most of the advice I have ever been given, although I may prepare in rough I usually find it better not to prepare lecture notes more than a week in advance. If I do, my intentions do not take the class reaction to the previous lecture into account; the lecture lacks spontaneity, and details of approach (which cannot always be noted) are sometimes forgotten.

Key Points

I do not always use the same form of preparation, although there are common features. Because Coats and Smidchens (1966) have shown that lecturers are more effective when they speak around a few points than when a lecture is read, the most important feature for me is the layout of the key points with headings and subheadings. These form the basis of the blackboard or projected summary. They also serve to jog my memory of each successive point when necessary. Because I need to see them during the lecture, I write them boldly, uncrowded by other notes, and preferably large enough to be recognized (not necessarily read) when standing at the screen or chalkboard in case I forget the wording of a key phrase. For this reason I use plain paper because lines are too narrow and detract from clarity. If you are using a word processor, make the key words at least 16 points and in a bold font. (Typewritten notes are certainly too small. They are designed to be read from a distance of only ten to twelve inches.) So that I can find my place quickly, the key phrases are the only words written between one-and-a-half and four inches from the left-hand side of the page (see Figure 21.1).

Objectives and Introduction

I do not always write out my objectives separately because these are often virtually the same as knowledge of key points. But I usually do when the objectives are concerned with promoting thought and attitudes, in which case I write them across the top of the first page as a constant reminder.

Any jottings for the introduction (such as a quotation) I also write near the top, usually in a smaller hand. But there is a trap to be avoided here. Be prepared to ditch your prepared introduction at the last moment if it does not feel right. That witty anecdote you thought would get everyone's attention and bonhomie

FIGURE 21.1. A POSSIBLE SCHEMA FOR
THE PREPARATION OF A LECTURER'S NOTES.

Title or Topic

Apparatus

Objectives of lecture . . . .   _____

. . . .   _____

. . . .   _____

Possible introduction

Timing and reminders	Key Points	Elaboration	References
10:05	1. _____		_____
	a. _____	_____	_____
show slide . . . . b. _____		_____	_____
	c. _____		_____
10:20	2. _____		_____
	a. _____	_____	_____
	b. _____	_____	_____
10:30 ───
Additional teaching method____	(e.g., Task to be given to groups)		
10:40	3. _____		_____
	a. _____	_____	_____
	b. _____	_____	_____
	c. _____		_____
10:50	Summary		

could achieve the opposite if the joke falls flat. It's a matter of sensing the mood of the class when the time comes.

Elaboration

Examples and other details of elaboration are usually written on the right half of the page opposite the appropriate key points, in the form of odd words to jog my memory. If there are any that are important, or that I know I tend to forget, I sometimes underline them lightly with a red ballpoint pen so that I may find them quickly.

References

On the right-hand edge of the page I write bibliographical references in different colors according to their use. Those that I wish to recommend to the students during the lecture are sometimes written in a bright color. They may include references to handouts, but sometimes those references are in a different color, signifying that I wish students to refer to them at that time and that I must bring my own copy to the lecture. References that indicate my own sources of information are written in a more subdued color; they are not used during the lecture unless I cannot answer a question, but they are useful if I wish to refer to my lecture notes on a later occasion or if I wish to check on detail.

Reminders About Procedure

The left-hand margin is reserved for reminders about procedure, but it is usually left blank. If timing is important, I may write what I reckon the time will be upon reaching certain key points. Because there are dangers in such self-imposed restrictions, this is exceptional; but it could be useful for a beginner inexperienced to know how long particular explanations take.

If some form of reorganization of the room is required in the middle of the lecture for the use of small groups or visual aids, a reminder to myself shortly before the time can sometimes save a moment of confusion. By writing the number of a color transparency in the margin, it is easier to select the right slide at the right time.

The variations in teaching method may also be noted in the left-hand margin if there is any likelihood of the notes being used on a later occasion. For example, I might remind myself in the margin to refer to a handout at a particular point, because I know that is the sort of thing I tend to forget.

Task Design

Tasks given to students when using alternative methods need careful thought. The wording of questions given to a buzz group, horseshoe group, or open-class discussion are worked out in terms of their psychological effects (such as the thought required, the objectives achieved, and the probable class reaction) and noted across the width of the page.

Equipment Required

When experienced teachers forget to bring a teaching aid to the lecture theater, they usually know how to manage; but it can be very disturbing for new lecturers. If I require items of apparatus that I am likely to forget to take, I sometimes list them in green at the top right-hand corner of the first page.

If you will need the help of a laboratory assistant, maybe you should review your notes and make a request the previous day (or whenever). I tend to work a lot at home, so I need to check the list the previous night. (If I leave it till breakfast I'll forget; as in most families, there's too much going on to remember.) The list also permits a quick last-minute check before going to class.

Handouts

One master copy of handouts that are an essential part of the lecture may be filed in my lecture notes if the folder is not made too voluminous as a result. This is useful because I usually prefer to mark them for easy reference to important points during the lecture. What is more, in broad principle I wish to have anything of this kind in front of me if the students can also refer to it.

Preparing the Conclusion

In lectures to teach information, I do not write a conclusion because it usually consists of standing at the chalkboard and reviewing the lecture summary written on it.

Lectures to promote thought usually require problems to be posed more than once, along with a reminder of reading or other work students may do to decide their own answers. In other words, rather than facts, I try to let the students go away with questions in their minds and some directions as to how the questions may be answered. These, too, are usually written elsewhere in the notes and do not need to be written again.

Conclusions to lectures primarily concerned with attitudes are superficially similar to those concerned with stimulating thought in that the issues are restated, but then I attempt to set out the alternatives with sentences of the form "if A then X, but if B then Y" so that students are left to choose between X and Y rather than only between A and B. In other words, the alternative conclusions are stated, not only the issues or problems considered.

There is a further, important reason why I do not prepare the conclusions of my lectures. Very few lectures ever go exactly according to plan. I nearly always find that I need to modify my intentions as a result of verbal or nonverbal feedback so that a prepared conclusion is rarely the precise thing that needs to be said.

The fact that lectures do not go as intended does not imply that preparation is not worthwhile. Quite the contrary, preparation needs to be broader than the ground that may actually be covered. Some contingencies need to be anticipated. Purists may say that a plan that has to be changed is not a good one, but in practice one cannot plan for every contingency in a complex interactive process. When lectures go exactly as planned, it may be more pertinent to question the lecturer's sensitivity to audience reaction. If planning implies some inflexibility, then good lectures may be prepared but not planned.

CHAPTER TWENTY-TWO

LECTURING FOR THE FIRST TIME

This chapter is a quiet word for beginners, but more experienced lecturers might like to check out their approach as well. Because it is a rather tense occasion, new lecturers, who have to go in front of a class for the first time, sometimes welcome very direct suggestions on what to do. Some have found the following suggestions helpful.

For lecturers who keep some of their lecture materials at home, it is worthwhile to glance at the list of apparatus (see in Figure 21.1) just before going home the previous day, to check on what will be needed.

If you read through your notes ten to fifteen minutes before going to class, the key points and overall organization will be fresh in your memory. In this way, a glance will be sufficient to remind you of each successive point during the lecture, so that you are not concentrating on your notes when you should be attending to the reactions of the students (see "Nonverbal Communication" in Chapter Twelve). The preview also gives reassurance of knowing where you are going so that the lecture easily flows from point to point.

If it is not absolutely your first lecture and you are reusing notes from a previous occasion, read through them carefully the day before, or at least half an hour before going to lecture. Why? This is the trap I mentioned in the last chapter. The first time you used the notes, there were probably some factual details, or details of how you would present them, that you did not record. If you don't remind yourself of these details before you go to lecture, you could feel that the result is embarrassing and your confidence could suffer.

On entering the room and reaching the lecturer's table, you should arrange notes and other apparatus for easy use. In particular, lecture notes need to be raised so that while referring to them, you will not easily lose visual contact with the class.

Most new lecturers start talking too soon. It is normally better to wait for a class to become quiet than to ask for silence, and when silence is obtained it is important to wait a few moments longer. This will seem a very long time indeed if you are a nervous baptismal lecturer, but you can use it to steady yourself, and without implying an atmosphere of discipline it places the responsibility for silence on the audience, sets the standards of attention the lecturer demands, allows the class time to adjust mentally to the task ahead, and raises the level of expectancy and sense of occasion.

Use that period of silence to engage eye contact with as many members of the audience as possible, particularly those at the back. Coats and Smidchens (1966) have shown that eye contact is important in establishing rapport with a class. Although personal interaction is important during the lecture, new lecturers sometimes find this easier to establish at the beginning, before part of their attention is directed toward the subject and their notes.

Some beginners realize that inaudibility is a common fault and overcompensate at first; then they find that the mouth becomes dry and the voice does not last. A glass of water can help, but some lecturers watch the reactions of the students at the back and adjust their voice accordingly.

We have seen that in the desire to appear confident it is easy to go too fast. Nevertheless, students are more likely to work well through the whole course if a businesslike tone is set from the start. Thus there is a need to be brisk, without being hurried. This may be achieved if the reexpression and elaboration of each point is carefully prepared so that while further details are being given, the few key points are being persistently driven home (Chapter Six). In this way, the lecture may command attention by seeming to move forward, while teaching is thorough because the movement is not too great. A working atmosphere can quickly be created by setting a small amount of work to be completed by the second meeting; but the work must be feasible, bearing in mind that students may not yet have bought basic textbooks, and library facilities may be limited. To give a handout to be read by the second lecture is one way of achieving this. If students discover they need not do such work, the working atmosphere is lost. Notice how Jenkins (1992) avoids this mistake at the end of Table 19.1.

It is fairly obvious that to stimulate students to work from the beginning of the course, major objectives of the first few weeks are to arouse the interest of the class and convince students that they can learn what is necessary. Because people like doing things at which they feel successful, to obtain confidence and motivation students need to feel they have learned something. Whether they have actually learned anything is less important than motivation at this stage because most information learned in the first few weeks is likely to be forgotten by the end of course examinations.

Many teachers begin their course by defining their subject, defining some of the common terms involved, and then perhaps giving a short history of the development of the subject. This approach may be all right for a textbook, but it is inappropriate for lectures. These things do not inspire students, and the significance of the history is often incomprehensible when the background issues are not known. It is not enough to provide a framework of ideas; the ideas are unintelligible if they cannot be related to the students' background knowledge. Consequently, a problem-centered lecture, where the problem is concerned with a broad spectrum of the principles of the subject applied to an everyday situation, is more suitable.

With classes of fewer than forty, new lecturers will enjoy teaching much more if they can get to know their students personally. It is well worthwhile to spend an afternoon looking at their college application forms for their personal, rather than their academic, background. This is particularly valuable for helping students with personal difficulties.

Once you begin to speak, your mind will be on what you are saying and how the audience reacts. Like a musician, actor, or sportsman, you will become yourself through your involvement in what you are doing. Thus conscious application of earlier advice at this stage risks producing a stiff and unnatural performance. I remember a cartoon of a man trying to read a book called *How to Dive* when he had left the high board and was plunging toward the swimming pool. It is a bit like that. For this reason, it is not desirable to make further suggestions here for you to remember to apply once the lecture has started.

CHAPTER TWENTY-THREE

CONCLUSION

What lectures can be used for (Part One).

Factors and techniques in their use (Parts Two and Three).

When lectures are not so useful (Part Four).

Preparing for their use (Part Five).

T he title of this book is deliberately ambiguous. It considers two questions: "What can lectures be used for?" and "How should they be used?"

What Lectures Can Be Used for (Part One)

It is concluded that they can be used to teach information, including the framework of a subject, but an expository approach is unsuitable to stimulate thought or change attitudes.

Factors and Techniques in Their Use (Parts Two and Three)

Although it is not normally possible to establish rules of lecturing technique, some suggestions are made in the light of psychological and experimental evidence, on ways of organizing information, teaching a single idea, using handouts and feedback techniques, and overcoming common difficulties. In each case, preparation is required to follow these suggestions.

When Lectures Are Not So Useful (Part Four)

It has been argued that the limitations of the lecture method commonly necessitate its use in combination with other teaching methods. The way methods are combined also requires preparation in light of the objectives to be achieved.

Preparing for Their Use (Part Five)

Thus answers to the second question require decisions at the time of preparation, in addition to those concerned with the selection of subject matter.

REFERENCES AND BIBLIOGRAPHY

Abercrombie, M.L.J. *The Anatomy of Judgment.* Hutchinson, 1960.

Abercrombie, M.L.J. *Aims and Techniques of Group Teaching.* Guildford, U.K.: Society for Research into Higher Education, 1978.

Abrami, P. C., Leventhal, L., and Perry, R. P. "Educational Seduction." *Review of Educational Research,* 1982, *52*(3), 446–464.

Abrami, P. C., Perry, R. P., and Leventhal, L. "The Relationship Between Student Personality Characteristics, Teacher Ratings, and Student Achievement." *Journal of Educational Psychology,* 1982, *74,* 111–125.

Abrami, P. C., Cohen, P. A., and d'Apollonia, S. "Implementation Problems in Meta-Analysis." *Review of Educational Research,* 1988, *58*(2), 151–179.

Abrami, P. C., d'Apollonia, S., and Cohen, P. A. "Validity of Student Ratings of Instruction: What We Know and What We Do Not." *Journal of Educational Psychology,* 1990, *82*(2), 219–231.

Adams, J. A. "A Source of Decrement in Psychomotor Performance." *Journal of Experimental Psychology,* 1955, *48,* 390–394.

Aiken, E. G., Thomas, G. S., and Shennum, W. A. "Memory for a Lecture: Effects of Notes, Lecture Rate, and Informational Density." *Journal of Educational Psychology,* 1975, *67*(3), 439–444.

Albanese, M. A., Schuldt, S. S., Case, D. E., and Brown, D. "The Validity of Lecturer Ratings by Students and Trained Observers." *Academic Medicine,* 1991, *66*(1), 26–28.

Annett, J. *Feedback and Human Behaviour.* New York: Penguin, 1969.

Annis, L. F. "Effect of Preference for Assigned Lecture Notes on Student Achievement." *Journal of Educational Research,* 1981, *74*(3), 179–182.

Annis, L. F., and Davis, J. K. "The Effect upon Preferred and Non-Preferred Method of Various Study Techniques and Cognitive Style on Recall and Recognition." Paper presented at the American Educational Research Association, New York, 1977.

Argyle, M., and Henderson, M. *The Anatomy of Relationships.* New York: Penguin, 1985.

Aronson, E., Turner, J. A., and Carlsmith, J. M. "Communicator Credibility and Communication Discrepancy as Determinants of Opinion Change." *Journal of Abnormal and Social Psychology,* 1963, *67,* 31–36.

Asch, S. E. "Effects of Group Pressure upon the Modification and Distortion of Judgments." In H. Guetzkow (ed.), *Groups, Leadership, and Men.* Pittsburgh, Pa.: Carnegie Press, 1951.

Ausubel, D. P. *Educational Psychology: A Cognitive View.* Austin, Tex.: Holt, Rinehart and Winston, 1968.

Ayer, W. W., and Milson, J. L. "The Effect of Notetaking and Underlining on Achievement in Middle School Life Science." *Journal of Instructional Psychology,* 1993, *20*(2), 91–95.

Baddeley, A. *Human Memory: Theory and Practice.* Hillsdale, N.J.: Erlbaum, 1996.

Baggett, J. L., Jr. "A Comparison Between the Use of Different Concept Maps as Advance Organizers to Supplement a Unit on Photosynthesis in a Community College Biology Course." *Dissertation Abstracts International,* Feb. 1994, *54A*(8), p. 2969.

Bakan, P. "Extroversion, Introversion, and Improvement in an Auditory Vigilance Task." *British Journal of Psychology,* 1959, *50,* 387–389.

Baker, G., Baker, C. S., and Blount, H. P. "Effects of Taking Notes on Learning from a Lecture." Paper presented at the American Educational Research Association, Chicago, 1974.

Baker, L., and Lombardi, B. "Students' Lecture Notes and Their Relation to Test Performance." *Teaching of Psychology,* 1985, *12*(1), 28–32.

Bakhtar, M., and Brown, G. "Styles of Lecturing: A Study and Its Implications." *Research Papers in Education,* 1988, *3*(2), 131–153.

Bane, C. L. "The Lecture Vs. the Class-Discussion Method of College Teaching." *School and Society,* 1925, *21,* 300–302.

Bane, C. L. *The Lecture in College Teaching.* Badger, 1931.

Barabasz, A. F. "A Study of Recall and Retention of Accelerated Lecture Presentation." *Journal of Communication,* 1968, *18*(3), 283–287.

Barnard, J. D. "The Lecture-Demonstration Versus the Problem-Solving Method of Teaching of a College Science Course." *Science Education,* 1942, *26,* 121–132.

Barnes, N. R., MacArthur, D., and Ballantine, P. R. "A Comparison of Alternative Techniques of Instruction." *South African Journal of Psychology,* 1983, *13*(1), 6–9.

Barnett, S. A. "An Experiment with Free Discussion Groups." *Universities Quarterly,* 1958, *12,* 175–180.

Barrett, J. E., Di Vesta, F. J., and Rogozinski, J. T. "What Is Learned in Note-Taking?" *Journal of Educational Psychology,* 1981, *73*(2), 181–192.

Barrington, H. "A Survey of Instructional Television Researches." *Educational Research,* 1965, *8*(1), 8–25.

Bassey, M. "Learning Methods in Tertiary Education." (Internal paper.). Nottingham Regional College of Technology, 1968.

Batson, C. D., and Johnson, A. "Arousing Intrinsic Motivation as a Goal for Introductory Classes: A Case Study." *Teaching of Psychology,* 1976, *3*(4), 155–159.

Bean, T. W., Searles, D., Singer, H., and Cowen, S. "Learning Concepts from Biology Text Through Pictorial Analogies and Analogical Study Guide." *Journal of Educational Research,* 1990, *83*(4), 233–237.

Beard, R. M. "On Evaluating the Success of Teaching." *British Journal of Medical Education,* 1967, *1*(4), 296–302.

Beard, R. M. *Teaching and Learning in Higher Education.* New York: Penguin, 1970.

Beard, R. M., Levy, P. M., and Maddox, H. "Academic Performance at University." *Educational Review,* 1964, *16*(3), 163–174.

Beard, R. M., and Pole, K. "Content and Purpose of Biochemistry Examinations." *British Journal of Medical Education,* 1971, *15*, 13–21.

Behr, A. L. "Exploring the Lecture Method: An Empirical Study." *Studies in Higher Education,* 1988, *13*(2), 189–200.

Beighley, K. C. "An Experimental Study of Three Speech Variables on Listener Comprehension." *Speech Monographs,* 1954, *21*, 248–253.

Bell, L. G. "Effects of Metaphorical Communication on the Acquisition, Retention, and Transfer of Counselor Goal-Setting Skills." *Dissertation Abstracts International,* Sept. 1983, *44A*(3), p. 670.

Bennett, E. B. "Discussion, Decision, Commitment, and Consensus in 'Group Decision.'" *Human Relations,* 1955, *8*, 251–273.

Benson, S. B. "A Comparison of the Effects of Short-Term Small Groups and Lectures on the Knowledge, Attitudes, and Behavior of Pharmacy Students Concerning Alcohol/ Alcoholism." *Dissertation Abstracts International,* Dec. 1996, *57A*(6), p. 2353.

Bentley, D. A., and Blount, H. P. "Testing the Spaced Lecture for the College Classroom." Paper presented to the Annual Meeting of the Georgia Psychological Association, Macon, 1980.

Benton, S. L., Kiewra, K. A., Whitfill, J. M., and Dennison, R. "Encoding and External Storage Effects on Writing Processes." *Journal of Educational Psychology,* 1993, *85*(2), 267–280.

Berliner, D. C. "Effects of Test-Like Events and Notetaking on Learning from Lecture Instruction." Paper presented to American Psychological Association, Washington, D.C., 1969.

Berliner, D. C. "Aptitude-Treatment Interactions in Two Studies of Learning from Lecture Instruction." Paper presented to American Educational Research Association, New York, 1971.

Berliner, D. C. "The Generalizability of Aptitude-Treatment Interactions Across Subject Matter." Paper presented to American Educational Research Association, Chicago, 1972.

Berlyne, D. E. *Conflict, Arousal, and Curiosity.* New York: McGraw-Hill, 1960.

Berry, R. "Rapid Reading Reconsidered." *Education,* Mar. 1965, 556.

Betts, D. S., and Walton, A. J. "A Lecture Match, or 'Anything You Can Do, I Can Do Better.'" *Physics Education,* 1970, *5*(6), 321–325.

Black, P. J. "University Examinations." *Physics Education,* 1968, *3*(2).

Bligh, D. A. "An Experiment to Compare the Teaching Effectiveness of a Tape-Recorded Lecture at Three Speeds of Delivery." (Unpublished.) 1970a.

Bligh, D. A. *Gropings for a Design of Objective Tests of the Effectiveness of Teaching Methods.* London: University Teaching Methods Unit, University of London, 1970b.

Bligh, D. A. "Are Varied Teaching Methods More Effective?" Doctoral dissertation, University of London, 1974.

Bligh, D. A. "Improving Teacher Performance Later in the Day." In *Improving University Teaching.* (Proceedings of international conference held at University of Maryland.). Heidelberg, 1975.

Bligh, D. A. "Explanatory Shifts." [www.dcs.ex.ac.uk/~donald/explain]. 1997.

Blizek, W. J., Jackson, K., and LaVoie, J. C. "Short Course Versus Conventional Structures for Teaching Philosophy." *Journal of Experimental Education,* 1974, *43*(1), 25–33.

Bloom, B. S. "Thought-Processes in Lectures and Discussions." *Journal of General Education,* 1953, *7,* 160–169.

Bloom, B. S. (ed.). *Taxonomy of Educational Objectives.* Vol. 1: *Cognitive Domain.* New York: McKay, 1956.

Bonwell, C. C., and Eison, J. A. "Active Learning: Creating Excitement in the Classroom." (Unpublished.) 1991. ERIC no. ED340272.

Boreham, N. C. "Personality Factors Related to Self-Reported Lapse of Attention During Lectures." *Psychological Reports,* 1984, *55*(1), 76–78.

Boreham, N. C., and Lilley, J. D. "Scales to Measure Listening Behavior During Lectures." *Perceptual and Motor Skills,* 1978, *47*(2), 673–674.

Bowles, C. R. "Teaching Practices of Two-Year College Science and Humanities Instructors." *Community/Junior College Quarterly of Research and Practice,* Jan.–Mar. 1982, *6,* 129–144.

Bramki, D., and Williams, R. "Lexical Familiarisation in Economics Text Books." *Reading in a Foreign Language,* 1984, *2*(1), 169–181.

Brant, G., Hooper, E., and Sugrue, B. "Which Comes First: The Simulation or the Lecture?" *Journal of Educational Computing Research,* 1991, *7*(4), 469–481.

Broadbent, D. E. "Review Lecture." *Proceedings of the Royal Society of London B,* 1970, *175,* 333–350.

Brobst, K. E. "The Process of Integrating Information from Two Sources, Lecture and Text (Reading, Comprehension, Memory)." *Dissertation Abstracts International,* Nov. 1996, *57A*(5), p. 1957.

Brown, D. E., and Clement, J. "Overcoming Misconceptions via Analogical Reasoning: Abstract Transfer Versus Explanatory Model Construction." *Instructional Science,* 1989, *18*(4), 237–261.

Brown, G. A., Bakhtar, M., and Youngman, M. B. "Toward a Typology of Lecturing Styles." *British Journal of Educational Psychology,* 1984, *54*(1), 93–100.

Browne, M. N., Hoag, J. H., and Berilla, B. "Critical Thinking in Graduate Programs: Faculty Perceptions and Classroom Behavior." *College Student Journal,* 1995, *29*(1), 37–43.

Bryant, J., Comiski, P. W., Cime, J. S., and Zillmann, D. "The Relationship Between College Teachers' Use of Humor in the Class Room and Students' Evaluations of Their Teachers." *Journal of Educational Psychology,* 1980, *72*(4), 511–519.

Buck, L. "Errors in the Perception of Railway Signals." *Ergonomics,* 1963, *6*(2), 181–192.

Burke, H. R. "An Experimental Study of Teaching Methods in a College Freshman Orientation Course." Doctoral dissertation, Boston University. *Dissertation Abstracts,* 1955, *16,* 77–78.

Busan, T. *Use Your Head.* London: British Broadcasting Corporation, 1974.

Cabral-Pini, A. M. "Cooperative Learning: Its Effect on Math Education." *Dissertation Abstracts International A,* 1995, *55,* 3772.

Camorosano, J. R., and Santapolo, F. A. "Teaching Efficiency and Class Size." *School and Society,* 1958, *86,* 338–341.

Camp, C. C. "A Comparison of the Math Anxiety and Math Self-Efficacy Constructs." *Dissertation Abstracts International,* June 1993, *53B*(12), p. 6541.

Campbell, J. O., and Lison, C. A. "New Technologies for Assessment Training." *College Student Journal,* 1995, *29*(1), 26–29.

Carlsen, W. S. "Teacher Knowledge and Discourse Control: Quantitative Evidence from Novice Biology Teachers' Classrooms." *Journal of Research in Science Teaching,* 1993, *30*(5), 471–481.

Carré, C. G. "Audio-Tutorials as Adjuncts to Formal Lecturing in Biology Teaching at the Tertiary Level." *Journal of Biological Education,* 1969, *3*(1), 57–64.

Carrier, C. A., and Titus, A. "Effects of Note-Taking Pretraining and Test Mode Expectations on Learning from Lectures." *American Educational Research Journal,* 1981, *18*(4), 385–397.

Carter, J. F., and Van Matre, N. H. "Note Taking Versus Note Having." *Journal of Educational Psychology,* 1975, *67*(6), 900–904.

Cartmell, A. E. "The Use of CCTV in the Assessment of Teacher Effectiveness." *Programmed Learning and Educational Technology,* 1971, *8*(3), 173–185.

Catts, D. C. "The Effects of Teaching Listening Versus Note-Taking Strategies on Lecture Performance and Note-Taking Strategy Awareness of Underprepared College Students." *Dissertation Abstracts International,* 1987, *48A*(11), p. 2816.

Cavanagh, S. J., Hogan, K., and Ramgopal, T. "The Assessment of Student-Nurse Learning Styles Using the Kolb Learning Styles Inventory." *Nurse Education Today,* 1995, *15*(3), 177–183.

Chafe, W. L. "Integration and Involvement in Speaking, Writing, and Oral Literature." In D. Tannen (ed.), *Spoken and Written Language.* Norwood, N.J.: Ablex, 1982.

Chaudron, C., and Richards, J. C. "The Effect of Discourse Markers on the Comprehension of Lectures." *Applied Linguistics,* 1986, *7*(2), 113–127.

Chmielewska, E. "The Effects of a Lecture as a Function of Plan Presentation." *Polish Psychological Bulletin,* 1976, *7*(2), 105–114.

Chu, G. C., and Schramm, W. *Learning from Television: What the Research Says.* Stanford, Calif.: Institute for Communication Research, Stanford University, 1967.

Cicirelli, V. G. "University Supervisors' Creative Ability and Their Appraisal of Student Teachers' Classroom Performance: An Exploratory Study." *Journal of Educational Research,* 1969, *62*(8), 375–381.

Clark, G. K., and Clark, E. B. *The Art of Lecturing.* Cambridge: Heffers, 1957.

Coats, W. D., and Smidchens, U. "Audience Recall as a Function of Speaker Dynamism." *Journal of Educational Psychology,* 1966, *57*(4), 189–191.

Cohen, A. R. *Attitude Change and Social Influence.* New York: Basic Books, 1964.

Cohen, P. A. "Student Ratings of Instruction and Student Achievement: A Meta-Analysis of Multisection Validity Studies." *Review of Educational Research,* 1981, *51,* 281–309.

Collard, T. Y. "'Hello . . . Hello? Is Anybody Listening?' Teacher as Listener in the Classroom." Paper presented to the International Listening Association, Boston, 1994. ERIC no. ED371413.

Collier, K. G. "An Experiment in University Teaching." *Universities Quarterly,* 1966, *20*(3), 336–348.

Collingwood, V., and Hughes, D. C. "Effects of Three Types of University Lecture Notes on Student Achievement." *Journal of Educational Psychology,* 1978, *70*(2), 175–179.

Corey, S. M. "Learning from Lectures Versus Learning from Reading." *Journal of Educational Psychology,* 1934, *25,* 459–470.

Corman, B. R. "The Effect of Varying Amounts and Kinds of Information as Guidance in Problem Solving." *Psychological Monographs,* 1957, *71* (entire issue 2).

Correa, H. "Optimal Allocation of Time Between Lectures and Examinations for Student Motivation." *Scientia Paedagogica Experimentalis,* 1994, *31*(1), 87–100.

Costin, F. "Lecturing Versus Other Methods of Teaching: A Review of Research." *British Journal of Educational Technology,* 1972, *3*(1), 4–31.

Costin, F., Greenough, W. T., and Menges, R. J. "Student Ratings of College Teaching: Reliability, Validity, and Usefulness." *Review of Educational Research,* 1971, *41,* 511–536.

Couch, R. W. "Individualized Instruction: A Review of Audio-Tutorial Instruction, Guided Design, the Personalized System of Instruction, and Individualized Lecture Classes." Ph.D. dissertation, University of Kansas, 1983. ERIC no. ED252178.

Craik, F.I.M., and Lockhart, R. S. "Levels of Processing: A Framework for Memory Research." *Journal of Verbal Learning and Verbal Behavior,* 1972, *11,* 671–684.

Cranton, P., and Smith, R. A. "Reconsidering the Unit of Analysis: A Model of Student Ratings of Instruction." *Journal of Educational Psychology,* 1990, *82*(2), 207–212.

Crawford, C. C. "The Correlation Between College Lecture Notes and Quiz Papers." *Journal of Educational Research,* 1925a, *12,* 282–291.

Crawford, C. C. "Some Experimental Studies of the Results of College Note-Taking." *Journal of Educational Research,* 1925b, *12,* 379–386.

Creswell, K. W., and Lin, C. A. "Effects of Televised Lecture Presentation Styles on Student Learning." *Journal of Educational Television,* 1989, *15*(1), 37–52.

Cryer, P. "Video Feedback Sessions for Improving Lecturing: Participants' Reactions to this Method of Academic Staff Development." *Programmed Learning and Educational Technology,* 1988, *25*(2), 112–117.

Culbertson, F. M. "Modification of an Emotionally Held Attitude Through Role Playing." *Journal of Abnormal and Social Psychology,* 1957, *54,* 230–233.

Daines, J. M., and Brown, G. A. "Evaluating a Training Programme on Lecturing." In A. Trott, H. Strongman, and L. Giddens (eds.), *Aspects of Educational Technology.* Vol. 15: *Improving Efficiency in Education and Training.* Proceedings of 15th annual conference of AETT, 1983.

Dansereau, D. F., and others. "Evaluation of a Learning Strategy System." In H. F. O'Neil and C. D. Spielberger (eds.), *Cognitive and Affective Learning Strategies.* New York: Academic Press, 1979.

Davies, B. "Physics Lectures and Student Notes." *Physics Education,* 1976, *11*(1), 33–36.

Davis, W. K., and others. "Influence of a Highly Focused Case on the Effect of Small-Group Facilitators' Content Expertise on Students' Learning and Satisfaction." *Academic Medicine,* 1994, *69*(8), 663–669.

Davy, S., and Dunkel, P. A. "The Heuristic of Lecture Note-Taking: Perceptions of American and International Students Regarding the Value and Practice of Note-Taking." *English for Specific Purposes,* 1989, *8*(1), 33–50.

Dawson, M. D. "Lecture vs. Problem-Solving in Teaching Elementary Social Sciences." *Science Education,* 1956, *40,* 395–404.

DeCarrico, J., and Nattinger, J. R. "Lexical Phrases for the Comprehension of Academic Lectures." *English for Specific Purposes,* 1988, *7*(2), 91–102.

De Cecco, J. P. "Class Size and Co-Ordinated Instruction." *British Journal of Education Psychology,* 1964, *34,* 65–74.

Deutsch, M. "Experimental Study of Effects of Co-Operation and Competition upon Group Process." *Human Relations,* 1949, *3,* 199–231.

Di Vesta, F. J., and Gray, G. S. "Listening and Note-Taking." *Journal of Educational Psychology,* 1972, *63,* 8–14.

Di Vesta, F. J., and Gray, G. S. "Listening and Note-Taking II." *Journal of Educational Psychology,* 1973, *64,* 278–287.

Di Vesta, F. J., and Smith, D. A. "The Pausing Principle: Increasing the Efficiency of Memory for Ongoing Events." *Contemporary Educational Psychology,* 1979, *4*(3), 288–296.

Dorward, N., and Wiedemann, P. "An Evaluation of the Mass Lecture as a Teaching Technique in First-Year Economics." *Economics,* 1977, *13*(part 4), 110–111.

Dowell, D. A., and Neal, J. A. "A Selective Review of the Validity of Student Ratings of Teaching." *Journal of Higher Education,* 1982, *53,* 51–62.

Dowell, D. A., and Neal, J. A. "The Validity and Accuracy of Student Ratings of Instruction: A Reply to Peter Cohen." *Journal of Higher Education,* 1983, *54,* 459–463.

Downs, V. C., Javidi, M. M., and Nussbaum, J. F. "An Analysis of Teachers' Verbal Communication Within the College Classroom: Use of Humor, Self-Disclosure, and Narratives." *Communication Education,* 1988, *37*(2), 127–141.

Dresner, M. "Changing Energy End Use Patterns as a Means of Reducing Global Warming Trends." *Journal of Environmental Education,* 1989–1990, *21*(2), 41–46.

Drew, C. P. "Are You Spoon-Feeding Your Students? A Paper on Facilitating a Collaborative Learning Experience." (Unpublished.) 1990. ERIC no. ED324046.

Dubin, R., and Hedley, R. A. *The Medium May Be Related to the Message: College Instruction by TV.* Eugene: Center for the Advanced Study of Educational Administration, University of Oregon, 1969.

Dubin, R., and Taveggia, T. C. *The Teaching-Learning Paradox.* Monograph no. 18. Eugene: Center for the Advanced Study of Educational Administration, University of Oregon, 1968.

Dudley-Evans, A., and Johns, T. F. "A Team Teaching Approach to Lecture Comprehension for Overseas Students." In British Council English Language Division, *The Teaching of Listening Comprehension.* London: British Council, 1981.

Dunkel, P. A., and Davis, J. N. "The Effects of Rhetorical Signaling Cues on Recall." In J. Flowerdew (ed.), *Academic Listening: Research Perspectives.* Cambridge University Press, 1994, 55–74.

Dunn, W. R. "Programmed Learning News: Feedback Devices in University Lectures." *New University,* 1969, *3*(4), 21–22.

Einstein, G. O., Morris, J., and Smith, S. "Note-Taking, Individual Differences, and Memory for Lecture Information." *Journal of Educational Psychology,* 1985, *77*(5), 522–532.

Eisner, S., and Rohde, K. "Note-Taking During and After the Lecture." *Journal of Educational Psychology,* 1959, *50,* 301–304.

Ekman, P., and Friesen, W. V. "Categories, Origins, Usage, and Coding: The Basis for Five Categories of Non-Verbal Behavior." *Semiotica,* 1969, *1,* 49–98.

Ellis, A. W., and Young, A. W. *Human Cognitive Neuropsychology.* Hillsdale, N.J.: Erlbaum, 1988.

Elton, L.R.B. "The Use of Duplicated Notes and Self-Tests in University Teaching." Paper read at the 1970 National Conference of the Association for Programmed Learning and Educational Technology, Loughborough, U.K., 1970.

English, S. L. "Kinetics in Academic Lectures." *ESP Journal,* 1985, *4*(2), 161–170.

Entwistle, N. J., and Entwistle, D. "The Relationships Between Personality Study Methods and Academic Performance." *British Journal of Educational Psychology,* 1970, *40*(2), 132–143.

Entwistle, N. J., and Marton, F. "Knowledge Objects: Understandings Constituted Through Intensive Academic Study." *British Journal of Educational Psychology,* 1994, *64*(1), 161–178.

Entwistle, N. J., and Wilson, J. D. "Personality Study Methods and Academic Performance." *Universities Quarterly,* 1970, *24*(2), 147–156.

Erlich, R. "Anxiety Reduction in Small Groups Learning and in Frontal Instruction Classroom." *Israeli Journal of Psychology and Counseling in Education,* Feb. 1979, no. 10, 38–44.

Erskine, C. A., and O'Morchoe, C.C.C. "Research on Teaching Methods: Its Significance for the Curriculum." *Lancet,* 1961, *23,* 709–711.

Evans, G. E. "Metaphors as Learning Aids in University Lectures." *Journal of Experimental Education,* 1988, *56*(2), 91–99.

Evans, K. M. "Teacher-Training Courses and Students' Personal Qualities." *Educational Research,* 1967, *10*(1), 72–77.

Evans, R. D., and Evans, G. E. "Cognitive Mechanisms in Learning from Metaphors." *Journal of Experimental Education,* 1989, *58*(1), 5–19.

Facinelli, J. *Music Students and Bibliography Instruction: A Study.* Akron, Ohio: University of Akron, 1982. ERIC no. ED242322.

Falchikov, N. "Attitudes and Values of Lecturing Staff: Tradition, Innovation and Change." *Higher Education,* 1993, *25*(4), 487–510.

Falk, B. "The Use of Student Evaluation." *Australian University,* 1967, *5*(2), 109–121.

Feather, N. T. "Preference for Information in Relation to Consistency, Novelty, Intolerance of Ambiguity, and Dogmatism." *Australian Journal of Psychology,* 1969, *21*(3), 235–250.

Feldman, K. A. "The Superior College Teacher from the Student's Point of View." *Research in Higher Education,* 1976, *5,* 243–288.

Feldman, K. A. "Consistency and Variability Among College Students in Rating Their Teachers and Courses." *Research in Higher Education,* 1977, *6,* 223–274.

Feldman, K. A. "Course Characteristics and College Students' Ratings of Their Teachers and Courses: What We Know and What We Don't Know." *Research in Higher Education,* 1978, *9,* 199–242.

Feldman, K. A. "The Significance of Circumstances for College Students' Ratings of Their Teachers and Courses." *Research in Higher Education,* 1979, *10,* 149–172.

Feldman, K. A. "Instructional Effectiveness of College Teachers as Judged by Teachers Themselves, Current and Former Students, Colleagues, Administrators, and External (Neutral) Observers." *Research in Higher Education,* 1989, *30,* 137–194.

Feldman, K. A., and Newcomb, T. M. *The Impact of College on Students.* Vol. 2. San Francisco: Jossey-Bass, 1973.

Festinger, L. *A Theory of Cognitive Dissonance.* New York: HarperCollins, 1957.

Fielding, G. D., Kameenui, E., and Gersten, R. M. "A Comparison of an Inquiry and a Direct Instruction Approach to Teaching Legal Concepts and Applications to Secondary School Students." *Journal of Educational Research,* 1983, *76*(5), 287–293.

Firstman, A. "A Comparison of Traditional and Television Lectures as a Means of Instruction in Biology at a Community College." (Unpublished.) 1983. ERIC no. ED230264.

Fisher, J. L., and Harris, M. B. "The Effect of Note-Taking and Review on Recall." *Journal of Educational Psychology,* 1973, *65,* 321–325.

Fisher, J. L., and Harris, M. B. "Note-Taking and Recall." *Journal of Educational Research,* 1974a, *67,* 291–292.

Fisher, J. L., and Harris M. B. "The Effect of Note-Taking Preferences and Type of Notes Taken on Memory." *Psychological Reports*, 1974b, *35*, 384–386.

Fitch, M. L., Drucker, A. J., and Norton, J. A., Jr. "Frequent Testing as a Motivating Factor in Large Lecture Classes." *Journal of Educational Psychology*, 1951, *42*, 1–20.

Flood Page, C. "Students' Reactions to Teaching Methods." *Universities Quarterly*, July 1970, 266–272.

Flowerdew, J. "Pragmatic Modifications on the 'Representative' Speech Act of Defining." *Journal of Pragmatics*, 1991, *15*(3), 253–264.

Flowerdew, J. "Definitions in Science Lectures." *Applied Linguistics*, 1992, *13*(2), 202–221.

Fodor, J. T. "A Comparative Study of Two Approaches to Health Instruction at the College Level." Unpublished doctoral dissertation, University of California, 1963.

Fontenot, D. W. "The Effects of Cooperative Learning Methods in Conjunction with Traditional Lectures in Seventh-Grade Science Classes." *Dissertation Abstracts International A*, 1996, *57*(1), 86.

Fortune, J. C., Gage, N. L., and Shutes, R. E. "The Generality of the Ability to Explain." Paper presented to the American Educational Research Association, Chicago, Feb. 1966.

Fox, D. "What Are the Principal Concerns of New Lecturers?" In R. Oxtoby, SRHE (ed.), *Higher Education at the Crossroad*. Guildford, U.K.: Society for Research into Higher Education, 1980.

Foy, J. M. "A Note on Lecturer Evaluation by Students." *Universities Quarterly*, 1969, *23*(3), 345–348.

Frank, B. M. "Effect of Field Independence-Dependence and Study Technique on Learning from a Lecture." *American Educational Research Journal*, 1984, *21*(3), 669–678.

Frank, R. E., and Lesher, R. E. "An Evaluation of the Effectiveness of Taped Lectures in a Community College Setting." *Scientia Paedagogica Experimentalis*, 1971, *8*(1), 16–21.

Freyberg, P. D. "The Effectiveness of Note-Taking." *Education for Teaching*, Feb. 1956, 17–24.

Friedman, H. L., and Johnson, R. L. "Compressed Speech: Correlates of Listening Ability." *Journal of Communication*, Sept. 1968, *18*, 207–218.

Furneaux, W. D. "The Psychologist and the University." *Universities Quarterly*, 1962, *17*, 33–47.

Gage, N. L. *Handbook of Research on Teaching*. New York: Rand McNally, American Educational Research Association, 1963.

Gage, N. L. "An Analytical Approach in Research on Instructional Methods." *Phi Delta Kappan*, June 1968, 601–606.

Gage, N. L., and others. *Explorations of the Teacher's Effectiveness in Explaining*. Technical Report no. 4 of the Stanford Center for Research and Development in Teaching, School of Education, Stanford University, 1968.

Gage, N. L., and Unruh, W. R. "Theoretical Formulations for Research on Teaching." *Review of Educational Research*, 1967, *37*, 358–370.

Gagne, R. M. *The Conditions of Learning*. Austin, Tex.: Holt, Rinehart and Winston, 1965.

Galotti, K. M. "Reasoning About Reasoning: A Course Project." (Special issue: "Psychologists Teach Critical Thinking.") *Teaching of Psychology*, 1995, *22*(1), 66–68.

Gane, C. "Educational Technology Vs. the Technology of Education." *Royal Television Society Journal*, 1969, *12*(5), 101–104.

Gauger, P. W. "The Effect of Gesture and the Presence or Absence of the Speaker on the Listening Comprehension of 11th and 12th Grade High School Pupils." Ph.D. dissertation, University of Wisconsin, 1951.

Gauvain, S. "The Use of Student Opinion in the Quality Control of Teaching." *British Journal of Medical Education,* 1968, *2*(1), 55–62.

Geller, E. S., Chaffee, J. L., and Farris, J. C. "Research in Modifying Lecturer Behavior with Continuous Student Feedback." *Educational Technology,* 1975, *15*(12), 31–35.

Gerberich, J. R., and Warner, K. O. "Relative Instructional Efficiencies of the Lecture and Discussion Methods in a University Course in American National Government." *Journal of Education Research,* 1936, *29,* 574–579.

Gibbs, G. *Improving the Quality of Student Learning.* Bristol, U.K.: Technical and Educational Services, 1992.

Gibbs, G., Lucas, L., and Simonite, V. "Class Size and Student Performance: 1984–1994." *Studies in Higher Education,* 1996, *21*(3), 261–273.

Giles, R. M., and others. "Recall of Lecture Information: A Question of What, When and Where." *Medical Education,* 1982, *16*(5), 264–268.

Gimson, A. C. "The Twentyman Lecture: The Pronunciation of English." *Modern Languages,* 1981, *62*(2), 61–68.

Gist, M. E. "The Influence of Training Method on Self Efficacy and Idea Generation Among Managers." *Personnel Psychology,* 1989, *42*(4), 787–805.

Glanzer, M., and Cunitz, A. R. "Two Storage Mechanisms in Free Recall." *Journal of Verbal Learning and Verbal Behaviour,* 1966, *5,* 351–360.

Glass, G. V. "Class Size." In M. J. Dunkin (ed.), *International Encyclopedia of Teaching and Teacher Education.* New York: Pergamon Press, 1987.

Glogovsky, R. J. "A Comparison of Graphic Arts Processes Practiced by Contemporary Industry with Those Taught in Industrial Arts Teacher Education." Ed.D. dissertation, University of Northern Colorado, 1970.

Goodhue, D. "Tape-Recorded Lectures with Slide Synchronization: A Description of the Method." *Journal of Biological Education,* 1969, *3*(4), 311–319.

Gore, A. E. "Individualized Instruction Through Team Learning in a College Course in General Psychology." Doctoral dissertation, Boston University. Reprinted in *Dissertation Abstracts,* 1962, *23*(4), p. 1273.

Greene, E. B. "Certain Aspects of Lecture, Reading, and Guided Reading." *School and Society,* 1934, *39,* 619–624.

Grobe, R. P., and Pettibone, T. J. "Effect of Instructional Pace on Student Attentiveness." *Journal of Educational Research,* 1975, *69*(4), 131–134.

Gruber, A. "Sensory Alternation and Performance in a Vigilance Task." *Human Factors,* 1964, *6,* 3–12.

Guetzkow, H., Kelly, L. E., and McKeachie, W. J. "An Experimental Comparison of Recitation, Discussion, and Tutorial Methods in College Teaching." *Journal of Educational Psychology,* 1954, *45,* 193–207.

Guilford, J. P. "Three Faces of Intellect." *American Psychologist,* 1959, *14,* 469–479.

Gulo, E. V., and Baron, A. "Classroom Learning of Meaningful Prose by College Students as a Function of Sensory Mode of Stimulus Presentation." *Perceptual and Motor Skills,* 1965, *21,* 183–186.

Gulo, E. V., and Nigro, M. R. "Classroom Learning as a Function of Method of Presenting Instructional Materials." *Psychological Reports,* 1966, *19,* 971–977.

Gunter, B., Berry, C., and Clifford, B. R. "Proactive Interference Effects with Television News Items: Further Evidence." *Journal of Experimental Psychology: Human Learning and Memory,* 1981, *7,* 480–487.

Gunzburger, L. K. "U.S. Medical Schools' Valuing of Curriculum Time: Self-Directed Learning Versus Lectures." *Academic Medicine,* 1993, *68*(9), 700–702.

Guthrie, E. R. *The Evaluation of Teaching: A Progress Report.* Seattle: University of Washington, 1954.

Hale, E. *Report of the Committee on University Teaching Methods: Chairman Sir E. Hale.* University Grants Committee. London: Her Majesty's Stationery Office, 1964.

Halpin, F. B. "A Predictive Failure of Veterinary Students: A Method of Selection for Counselling." *British Journal of Medical Education,* 1968, *2*(3), 200–203.

Hamp-Lyons, E. "Survey Review of Materials for Teaching Advanced Listening and Note-Taking." (Unpublished.) 1982. ERIC no. ED225359.

Hancock, D. R. "Motivating Adults to Learn Academic Course Content." *Journal of Educational Research,* 1994, *88*(2), 102–108.

Hansen, C., and Jensen, C. "Evaluating Lecture Comprehension." In J. Flowerdew (ed.), *Academic Listening, Research Perspectives.* Cambridge, U.K.: Cambridge University Press, 1994.

Harden, R. M., Wayne, E., and Donald, G. "An Audio-Visual Technique for Medical Teaching." *Journal of Medical and Biological Illustration,* 1968, *18*(1), 29–32.

Harlow, H. F. "The Formation of Learning Sets." *Psychological Review,* 1949, *56,* 51–56.

Harris, W. G., Jr. "A Comparison of Student Performance in a College Engineering Course Between Two Lecture Methods: A Taped Recording and a Printed Transcription." Ed.D. dissertation, Oklahoma State University, 1971. ERIC no. ED076322.

Hartley, J. "Lecture Handouts and Student Note-Taking." *Programmed Learning and Educational Technology,* 1976, *13*(2), 58–64.

Hartley, J., and Cameron, A. "Some Observations on the Efficiency of Lecturing." *Educational Review,* 1967, *20*(1), 30–37.

Hartley, J., and Davies, I. K. "Note-Taking: A Critical Review." *Programmed Learning and Educational Technology,* 1978, *15,* 207–224.

Hartley, J., and Marshall, S. "On Notes and Note-Taking." *Universities Quarterly,* 1974, *28*(2), 225–235.

Harvey, J. N., and Barker, D. G. "Student Evaluation of Teaching Effectiveness." *Improving College and University Teaching,* 1970, *18,* 275–278.

Heilman, J. D., and Armentrout, W. D. "The Rating of College Teachers on Ten Traits by Their Students." *Journal of Educational Psychology,* 1936, *27,* 197–216.

Henderson, N. K. *University Teaching.* Oxford University Press, 1970.

Henk, W. A., and Stahl, N. A. "A Meta-Analysis of the Effect of Note-Taking on Learning from Lecture." *National Reading Conference Yearbook,* 1985, no. 34, 70–75.

Hertz-Lazarowitz, R., and others. "Student-Student Interaction in the Classroom: A Naturalistic Study." Paper presented to the summer workshop of the Association of Teacher Educators, Institute for Research on Teaching, East Lansing, Mich., 1981.

Hildum, D. C., and Brown, R. W. "Verbal Reinforcement and Interviewer Bias." *Journal of Abnormal and Social Psychology,* 1956, *53,* 108–111.

Hiller, J. H. "Verbal Response Indicators of Conceptual Vagueness." *American Educational Research Journal,* 1971, *8,* 151–161.

Hiller, J. H., Fisher, G. A., and Kaess, W. "A Computer Investigation of Verbal Characteristics of Effective Classroom Lecturing." *American Educational Research Journal,* 1969, *6,* 661–675.

Himmelweit, H. T., and Swift, E. "The Class as a Reference Group." Report to the British Psychological Society Annual Conference, University of Exeter, Devon, United Kingdom, 1971.

Hingorani, H. K. "Information Technology Supported Case Studies for Teaching Higher Level Cognitive Skills: A Comparative Evaluation of Methodologies (Professional Development)." *Dissertation Abstracts International A,* 1996, *56*(12), 4852.

Hinkle, S., and Hinkle, A. "An Experimental Comparison of the Effects of Focused Freewriting and Other Study Strategies on Lecture Comprehension." *Teaching of Psychology,* 1990, *17*(1), 31–35.

Hodgson, V., and McConnell, D. "The Development of Student Constructed Lecture Feedback Questionnaires." *Assessment and Evaluation in Higher Education,* 1985, *10*(1), 2–27.

Hohn, R. L., Gallagher, T., and Byrne, M. "Instructor Supplied Notes and Higher Order Thinking." *Journal of Instructional Psychology,* 1990, *17*(2), 71–74.

Holen, M. C., and Oaster, T. R. "Serial Position and Isolation Effects in a Classroom Lecture Simulation." *Journal of Educational Psychology,* 1976, *68*(3), 293–296.

Hollingsworth, P. M. "Enhancing Listening Retention: The Two Minute Discussion." *College Student Journal,* 1995, *29*(1), 116–117.

Holloway, P. J. "The Effect of Lecture Time on Learning." *British Journal of Educational Psychology,* 1966, *31*(3), 255–258.

Hood, K. R. "Effects of a Lecturer's Use of Synchronous Whole-Body Locomotion on Student Attitudes Towards Instruction." Ed.D. dissertation, Texas Tech University. See also *Dissertation Abstracts International,* 1988, *49*(3A), p. 441, no. 098758.

Horak, V. M., and Horak, W. J. "The Influence of Student Locus of Control and Teaching Method on Mathematics Achievement." *Journal of Experimental Education,* 1982, *51*, 18–21.

Houtman, I. L., and Bakker, F. C. "Stress in Student Teachers During Real and Simulated Standardized Lectures." *Journal of Human Stress,* 1987, *13*(4), 180–187.

Houtman, I. L., and Bakker, F. C. "Individual Differences in Reactivity to and Coping with the Stress of Lecturing." *Journal of Psychosomatic Research,* 1991a, *35*(1), 11–24.

Houtman, I. L., and Bakker, F. C. "Stress and Coping in Lecturing, and the Stability of Responses Across Practice." *Journal of Psychosomatic Research,* 1991b, *35*(2–3), 323–333.

Hovland, C. I., and Janis, I. L. (eds.). *Personality and Persuasibility.* New Haven: Yale University Press, 1959.

Hovland, C. I., Janis, I. L., and Kelley, H. H. *Communication and Persuasion.* New Haven: Yale University Press, 1953.

Hovland, C. I., Lumsdaine, A. A., and Sheffield, F. D. *Experiments on Mass Communication.* Princeton, N.J.: Princeton University Press, 1949.

Hovland, C. I., and Mandell, W. "An Experimental Comparison of Conclusion-Drawing by the Communicator and by the Audience." *Journal of Abnormal and Social Psychology,* 1952, *47*, 581–588.

Howe, M.J.A. "Notetaking Strategy, Review, and Long-Term Retention of Verbal Information." *Journal of Educational Research,* 1970a, *63*, 285.

Howe, M.J.A. "Using Students' Notes to Examine the Role of the Individual Learner in Acquiring Meaningful Subject Matter." *Journal of Educational Research,* 1970b, *64*, 61–63.

Howe, M.J.A. "Learning and the Acquisition of Knowledge by Students: Some Experimental Investigations." In M.J.A. Howe (ed.), *Adult Learning: Psychological Research and Applications.* London, Wiley, 1977.

Howe, M. J. A., and Godfrey, J. *Student Note-Taking as an Aid to Learning.* Exeter, U.K.: Exeter University Teaching Services, 1977.

Howe, M.J.A., Ormond, V., and Singer, L. "Recording Activities and Recall of Information." *Perceptual and Motor Skills,* 1974, *39*, 309–310.

Hubbard, R. "Tertiary Mathematics Without Lectures." *International Journal of Mathematical Education in Science and Technology,* 1990, *21*(4), 567–571.

Hudelson, E. *Class Size at the College Level.* Minneapolis: University of Minnesota Press, 1928.

Hughes, C. A., and Suritsky, S. K. "Notetaking Skills and Strategies for Students with Learning Disabilities." *Preventing School Failure,* 1993, *38*(1), 7–11.

Hult, R. E., and others. "Differential Effects of Note Taking Ability and Lecture Encoding Structure on Student Learning." Paper presented to the annual meeting of the Eastern Educational Research Association, West Palm Beach, Florida, 1984.

Hunkins, A. Papers read to American Educational Research Association, 1967, 1968.

Hyde, R. M., and Flournoy, D. J. "A Case Against Mandatory Lecture Attendance." *Journal of Medical Education,* 1986, *61*(3), 175–176.

Isaacs, G. "Lecture Note-Taking, Learning, and Recall." *Medical Teacher,* 1989, *11*(3/4), 295–302.

Isaacs, G. "Lecturing Practices and Note-Taking Purposes." *Studies in Higher Education,* 1994, *19*(2), 203–216.

Jackson, J., and Bilton, L. "Lecture Comprehension and Note-Taking for L2 Students." (Unpublished.) 1990a. ERIC no. ED323785.

Jackson, J., and Bilton, L. "Listening and Note-Taking in Higher Education." (Unpublished.) 1990b. ERIC no. ED366189.

Jackson, J., and Bilton, L. "Stylistic Variations in Science Lectures: Teaching Vocabulary." *English for Specific Purposes,* 1994, *13*(1), 61–80.

James, D. W., Johnson, M. L., and Venning, P. "Testing for Learnt Skill in Observation and Evaluation of Evidence." *Lancet,* 1956, *2,* 379–383.

Jamieson, G. H., James, P. E., and Leytham, G.W.H. "Comparisons Between Teaching Methods at the Post-Graduate Level." *Programmed Learning,* Oct. 1969, 243–249.

Janis, I. L. "Motivational Effects of Different Sequential Arrangements of Conflicting Argument: A Theoretical Analysis." In C. I. Hovland (ed.), *The Order of Presentation in Persuasion.* New Haven: Yale University Press, 1957.

Janis, I. L., and Feshbach, S. "Effects of Fear-Arousing Communications." *Journal of Abnormal and Social Psychology,* 1953, *48,* 78–92.

Janis, I. L., and Field, P. B.. "A Behavioral Assessment of Persuasibility: Consistency of Individual Differences." In C. I. Hovland and I. L. Janis, *Personality and Persuasibility.* New Haven: Yale University Press, 1959. (Reprinted in A. R. Cohen, *Attitude Change and Social Influence,* New York: Basic Books, 1963.)

Javidi, M. N., and Long, L. W. "Teachers' Use of Humor, Self-Disclosure, and Narrative Activity as a Function of Experience." *Communication Research Reports,* 1989, *6*(1), 47–52.

Jenkins, A., cited by Gibbs, G. "Break Up Your Lectures: Or Christaller Sliced Up." *Journal of Geographical Higher Education,* 1984, *8*(1), 232, 252, 253, 266.

Jenkins, A. "Encouraging Active Learning in Structured Lectures." In G. Gibbs (ed.), *Improving the Quality of Student Learning.* Bristol, U.K.: Technical and Education Services, 1992.

Jensen, P. H. "The Application of Kolb's Experiential Learning Theory in a First Semester College Accounting Course." *Dissertation Abstracts International A,* 1996, *56,* 3201.

Johnson, J. A. "Instruction: From the Consumer's Point of View." In C.B.T. Lee, *Improving College Teaching.* Washington, D.C.: American Council on Education, 1967.

Johnson, P. E. "Some Psychological Aspects of Subject Matter Structure." *Journal of Educational Psychology,* 1967, *58*(2), 75–83.

Johnston, J. O., and Calhoun, T.A.P. "The Serial Position Effect in Lecture Material." *Journal of Educational Research*, 1969, *62*(6), 255–258.

Johnstone, A. H., and Percival, F. "Attention Breaks in Lectures." *Education in Chemistry*, 1976, *13*(2), 49–50.

Jones, H. E. "Experimental Studies of College Teaching." *Archives of Psychology*, 1923, no. 68.

Joyce, C.R.B., and Weatherall, M. "Controlled Experiments in Teaching." *Lancet*, 1957, *2*, 402–407.

Kaplan, R. M., and Pascoe, G. C. "Humorous Lectures and Humorous Examples: Some Effects upon Comprehension and Retention." *Journal of Educational Psychology*, 1977, *69*(1), 61–65.

Karp, H. J. "The Use of Keller's Personalized System of Instruction." *College Student Personnel Abstracts*, no. 0298–19, 1983, *19*(1), 146.

Katona, G. *Organizing and Memorizing*. New York: Columbia University Press, 1940.

Katz, D. *Gestalt Psychology*. Somerset, N.J.: Ronald Press, 1950.

Katz, N. "Problem Solving and Time: Functions of Learning Style and Teaching Methods." *Occupational Therapy Journal of Research*, 1990, *10*(4), 221–236.

Kaul, P. N. "Teaching Styles and Attitudes Towards Extension Education." *Asian Journal of Psychology and Education*, 1976, *1*(1), 24–28.

Kelly, A. E., and O'Donnell, A. "Hypertext and the Study Strategies of Preservice Teachers: Issues in Instructional Hypertext Design." *Journal of Educational Computing Research*, 1994, *10*(4), 373–387.

Kelly, N., and Kelly, B. "Backgrounds, Education, and Teaching Styles of Teaching Award Winning Professors." Unpublished paper, 1982. ERIC. No. ED230080.

Khoiny, F. E. "The Effectiveness of Problem-Based Learning in Nurse Practitioner Education." *Dissertation Abstracts International A*, 1996, *57*(1), 88.

Kiewra, K. A. "Learning from a Lecture: An Investigation of Notetaking, Review and Attendance at a Lecture." *Human Learning Journal of Practical Research and Applications*, 1985, *4*(1), 73–77.

Kiewra, K. A., and Frank, B. M. "Encoding and External Storage Effects of Personal Lecture Notes, Skeletal Notes, and Detailed Notes for Field-Independent and Field-Dependent Learners." *Journal of Educational Research*, 1988, *81*(3), 143–148.

Kiewra, K. A., DuBois, N. F., Christian, D., and McShane, A.. "Providing Study Notes: Comparison of Three Types of Notes for Review." *Journal of Educational Psychology*, 1988, *80*(4), 595–597.

Kiewra, K. A., and others. "A More Equitable Account of the Note Taking Functions in Learning from Lecture and from Text." *Instructional Science*, 1989, *18*(3), 217–232.

Kiewra, K. A., and others. "Note Taking Functions and Techniques." *Journal of Educational Psychology*, 1991, *83*(2), 240–245.

King, M. "The Anxieties of University Teachers." *Universities Quarterly*, 1973, *28*, 69–83.

King, A. "Effects of Self-Questioning Training on College Students' Comprehension of Lectures." *Contemporary Educational Psychology*, 1989, *14*(4), 366–381.

King, A. "Enhancing Peer Interaction and Learning in the Classroom Through Reciprocal Questioning." *American Educational Research Journal*, 1990, *27*(4), 664–687.

King, A. "Improving Lecture Comprehension: Effects of a Metacognitive Strategy." *Applied Cognitive Psychology*, 1991, *5*(4), 331–346.

King, A. "Facilitating Elaborative Learning Through Guided Student Generated Questioning." *Educational Psychologist*, 1992, *27*(1), 111–126.

King, A. "Autonomy and Question Asking: The Role of Personal Control in Guided Student Generated Questioning." (Special Issue: Individual Differences in Question Asking and Strategic Listening Processes.) *Learning and Individual Differences,* 1994, *6*(2), 163–185.

King, A. "Inquiring Minds Really Do Want to Know: Using Questioning to Teach Critical Thinking." *Teaching of Psychology,* 1995, *22*(1), 13–17.

King, B. T., and Janis, I. L. "Comparison of the Effectiveness of Improvised Versus Non-Improvised Role-Playing in Producing Opinion Changes." *Human Relations,* 1956, 9, 177–186.

Kintsch, W., and Bates, E. "Recognition Memory for Statements from a Classroom Lecture." *Journal of Experimental Psychology: Human Learning and Memory,* 1977, *3*(2), 150–159.

Kintsch, W., and Yarbrough, J. C. "Role of Rhetorical Structure in Text Comprehension and Production." *Journal of Educational Psychology,* 1982, *74*(6), 828–834.

Kipper, D. A., and Ben-Ely, Z. "The Effectiveness of the Psychodramatic Double Method, the Reflection Method, and Lecturing in the Training of Empathy." *Journal of Clinical Psychology,* 1979, *35*(2), 370–375.

Klein, J. *Working with Groups.* London: Hutchinson, 1961.

Kletz, T. A. "Putting Knowledge to Use." *Education in Chemistry,* 1970, *7*(6), 229.

Klinzing, H. G. "Skill Acquisition and Reflection-Based Decision Making in a Teaching Laboratory: An Evaluative Study." *European Journal of Teacher Education,* 1988, *11*(2–3), 167–175.

Koo, A., Wong, R., and Tam, M. "Improving Lectures by Using Interactive Handouts." *British Journal of Educational Technology,* 1993, *24*(2), 139–145.

Kozoil, E. M. "Kinetic Structural Analysis of Selected College Mathematics Lectures (Remedial)." *Dissertation Abstracts International,* Mar. 1986, *46A*(9), p. 2606.

Kulik, J. A., Kulik, C.-L. C., and Smith, B. B. "Research on the Personalized System of Instruction." *Programmed Learning and Educational Technology,* 1976, *13*, 23–30.

Kuz'mina, L. S. "Mental Work Capacity of Students in Listening to Text Materials and Lectures." *Voprosy Psikhologii,* 1976, no. 5, 128–133.

Lacroix, P. S. "The Effects of Cognitive Style, Notetaking, and Instructor-Prepared Handout Materials on Learning from Lecture Instruction." *Dissertation Abstracts International,* 1987, *48A*(5), p. 1104.

Ladas, H. "Summarizing Research: A Case Study." *Review of Educational Research,* 1980, *50*(4), 597–624.

Lam, Y. J. "Longitudinal Relationships of Selected Course Structure, Cognitive and Affective Factors and Classroom Behaviors of Adult Learners." *Educational Research Quarterly,* 1984–1985, *9*(3), 28–36.

Lambiotte, J. G., Skaggs, L. P., and Dansereau, D. F. "Learning from Lectures: Effects of Knowledge Maps and Cooperative Review Strategies." *Applied Cognitive Psychology,* 1993, *7*(6), 483–497.

Lambiotte, J. G., and Dansereau, D. F. "Effects of Knowledge Maps and Prior Knowledge on Recall of Science Lecture Content." *Journal of Experimental Education,* 1992, *60*(3), 189–201.

Land, M. L. "Combined Effect of Two Teacher Clarity Variables on Student Achievement." *Journal of Experimental Education,* Fall 1981, *50*, 14–17.

Land, M. L., and Combs, N. "Teacher Behavior and Student Ratings." *Educational and Psychological Research,* Winter 1982, *2*, 63–66.

Lazarus, B. D. *Using Guided Notes to Aid Learning-Disabled Students in Secondary Mainstream Settings. Pointer,* 1988, *33*(1), 32–35. ERIC no. EJ384022.

LeBlanc, P. A. "Attitudes of Nursing Students Toward the Elderly as Influenced by Lecture-Discussion with and Without Simulation." *Dissertation Abstracts International A,* 1996, *56*(11), 4247.

Lesniak, S. L. "Active Learning and Other Teaching Activities as Perceived by Part-Time Faculty and Students in a Professional Degree Program Designed for Adult Learners." *Dissertation Abstracts International,* July 1996, *57A*(1), p. 127.

Lewin, K. "Forces Behind Food Habits and Methods of Change." *Bulletin of the National Research Council,* 1943, no. 108, 36–65. (Reprinted in A. R. Cohen, *Attitude Change and Social Influence,* New York: Basic Books, 1964.)

Linn, M. D. "Urban Black Speech as the Sixth Clock." Paper presented at the 63rd annual meeting of the National Council of Teachers of English, Philadelphia, Nov. 1973. ERIC no. ED094376.

Little, C. E. "An Experimental Study of Programmed Instruction in College Algebra at Colorado State College." Doctoral dissertation, Colorado State College, 1964.

Lloyd, D. H. "A Concept of Improvement of Learning Response in the Taught Lesson." *Visual Education,* Oct. 1968, pp. 23–25.

Locke, E. A. "An Empirical Study of Lecture Note-Taking Among College Students." *Journal of Educational Research,* 1977, *71*, 93–99.

Loomis, S. D., and Greene, A. W. "The Pattern of Mental Conflict in a Typical State University." *Journal of Abnormal and Social Psychology,* 1947, *42*, 342–355.

Lovell, G. D., and Haner, C. F. "Forced Choice Applied to College Faculty Rating." *Educational and Psychological Measurement,* 1955, *15*, 291–304.

Lumsdaine, A. A., and Janis, I. L. "Resistance to 'Counter Propaganda' Produced by One-Sided and Two-Sided 'Propaganda' Presentations." *Public Opinion Quarterly,* 1953, *17*, 311–318.

MacDonald M., and Romano, S. "An Investigation into Student and Teacher Attitudes Towards the Value of Handouts." *British Journal of In-Service Education,* 1983, *9*(3), 149–158.

Mackworth, J. *Vigilance and Habituation.* New York: Penguin, 1970.

Mackworth, N. H. *Researches in the Measurement of Human Performance.* London: Her Majesty's Stationery Office, 1950.

MacManaway, L. A. "Using Lecture Scripts." *Universities Quarterly,* June 1968, pp. 327–336.

MacManaway, L. A. "Teaching Methods in Higher Education: Innovation and Research." *Universities Quarterly,* 1970, *24*(3), 321–329.

MacMillan, M. "Efficiency in Reading." Occasional Paper no. 6. London: English-Teaching Information Centre, 1965.

Macomber, F. G., and Siegel, L. *Final Report of the Experimental Study in Instructional Procedures.* Oxford, Ohio: Miami University, 1960.

Maddox, H., and Hoole, E. "Performance Decrement in the Lecture." *Educational Review,* 1975, *28*, 17–30.

Magnusson, J. L., and Perry, R. P. "Stable and Transient Determinants of Students' Perceived Control: Implications for Instruction in the College Classroom." *Canada Journal of Educational Psychology,* 1989, *81*(3), 362–370.

Malleson, N. "Medical Students' Study: Time and Place." *British Journal of Medical Education,* 1967, *1*(3), 169–177.

Maqsud, M. "Effects of Personal Lecture Notes and Teacher-Notes on Recall of University Students." *British Journal of Educational Psychology,* 1980, *50*(3), 289–294.

Marks, L. E., and Miller, G. A. "The Role of Semantic and Syntactic Constraints in the Memorisation of English Sentences." *Journal of Verbal Learning and Verbal Behaviour,* 1964, *3,* 1–5.

Marris, P. *The Experience of Higher Education.* New York: Routledge, 1964.

Marsh, H. W. "Experimental Manipulation of Student Motivation and Their Effects of Examination Performance." *British Journal of Educational Psychology,* 1984a, *54*(2), 206–213.

Marsh, H. W. "Students' Evaluations of University Teaching: Dimensionality, Reliability, Validity, Potential Biases, and Utility." *Journal of Educational Psychology,* 1984b, *76*(5), 707–754.

Marsh, H. W. "Students' Evaluations of University Teaching: Research Findings, Methodological Issues, and Directions of Future Research." *International Journal of Educational Research,* 1987, *11*(3), 253–388.

Marsh, H. W., Overall, J. U., and Kesler, S. P. "Class Size, Student Evaluations, and Instructor Effectiveness." *American Educational Research Journal,* 1979, *16,* 57–69.

Marton, F., Hounsell, D., and Entwistle, N. J. (eds.). *The Experience of Learning.* Edinburgh: Scottish Academic Press, 1984.

Mastin, V. E. "Teacher Enthusiasm." *Journal of Educational Research,* 1963, *56,* 385–386.

McAleese, R. "Density and Vagueness in Lecturing: A Learning Theory Explanation." *Research Intelligence,* 1978, *4,* 16–18.

McCarthy, P. R., and Schmeck, R. R. "Effects of Teacher Self-Disclosure on Student Learning and Perceptions of Teacher." *College Student Journal,* Spring 1982, *16,* 45–49.

McCarthy, W. H. "Improving Large Audience Teaching: The 'Programmed' Lecture." *British Journal of Medical Education,* 1970, *4*(1), 29–31.

McClain, A. "Improving Lectures: Challenge Both Sides of the Brain." (Unpublished.) 1986. ERIC no. ED274954.

McClendon, P. I. "An Experimental Study of the Relationship Between Notetaking Practices and Listening Comprehension of College Freshman During Expository Lectures." *Speech Monographs,* 1958, *25,* 222–228.

McCord, W. B. "Speech Factors Relating to Teaching Efficiency." *Speech Monographs,* 1944, *11,* 53–64.

McDonald, R. J., and Taylor, E. G. "Student Note-Taking and Lecture Handouts in Veterinary Medical Education." *Journal of Veterinary Medical Education,* 1980, *7*(3) 157–161.

McDougall, I. R., Gray, H. W., and McNichol, S. P. "The Effect of Timing and Distribution of Handouts on Improvement of Student Performance." *British Journal of Medical Education,* 1972, *6,* 155–157.

McGuire, C. H. "A Process Approach to the Construction and Analysis of Medical Examinations." *Journal of Medical Education,* 1963, *38,* 556.

McHenry, D. E. *The Effect of Notetaking Activity on Listening Comprehension in an Immediate Recall Situation.* USAFA Educational Research Report 69–2. Colorado Springs, Colo.: Directorate of Educational Research, U.S. Air Force Academy, 1969.

McKeachie, W. J. "Research on Teaching at the College and University Level." In N. Gage (ed.), *Handbook of Research on Teaching.* New York: Rand McNally, 1963.

McKeachie, W. J. *Teaching Tips.* (5th ed.). Lexington, Mass.: Heath, 1965.

McKibben, M. L. "Listening, Study Skills, and Reading: Measuring and Meeting College Freshman Needs in the 1980s." (Unpublished.) 1982. ERIC no. ED214111.

McLeish, J. *The Lecture Method.* Cambridge Monographs on Teaching Methods no. 1. Cambridge, U.K.: Cambridge Institute of Education, 1968.

McLeish, J. *Students' Attitudes and College Environments.* Cambridge Monographs on Teaching Methods no. 3. Cambridge, U.K.: Cambridge Institute of Education, 1970.

McMinn, M. R., Troyer, P. K., Hannum, L. E., and Foster, J. D. "Teaching Nonsexist Language to College Students." *Journal of Experimental Education,* 1991, *59*(2), 153–161.

McQueen, W., Meschino, R., Pike, P., and Poelstra, P. "Improving Graduate Student Performance in Cognitive Assessment: The Saga Continues." *Professional Psychology Research and Practice,* 1994, *25*(3), 283–287.

Menec, V. H., and others. "Assisting At-Risk College Students with Attributional Retraining and Effective Teaching." *Journal of Applied Social Psychology,* 1994, *24*(8), 675–701.

Meredith, G. M., and Ogasawara, T. H. "Instructional Format and Impact of Graduate Level Teaching Assistants." *Psychological Reports,* 1982a, *50*(3, part 2), 1085–1086.

Meredith, G. M., and Ogasawara, T. H. "Preference for Class Size in Lecture Format Courses Among College Students." *Psychological Reports,* 1982b, *51*(3, part 1), 961–962.

Miller, G. A. "The Magical Number Seven, Plus or Minus Two: Some Limits on Our Capacity for Processing Information." In *The Psychology of Communication.* New York: Penguin, 1967.

Miller, N. P. "The Effect of Working Memory, an Advance Organizer and Modeled Note-taking on Listening Comprehension of Inner-City Fifth Graders." *Dissertation Abstracts International,* Dec. 1996, *57A*(6), p. 2344.

Miller, N., and Campbell, D. T. "Recency and Primacy in Persuasion as a Function of the Timing of Speeches and Measurements." *Journal of Abnormal and Social Psychology,* 1959, *59,* 1–9.

Mills, D. G. "The Use of Closed-Circuit Television in Teaching Geography and in Training Teachers of Geography." *Geography,* 1966, *51*(3), 218–223.

Milton, O. "Two Year Follow-up: Objective Data After Learning Without Class Attendance." *Psychological Reports,* 1962, *11,* 833–836.

Miron, M. S., and Brown, E. R. "Stimulus Parameters in Speech Compression." *Journal of Communication,* 1968, *18*(3), 319–325.

Mitnick, L. L., and McGinnies, E. "Influencing Ethnocentrism in Small Discussion Groups Through a Film Communication." *Journal of Abnormal and Social Psychology,* 1958, *56,* 82–90.

Mohr, P. H. "Cognitive Development in College Men and Women as Measured on the Perry Scheme When Learning and Teaching Styles Are Addressed in a Chemical Engineering Curriculum." *Dissertation Abstracts International A,* 1996, *56*(8), 3020.

Morgan, C. H., Lilley, J. D., and Boreham, N. C. "Learning from Lectures: The Effect of Varying the Detail in Lecture Handouts on Note-Taking and Recall." *Applied Cognitive Psychology,* 1988, *2*(2), 115–122.

Morgan, S. V., and Puglisi, J. T. "Enhancing Memory for Lecture Sentences: A Depth Perspective." *Psychological Reports,* 1982, *51*(2), 675–678.

Murdock, B. B. "The Retention of Individual Items." *Journal of Experimental Psychology,* 1961, *62,* 618–625.

Murray, H. G., Rushton, J. P., and Paunonen, S. V. "Teacher Personality Traits and Student Instructional Ratings in Six Types of University Courses." *Journal of Educational Psychology,* 1990, *82*(2), 250–261.

Nager, N. R. "How to Create One-on-One Feedback System for Students and, at the Same Time, Organize Notes for Books, Lectures with Interactive Electronic Index Card Software." Classroom teaching guide and paper, presented at the 69th annual meeting of the Association for Education in Journalism and Mass Communication, Corvallis, Oregon, 1983. ERIC no. ED237976.

Nance, J. L., and Nance, C. E. "Does Learning Occur in the Classroom?" *College Student Journal,* 1990, *24*(4), 338–340.

Natfulin, D. H., Ware, J. E., and Donnelly, F. A. "The Dr. Fox Lecture: A Paradigm of Educational Seduction." *Journal of Medical Education,* 1973, *48,* 630–635.

Nelson, W. B. "An Experiment with Class Size in the Teaching of Elementary Economics." *Educational Record,* 1959, *4,* 330–341.

Nelson, G. L. "The Relationship Between the Use of Personal Examples in Foreign Teaching Assistants' Lectures and Uncertainty Reduction, Student Attitude, Student Recall, and Ethnocentrism." Ph.D. dissertation, University of Minnesota (no. 0130). See also *Dissertation Abstracts International,* 1989, *50A*(11), p. 3414.

Nelson, G. L. "The Relationship Between the Use of Personal, Cultural Examples in International Teaching Assistants' Lectures and Uncertainty Reduction, Student Attitude, Student Recall, and Ethnocentrism." *International Journal of Intercultural Relations,* 1992, *16*(1), 33–52.

Nisbet, J. "Papers for a Short Course on University Teaching Methods." (Mimeographed papers.) Aberdeen, U.K.: Department of Education, University of Aberdeen, 1966.

Nisbet, J., and Welsh, J. "Predicting Student Performance." *Universities Quarterly,* 1966, *20*(4), 468–480.

Northcraft, G. B., and Jernstedt, G. C. "A Comparison of Four Teaching Method Styles for Large Lecture Classes." *Psychological Reports,* 1975, *36,* 599–606.

Nye, P. A. "Student Variables in Relation to Note Taking During a Lecture." *Programmed Learning and Educational Technology,* 1978, *15*(3), 196–200.

O'Donnell, A. "Searching for Information in Knowledge Maps and Texts." *Contemporary Educational Psychology,* 1993, *18*(2), 222–239.

O'Donnell, A., and Dansereau, D. F. "Learning from Lectures: Effects of Cooperative Review." *Journal of Experimental Education,* 1993, *61*(2), 116–125.

Oaks, T. D. "Storytelling: A Natural Mnemonic. A Study of a Storytelling Teaching Method to Positively Influence Student Recall of Instruction (Memory)." *Dissertation Abstracts International,* Aug. 1996, *57A*(2), p. 579.

Orr, D. B. "Time Compressed Speech: A Perspective." *Journal of Communication,* 1968, *18*(3), 288–292.

Osterman, D., and others. "The Feedback Lecture." Idea paper no. 13. (Unpublished.) Manhattan: Center for Faculty Education and Development in Higher Education, Kansas State University, Jan. 1985. ERIC no. ED302562.

Oswald, I. *Sleep.* New York: Penguin, 1966.

Ovaiza, S. "Listening Comprehension: A Lecture-Based Approach." *ELT Journal,* 1985, *39*(3), 187–192.

Palkovitz, R. J., and Lore, R. K. "Note Taking and Note Review: Why Students Fail Questions Based on Lecture Material." *Teaching of Psychology,* 1980, *7*(3), 159–161.

Parlett, M. R. "The Syllabus Bound Student." In L. Hudson (ed.), *Ecology of Human Intelligence.* New York: Penguin Modern Sociology Readings, 1970.

Parnes, S. J., and Meadow, A. "Effects of 'Brainstorming' Instructions on Creative Problem Solving by Trained and Untrained Subjects." *Journal of Educational Psychology,* 1959, *50,* 171–176.

Patton, J. A. "A Study of the Effects of Student Acceptance of Responsibility and Motivation on Course Behaviour." *Dissertation Abstracts,* 1955, *15,* 637–638.

Pauk, W. "Does Note-Taking Interfere with Listening Comprehension?" *Journal of Developmental Reading,* 1963, *6,* 276–278.

Pederson, C. "Promoting Nursing Students' Positive Attitudes Toward Providing Care for Suicidal Patients." *Issues in Mental Health Nursing,* Jan–Mar. 1993, *14,* 67–84.

Pennington, D. F., Jr., Haravey, F., and Bass, B. M. "Some Effects of Decision and Discussion on Coalescence, Change, and Effectiveness." *Journal of Applied Psychology,* 1958, *42,* 404–408.

Pennington, H. "Excerpts from Journal Articles as Teaching Devices." *Teaching of Psychology,* 1992, *19*(3), 175–177.

Peper, R. J., and Mayer, R. E. "Note Taking as a Generative Activity." *Journal of Educational Psychology,* 1978, *70*(4), 514–522.

Peper, R. J., and Mayer, R. E. "Generative Effects of Note-Taking During Science Lectures." *Journal of Educational Psychology,* 1986, *78*(1), 34–38.

Pepler, R. D. "Warmth and Lack of Sleep: Accuracy or Activity Reduced." *Journal of Comparative and Physiological Psychology,* 1959, *52,* 446–450.

Perry, R. P., Abrami, P. C., and Leventhal, L. "Educational Seduction: The Effect of Instructor Expressiveness and Lecture Content on Student Ratings and Achievement." *Journal of Educational Psychology,* 1979, *71*(1), 107–116.

Perry, W. G. *Forms of Intellectual and Ethical Development in the College Years: A Scheme.* Austin, Tex.: Holt, Rinehart and Winston, 1970.

Peters, D. L. "Effects of Note-Taking and Rate of Presentation on Short-Term Objective Test Performance." *Journal of Educational Psychology,* 1972, *63*(3), 276–280.

Peters, D. L., and Harris, C. "Note-Taking and Review in Recognition Learning." In F. Di Vesta and others (eds.), *Instructional Strategies: Multivariable Studies in Psychological Processes Related to Instruction.* ARPA Annual Report, 1970. (Advanced Research Projects Agency, Pennsylvania State University.)

Peterson, L. R. "Short-Term Memory." *Scientific American,* 1966, *215*(1), 90–95.

Peterson, L. R., and Peterson, M. J. "Short-Term Retention of Individual Verbal Items." *Journal of Experimental Psychology,* 1959, *58,* 193–198.

Pettibone, T. J., and Martin, D. W. "Effects of Lecturer Pace on Noise Level in a University Classroom," *Journal of Educational Research,* 1973, *67*(2), 73–75.

Poincaré, H. "Mathematical Creation." In P. E. Vernon (ed.), *Creativity.* New York: Penguin, 1970.

Pollio, H. R. "Remembrances of Lectures Past: Notes and Note-Taking in the College Classroom." *Teaching/Learning Issues,* Fall 1990.

Poppleton, P. K., and Austwick, K. "A Comparison of Programmed Learning and Note-Making at Two Age Levels." *British Journal of Educational Psychology,* 1964, *34,* 43–50.

Poulton, E. C. "British Courses for Adults on Effective Reading. *British Journal of Educational Psychology,* 1961, *31*(part 2), 128–137.

Ramsden, P. *Learning to Teach in Higher Education.* New York: Routledge, 1992.

Ransdell, S. "Incorporating Educational Software into Large Introductory Psychology Lectures and Labs." (21st annual meeting of the Society for Computers in Psychology, San Francisco.) *Behavior Research Methods, Instruments, and Computers,* 1992, *24*(2), 172–173.

Rasor, R. A. "Correlates of Classroom Retention." (Unpublished report.) Department of Psychology, American River College, 1980.

Razzell, P., and Weinman, J. "The Pre-Clinical Curriculum and Information Processing Problem." *Medical Education,* 1977, *11,* 257–261.

Reid, R. H. "Grammatical Complexity and Comprehension of Compressed Speech." *Journal of Communication,* 1968, *18*(3), 236–242.

Reid-Smith, E. R. "The Measurement of Level of Student Satisfaction by Means of a Course Assessment Questionnaire." *Research in Librarianship*, 1969, *10*(2), 100–107.

Remmers, H. H. "Reliability and Halo Effect of High School and College Students Judgments of Their Teachers." *Journal of Applied Psychology*, 1934, *18*, 619–630.

Remmers, H. H. "Rating Methods in Research on Teaching." In N. L. Gage (ed.), *Handbook of Research on Teaching*. Skokie, Ill.: Rand McNally, 1963.

Rickards, J. P., and McCormick, C. B. "Effect of Interspersed Conceptual Prequestions on Note-Taking in Listening Comprehension." *Journal of Educational Psychology*, 1988, *80*(4), 592–594.

Rock, I. "The Role of Repetition in Associative Learning." *American Journal of Psychology*, 1957, *70*, 186–193.

Rohrer, J. H. "Large and Small Sections in College Classes." *Journal of Higher Education*, 1957, *28*, 275–279.

Rosenshine, B. "Objectively Measured Behavioral Predictors of Effectiveness in Explaining." Unpublished doctoral dissertation, Stanford University, 1968.

Rosenshine, B. "Enthusiastic Teaching: A Research Review." *School Review*, 1970, *78*, 499–514.

Ross, J. M. "Critical Teaching Behaviours as Perceived by Adult Undergraduates." Paper presented at the American Educational Research Association annual meeting, Mar. 1989.

Royer, P. N. "Effects of Specificity and Position of Written Instructional Objectives on Learning from Lecture." *Journal of Educational Psychology*, 1977, *69*(1), 40–45.

Rugg, H. "Is the Rating of Human Character Possible?" *Journal of Educational Psychology*, 1921, *12*, 425–438, 485–501.

Rugg, H. "Is the Rating of Human Character Possible?" *Journal of Educational Psychology*, 1922, *13*, 30–42, 81–93.

Ruhl, K. L., Hughes, C. A., and Gajar, A. H. "Efficacy of the Pause Procedure for Enhancing Learning Disabled and Nondisabled College Students' Long and Short Term Recall of Facts Presented Through Lecture." *Learning Disability Quarterly*, 1990, *13*(1), 55–64.

Ruhl, K. L., and Suritsky, S. "The Pause Procedure and/or an Outline: Effect on Immediate Free Recall And Lecture Notes Taken by College Students with Learning Disabilities." *Learning Disability Quarterly*, 1995, *18*(1), 2–11.

Ruskin, R. S., and Hess, J. H. *The Personalized System of Instruction: An Annotated Review of the Literature*. Washington, D.C.: Georgetown University, 1974.

Russell, I. J., Hendricson, W. D., and Herbert, R. J. "Effects of Lecture Information Density on Medical Student Achievement." *Journal of Medical Education*, 1984, *59*(1), 881–889.

Saunders, M., and others. *Report of the Commission on Teaching in Higher Education, National Union of Student.*, 1969.

Sawyer, H. W., and Sawyer, S. H. "A Teacher-Parent Communication Training Approach." *Exceptional Children*, 1981, *47*(4), 305–306.

Sazar, L., and Kassinove, H. "Effects of Counselor's Profanity and Subject's Religiosity on Content Acquisition of a Counseling Lecture and Behavioral Compliance." (Special issue.). *Psychological Reports*, 1991, *69*(3, part 2), 1059–1070.

Scerbo, M. W., Warm, J. S., Dember, W. N., and Grasha, A. F. "The Role of Time and Cueing in a College Lecture." *Contemporary Educational Psychology*, 1992, *17*(4), 312–328.

Schachter, S., Christenfeld, N., Ravina, B., and Bilous, F. "Speech Disfluency and the Structure of Knowledge." *Journal of Personality and Social Psychology*, 1991, *60*(3), 362–367.

Schachter, S., Rauscher, F., Christenfeld, N., and Crone, K. T. "The Vocabularies of Academia." *Psychological Science,* 1994, *5*(1), 37–41.

Scott, W. A. "Attitude Change Through Reward of Verbal Behaviour." *Journal of Abnormal and Social Psychology,* 1957, *55,* 72–75.

Self, D. J., Wolinsky, F. D., and Baldwin, De W. C. "The Effect of Teaching Medical Ethics on Medical Students' Moral Reasoning." *Academic Medicine,* 1989, *64*(12) (special issue), 755–759.

Seymour, W. D. "An Experiment Showing the Superiority of a Light-Colored 'Blackboard.'" *British Journal of Educational Psychology,* 1937, *7*(3), 259–268.

Shaw, R. "Determining Register in Sign-to-English Interpreting." *Sign Language Studies,* Winter 1987, *57,* 295–322.

Sherif, M. A., and Sherif, C. W. *An Outline of Social Psychology.* (Rev. ed.). New York: Harper-Collins, 1956.

Sherwood, J. J. "A Relation Between Arousal and Performance." *American Journal of Psychology,* 1965, *78,* 461–465.

Siegel, H. B. "McLuhan, Mass Media, and Education." *Journal of Experimental Education,* 1973, *41*(3), 68–70.

Siegel, L., Adams, J. F., and Macomber, F. G. "Retention of Subject Matter as a Function of Large Group Instructional Procedures." *Journal of Educational Psychology,* 1960, *51,* 9–13.

Siegel, L., and others. "Students' Thoughts During Class: A Criterion for Educational Research." *Journal of Educational Psychology,* 1963, *54*(1), 45–51.

Sime, M., and Boyce, G. "Overt Responses, Knowledge of Results, and Learning." *Programmed Learning and Educational Technology,* 1969, *6*(1), 12–19.

Singer, R. D. "Verbal Conditioning and Generalization of Pro-Democratic Responses." *Journal of Abnormal and Social Psychology,* 1961, *63,* 43–46.

Smeltzer, L. R., and Watson, K. W. *Improving Listening Skills Used in Business: An Empirical Comparison of Discussion Length, Modeling, and Level of Incentive.* American Business Communication Association, 1983. ERIC no. ED229809.

Smith, C. W. "The Effect of Class Size on Student Achievement in the Principles of Economics Courses." *Dissertation Abstracts International,* Apr. 1996, *56A*(10), p. 4063.

Smith, D. L. "The Effects of Cooperative Learning in a Short-Term, Intensive, Adult, Religious Education Seminar." *Dissertation Abstracts International A,* 1995, *56*(7), 2549.

Smith, G., and Wyllie, J. H. "Use of Closed-Circuit Television in Teaching Surgery to Medical Students." *British Medical Journal,* July 10, 1965, pp. 99–101.

Smith, H. C. "Team Work in the College Class." *Journal of Educational Psychology,* 1955, *46,* 274–286.

Smith, L. R. "Effect of Teacher Vagueness and Use of Lecture Notes on Student Performance." *Journal of Educational Research,* 1984, *78*(2), 69–74.

Smithers, A. "Some Factors in Lecturing." *Educational Review,* 1970a, *22*(2), 141–150.

Smithers, A. "What Do Students Expect of Lectures?" *Universities Quarterly,* 1970b, *24*(3), 330–336.

Snowberg, R. L. "Bases for Selection of Background Colours for Transparencies." *Audio Visual Communication Review,* 1973, *21*(2).

Sox, H. C., Marton, K. I., Higgins, M. C., and Hickam, D. H. "Tutored Video-Tape Instruction in Clinical Decision-Making." *Journal of Medical Education,* 1984, *59*(3), 188–195.

Spencer, R. E., and Aleamoni, L. M. "A Student Course Evaluation Questionnaire." *Journal of Educational Measurement,* 1970, *7,* 209–210.

Spender, S. "The Making of a Poem." In B. Ghiselin (ed.), *The Creative Process: A Symposium.* Berkeley: University of California Press, 1952.

Sperling, G. "The Information Available in Brief Visual Presentations." *Psychological Monographs*, 1960 (whole of no. 498).

Spires, H. A. "Learning from a Lecture: Effects of Comprehension Monitoring." *Reading Research and Instruction*, 1993, *32*(2), 19–30.

Stanton, D. G. "Utilizing Hypercard for Tutorial CAI in Advanced Professional Training (Macintosh)." *Dissertation Abstracts International A*, 1994, *54*(10), 3722.

Stanton, H. E. "Confidence Building in the University Lecturer." *Contemporary Educational Psychology*, 1978.

Stanton, H. E. "Increasing Lecturer Self-Confidence." *Australian Psychologist*, 1979, *14*(3), 329–335.

Startup, R. "Staff Experience of Lectures and Tutorials." *Studies in Higher Education*, 1977, *2*(2), 191–201.

Stewart, R. A. "Interaction Effects of Teacher Enthusiasm and Student Notetaking on Recall and Recognition of Lecture Content." *Communication Research Reports*, 1989, *6*(2), 84–89.

Sticht, T. G. "Some Relationships of Mental Aptitude, Reading Ability, and Listening Ability Using Normal and Time-Compressed Speech." *Journal of Communication*, 1968, *18*(3), 159–171.

Stolurow, L. M. "Teaching Machines and Special Education." *Educational Psychology Measurement*, 1960, *20*, 429–448.

Stones, E. "Students' Attitudes to the Size of Teaching Groups." *Educational Review*, 1970, *21*(2), 98–108.

Strasser, S. E., and Ozgur, C. "Undergraduate Business Statistics: A Survey of Topics and Teaching Methods." *Interfaces*, 1995, *25*(3), 95–103.

Strodt-Lopez B. "Tying It All In: Asides in University Lectures." *Applied Linguistics*, 1991, *12*(2), 117–140.

Tannenbaum, P. H. "Attitudes Toward Source and Concept as Factors in Attitude Change Through Communication." Unpublished doctoral dissertation, University of Illinois, 1953.

Tannenbaum, P. H. "Effect of Serial Position on Recall of Radio News Stories." *Journalism Quarterly*, 1954, *31*, 319–323.

Tanner, D. "Influencing Student Opinion in the College Classroom." *Journal of Educational Research*, 1968, *62*(1), 30–33.

Taplin, G. "The Cosford Cube: A Simplified Form of Student Feedback." *Industrial Training International*, 1969, *4*(5), 218–219.

Taylor, D. W., Berry, P. C., and Block, C. H. "Does Group Participation When Using Brainstorming Facilitate or Inhibit Creative Thinking?" *Administrative Science Quarterly*, 1958, *3*, 23–47.

Thoday, D. "How Undergraduates Work." *Universities Quarterly*, 1957, *11*, 172–181.

Thomas, E. J. "The Variation of Memory with Time for Information Appearing During a Lecture." *Studies in Adult Education*, 1972, *4*, 57–62.

Thomas, G. S., Aiken, E. G., and Shennum, W. A. *Further Investigations of Coding/Rehearsal Strategies During a Segmented Lecture Format*. (NPRDC TR 76–15.) San Diego: U.S. Navy Personnel Research and Development Center, 1975.

Thompson, S. "Frameworks and Contexts: A Genre-Based Approach to Analysing Lecture Introductions." *English for Specific Purposes*, 1994, *13*(2), 171–186.

Thorson, E., and Lang, A. "The Effects of Television Videographics and Lecture Familiarity on Adult Cardiac Orienting Responses and Memory." *Communication Research*, 1992, *19*(3), 346–369.

Tillman, B. A. "A Study of the Use of Case Methods in Preservice Teacher Education." *Dissertation Abstracts International A*, 1993, *56*(8), 3201.

Treisman, A. "Human Attention." In B. Foss (ed.), *New Horizons in Psychology*. New York: Penguin, 1966.

Trimble, L. *English for Science and Technology: A Discourse Approach*. Cambridge, U.K.: Cambridge University Press, 1985.

Troisi, N. F. *Effective Teaching and Student Achievement*. National Association of Secondary School Principals, 1983. ERIC no. ED231067.

Trown, A. "Some Evidence on the 'Interaction' Between Teaching Strategy and Personality." *British Journal of Educational Psychology*, 1970, *40*(2), 209–211.

Trueman, M., and Hartley, J. "Note-Taking in Lectures: A Longitudinal Study." *Bulletin of the British Psychological Society*, 1978, *31*, 37–39.

Tucker, B. N. "A Comparison of Three Note-Taking Strategies on Immediate Recall and Retention." *Dissertation Abstracts International*, 1989, *49A*(10), p. 3003.

Tuohimaa, P., Tamminen, T., and Fabrin, V. "Is It Appropriate to Speak of Death During a Dissection Course?" *Teaching and Learning in Medicine*, 1993, *5*(3), 169–173.

Unruh, W. R. "The Modality and Validity of Cues to Lecture Effectiveness." Unpublished doctoral dissertation, Stanford University, 1968.

Uren, O. "The Use of Texts in Language Skill Development: Some Problems, Innovations, and Experiments in University Teaching Methods." Report of the 3rd conference organized by the University Teaching Methods Unit, University of London Institute of Education, Apr. 1968.

Van Dijk, T. A., and Kintsch, W. "Cognitive Psychology and Discourse." In W. U. Dressler (ed.), *Current Trends in Text Linguistics*. 1978.

Van Matre, N. H., and others. *Learning from Lecture: Investigations of Study Strategies Involving Note-Taking*. San Diego: U.S. Navy Personnel Research and Development Center, 1975. ERIC no. ED120684.

Van Metre, P., Yokoi, L., and Pressley, M. "College Students' Theory of Note-Taking Derived from Their Perceptions of Note-Taking." *Journal of Educational Psychology*, 1994, *86*(3), 323–338.

Van Patten, J., Chao, C-I., and Reigeluth, C. "Knowledge Restructuring." *Review of Educational Research*, 1986, *56*(4), 437–471.

Vogel, M. R. "Is Humor a Useful Teaching Tool in Human Sexuality Education? Perspectives of Sixth-Grade Students." *Dissertation Abstracts International*, Feb. 1996, *56*(8), p. 3012.

Walbaum, S. D. "Notetaking, Verbal Aptitude, and Listening Span: Factors Involved in Learning from Lectures." Paper presented to the annual meeting of the American Educational Research Association, San Francisco, 1989.

Walton, H. J., and Drewery, J. "The Objective Examination in the Evaluation of Medical Students." *British Journal of Medical Education*, 1967, *1*(4), 255–264.

Warburton, F. W., Butcher, H. J., and Forrest, G. M. "Predicting Student Performance in a University Department of Education." *British Journal of Educational Psychology*, 1963, *33*, 68–79.

Weaver, R. L., and Cotrell, H. W. "Mental Aerobics: The Half-Sheet Response." *Innovative Higher Education*, 1985, *10*(1), 23–31.

Weiland, A., and Kingsbury, S. J. "Immediate and Delayed Recall of Lecture Material as a Function of Note Taking." *Journal of Educational Research*, 1979, *72*(4), 228–230.

Wertheimer, M. *Productive Thinking.* New York: HarperCollins, 1945.

White, L. D., and Chavigny, K. H. "Direct Tape Access as an Adjunct to Learning." *Nursing Research*, 1975, *24*(4), 295–298.

Wijasuriya, B. A. "The Occurrence of Discourse Markers and Intersentence Connectives in University Lectures and Their Place in Testing and Teaching of Listening Comprehension in English as a Foreign Language." Medical thesis, University of Manchester, U.K., 1971.

Wilding, J. M., and Hayes, S. "Relations Between Approaches to Studying and Note-Taking Behaviour in Lectures." *Applied Cognitive Psychology*, 1992, *6*(3), 233–246.

Wilkinson, R. T. "Rest Pauses in a Task Affected by Lack of Sleep." *Ergonomics*, 1959, *2*, 373–380.

Wilkinson, R. T. "Interaction of Lack of Sleep with Knowledge of Results, Repeated Testing, and Individual Differences." *Journal of Experimental Psychology*, 1961, *62*, 263–271.

Wilkinson, R. T. "After-Effect of Sleep Deprivation." *Journal of Experimental Psychology*, 1963a, *66*, 439–442.

Wilkinson, R. T. "Interaction of Noise with Knowledge of Results and Sleep Deprivation." *Journal of Experimental Psychology*, 1963b, *66*, 332–337.

Williams, R. G., and Ware, J. E. "An Extended Visit with Dr. Fox: Validity of Student Satisfaction with the Instruction Ratings After Repeated Exposures to a Lecturer." *American Educational Research Journal*, 1977, *14*(4), 449–457.

Winocur, S., and others. "Perceptions of Male and Female Academics Within a Teaching Context." *Research in Higher Education*, 1989, *30*(3), 317–329.

Wiseman, S., and Start, K. B. "A Follow-up of Teachers Five Years After Completing Their Training." *British Journal of Educational Psychology*, 1965, *35*, 342–361.

Witkin, H. A. (ed.). *Psychological Differentiation.* New York: Wiley, 1962.

Wood, C. C., and Hedley, R. L. "Student Reaction to VTR in Simulated Classroom Conditions." *Canadian Educational Research Digest*, 1968, *8*(1), 46–59.

Woodcock, R. W., and Clark, G. R. "Comprehension of a Narrative Passage by Elementary School Children as a Function of Listening Rate, Retention Period, and IQ." *Journal of Communication*, 1968, *18*(3), 259–271.

Woolford, G. A. "Teacher Influence in a College of Education." *Educational Research*, 1969, *11*(2), 148–152.

Wyckoff, W. L. "The Effect of Stimulus Variation on Learning from Lecture." *Journal of Experimental Education*, 1973, *41*(3), 85–90.

Yorde, B. S., and Witmer, J. M. "An Educational Format for Teaching Stress Management to Groups with a Wide Range of Stress Symptoms." *Biofeedback and Self-Regulation*, 1988, *5*(1), 75–90.

Young, L., and Fitzgerald, B. *Listening and Learning.* Boston: Newbury House, 1982.

Zacharakis-Jutz, J. "Adult Education Guided Design and Student Participation." (Unpublished.) 1983. ERIC no. ED244052.

Zillmann, D., and Cantor, J. R. "Induction of Curiosity Via Rhetorical Questions and Its Effect on the Learning of Factual Materials." *British Journal of Educational Psychology*, 1973, *43*(2), 172–180.

Zimbardo, P. J. "Involvement and Communication Discrepancy as Determinants of Opinion Conformity." *Journal of Abnormal and Social Psychology*, 1960, *60*, 86.

NAME INDEX

SUBJECT INDEX